C000194829

Religion: Contemporary Issues

RELIGION: CONTEMPORARY ISSUES

The All Souls Seminars
in the Sociology of Religion

Edited by Bryan Wilson

Bellew Publishing
London
1992

First Published in Great Britain in 1992 by
Bellew Publishing Company Limited
8 Balham Hill, London SW12 9EA

The collection copyright © Bellew Publishing 1992

All rights reserved. No part of this publication may
be reproduced, stored in a retrieval system or
transmitted, in any form or by any means, electronic,
mechanical, photocopying, recording or otherwise
without the prior permission of the publisher

ISBN 1 85725 045 1

Phototypeset by Intype, London
Printed and bound in Great Britain by
Billing and Sons Ltd, Worcester

Contents

Introduction

Like all the sub-divisions of sociology, the sociology of religion is something of a hybrid. Its origins can be traced, on the one hand, to the significant role accorded by the classical sociologists to religion in the evolution of society, and, on the other, to the interest of some among the clergy to acquire more precise knowledge of the social aspects of religious practice. The two orientations were radically different. The classical theorists – Comte, Durkheim, Weber, Veblen and Freud – all recognized that earlier societies had based their sense of social cohesion, their values, their very *raison d'être*, on supernaturalist conceptions. Religion had functions for those societies, and the welding together of tribes or larger collectivities had been one effect of common religious practice. Although, in their different ways, all saw that religion was destined to be superseded by some alternative basis for social integration, this did not derogate from the importance which they ascribed to its role in pre-modern societies. The expectation, shared no less by the thinkers of the Enlightenment and by Marx, that religion was doomed to disappear, in no way diminished their interest in appraising its functions in past societies. Religion as a source of values had been a transformative agency in society; it had underwritten a collective consciousness; it had provided the sub-stratum of thought, feeling and evaluation in which the collective *mentalité* was grounded. From its very beginning, and in spite of the evolutionist perspective so vigorously canvassed by Saint-Simon and Comte, which was also implicit in Weber, Durkheim and others, religion featured centrally in sociological theory.

Once it became apparent, as it gradually did, that the evolutionary prognosis erred in supposing that functional alternatives to religion – in regard to its role in sustaining social cohesion, reinforcing social control and providing ultimate legitimacy both for authority and for the corpus of intellectual knowledge – would bring about its demise, the nature of the questions concerning its social role necessarily underwent some change of direction. Religion persisted. How was that to be explained, given its loss of social functions and the manifest transformation of society? That question, among others, became itself a stimulus to the development of a specialist branch of sociology, one cultivated in response to, and in interaction with the sceptical tradition that had developed within sociology proper.

As it was steadily appreciated that religion was a persisting phenomenon, other questions suggested themselves. Religion was an organized human activity: thus, its effectiveness; the appeal that it exercised; the techniques of persuasion; its resistance to, or its acceptance of, change; its systems of internal authority – all became issues of direct intellectual concern to those engaged in explaining social processes. Religion changed; became the subject of disputation; harboured the socially dissident as well as those who endorsed existing political and social arrangements. Religion interacted with other spheres of social activity and maintained, if on newly negotiated terms, relationships with other social institutions – most conspicuously perhaps with the provision for education. But there is no need here to attempt to catalogue the diverse issues that sociologists might designate as topics of interest and importance in establishing a sociological understanding of religion.

The other stimulus to the development of a sociology of religion as a subject in its own right came, as indicated above, from churchmen who recognized that manifestations of religious commitment and the incidence of religious practice (whether in quotidian life, church attendance, daily prayers, or the more occasional rites of passage, pilgrimages and so on) were not vouchsafed by the promptings of the Holy Spirit alone. Social influences could not be ignored: religion was, at least partly, perhaps largely or even wholly, to be understood in relation to prevailing social conditions. Such matters as the past history of a region, its earlier exposure to mission activity, the general demographic pattern of its population, ethnic composition, the nature of occupations, the authority structure of local political life and so on – all might affect what was believed and by whom, and the incidence of religious practice. The surveys of a Booth or the stimulation of such research directives as those of Gabriel Le Bras made it clear that inquiries on these issues were practical and informative. The development, in other branches of sociology, of questionnaire surveys, opinion polls and census data opened up lines of empirical inquiry which augmented, and to some extent tested, the propositions advanced by the theorists. That some of this work was prompted from within the churches and was ultimately in their service did not, in the long term, prevent closer association between those who saw their field as the sociology of religion and those, Christian-committed, researchers whose work was more typically defined (in France) as *sociologie religieuse*. Those in the tradition of the classic theorists have generally qualified the evolutionary framework in which the total demise of religion was explicitly envisaged. Those still motivated by the need to understand from a pastoral perspective the changing pattern of religiosity, now generally recognize the distinction to be made between scientific inquiry, on the one hand, and the purposes for which it might be undertaken and subsequently employed, on the other.

The coming together of these different traditions has resulted not so much in a synthesis as in a proliferation of concerns. The question of secularization came to loom large in the context of the structural differentiation of society, in which different institutions acquired virtual autonomy in their operation (government; judicature; education, etc.) as religion lost its earlier influence over these various social activities. Yet, despite this secularizing process, religion showed no signs of disappearing. True, there were fewer people in the churches, and there were steadily fewer and fewer clergymen, and churches and dioceses find it harder and harder to finance their activities. None the less, the majority of people have continued to claim that they hold religious beliefs. The issue, discussed in one context in the following pages by Michael Hornsby-Smith, has been the stuff of extensive debate. How are professed beliefs to be related to church attendance and religious practice generally, and what, if any, are the consequences in the way of life that believers conduct?

To put the problems in these terms is to seek answers by empirical study at the grass roots, by surveys of religious belief and practice as indices of the process of change in people's attitudes and behaviour. It is the bedrock of sociological knowledge, but the data supplied by such methods always stand in need of interpretation, and interpretation readily brings about recourse to more theoretical levels of discourse. Appropriately, it is to discussion of these more general aspects of sociological theory that the reader is directed in the first two chapters of this book. James Beckford seeks to relate religious change to the phenomenon of modernity and – in recognition of one of the impulses of current thinking – of post-modernity. In so doing, he seeks to indicate the nature of the relationship of religion, or at least of Christianity, to modern society. The problems that he airs remain central to the sociology of religion, even if they are not always accorded the highest significance by those engaged more exclusively with sociological theory. Beckford is keen to illustrate what the sociology of religion loses by its general detachment from sociological theory, but conversely, the theorists, unlike their classical predecessors, attach little importance in their analyses to the role of religion. It might be disputed whether this is a consequence of the relative insularity of the sociology of religion or the changing, perhaps diminished, effect of religion on contemporary society. This substantive issue, loosely designated as the secularization thesis, remains the central and most contentious, if not always fully articulated, current concern of the sociology of religion.

Two phenomena must give pause to those who argue that the

influence of religion necessarily wanes in modernizing societies: the incidence of new modes of spirituality, evident in the New Age movements, with their fashionable congruity with post-modernist theories; and the resilience, in some parts of the world, of fundamentalism. Neither New Age spirituality nor fundamentalism is easily defined, however, and much that passes under each of these labels might be of disputed provenance, but both might be seen as reactions to modernity. Stephen Sharot puts the debate about fundamentalism into the comparative perspective of Judeo–Christian–Islamic traditions, and indicates the confusion which readily arises when an inadequately examined concept which carries distinct cultural connotations in one culture is employed for phenomena in another context in which these connotations might be irrelevant, or, indeed, entirely alien.

The connection between what passes as fundamentalist movements and the sponsorship of moral crusades has certainly been evident in both Christianity and Islam. Indeed, in the Christian case, and perhaps no less in Islam, fundamentalism has often been publicly more conspicuous for, and more readily identified with, the defence of traditional moral norms than for the endorsement of specific sets of beliefs based on literal interpretations of sacred scriptures. Using specific cases drawn from the various issues on which fundamentalists have been embattled in Britain and the United States, Christie Davies adds another dimension to the debate by indicating the significant role which religiously-inspired interdictions perform in reinforcing and conveying a sense of social – specifically regional, national or ethnic – identity. The attempt to preserve or restore traditional morality, if need be by force of law, has a clear political dimension, as the operation of the Moral Majority in the years of the Reagan presidency of the United States made apparent. Right-wing parties, particularly those committed to *laissez-faire* liberalism may not always be committed to the reassertion of traditional moral injunctions. Indeed, there is a sense in which it may be said that implicit in *laissez-faire* economics is an acceptance of a *laissez-faire* morality. Choice in the market may imply a parallel choice of life-style, and the commitment to reduce, and if possible to eliminate, restraints on business may be matched by the diminution of moral inhibitions which limit freedom in personal behaviour. But modern right-wing parties often embrace elements which espouse an older version of conservatism, in which crown and Church, nation and family are the structures to be sustained, and church-prescribed morality is the social cement with which their conservation is to be effected. Uneasily as such values sit with the neo-liberalism that endorses moral freedom and, at times, libertarianism, they have not been jettisoned, and are, indeed, often essential as the substance of election rhetoric for parties with practical programmes dictated by rather different philosophies. One need not attribute the inner contradictions of such party policies to deliberate deceit, but only suspect profound muddle at the heart of party propaganda which demands the restoration of Victorian values while simultaneously denying the very existence of anything called 'society'. William Thompson, with instructive comparisons with the situation in the United States, examines the constituency of particular groups which, almost as vigilantes, have promoted moral crusades, and provides an appraisal of the extent of their success and their future prospects.

The late twentieth century is an age of rapid moral change, not only involving a change in personal habits (facilitated by technical innovations such as the ready availability of contraceptive devices) but inducing widespread differences of opinion even among clergy about moral norms and religious truths. Yet, despite the prevailing confusion, society has in place institutions one traditional function of which is the transmission of beliefs, attitudes and values. Despite moral dilemmas and ethical divergence, the prevailing view remains that such institutions must continue in that role. The school is the essential agency in that socializing process. The concern of Leslie Francis, in the paper that he contributes, is with the communication by church schools of religious beliefs and the extent to which they transmit a distinctive ethos. Even though he does not directly address the question of morals, the function of church schools has certainly been conceived by their personnel as helping to lay the religious groundwork on which a moral community might subsist. That state schools in Britain are also charged to establish such a basic religious understanding in pupils provides a framework for comparison of just what difference church-sponsorship achieves in schooling. And that is a matter of some importance when other, minority, religious groups, with different beliefs and a different ethos, are pressing to be accorded similar rights and similar subsidies in setting up schools of their own.

In a wide-ranging review of contemporary Catholicism, Karel Dobbelaere returns to an issue fundamental to so much work in the sociology of religion, namely the role of the Church in societies becoming increasingly secularized. Is the Church to engage in social and political action ('performance') or is it rather to confine itself to the functions that remain to it as explicitly and exclusively religious goals? He covers organizational dilemmas, the problem of acculturation of religious styles and values to particular national contexts, and the extent to which clerical personnel are today deployable, as once they so readily were, in territories remote from the lands of their birth and their upbringing. If this is a comprehensive commentary on the effects on the Church of the process of secularization in western society, the essay which follows, by Michael Hornsby-

Smith, takes as its focus the apparent discrepancy in the numbers
of those who profess to believe and those who actually belong. One
might surmise that, for some, a profession of belief might be easier
than an actual appearance in church – and it is not altogether inappropriate to suggest that actions may speak louder than words. After
all, for many modern people, the question might be 'What else is
there to believe?', while they can hardly ask the parallel question of
where, on Sundays, other than church, could they possibly spend
their time. But the disparity between believers and attenders may
also indicate the cultural incongruity in the modern world of traditional church structures. Congregational activity under the guidance of a star performer who, if not quite the possessor of a total
monopoly of spiritual power, is at least the vehicle through whom
that power is approached and communicated, may sit ill with the
demotic and democratic ethos of contemporary society.

Alien as traditional church structures may have become to modern
people, belief, even though it might make a better showing in surveys and opinion polls than does religious practice, might be
revealed to harbour its own problems were research investigation
to penetrate deeper. The churches scarcely speak with one voice:
indeed, no one church, not even the most hierocratic, speaks
unequivocally. What then should laymen believe, and what actually
do they believe? In the face of an increasingly strident evangelical
assault, and of a more explicitly biblical fundamentalism, those who
consider themselves as liberal Christians, soft-spoken as they generally are, may find difficulty in being heard at all. The very stance
they take is on a slippery patch as they seek to present themselves
as enlightened churchmen who try to bring secular and scientific
knowledge into harmony with at least a version of Christian commitment, while acknowledging that much of what that commitment
used to be is now subject to a multitude of qualifications and reservations. The dilemma, seen from a liberal Christian perspective, is
explored by Peter Gee, particularly with regard to the part that
liberal clergy play in the higher reaches of the Established Church.
The endeavour to hold on to certain charter values in a society where
quite different values are more widely canvassed and more readily
taken for granted, and yet to claim that the Church and what it
proclaims is relevant to people's contemporary needs, at times risks
exposing liberal clergy to the charge of *trahison des clercs*.

It is virtually that charge which Kenneth Minogue, writing from
a different vantage point, levels against a contemporary church that
is more concerned with what, in his earlier essay, Dobbelaere designated 'performance', than with the maintenance of the traditional
terms of its mission. The virtual surrender of that ascetic ethic which
formed the Christian hero, the tendency to lose sight of the original
Christian truth that man must always be seen as a sinner, have

made it easy for some of those who pass as liberal clergymen to talk and act as if redemption could come only through reformed social institutions, and not through that agency which is at the core of traditional Christian belief. The vital difference between a Rousseau-esque socialism which regards good men as the products of good institutions, and the evangelical opposite premiss that a good society could arise only if individuals were good or redeemed, is at the heart of the debate on a wide variety of issues exercising contemporary Christians.

Among those numerous issues to which Minogue points is the fashionable demand for women priests, which is perhaps the most explosive and most clearly crystallized of any of the Church's current disputes. In itself, it is not a matter on which a sociologist need, or should, take sides, but the debate between the contending parties is certainly an area of sociological interest, explored in these pages by Alan Aldridge, who examines the rhetoric and the devices of legitimation which the two sides employ in seeking to present a coherent statement of policy. The subject polarizes the parties, one of which sees the Church's teaching and organization as timelessly valid, and the other whose current advocacy must imply that structures and practice of the past were not valid, and the teachings that justified them were neither timeless nor true.

The question of women's eligibility for admission to the priesthood immediately raises profound and contentious theological arguments. Not so the question of the use for religious ends of the mass media of communication, where the debate is more in terms of what is expedient. Yet, new technology does challenge some assumptions that have been basic to religious performance in the past, in particular the extent to which spiritual ministrations necessitate a direct relationship between priest (or minister) and laity. Certainly, for the vital symbolic acts of the sacraments, personal mediation of sacred power has traditionally been seen as indispensable. Radio and television religion which seeks to go beyond mere evangelism might challenge those dependencies, and it is no accident that broadcast religion has found endorsement most readily, and particularly in America, among evangelical Protestants, for whom the expounding of the word is often seen as a more urgent concern than is the administration of the sacraments. Churches with a sacerdotal tradition have seen the mass media as perhaps less valuable as an alternative to church attendance and participation, and an account of this guarded approach, and the often lukewarm embrace of media managers are the subject of Kenneth Wolfe's discussion. How readily the de-regulation of broadcasting in Britain and, indeed, in Europe, will be seen as an opportunity for American styles of televangelism and solicitation of funds is an issue which may exercise the minds and hearts of a far wider public than those who constitute the religiously committed, and may represent the most dramatic, and in many respects the most practical, example of how British religion will grapple with the technologies of modernity.

The sociology of religion has never neglected minority religious organizations. Indeed, the discipline has at times been criticized for giving sects and new movements disproportionate attention. But such bodies inevitably demand more explanation than does the comfortable orthodoxy of the majority of church-goers, since the votaries of these smaller groups generally manifest a measure of commitment which far exceeds that of most of the members of the major churches. These bodies are often more coherent in doctrine and organization, present a more distinctive pattern of belief and practice, and raise for the sociologist more acutely the question of the relative influence of values over material interests that has been a central sociological concern at least since Weber challenged Marxist economic determinism. It is, then, no less than appropriate that a graduate seminar in the sub-discipline should devote attention to religious minorities. The Adventists are a sizeable sect in world terms which, until recent years, had not attracted much attention from sociologists, even while stimulating an informed corpus of literature from scholars among their own members. D. S. Porter provides an encompassing overview of the remarkable vicissitudes which Adventism has experienced in recent decades, not least among which, in Britain, has been the changing racial composition of this movement.

Today, many sects and even more certainly many new religious movements operate as world-wide organizations, even though they may also give rise to imitators and derivatives, and, in the case of new movements, which some sociologists designate as 'cults', they may create a cultic milieu in which one movement may be said to open the way for numerous others. It is this milieu and its congruence with the materialism and the individualism of contemporary western society which Michael Hill discusses in the penultimate chapter of this volume, linking this phenomenon with the neglected category of religiosity which Ernst Troeltsch depicted as mysticism in his writings of eighty years ago. Thus, Hill roots the prognosis that he offers for the future of religion firmly in the classical sociological tradition, invoking not only the prescient insights of Troeltsch, but also those of Émile Durkheim.

New movements are not all committed to the individualism and self-enhancement of the type of human potential movements which form much of the content of Hill's analysis: some are movements with strong authoritarian characteristics which have had levelled against them in the media regular charges of brainwashing, mind control and even of reducing converts to a state of virtual servitude. The terms used by the media are crude and sensational. The reality of the relationships between follower and leader are often much more subtle, and it is the subtlety of these connections that is the focus of attention for Eileen Barker who tackles directly the contentious issue of the extent to which devotees of some of the new religions develop a real dependence on the organization to which they belong and the leaders whom they follow. Among the various disputable subjects which form the content of the papers gathered in this collection, this one, because of the sensationalist press, is the most contentious and the one which has had the widest exposure to the general public. Dr Barker's analysis is essential background for an understanding of a subject which public and press comment have often obfuscated rather than clarified.

For almost thirty years, the All Souls Seminar in the Sociology of Religion has been a forum of debate for both historical and contemporary sociological issues. The papers in this book are a sample of some of those presented in recent months on matters of contemporary importance in the broad arena of western religion. Obviously, they are far from exhausting the subjects that have engaged the seminar, much less the range of topics exercising either secular sociologists or religious professionals. These papers are, I believe, all contributions to informed debate that deserve more of an airing than is afforded by a gathering of fifteen or twenty young scholars, and it is in that belief that they are here offered to a wider interested public.

B. R. WILSON

Chapter 1

Religion, Modernity and Post-modernity[1]

James A. Beckford

I have been arguing for a long time that the sociology of religion is excessively insulated against and isolated from developments in other parts of sociology.[2] Roy Wallis and Steve Bruce have tried to refute this argument.[3] Their view is that 'work in the sociology of religion has been influential upon and interacted frequently and effectively with a wide range of cognate concerns both within and beyond the sociology of religion'.[4]

I want to argue here that this judgement is misguided. It flies in the face of the facts agreed by many other specialists.[5] My opinion is that the concerns of many sociologists of religion are indeed isolated from the currents of thought and the debates of interest to other social scientists. They therefore need to shift the prevailing focus of their work away from the alleged secularization of religion and to concentrate, instead, on the more sociologically interesting question of the relationship between religion and, say, *modernity*. Such a move would put sociologists of religion in a better position to examine the links between (i) religion and other social phenomena, and (ii) theorizing about religion and theorizing about societal change. It would have the additional advantage of giving research into religion the opportunity to shape general sociological thought about the nature of present-day society and culture.

The first objective of this chapter is, therefore, to see to what extent concepts of modernity can help us to make sociological sense of religion in the UK. The second objective is to assess the extent to which various notions of modernity help to explain some recent changes in British religion. And the third task will be to decide whether concepts of *post-modernity* have anything to add to the explanation. I tackle the third topic with no great hopes of making much progress (which is appropriate to a post-modernist perspective, of course). But I tackle it more in the originally sceptical spirit of 'What do I know?' Until I have asked myself what the notions of modernity and post-modernity can contribute towards a sociological understanding of religion I do not consider that I have done my job.

My conclusion will propose an alternative way of interpreting some recent changes in British religion.

Modernity and Religion

It is virtually a truism to say that all the formative contributions towards classical sociology were preoccupied with trying to understand modernity. I think that this remains true of a great deal of sociology in the most general sense of pondering 'How did we get from there to here?' and, 'What is it like now that we have arrived?' (Or, better, 'Have we even arrived yet?') But beneath these very broad characterizations of the sociological vocation lie many variations in approach. Each of them is preoccupied with trying to specify the distinctiveness of the most general frameworks of ideas, sentiments and social relationships which make life modern and therefore significantly different from traditional or pre-modern life. The range of such characterizations is enormously broad, but recurrent themes include a faith in the power of applied reason and reliable knowledge to generate order, purpose, progress, efficiency and growth even if the costs include fragmentation of communal or personal identity and constant change. A more detailed specification of the notion of modernity is unnecessary for present purposes. My aim is simply to sketch the most general outlines of the notion as a backdrop for the following delineation of three authoritative elaborations of the place of religion in modernity broadly conceived.

Instead of trying to legislate for an essential meaning of 'modernity', then, I shall sketch three uses of the term which have been very influential in the sociology of religion. I shall then ask how each of them makes sense of some aspects of the pattern of religious change in the UK. For the sake of convenience I shall call these models of the relationship between modernity and religion, respectively, 'embrace', 'ambivalence' and 'exclusion'.

(a) The first sense of 'modernity' is epitomized in the work of Talcott Parsons and of the many social scientists who were strongly influenced by him in the 1960s and 1970s. Parsons laid down the framework of the normative functionalist approach to religion in *The Social System, Toward a General Theory of Action* and two influential articles.[6] It all added up to the claim that Christianity generated and legitimated the values and norms which were essential to the stability *and* economic development of modern social systems.[7] He argued that the process of modernization involved the extension of Christian values to more and more spheres of life, the differentiation of religious organizations from the rest of society, and the evolutionary upgrading of ethical conduct. He denied that this amounted to secularization, however, because religion remained essential in

linking individual conduct to core values. The more religious institutions were differentiated from politics, education, law and medicine, for example, the more likely it was for Parsons that religious
values would become refined, rationalized and diffused throughout
society. Civil religion was believed to fulfil the function of sanctifying
a society's highest ideals and of preventing governments from claiming divine sanction for their actions. Meanwhile, Christian values
were supposedly sufficient to drive individuals to seek new achievements and thereby constantly to modernize their society.[8]

Far from being at odds with modernity, then, the Christian
religion, according to Parsons, was actually a prerequisite for modernization. The prospects for modernity in non-Christian culture
areas were correspondingly poor – a recurrent theme of the huge
American literature on modernization in the 1960s. Robert Bellah,
for example, defined modernization as the construction of social
systems 'with a built-in tendency to change in the direction of greater
value realization' (i.e. influence of Protestant-type values of discipline, rationality and inner-worldly asceticism).[9] He explained the
modernization of Japan in terms of the eventual realization of poli-
tico-economic and religious values which had been fostered by the
samurai and merchant class during the Tokugawa period. Again,
there is no conflict between religion and modernity. On the contrary,
modernity and religion embrace each other.[10] Bellah quotes a fif-
teenth-century monk to the effect that 'If we engage in business, we
must realize that it is in the service of Buddhism.'[11]

(b) The second sense of modernity, with an emphasis on rationalization, places the relationship between religion and modernity on a
different footing. In the hands of Peter Berger, in particular, religion
becomes both a victim of modernity *and* a potential source of resistance. The relationship is therefore ambivalent.[12]

Berger's argument is that the process of rationalization (i.e. consistently seeking a more efficient relationship between means and
ends) had its roots in ancient Judaism, was nurtured by Christianity
but has now become independent and threatening to religion. Technological rationality is particularly threatening because it leads to
the fragmentation of social and moral life. It allegedly drives individuals into privatized isolation and permits bureaucracy, the State
and big business to impose a single, instrumental standard of rationality on all spheres of life. The modern logics of business, government and employment not only lack moral legitimation but they
also erode human meanings and personal identity.

The antidote that Berger proposes against the acids of modernity
is, à la Tocqueville and Durkheim, to foster 'intermediary structures'
which can provide meaningful anchorage for personal identity *and*
some politico-moral leverage on the hyper-rational and authoritarian
practices of government and business. He believes that the chances

of successfully resisting crass rationality would be even greater if the intermediary structures were grounded in prophetic religion. For this would give them the transcendental warrant to challenge the dominant rationalities in the name of eternal truths and thereby to subordinate politics to religious critique.

Berger remains stoically ambivalent towards modernity: he recognizes its religious origins and material benefits but he also insists on its threats to meaningfulness and identity. He seems confident that, as long as the Two Kingdoms of politics and religion are kept separate, the capacity of the supernatural to relativize all human activity still stands a chance of resisting or neutralizing the acids of modernity.[13] There may only be a Rumour of Angels but it is strong enough to sustain Berger's faith in both God and modernity.

(c) The third authoritative version of the relationship beween religion and modernity implies that they are, to all practical purposes, mutually exclusive. One of the clearest statements of this position is that 'Whereas religion once entered into the very texture of community life, in modern society it operates only in interstitial places in the system . . . One might, then, juxtapose the two phenomena: the religious community and the secular society.'[14]

The explanation for this exclusion of religion from all but the margins of the modern world is that the logic of rationality, function, system and utility is sufficient to integrate the increasingly differentiated modern society. Consequently, 'Industrial society needs no local gods, or local saints; no local nostrums, remedies, or points of reference . . . The large-scale societal system does not rely, or seeks not to rely, on a moral order, but rather, wherever possible, on technical order.'[15]

Religion, or 'the ideology of community', has therefore been marginalized by the integration of local communities into whole societies through a process that Bryan Wilson calls 'societalization'.

Of course, religion survives on the margins of modern society – often in forms of noisy and intense commitment. But, according to this view, it still has no consequence for the social integration or moral direction of society. In other words, modernity prevents religion from fulfilling its societal functions. They virtually exclude each other.

In the hands of authoritative sociologists, then, modernity is given the appearance of being, variously, constitutive of religion, ambivalent towards religion or exclusive of religion. The more subtle combinations and nuanced versions of these basic theoretical positions are of no concern to me here; my aim is simply to establish the broad range of possible relations between religion and modernity. The next part of my argument will try to gauge to what extent each of these three theoretical positions can account for recent developments in British religion.

Religion in the UK

Religion is such a complex and subtle phenomenon that we are unlikely to be able to find clear-cut and unambiguous evidence for or against the relative usefulness of the three models of the relationship between religion and modernity. Certainly, it would be unwise even to look for anything more decisive than their respective degrees of plausibility. Fortunately from my point of view, the broad patterns of change in the readily observable aspects of religious conduct are quite clear.

Beginning with the evidence concerning participation in formal religious organizations, it is clear that religious activity is far from being completely marginal.[16] But the pattern of church membership falls into two different categories: the mainstream of Anglicans, Methodists, Presbyterians and Catholics is shrinking by about 5 per cent per annum, while the minority Christian groups seem to be static or growing. If we include the sectarian, cultic and New Age expressions as well, the picture of one-sided growth is even more pronounced. Finally, the growth rates among Muslim, Hindu and Sikh religions complete the two-pattern picture of uneven development.[17]

As far as the Christian churches are concerned, the evidence from the USA and Canada indicates that the number of drop-outs from religion altogether is rising only slowly and is still quite small. Similarly for the UK, no more than about 4 per cent of British adults describe themselves as atheists.[18] But the situation is not static. A 'circulation of the Saints'[19] or a game of religious musical chairs[20] is occurring, with Protestants either re-joining conservative churches or migrating from the mainstream to the more conservative groups. There are also pressures within sections of the mainstream for the adoption of more conservative and even sectarian stances on doctrine, liturgy and ethics.

In any case, as would be expected on the basis of theories about 'lazy monopolies'[21] or about the mis-timing of church-building programmes,[22] the decline in the numbers of ministers and churches or congregations in the mainstream is much less sharp than the decline in members.

But some advocates of the view that modernity is incompatible with religion would still insist that evidence of participation in religious organizations was partly irrelevant to their argument about the declining power of churches and other religious organizations to influence public life. From this point of view, religion could still be marginal despite the evidence about participation levels especially if people no longer held religious beliefs. If we turn to evidence about levels of reported religious beliefs, however, we discover that about 76 per cent of adults in the UK profess to believe in God; 58

per cent define themselves as religious; 50 per cent think God is important in their life; but only 27 per cent believe in the devil. Admittedly, we have no way of knowing precisely what it means when a respondent affirms one of these beliefs. Nor is there much reliable evidence about the way in which people translate their stated beliefs into practical conduct. But at least the levels of consistency between the findings of separate surveys are impressively high. They display the same kinds of patterns and trends, for example. Moreover, nobody has collected reliable evidence of either system- atic or random attempts to give misleading responses to survey questions. In the circumstances, caution is needed in the interpre- tation of the findings about reported beliefs; but the findings cannot simply be discounted.

The persistence on a large scale of what Towler[23] called 'conven- tional religion' also indicates that Berger's scenario of a beleaguered minority of religious believers battling against the forces of mod- ernity is also an exaggeration as far as the UK is concerned. Indeed, religious commitments are in the majority in some regions, age groups, social classes and professional categories. For example, 75 per cent of adults belong to religious organizations in Northern Ireland.

On the other hand, Berger's prescription for a system of religious checks and balances on politics in modern societies seems to be at odds with some tendencies. Both in the UK and in many developing countries there is a growing affinity between religious and political forces for radical change. Indeed, religious voices are being increa- singly heard in campaigns for a change in government policy on a wide range of issues from poverty and the poll tax to nationality laws and nuclear weapons.[24] The evidence is inconclusive at present, but there are certainly grounds for suggesting that the anticipated privatization of religion is at least being paralleled by a process whereby religion is also becoming more publicly visible and contro- versial.[25]

It is difficult to imagine what kind of evidence would count for or against Talcott Parsons's version of the relation between religion and modernity, but he might have regarded the diversity of religion in the UK and the increasing pressure for a sharper division between Church and State as at least partial confirmation of his views. On the other hand, the religious diversity in the UK is not the same as pluralism in the USA. In fact, it reflects deep-rooted divisions and conflicts over fundamental beliefs and values rather than universal equality and tolerance.[26] Significantly, the less tolerant and the less universalistic churches and synagogues are among the religious groups which are growing. Rather than striving towards a more abstract and diffuse kind of spirituality, they offer a more literal, practical and particularistic style of religion. This is not to say that

Parsons was entirely wrong about the direction of change in modern religion: it is merely to point out that the expected process of benign value-rationalization has been matched, if not eclipsed, by the contrary development of a type of religion characterized in Parsons's own terms by particularism, affectivity, ascription and specificity. These characteristics are the very opposite of a modern pattern in Parsons's terms.

In short, although the case is not clear-cut, there are plenty of reasons for thinking that the three main versions of the relation between religion and modernity in the sociology of religion – embrace, ambivalence and exclusion – may have overlooked something. But perhaps the most telling reason for questioning the received wisdoms is that none of the prevailing versions pays more than passing attention to what I believe to be the most important aspect of religious change in recent years. I am referring to the growth of parallel, yet contrasting, types of religion. On the one hand, Christian churches and Jewish groups with strict and very conservative outlooks are growing. And, on the other, a relatively new form of liberal and tolerant spirituality is spreading both inside and outside religious organizations. I shall refer to the latter as 'holistic' spirituality. The combination of these two contrasting developments wreaks havoc with prevailing ideas about religion and modernity. Let me be more specific about the new spirituality.

The first major characteristic of the new spirituality is that, although it is sensitive to considerations transcending the mundane world of individual and sectional interests, it does not necessarily refer to the supernatural. Instead, it strains towards a holistic perspective which emphasizes the inter-connectedness between, for example, human and non-human, personal and public, physical and mental, or national and international. It therefore involves what Luckmann terms 'a little transcendence' rather than the 'great transcendences' at the centre of the major world religions.[27]

The second major characteristic is the belief that the adoption of a holistic perspective can provide access to, or can release, new sources of power. The new spirituality tends to be focused on application of this power to practical problems to do with, for example, health, the quality of food, the natural environment, human rights, justice and peace. The underlying optimism is strong in the conviction that the power to solve many problems is available to human beings but is conditional upon their abandonment of ways of thinking which are analytic rather than synthetic, dualist rather than monist, divisive rather than constructive.

The third major characteristic of this new spirituality is that it seems to be compatible with a wide range of specific ideologies and practices. Although some New Age groups try to foster particular forms and applications of holism, this is not the significant point for me. Much more important from a sociological point of view is the fact that holistic spirituality is being adopted and adapted by many different agencies for their own purposes. It represents a general shift in sensibility and ethos: not a specific programme of social change or a separate form of religious practice. It would be wrong, therefore, to adopt what Gusfield called a 'linear perspective' on holism, i.e. the expectation that this movement would have clearly defined origins, forms of organization and consequences.[28] Instead, we need a 'fluid perspective' in order to appreciate how the movement is slowly influencing ways of feeling, perceiving and interacting, especially by eroding the barriers between politics and personal life.

I am not suggesting that a wave of holism is threatening to sweep away patterns of religious culture which have been sedimented over centuries. My claim is the more modest one that a relatively new sensibility to holistic considerations is working its way into organized religion and other social spheres. I am thinking particularly about the recent evolution of some ways of thinking about medicine, sport, leisure, education, peace, ecology, dying and grieving, self-help, gender, relations with non-human animals, social work, and even management training. There is a growing recognition in each of these spheres of the strengths that can be derived from emphasizing the wholeness of the human person, the inter-connectedness of the human/non-human environment, and the essentially global nature of social and natural processes.[29] The thrust is towards a transcendent, but not necessarily supernatural, point of reference. An echo of this 'transcendent humanism' has been detected even in the rural French Catholic Church.[30]

Now, there will no doubt be objections (i) that this holistic current is confined to a tiny proportion of the population, and (ii) that spirituality is not the same as religion. On the first point, I have to admit that the number of activists and true believers deliberately pursuing or cultivating holism may still be relatively small. But I contend that holistic consciousness has already made inroads deep into public thinking about ecology, peace, gender and health.[31] On the second point, it seems to me that there is far more overlap than difference between 'religion' and 'spirituality' in so far as they both denote ways of thinking, feeling and acting which are oriented towards the highest sources of meaning and value. If spirituality lacks the sense of communal obligation and collective ritual attaching to public religion, it is only appropriate that it should expand at a time when personal choice seems to be the criterion of well-being in so many areas of life.[32]

My preference is to examine the emerging forms of the new spirituality and the range of occasions and places where it is having an impact without worrying too much about definitional matters. The important thing is to get on with the task and not to be constrained by the vocabulary which currently prevails in the sociology of religion. At least, it is clear to me that the current vogue for holistic forms of spirituality makes little or no sense in terms of the three models of the relations between religion and modernity that I outlined above. The next question to tackle is whether it would be more profitable to interpret the 'holistic shift' as a feature of post-modernity.

The Post-modern Possibility

If one of the prominent changes taking place in religion in the UK fails to fit into the dominant models of the relations between modernity and religion, perhaps the notion of 'post-modernity' is better adapted to the task of understanding the change. It would be naive to expect help from a concept which is even more heavily contested than that of 'modernity', but the exercise may prove useful if it compels us to question some of our routine ways of thinking.

The first difficulty with my plan is that the term 'post-modernity' is not only contestable in its details but is also construed as serving different functions. It can serve, for example, as the label of an artistic style, a periodization of history, or a shift of sensibility. In order to reduce the difficulty, let me simply stipulate that I shall use it in the sense of a shift of sensibility without presuming anything about style or periodization. I shall ignore all questions about the causes of post-modernity.[33]

The next difficulty is to reduce to a manageable number the characteristics imputed to the new sensibility. Here again I propose to make a selection and not to try to embody every conceivable characteristic. It seems to me that the following are most commonly associated with post-modernity:

1 A refusal to regard positivistic, rationalistic, instrumental criteria as the sole or exclusive standard of worthwhile knowledge.
2 A willingness to combine symbols from disparate codes or frameworks of meaning, even at the cost of disjunctions and eclecticism.
3 A celebration of spontaneity, fragmentation, superficiality, irony and playfulness.
4 A willingness to abandon the search for over-arching or triumphalist myths, narratives or frameworks of knowledge.

If these characteristics are the hallmarks of the post-modern sensibility in general, then one might expect, on the analogy with post-modern fine arts, architecture and literature, that it would receive a distinctive expression in religion. My expectation would be that

putatively post-modern forms of religion would embrace diversity
of discourse and the abandonment of unitary meaning systems;
cross-references between, and pastiches of, different religious traditions; collapse of the boundary between high and popular forms
of religion; and an accent on playfulness or cynicism.

It would be no exaggeration to describe a few New Age groups
and new religious movements as post-modern in these terms. The
Neo-Sannyas movement of the Bhagwan Shree Rajneesh, for
example, epitomizes anti-rationalism, pastiche, populism and playfulness.[34] Some Buddhist spiritualities 'deconstruct' identity into
experiences of fragmentation. And an avowedly post-modern theologian like Robert Bellah celebrates the fact that monks and guests
at a Benedictine retreat in California contemplated the sacrament of
the Eucharist 'in the posture of zazen'.[35] But these examples are
purely illustrative: not representative. More to the point, they are
definitely rare and marginal to most forms of present-day religion
in the UK. This raises the point that *many* examples of post-modernism are precisely rare and of élitist concern. They may 'quote' from
mass-cultural styles but they do not represent mass products. Perhaps they attract a disproportionate amount of attention not only
because of their sheer exoticism but also because the majority of
British adults have become illiterate or 'deskilled' in matters of
religion. As a result, there are fewer standards and fixed points of
reference by which to place novelties such as NRMs in any wider
perspective.

If we disregard the glittering baubles on the exotic fringe of
religion, it is much harder to find illustrations of post-modern sensibility. Indeed, many of the relatively thriving groups and movements tend to veer in the opposite direction towards a reliance on
very univocal, would-be universalistic, fundamental and definitely
'triumphalist' principles of truth. Even the cultivation of ecstatic
experiences and heightened emotion in, for example, Pentecostalism
or charismatic movements is based on principles derived from the
Bible, presumably a source of ultimate truth. The fashion for 'house
churches' and Christian communities also reflects much greater continuity than discontinuity with the strong Christian meta-narratives
about hope, heaven on earth and salvation. And, despite the form
of the medium, the style of televangelism is remarkably derivative
from traditional evangelism.

In short, it seems that the British expressions of Christianity and
other world religions which have fared relatively well in recent years
have been resolutely transcendental rather than immanent, serious
rather than playful, in good faith rather than cynical, univocal rather
than fragmented, and so on.

My assessment of the new spiritualities that I discussed earlier is
the same, namely, that their very holism locates them much more

firmly in the traditions of modernity than of post-modernity. The stress on the inter-connectedness of all living things, the heightened awareness of 'the global circumstance',[36] the strong sense of evolutionary equilibrium and change, the belief in the possibility of personal and social transformation, and the affirmation of non-instrumental rationalities are all redolent of a revised 'Enlightenment project' with the emphasis more firmly placed on the human scale and spiritual implications of science, politics and State administration. There is explicit condemnation of the elision which has taken place between technology as a force for controlling nature and modernity as a force for controlling human beings.

Some of the most visible and controversial aspects of religion nowadays include religiously-inspired attempts to bring the forces of science, technology and bureaucracy back under human control. The *contretemps* between senior clergy and government are not entirely new, of course, but the scale and frequency of the disagreements are unusual. Again, I think that they indicate a determination to harness the benefits of modernity without abandoning faith in rational planning and profitable business. There is nothing post-modern about the Bishop of Durham or the Roman Catholic Archbishop of Liverpool.

Nevertheless, the fragmentation of formerly unitary systems of religious meaning has undoubtedly taken place in many western societies; and the juxtaposition of formerly separate religions may have created the impression more of a patchwork quilt than of a sacred canopy. But it does not follow that many religious collectivities have abandoned their claims to universal truth. Nor is there much evidence of a distinct turn away from belief in scientific principles. All that has happened in some cases is that the more narrowly empiricist and positivist versions of science have been modified to suit supernaturalist or humanistic criteria of truth. In any case, there is a widespread belief in many religious circles that scientific thinking is moving closer to religious sensibilities.[37] I fail to see why this amounts to post-modernism[38] and not simply another instance of epistemological change. There has always been a tension within *modern* thought between triumphalist science and symbolic realism.

Conclusion

If my claim is correct that some recent changes in the pattern of religion and spirituality in the UK defy interpretation in terms of the dominant models of modernity *and* post-modernity, does it follow that sociologists of religion are bereft of a suitable explanation? I want to argue that one alternative way of making sense of the puzzling pattern of religious change is to examine the social transformations which have allowed religious symbols to float free to some extent from their former points of anchorage in religious organizations and institutions.

It is clear that religion (including holistic spirituality) can still convey convincing symbols of various transcendent realities. It can serve as a language for representing powerful inspirations, perceptions, sufferings and aspirations even though the users of this language may not associate with any religious organization. In some cases, religion conveys conservative ideas of national, tribal or cultural integrity. In other cases, it conveys new and challenging ideas of personhood, wholeness, peace and justice. In all cases, however, it is apparent that the *use* of religious symbols is increasingly likely to be controversial and contested these days because they are no longer necessarily tied to age-old communities or other so-called natural groupings.[39] It can no longer be taken for granted that most uses of religion will, by definition, be for the straightforward benefit of any entire community. Religion has come adrift from its former points of social anchorage but is no less potentially powerful as a result. It remains a potent cultural resource which may act as the vehicle of change, challenge or conservation. Consequently, religion has become less predictable. The capacity of religion to mobilize people and material resources remains strong, but the decline of various religious monopolies and other powerful religious organizations has increased the possibility that it can be mobilized in unexpected places and in ways which may be in tension with 'establishment' practices and public policy.[40]

This argument about what Georg Simmel might have called the 'autonomization' of religion amounts to much more than the claim that religion can nowadays be marketed in a quasi-commercial fashion. This is only part of the picture. The freeing of religion from its points of anchorage in age-old communities and natural social groupings has also turned it into a resource which may be invested with highly diverse meanings and used for a wide variety of purposes. Religion can now be put to varied uses both within and outside the framework of religious organizations and, where they exist, State religions. Civil religions, for example, are best thought of as symbolic resources employed by politicians independently of religious organizations. Religious symbols frequently serve the interests of revolutionaries and political radicals as well. Health care and movements for the protection of the environment or the promotion of human rights or peace are other spheres in which religious symbolism is increasingly being appropriated.

The profound and continuing transformations of advanced industrial societies since the 1960s have tended to undermine the communal, familial and organizational bases of religion. But religious and spiritual forms of sentiment, belief and action have survived as relatively autonomous resources. They retain the capacity to symbolize, for example, ultimate meaning, infinite power, supreme indignation and sublime compassion. And they can be deployed in the service of virtually any interest-group or ideal: not just organizations with specifically religious objectives. This presents obvious advantages in states which offer constitutional protections for religious activity. But it also leads to problems if the 'protected' use of religion falls foul of public opinion or government policy.

This can all be summarized in the statement that, from a sociological point of view, it is nowadays better to conceptualize religion as a cultural resource or form than as a social institution. As such, it is characterized by a greater degree of flexibility and unpredictability. For the decline of the great religious monopolies in the West has been accompanied by the sporadic deployment of religion for a great variety of new purposes. Religious symbols can be combined with virtually any other set of ideas or values. And the chances that religion will be controversial are increased by the fact that it may be used by people having little or no connection with formal religious organizations. The deregulation of religion is one of the hidden ironies of so-called secularization. It helps to make religion sociologically problematic in ways which are virtually inconceivable in the terms of the sociological classics. We therefore need to adjust our ideas about modernity, but without necessarily accepting the logic of post-modernity.

Chapter 2

Religious Fundamentalism: Neo-traditionalism in Modern Societies

Stephen Sharot

'Fundamentalism' as Label

There has been little comparative analysis of modern religious movements across religious traditions and almost no discussions of the goals, analytical problems or suitable conceptual frameworks for such comparisons. There have, however, been a few attempts to compare 'fundamentalist' movements from different religious traditions. These comparisons have followed the frequent use of the term in recent years both in the mass media, where it is often used to denote religious extremism or fanaticism, and in scholarly works. The wide variety of understandings and definitions that have accumulated has led some scholars to question whether the extensive use of the term is likely to lead to analytical precision or explanations,[1] but a number of analyses have sought to define fundamentalism in a way that will allow for comparative analysis. The critical review of these attempts in this chapter is intended to clarify conceptual and analytical problems in the comparative analysis of religious movements across religious traditions. In its details, the critique is confined to the three monotheistic religions. The reason for this is that, although the term fundamentalism has been used to refer to movements in non-monotheistic traditions (the collection edited by Caplan includes examples),[2] I have not encountered an attempt at a systematic comparison that extends beyond the three monotheistic traditions. Movements that have been designated as fundamentalist include the Muslim Brethren and its more radical offshoots and successors among the Sunni, the Shiites in Iran, Protestant conservative and evangelical movements, ultra-Orthodox Jewish communities, and the messianic Gush Emunim movement in Israel.

Some scholars would prefer to restrict the term 'fundamentalism' to specific movements in Protestantism, but a distinction should be made here between the objection that movements in different religious traditions that have been called fundamentalist are not sufficiently similar to justify a common label, and the objection that the particular label is not an appropriate one for the category of religious movements that has been delineated. Shepard has argued that, although the similar reaction against modernity of Protestant fundamentalist and Islamic radical movements warrants a common label, the label should not be 'fundamentalism' because it has emotive connotations and, even more importantly, specific cultural content is implicit in the western usage.[3] Lawrence, on the other hand, objects to arguments that the label should be restricted to movements from the religious tradition in which the term originated (in this case Protestantism) or to those who identify themselves by it.[4]

My preference is to adopt the term 'neo-traditionalism' to refer to religious movements that self-consciously attempt to represent or reassert what they regard as their authentic religious tradition against what they perceive as threats in modern developments. A past society is believed to have embodied the authentic tradition, and this provides a model to be reconstituted or emulated. Understood in this way, the term encompasses movements that are often called 'fundamentalist' (Protestant fundamentalism, Jewish ultra-Orthodoxy and Islamic radicalism) as well as others that have been rarely so called (e.g. the Catholic opposition to Vatican II), but it excludes some movements that have also been labelled 'fundamentalist'. Pentecostal and millenarian movements have often been labelled 'fundamentalist',[5] but I would exclude them because, although they might include elements of neo-traditionalism, this does not constitute the core of their self-definitions. The distinctive characteristic of Pentecostal movements is their focus on the gifts of the Spirit in the here and now, and that of millenarian or messianic movements is their belief that the time of Redemption is underway or to begin in the near future. Neo-traditional movements may have messianic beliefs, but these are of much less immediate concern than the rebuilding in 'normal times' of a society that conforms to what is believed to be the authentic religious tradition. The reasons for preferring the label 'neo-traditionalism' will become evident in the discussion, but the arguments over terminology are secondary to the question of whether or not the various religious movements that are frequently labelled fundamentalist have common characteristics that are the consequences of common social processes.

From the Specific to the General and in between

Definitions or understandings of fundamentalism can be placed on a scale of generality, ranging from those that restrict it to a single religious tradition (usually Protestantism) to those that view it as a global phenomenon. An example of the former is that of Ammerman who writes that her working definition of fundamentalism includes three elements: separation from the world, dispensational pre-millenarianism and biblical literalism. Separation from the world could of course be extended as a criterion to other religious contexts, but biblical literalism considerably narrows the focus and dispensational pre-millenarianism narrows it much further, restricting its usage to those who believe that Christ will return to 'rapture' the true believers away from the world which will then suffer the reign of the anti-Christ before his defeat and the coming of the millennium.[6]

Some scholars of Protestant fundamentalism in the United States have argued that religious developments elsewhere, such as those in Iran, are not comparable to the American case. If fundamentalism is restricted to the Christian context, the major comparative question becomes why fundamentalistic movements have been far more important in the United States than in other western countries. There have been few attempts to confront this question, but among the factors that have been presented as contributing to or enabling fundamentalism and evangelicalism in America are the country's structure of Church–State relations, the religious legacy of the American south, and the decentralized polity which permits strong sub-cultures and puts fewer obstacles in the way of independent religious formation.[7]

At the other end of the scale of generality is the approach that views fundamentalism as a global phenomenon in the modern world. Roland Robertson writes that the upsurge of fundamentalist movements around the world is a particularizing reaction to the universalistic and relativistic tendencies of what he calls the globalization process. The making of the world into 'a single sociocultural place' has involved, among other relativizations, the relativization of religious traditions, and fundamentalists seek to reassert the 'real' identity of their societies and the primordial 'truth' of their traditions.[8] Following Robertson, Shupe and Hadden argue that global fundamentalism represents a resistance in many societies to secularization or the process in which religion becomes institutionally differentiated and loses its relevance in the general culture. They define fundamentalism as 'a proclamation of reclaimed authority of a sacred tradition which is to be reinstated as an antidote for a society that has strayed from its cultural moorings'. The movements proclaim their continuities with a traditional faith that they believe had previously existed in a pure form, but their attempts at restoration involve them in the promotion of new social arrangements.[9]

There has been little documentation of fundamentalism as a global phenomenon. Shupe and Hadden note that militant Sikhs are sometimes referred to as fundamentalist,[10] but all their other examples come from Protestantism, Islam and Judaism, and the extent to which the movements in these traditions have common fundamentalist features is not analysed. Robertson's analysis remains throughout at a highly abstract level, but he does write that, although he wishes to confine himself to an analysis of the global processes, ideally it should be combined with a comparative analysis. Presumably, only a comparative analysis of religious movements in different societies will answer the question of whether there is a common fundamentalist reaction to globalization processes.

Comparative analyses of fundamentalism have been attempted by authors whose approach may be placed within the middle of the scale of generality, encompassing movements in either two or three of the monotheistic faiths.[11] Not all these authors justify their focus on the monotheistic faiths, but those who do argue that only the monotheistic traditions have characteristics which make possible a fundamentalist response to modernity. Lawrence emphasizes the similarities in the doctrines and orientations of the monotheistic religions, and he suggests that only in these faiths is there likely to be a focus on irreducible core elements. The monotheistic traditions are characterized by the centrality of core religious texts, the Jewish Bible, the Christian Bible and the Qur'ān, and it is the particular orientation towards these texts that is claimed to be the core of the self-definition of the fundamentalist movements in all three faiths.[12] This orientation is variously termed literalism, inerrancy or spiritual absolutism.

A Religious Parameter to Fundamentalism?

Robin Gill defines fundamentalism as 'a system of beliefs and practices which treat scriptural absolutism as *the* way to counter the pluralism and relativism engendered by modernity', and writes that the term 'spiritual absolutism' is used in order to define fundamentalism in terms that are not solely Christian.[13] Lawrence, on the other hand, writes that many scholars restrict the term 'fundamentalism' to Protestant movements precisely because of their scriptural absolutism, and he attempts to justify the comparative approach by claiming that the potential for scriptural absolutism is at least as high in Judaism and Islam as in Protestantism.[14] This potentiality is presumably based on the centrality of core scriptures in all three faiths, but problems of comparison arise if this is taken to mean that the scriptures are the focus of authority in all the monotheistic traditions.

Shepard justifies confining his comparison to Protestantism and Islam because they are the only two religious traditions where a fixed written scripture, rather than priesthood, sacramentalism or mysticism, is the focus of authority. He justifies excluding Judaism from his comparison because, although Jews have a scripture, the emphasis on talmudic–rabbinical interpretation has made Judaism an ongoing tradition rather than a religion based primarily on a scripture.[15] Presumably, anti-modernist movements in Catholicism will not be fundamentalist because scripture is recognized by Catholics as mediated by the more basic authority of the Church. The restriction of scriptural absolutism to Protestantism and Islam does not, however, overcome problems of comparison.

One problem is that there are differences between the Sunni and Shiite traditions that are reflected in the neo-traditionalist movements. The Shiite tradition may be regarded as less scripturalist than the Sunni; whereas the authority of the Sunni *ulema* depends on their erudition, the authority of the Shiite *ulema* is believed to be derived from the Hidden Imam whom they represent in his absence. Sunni neo-traditionalists believe that the religious law should be inspired directly by the Qur'ān, abhore the official *ulema*, and call for the purification of the law from what they perceive as obscure legal interpretations and decisions of generations of official religious functionaries. The Shiite, in contrast, regard their official religious leaders as the custodians and authoritative interpreters of the law, and the principle of legitimate reinterpretation of the law by the Imam or religious leaders who speak in his name was fully exploited by Khomeini in Iran.[16]

Another problem is that, depending on the meaning attributed to scripturalism, Islam can be said to be both more scriptural and less scriptural than Protestantism, and in the sense that it is less scriptural (and more legalistic) a comparison with Judaism is more appropriate than a comparison with Protestantism. It is more scriptural (and more literalist) in the sense that the whole of the Qur'ān is believed to be the speech of God transmitted to Muhammad by the angel Gabriel. It followed from this belief that the Qur'ān was the eternal and unalterable Word of God, that it was revealed in Arabic and should not be translated, and that the integrity of the text had to be defended. This differed from Christianity where, because the Word of God was considered to be manifested in Christ's person, it was the nature of the Incarnation rather than the exact nature of God's speech that became the central issue in the formative period.[17] It may be said that because inerrancy and literalism are so central (or taken for granted) in the Muslims' conception of the Qur'ān, they are much less important than in Protestantism in differentiating between a fundamentalist and non-fundamentalist stance. Since Shepard recognizes this point it is not clear why he regards the scriptural bases of Protestantism and Islam as an important parameter in a comparison of 'fundamentalisms'.

In the sense that Islam, like Judaism, puts a primary emphasis on the practice of the religious law, it is less scripturalist than Protestantism. It might well be argued that, in order to interpret contemporary neo-traditionalism, the similarities in the developments of Judaism and Islam are more relevant than the emphasis on scripture in Protestantism and Islam. In Islam, like Judaism, the 'written law' was expanded in an oral tradition that was later set down in writing, and the *sharia* came to resemble the *halacha* in its details and range of jurisdiction. In both traditions, religious authority came to be vested in their religious scholars who codified and interpreted the law, applying the principles of logic, antecedents and analogy.[18] Sunni radicals condemn the Sunni religious establishment, but they emphasize conformity to the religious law and they justify their actions by reference to past scholars.

In addition to their concern with the fundamentals of their faith, Protestant neo-traditionals have been characterized by a strong, usually literal belief in the inerrancy of their scriptures. Lazarus-Yafeh writes that inerrancy can be traced, not only to early Protestant theology, but also to medieval Islamic thought, and that it is a more recent development in Jewish thought.[19] However, the far greater emphasis on the inerrancy of the scriptures in Protestant fundamentalism has led some commentators to seek parallels by arguing that literalism or inerrancy in fundamentalist Islam and Judaism is evident in their orientations towards their systems of religious laws. Islamic movements have been termed literalist when they have emphasized a literal obedience to the *sharia* (stoning for adultery, for example), but this approach is difficult to justify because there is no single authoritative legal text and there are four Sunnite schools of law.[20] Ultra-Orthodox Jews may be said to regard the *halacha* as inerrant because they accept the rabbinical interpretations,[21] but the Jewish tradition of seeking out apparent contradictions in *halachic* writings in order to reconcile them is clearly distant from inerrancy in Protestantism.

The attempts to find parallels or analogies in Judaism and Islam to scriptural absolutism or inerrancy in Protestantism only serve to obscure critical differences between Protestantism, on the one hand, and Islam and Judaism (and possibly all other religious traditions) on the other. Charles Liebman writes that Judaism and Islam have, unlike Protestantism, religious traditions with many interrelated elements (beliefs, ceremonies, mythology, history, customs) which do not lend themselves to the kind of summary statements associated with Protestant fundamentalism. Protestants have the Bible in common, and their belief that it can be understood without the mediation of a tradition of authoritative commentaries accounts for the diversity of Protestant movements. The very notion of an unmediated interpretation is a dubious one in Judaism and Islam in which interpreters centre their debates on previous commentaries and interpretations, some of which may be considered equal with or even more important than the founding text.[22]

Formulated in such stark terms, Liebman's contrast fits ultra-Orthodox Judaism more than Islamic radicalism. Whereas ultra-Orthodox Jews stress continuity in the interpretation of the religious law, among Sunni radicals various views may be found regarding the traditional schools of Islamic legal interpretations. Although there may be few Muslims who would propose an entirely unmediated interpretation of the Qur'ān, some Sunni radicals have expressed a wish to remove the layers of past interpretations of the law which they feel have obscured its spirit and made it inaccessible to popular understanding. The difference remains, however, that, unlike Protestantism, a religion the core of which is doctrinal, the core of both Islam and Judaism is practice, and this difference is of central importance in comparing neo-traditionalism in Protestantism with neo-traditionalism in Islam and Judaism. In opposing religious modernism, it is natural for neo-traditional Protestants to state their position in terms of a number of fundamental doctrines, whereas for Muslim and Jewish neo-traditionals the central demand is conformity to the religious law.[23]

The conclusion that emerges from this part of the discussion is that, if fundamentalism is taken to mean scriptural absolutism or a focus on a few fundamental elements, the extension of usage from Protestantism to Islam and Judaism is not justified. If fundamentalism or neo-traditionalism is taken to mean the assertion of what is conceived as an authentic tradition against the incursion of what are conceived as the dangers in modernity, there is no analytical justification for restricting comparison to the monotheistic faiths. However, for reasons of economy of presentation, comparison will continue to be limited in this chapter to the monotheistic traditions.

Neo-traditionalism and Tradition

It is important to distinguish between the neo-traditionals' representation of the authentic tradition and their image of the traditional society that existed prior to the incursion of modernity. Neo-traditionalists are inventing tradition and this involves a stance towards the traditional society that ranges from the conservative to the radical. This is recognized, in part, by Shepard who wrote that whereas American fundamentalists are concerned to conserve elements from the period prior to the rise of modernity, the Muslims demand a radical reconstruction of their society.

Shepard argued that the two 'fundamentalisms' were similar in so far as both hark back to the past with visions of two golden ages, one quite far back and one relatively recent, that provide the standards by which modern developments are measured. For the Protestants, the two idealized images of the past are the early or 'primitive' Christian community, and the 'Great America' which was established by the Puritans and founding fathers and continued until about the mid-nineteenth century.[24] For the Muslims, it is the early Islamic society under Muhammad and (for Sunnis) the first caliphs, and the period just before the penetration of western imperialism.

Shepard's formulation does not emphasize sufficiently the differences between the American Protestant and Islamic Middle Eastern cases. Most Muslim neo-traditionals do not have as positive an image of the pre-colonialized Islamic society as American neo-traditionals have of pre-modernized America. Islamic religious radicals do not perceive themselves as part of a historically continuous traditional community, but rather as representing a return to a model society of the distant past which they must now rebuild in entirely new circumstances. For Sunni radicals, the fourteen centuries following the period of the Prophet and the four 'rightly guided caliphs' are of much less importance and contributed many deviations and distortions from the original Isamic message. Many believe that it was the decadence of the traditional Islamic community, its failure to adhere to a pure form of Islam, that made it susceptible to the inroads of western colonialization.[25] The model of the early Islamic community represents for them, not only rejection of the West, but also of the pre-westernized Islamic society that succumbed to western conquest and cultural influence.

The radical form of Islamic neo-traditionalism appears even more prominent when the comparison is extended to ultra-Orthodox Jews. They may be considered the most conservative of the neo-traditionals considered here in the sense that they see themselves as the carriers of a traditional society, formerly located in eastern Europe, which they seek to preserve and strengthen in new locations. In the last decades of the nineteenth century, there was a defection from the traditional religious society of east European Jewry, a defection that grew considerably during the inter-war years, but survivors of the Holocaust succeeded in establishing or considerably strengthening ultra-Orthodox communities in the West and in Israel. The greatly improved economic circumstances of the post-war period enabled them to build communities from which there was comparatively little defection and which grew significantly as a consequence of their high birth-rate.

The closest approximation in the Jewish context to the radical orientation towards tradition among many Islamic neo-traditionals was to be found among secular Zionists up to about 1967. They regarded the two thousand years diaspora between the ancient Jewish state and the new Israeli state as of little interest or even with contempt. The Jewish ultra-Orthodox, on the other hand, stress the historical continuity of the Jewish tradition, the need to follow the ways of their fathers, and the need for the non-Orthodox to return to the ways of their grandparents or great-grandparents. And indeed, for many *ba'alei teshuvah* (Jews from secular or non-Orthodox backgrounds who become Orthodox Jews), it is their grandparents or great-grandparents who have provided the appropriate model.[26] The traditional eastern European community remains the historical model for the ultra-Orthodox, but in fact the standards of the contemporary ultra-Orthodox community are more stringent and less compromising than those of the pre-war traditional community. The voluntaristic character of the contemporary community, based on members' commitment to the religious way of life, means that rabbis no longer have to soften their demands for stringency in order to cater to the less observant, and the tradition of the written law has come to triumph over the more compromising tradition anchored in the daily life of the local traditional community.[27]

Neo-traditionalist Selective Rejection of Modernity

In addition to their invention of tradition, neo-traditionals can be characterized by their selective opposition to dimensions of modernity. Most interpretations of fundamentalism have included in their definitions or characterizations an opposition to modernity, but there is a danger here of repeating the mistakes of those analyses of modernization which took as their framework the distinction between traditional and modern society. An attempt to understand the transformations of societies in 'modern times' by a single concept (modernity) has brought forth an attempt to understand religious oppositions to the transformations by another single concept (fundamentalism).

Although the rejection of modernity had been made central to an understanding of fundamentalism, the notion of modernity and its complex multi-dimensionality is rarely given detailed attention in discussions of fundamentalism. By omitting to break down modernity into its components and multiple contexts in time and space, the analyses fail to differentiate fundamentalist or neo-traditional movements from some other types of contemporary religious movements (for example, healing cults or millenarian movements) which, although they may have some common characteristics with some neo-traditional movements, differ considerably from them in their orientation towards important dimensions of modernity.

These problems are apparent in Lazarus-Yafeh's comparison of fundamentalism in the three monotheisms. She wrote that, although modernity may not have brought a greater resemblance among societies, it has brought forth universal negative reactions and is considered 'the great evil' by fundamentalists. She mentioned the impact of such social changes as the collapse of the family, intensive urbanization, rapid secularization, and the frustrations of those who are only partially absorbed in the expanding system of education. It is suggested that the impact of these changes will be so overwhelming that the fundamentalist religious reaction will be similar regardless of the differences among the religious traditions. She lists what she considers are nine 'astonishing' similarities of fundamentalist movements in the three monotheisms,[28] but some similarities are trivial in the sense that they are also found in religious movements that are not normally called fundamentalist (for example, a belief in Satan and spirits, apocalypticism), others do not apply to all three fundamentalisms (rejection of western ideologies and institutions can hardly be said to apply to American evangelicals), and certain features are far more significant in one of the fundamentalisms than in the other two (inerrancy in Protestant fundamentalism).

Lawrence listed five traits which, when found together, are intended to distinguish fundamentalist movements both from their modernist opponents and their contemporary co-religionists. The traits are: minority viewpoint, opposition to secular political or judicial powers, secondary-level male élites, a technical vocabulary and no ideological precursors. He admits, however, that other sectarian or separatist movements can be characterized by the initial four traits, and he claims that the one trait which is truly distinctive of fundamentalists is that they originated in direct response to the global pattern of modernization (and therefore have no ideological precursors).[29] Lawrence does introduce some clarification of his critical definitional and explanatory factor by distinguishing between modernization, the material elements of the modern world that fundamentalists accept and adopt, from modernism, the ideological response of the modern world that fundamentalists oppose. He writes that, fundamentalists 'accept the instrumental benefits of modernity but not its value reorientations',[30] and gives Khomeini as an example of a fundamentalist who relied on the instrumentalities of the modern world while rejecting its essential spirit.[31]

Lawrence's distinction between modernization and modernism follows what has been a widespread observation of fundamentalist movements: they tend to adopt and utilize the technological (and possibly also bureaucratic) dimensions of modernity and reject its cultural dimensions. The utilization of modern technology is most evident in the United States in the form of televangelism,[32] but effective use of modern media can also be observed by such groups as the Lubavitch Hasidim who broadcast their leader's speeches to their communities throughout the world and the Shiites in Iran who in the pre-revolution period spread the messages of Khomeini through cassettes. Fundamentalist or neo-traditional orientations towards science are somewhat more ambiguous and variable. Protestant fundamentalists have strongly opposed evolutionism and critical biblical scholarship, but, as Barr has shown, they tend to accept most findings of science and interpret their religious beliefs in conformity with them.[33]

A total resistance to modernity appears to occur only in its initial stages, during what Germani calls 'primordial modernization',[34] and in recent times anti-modernist movements can be distinguished in terms of the aspects of modernity that they oppose. The youth counter-culture of the 1960s rejected primarily the technological and bureaucratic dimensions of modernity, but in its cultural styles it either adhered to radical versions of modern secular ideologies or it took to extremes the individualist, self-expressive, pluralist and relativist themes in modern culture (encapsulated in such expressions as 'Do your own thing').[35] Many of the cultural themes that the counter-culture expressed are those that neo-traditionals oppose, but it is an over-simplification to characterize fundamentalism or neo-traditionalism as opposition to modernity as a single cultural process. Such an approach tends to reify modernity, ascribing to it an 'essential spirit', without reference to its multi-dimensionality and variant societal contexts. Differences among neo-traditional movements are to be understood, therefore, not only because they emerged in different religious traditions, but also because they emerged in a number of socio-cultural contexts which experienced modern trends in different ways and time frames.

One important contextual difference for neo-traditional movements is the extent to which modernist themes have been incorporated by other religious movements within their religious traditions. As many histories of Protestant fundamentalism have emphasized, its emergence in the late nineteenth and early twentieth centuries represented a reaction to critical biblical studies, liberal Protestantism and the social gospel. Against 'higher criticism' the fundamentalists claimed that the Bible was inerrant, free of any error. Against 'progressive revelation' fundamentalists stated the 'fundamental' beliefs of Christianity that were true for all time: the Genesis account of creation, the Virgin Birth, Christ's physical resurrection, and the certainty of his bodily return to earth. Against an emphasis on social reform and on worldly social action as a religious duty, fundamentalists reiterated the absolute centrality of personal salvation.[36]

At a later date, Protestant fundamentalism in America developed a broader critique of modernity in the ideological and mass cultural areas. The perception among fundamentalists of the 'moral decline' of America began after the First World War, but it became far more central from the 1960s with the changes in sexual norms, family patterns, and the emergence of the counter-culture and movements such as those of the feminists and gays. Watergate increased the sense of moral decay at the centre, and the feeling of a direct threat was made acute by the Supreme Court 1973 decision on abortion and government intervention in rules for Christian schools and colleges. Thus, in the 1970s and 1980s, American neo-traditionalism focused on moral and political issues such as opposition to the equal rights amendment, pornography, homosexuality, abortion, and support for prayer in public schools and the teaching of creationism. The many cultural grievances and threats were designated together as 'secular humanism', and this construction of a cultural threat replaced modernist theology as the fundamentalists' major enemy.[37]

In the Jewish context, it is important to distinguish between the Orthodox and ultra-Orthodox (or *haredi*) movements. Both reject the incorporation of modernist themes within the religion, but they differ considerably both in the nature of their response to modernity[38] and in their socio-historical origins. The Orthodox movement in Judaism was a response to religious modernism in the form of Reform Judaism that began in Germany in the first half of the nineteenth century. The characteristics and context of Jewish religious modernism were very different from those of Christianity. The centrality of post-biblical writings in Judaism meant that Orthodox Jews felt much less threatened by source criticism than Orthodox Christians. The disputes between Orthodox and Reform Judaism were, in contrast with the disputes over doctrine within Protestantism, focused on the form and content of the synagogue services and have to be seen in the context of the acculturation and assimilation of many Jews to the wider society. In its emphasis on decorum, its replacement of Hebrew by the vernacular, and its abolition or reformulation of traditional prayers referring to the messiah and the return to Zion, Reform Judaism represented an attempt to accommodate to the wider, more 'modern' non-Jewish cultural and national environment.[39] Orthodox Judaism would not countenance any change in the traditional prayers, but in Germany there developed a more compartmentalized response in what come to be known as neo-Orthodoxy or modern Orthodoxy, combining an adherence to the traditional religious laws with an accommodation to what were now considered the non-religious aspects of the wider culture.[40]

A Reform or modernist religious movement did not penetrate most eastern European communities (Hungary was an exception), and in those areas the ultra-Orthodox represented a reaction to general secular trends and to the secular Jewish socialist and Zionist movements.[41] The ultra-Orthodox rejection of Jewish accommodation to secular western culture was strengthened after the major centres of traditional Jewry were destroyed in the Holocaust, and in the post-Second World War period they have continued to represent a rejection of the wider secularized culture more than of religious modernism. This is particularly the case in modern Israel where the Reform and Conservative movements are small and uninfluential.

Religious modernism in Islamic countries has been confined mainly to small intellectual groups,[42] and has not, therefore, provided a major target of Islamic fundamentalists who are more likely to criticize traditional religious forms such as Sufism or the 'magical' practices in folk Islam. Islamic neo-traditionalism is directed against Muslim adoption of western secular culture and ideologies. Even by the beginning of the twentieth century, many Muslims had begun to distinguish the negative (moral) aspects of western civilization from its positive (material) aspects, but after the Second World War the criticisms of western culture grew and expanded. In recent years, radical Muslims have made vehement attacks on consumerism and other messages of the mass media that have penetrated their countries from the West.[43]

Differences among Neo-traditional Movements

It is evident that, although neo-traditional movements differ in the extent to which they originated as opponents of religious modernism, they all oppose what they perceive as the disintegration of moral codes and deregulation of behavioural patterns that have accompanied secularization, cultural pluralism and relativism. With respect to other dimensions of modernity, there are important differences among them. Most neo-traditional movements have not rejected political modernity in the sense of state-building or the replacement of multiple authorities by a single national authority, but they differ in their orientations towards the ideology of nationalism, the development of which accompanied these institutional processes.

In line with his attempt to define and explain fundamentalism in terms of its opposition to ideological modernity, Lawrence wrote that fundamentalism is in 'ideological conflict' with nationalism; they are 'archenemies' and 'incommensurate opposites'.[44] Many Islamic neo-traditionalists reject modern nationalism, not only because they recognize its non-Muslim origins, but also because it threatens to splinter the unity of the *umma*, the universal Muslim community. There are others, however, who combine radical Islam with a positive identity with Arabism or their national homeland or both. Lawrence acknowledges differences between the Sunni fundamentalists who are 'anti-nationalist' and the Twelver Shiites who are 'modified nationalist',[45] but the Muslim Brethren in both Egypt and Syria have taken positive positions towards Arab nationalism.[46]

Fundamentalist Protestants in the United States cannot be judged to be anti-nationalist; they have often emphasized that their nation has a special place in God's scheme for history. Lawrence can, however, point to the ultra-Orthodox Jewish Neterei Karta as a fundamentalist movement that fiercely opposes Zionism, and although most other ultra-Orthodox Jews have accommodated to Zionism and the Israeli State, only a few would endow them with positive religious meaning. An apparent contradiction to Lawrence's characterization of Jewish fundamentalism as anti-nationalist has to be dealt with when he includes as fundamentalist the ultra-nationalist religious movement Gush Emunim. Lawrence admits that Gush Emunim appears as a 'reverse image' of Neterei Karta in its view of the Israeli State, the less stringent style of its members' religiosity in daily life, and its willingness to compromise with secular society, but in spite of these differences he states that the two movements are 'complementary branches' of a single Jewish fundamentalist movement. This labelling of Gush Emunim as funda-mentalist appears to be justified in Lawrence's account by the movement's opposition to 'Enlightenment influence' and its 'theo-cratic' tendencies, but since he also characterizes fundamentalism by its unremitting opposition to nationalism, it is difficult to under-stand how an ultra-nationalist religious movement can be funda-mentalist.

Lawrence is not alone in including Gush Emunim within the category of fundamentalism; in fact, this is the opinion of most writers on fundamentalism who have included a reference to, or written about, Gush Emunim,[47] and other authors have claimed that it is similar in type to Islamic movements such as the Muslim Breth-ren and its radical offshoots.[48] These comparisons, stressing simi-larities, fail to recognize or appreciate significant differences with respect to orientations towards nationalism, an important dimension of modernity.

It is true that there is some similarity between Gush Emunim and the Islamic movements in that its members condemn the intrusion of materialism from western culture, but this is a relatively minor theme in the movement's ideology and is not emphasized when it seeks support among secularized Jews. In fact, the movement's interpretation of modern history in the framework of the process of redemption includes positive evaluations of certain secular develop-ments among Jews. Since it was secular Zionists who were the principal historical actors in the early modern Jewish settlement in the Land of Israel and in the establishment of the State and its institutions, Gush Emunim see them as having played an important role in the process of redemption, paving the way for the religious Zionists who have now the principal role in the process. Gush Emunim spokesmen have interpreted their settlements in 'Judea and Samaria' (the West Bank) as continuing the pioneering tradition of settlements of the secular Zionists in the early decades of the twentieth century, but since the secular Zionists are now in a state of moral confusion and decline they should make way for the religious Zionists who see themselves as the new authentic élite, the new pioneers of a transformed Zionism, who understand the deep meaning of historical events, will awaken the dormant forces within the Jewish people, and advance the process of redemption.[49]

The sacralization of Zionism by Gush Emunim and its interpretation of events, particularly the foundation of the Israeli State, the 'Six-Day War', and the settlement of 'Judea and Samaria' within the framework of the process of redemption is in radical contrast to the understanding of recent historical events by Neterei Karta and the Satmar hasidim who condemn Zionism and the Israeli State as blasphemous abominations and even blame the Holocaust on Zionism. Gush Emunim should not be classed as a fundamentalist or neo-traditionalist movement because it does not proclaim that the remedy for certain modern cultural developments that it opposes is to be found by attempting to approximate to a society of the past. The First and Second Jewish Commonwealths (thirteenth to sixth centuries BC; second century BC to second century AD) are important positive historical references for Gush Emunim, but these do no more than foreshadow the Third Commonwealth that is believed to be emerging in the messianic process.[50] It is true that Gush Emunim seeks to promote the sacred texts, the Torah, in the determination of public policy, and that it sees the laws embodied in these texts as absolute and indivisible. But unlike the neo-traditional movements in all three monotheistic traditions, Gush Emunim has not so much emphasized the need to implement the sacred texts as it has emphasized the sacred meaning of historical events and processes in recent times. Its sacralization of Zionism and the Israeli State indicates that its orientation towards modernity is, in some important respects, one of appropriation rather than rejection.[51]

Neo-traditional movements reject modern secular ideologies, but they are, nevertheless, influenced by them. Islamic radicals denounce nationalist and socialist ideologies, but their ideology bears the imprint of those modern ideologies that have self-consciously attempted to provide an all-encompassing way of life. The Islamic ideology has also appropriated the modern model of revolution; Islam is presented as a revolutionary ideology and practice that will destroy the social order and rebuild it on entirely different foundations. The difference from the secular revolutionary model is that the rebuilt Islamic society will not be a new society but rather a restoration of pristine Islam.[52]

All neo-traditionalist movements model themselves on an idealized image of a pre-modern society, but they differ in the ways that they hope to attain an approximation to this image: either by segregation from what they perceive as the impure world of modern society, or by actively attempting to transform that society in their image. There is a tendency for the more conservative form of neo-traditionalism to be associated with segregation, and the more radical form to be associated with activism.

There are some small, passive Islamic groups which strive to emulate the way of life of the early Islamic community by segregating themselves from the world,[53] but in general Islamic neo-traditionalism is the least separatist and most activist. Islamic activists aim at the attainment of political power because they believe that the full revival of Islam can occur only within the Islamic State. Among the most important goals of both Sunni and Shiite radicals are an Islamic penal code, an Islamic tax system, the demotion of non-Muslims to second-class citizenship, and warfare against non-Muslim nations to free Muslim populations from conquest and subordination.[54]

Jewish ultra-Orthodoxy inclines towards separatism, but there are important differences in degrees of separatism among its sectors. In Israel, extreme separatism is associated with Neterei Karta and the Satmar hasidim who try to keep their contacts with the wider Israeli society to an absolute minimum. Other ultra-Orthodox have accommodated to the existence of the Jewish State and have made a number of attempts to protect and increase the observance of the Jewish law at the public level. They are interested in the passing of religious legislation, such as a ban on pork and regulations against work or transport on the Sabbath, but because the observance of dietary laws and the Sabbath are dependent on the family they understand that there are limits to what can be achieved by State legislation. For the ultra-Orthodox, a truly Jewish State depends on the coming of the messiah, and this in turn is dependent on the repentance of the Jewish people and their observance of the religious law. Since there is little sign that this is occurring, ultra-Orthodox activism in politics and public life is confined mainly to promoting the interests of their own communities and protecting them from the influence of the wider culture.[55] Only the Lubavitch hasidim have an extensive campaign to attract secular Jews to Orthodox Judaism, and they attempt to carry this out without compromising the separatism of their communities. The task is given to young *yeshiva* students who, by trying to convince others, reinforce their own religious commitment.[56]

The distinction between separatism and activism in the United States has often been expressed in terms of a distinction between fundamentalism or hard-core fundamentalism and evangelicalism or neo-evangelicalism.[57] An activist phase among fundamentalists following the First World War was shortlived, and after the Scopes trial of 1925, fundamentalists tended to turn inward, representing themselves in the 1930s as the 'faithful remnant'. Tension between separatists and activists became evident in the early 1940s with the resurgence of mass evangelicalism and the foundation of two movements representing the two stances. By the late 1950s there was a tendency for only strict separatists to retain the term fundamentalism, and a much larger non-separatist evangelical movement dropped the doctrine of dispensationalism and presented a more sophisticated attack on modern theology and culture. The evangelical movement became far more diverse in its social and religious opinions in the 1970s and 1980s, but the distinction between fundamentalism and evangelicalism in terms of separatism and outreach made less sense as many of those with the most fundamentalist beliefs began to take an activist stance and become politically involved.[58]

The Social Determinants of Differences among Neo-traditional Movements

Differences among fundamentalist or neo-traditional movements can be explained, in part, by the tendency of each movement to emphasize what is distinctive in its own religious tradition.[59] All propagate strict moral codes but, in keeping with their historical legacies, Protestant fundamentalists focus on doctrinal matters and the saving of individual souls, Jewish ultra-Orthodox emphasize conformity to the *halacha*, and Islamic radicals seek legal, political and social reform in accordance with the *sharia*. In the case of Islamic neo-traditionalism, the desire to fuse religious and political authority in a single community can be traced back to the historical circumstances in which Islam emerged. Whereas Christianity emerged within an already established State and Judaism was practised for most of its history under non-Jewish rule, Islam began as the very foundation of a political community, and the ideal of a fusion of religion and political community has remained throughout its history. Thus, in contrast with other neo-traditional movements, the Islamic movements see the achievement of political power as not just a means to achieve religious aims but as a religious end in itself.

The political component in the legacy of Islam does not, however, account for the rise in political activity in recent years. In the past, both Sunni and Shiite doctrines encouraged accommodation to ruling governments. The Sunni tradition legitimized Muslim rulers as long as they did not publicly reject Islam and condemned any act that was likely to lead to civil strife. Shiites have regarded States not ruled by the descendants of Ali as illegitimate, but the traditional approach recommended patience and pragmatic accommodation until the coming of the Imam. Sunni radicals have had to search out texts, such as that of the fourteenth-century Ibn Taymiyya, that justify rebellion, and Shiite radicals have emphasized the need to take action in order to create the conditions for the appearance of the last Imam.[60]

The transition to political confrontism is related to the effects of modernity; there is a strengthened feeling of political entitlement and more optimistic assessments of the effectiveness of political involvement. There is also, in the Islamic case, the image of a modernist threat that originates from outside the society and then corrupts from within. Religious movements that represent a reaction or revolt against the penetration of an external religion or culture have arisen in many periods, but the pervasiveness of modern western culture as communicated by the mass media has meant that the threat to the indigenous religion has been felt in an especially acute way in recent times. Thus, militant Islam can be represented as a reaction to what many Muslims see as western cultural imperialism, and to the devaluation and desecration of the indigenous culture by the West and westernized natives.[61]

Among the internal societal features that are likely to influence whether neo-traditional movements tend towards activism or separatism is the level of pluralism. Although a pluralistic political structure might provide more opportunities for unimpeded political action, cultural and religious pluralism is likely to lead to tension within activistic neo-traditional movements. In their battle over such issues as abortion and pornography, some Protestant fundamentalists, such as those in the Moral Majority movement, attempted to compartmentalize their religious from their socio-moral positions and sought out political allies among Catholics and Jews. This reaching out was criticized by stricter fundamentalists who believed that their essentially religious message was being diluted by 'pseudo-fundamentalists' or 'neo-evangelists'. In fact, it would appear that activism and a concern with growth was leading American fundamentalists to accommodate many of the features of secular culture: televangelists used the same entertainment techniques as secular entertainers, religious television channels presented their own soap operas, and fundamentalist literature came to include popular psychology, money guides and sex manuals.[62]

These developments indicate that, in a democratic and pluralistic society, the fundamentalist claim that they embody the single unique truth can be preserved only in a sectarian enclave. An attempt to mobilize widespread support outside that enclave requires them to accept diversity and thereby to lose their distinctiveness. To seek support among conservative Catholics and Jews constituted an accommodation to pluralism, and was recognized as such by the more sectarian fundamentalists. The separation of politics from religion represented a contradiction for those whose involvement in politics was justified by their religion.[63] The promotion of fundamentalism throughout a society without compromising basic positions appears more feasible when there is little democracy and pluralism, as in the case of many Muslim Middle Eastern societies.

Another factor that will influence the features of neo-traditionalism is the position of its social carriers within the processes of modernity. Supporters are likely to be drawn from two major types of groups and strata. First, those whose social life and cultural identity are anchored in communities that retain traditional features but feel threatened by modern developments. And second, those who have abandoned or been cut off from their traditional social life and cultural identity without being absorbed or being able to find a secure position within modern settings.

The closest approximation to the first pattern are the ultra-Orthodox Jews who are the most conservative of the neo-traditionals considered here in the sense that they seek to preserve and strengthen the kind of community into which most of them were born. The radical nature of Islamic neo-traditionalism, on the other hand, can be understood as a consequence of the experiences of disjuncture, social, cultural and religious, in the biographies of its supporters. The Muslim Brothers arrested in Egypt tended to be recent migrants to the cities with white-collar salaried jobs, and those who had returned to rural areas tended to be school teachers.[64] The members of the more militant successor movements who were brought to trial in Egypt were mostly in the twenty to twenty-five age group, from rural or small town backgrounds, and lived in poor areas on the outskirts of the large cities. Many were artisans and merchants but about half were students, especially in medicine and engineering.[65] Coming from traditionally illiterate strata, their education gave them access to the written scriptures and they can be considered upwardly mobile, but the form of education provided by the universities, consisting largely of the routine memorization of lecturers' manuals of narrowly conceived subjects, had little effect on their cultural identities. Students had to suffer the deficient infrastructure of the universities and overcrowded lodgings, and they realized that their education was unlikely to provide them with a prestigious occupation or comfortable standard of living.[66]

The Islamic radicals tended to come from relatively stable and cohesive family backgrounds, but the relocation of their families in urban environments and their experiences in the universities led to an awareness of cultural discontinuity without a substantive adoption of western ideas. This led them to support a holistically conceived Islam, seen as encompassing all aspects of existence, that was purified from the religious superstitions of their rural backgrounds and was opposed to all western influences.[67]

In terms of its relation to the past, Protestant fundamentalism is closer to the pattern of the conservative form of neo-traditionalism of

Jewish ultra-Orthodoxy than to the radical form, based on the pure image of the founding community, of Islamic neo-traditionalism. The early Christian community is an important positive reference, but the image of nineteenth-century Protestant America probably has more meaning for most American fundamentalists. In contrast with Jewish ultra-Orthodoxy, however, most Protestant fundamentalists are far less enclosed within a largely self-contained and historically continuous community. Many Protestant fundamentalists are members of major denominations, but even those who are members of independent fundamentalist congregations and send their children to fundamentalist schools spend their working lives in the 'outside world' and participate in the institutions of the wider civic society. They may be members of fundamentalist special purpose groups and support a movement such as the Moral Majority,[68] but their levels of participation in the wider society are far more extensive than those of the Jewish ultra-Orthodox, the boundaries of whose communities separating them from the wider society (including other Jews) are maintained by their distinctive appearance, language, and comprehensive array of community institutions.[69]

In the past, fundamentalists in America tended to include disproportionate numbers from rural areas, the lower socio-economic strata and older age groups. The socio-economic and age distribution of fundamentalists has become far more heterogeneous and now includes many middle-class, educated and young members, but religious conservatives (evangelicals and fundamentalists) still tend to be more rural, less affluent, and have less education than religious liberals. The growth of American fundamentalism in recent decades has been interpreted as a reaction to the norms and patterns of behaviour of the college-educated 'new class' that grew considerably, as a result of the rapid expansion of higher education, in the 1960s and 1970s. At the same time, the increase in the urban membership and educational and class levels of fundamentalists gave them greater resources and knowledge to promote their cause effectively, using modern technology.[70] In sum, the variations among neo-traditional movements can be understood as consequences of the historical legacies of the religious traditions in interaction with particular patterns of modernity, and the varied effects of these conjunctures on different groups and strata.

Conclusions

The term 'fundamentalist' will no doubt continue to be used in a wide variety of contexts, but if it is taken to mean the presentation of a religious perspective by reference to the 'fundamentals' of the religion, its usage outside Protestantism is not justified. There are also problems of extended usage when 'fundamentalism' is understood to mean literalism, inerrancy or scriptural absolutism. The element that is common among movements that are often called 'fundamentalist' is that they oppose important components of cultural modernism and advocate in its place religious societies modelled on societies of the past. It is the combination of opposition to cultural dimensions of modernity and the invention of tradition that distinguishes what I prefer to call neo-traditionalist movements from other contemporary religious movements.

In categorizing contemporary religious movements, it is important to recognize the multi-dimensionality of modernity and the range of religious responses to it. Opposition to the technological component of modernity is rare among religious movements that have emerged in recent times, and an understanding of the differences between neo-traditional and other movements is furthered by focusing on their religious responses to the cultural dimensions of modernity. These dimensions include secular ideologies, such as socialism and nationalism, scientism, a permissive ethos, liberal individualism, pluralism and ethical relativism. The possible religious responses are: religious modernism or incorporation (that is, the adoption of modernist themes into the religion itself), compartmentalization (involvement in modernism while adhering to a traditional religion with minimal change), appropriation (encompassing modern phenomena as sacred) and rejectionism.

If the modernist themes are rejected in favour of a religious society modelled on images of a past society (rather than on what is believed to be a new religious vision), the term neo-traditional would appear appropriate. The term denotes movements that not only readily accept certain dimensions of modernity, particularly modern technology, but are also influenced by the components of modernity that they reject. They model themselves on past or traditional societies, but their images of such societies are filtered through their contemporary perspectives. Their encounter with modernity has moulded their invention of tradition.

Once the possible religious responses to a multi-dimensionally conceived modernity are distinguished, it becomes clear that there are considerable differences between movements that have all been labelled 'fundamentalist'. In particular, the inclusion of Gush Emunim with such movements as the Muslim Brethren and the Moral Majority under a common label appears ill-conceived. Gush Emunim's orientation towards modern nationalism and the secular Israeli State is one of appropriation rather than rejection; it has sacralized rather than rejected modern nationalism and the secular State. The similarities that have been made between Gush Emunim and rejectionist movements relate more to their political activism than to their religious orientations towards modernity.

Once the comparative focus is narrowed down to neo-traditionalist movements, it is evident that there are important differences between them, particularly the difference between conservative and radical forms of neo-traditionalism. These differences can be related to the historical heritages of the traditions from which they emerged, the particular components of the modernity process in their societal contexts, and the social strata that are drawn to neo-traditionalism. The conservative case (the ultra-Orthodox Jews) includes a wide range of socio-economic statuses within a boundary-maintaining community which seeks to segregate itself from the penetration of the cultural components of modernity. In the radical case (Islamic radical movements) the greatest appeal has been to those who have experienced disjuncture from the traditional society and have been frustrated in their experiences of a modernity that is seen to originate from outside the society. American fundamentalists combine a defence of traditionally-conceived patterns with a rejection of the cultural patterns represented by the 'new class' of the modernizing society. Thus, the divergent forms of neo-traditionalism are the consequences of a complex interaction of religious heritages and processes of modernity among groups and strata who construct alternative worlds in their invention of tradition.

Chapter 3

Religion, Identity and the Enforcement of Morality

Christie Davies

Controversies as to whether particular moral precepts should be enforced by law are often discussed in a universal way, as if there were merely a series of general collisions between, on the one hand, attempts to use the power of the State to uphold virtue and punish wickedness and, on the other, the rights of the individual to choose for him- or herself or the negative utilitarian presumption that harm and suffering should be minimized even where they fall on those who have broken moral rules.[1] Yet in practice all such arguments occur within a social and historical context and those seeking to use the law to enforce morality may do so as much because it is perceived as necessary to the maintaining of a *particular* communal identity as for the reason that the transgressors are seen as violating a universal moral rule. The identity of a nation or a people is, of course, often defined or at least shaped by their historic allegiance to a particular religious tradition.[2] Even when questions of religious faith, belief and observance are, or have become, a private matter for the individual to decide, the State or, indeed, a local or regional political unit may continue to enforce moral rules derived from the traditionally predominant religion of the people, and attempts to overturn such laws will be resisted as a threat to the distinctive national or ethnic identity of the society. In such cases, religion, national identity and the legal enforcement of a particular morality are seen as all part of a single seamless web.[3] Yet even a seamless web can be unravelled, and in Britain, and indeed in much of western Europe generally, during the last forty years secularization and a declining sense of unique and separate national identities have gone together such that it has become more difficult to justify the use of the criminal law to enforce morality. These changes can be demonstrated by examining in detail the cases of Sunday trading, abortion and homosexual behaviour.

Sunday, Sunday . . . Sunday?

The issue of Sabbath observance is one in which the influence of
the religious forces upholding a specific national or ethnic identity on
the relationship between law and morality has long been explicitly
recognized, notably by Basil Mitchell in his Edward Cadbury lectures
at the University of Birmingham in 1966. The central theme of these
lectures (published the following year as *Law, Morality and Religion
in a Secular Society*)[4] was the debate that had taken place between
Lord Devlin and H. L. A. Hart[5] on whether it was the business of
the State to enforce morality. Basil Mitchell suggested that:

> In point of fact it sometimes happens that an effort is made by law to
> safeguard institutions less because they are thought to be good than
> because they are thought to be characteristic. No doubt in all such cases
> motives are mixed, but it is reasonable to suspect that some of those who
> want to preserve the Welsh language and the Welsh Sunday do so not
> because they believe these institutions have peculiar merits, but because
> they are characteristically Welsh. They want to preserve the Welshness of
> Wales, even if it means that the majority have to learn a minority language
> and those who want to drink on Sunday are frustrated . . . Without the
> Welsh language and the Welsh Sunday, Wales would suffer no greater
> injury than that of becoming largely indistinguishable from England. One
> would have to say something like that the survival of the Welsh way of
> life was at stake, not what makes Wales viable, or what makes it civilized
> but what makes it Welsh.[6]

At the time when Basil Mitchell wrote, the law prohibiting the
sale of alcohol in public houses on Sunday in Wales (and Monmouthshire, which thus showed itself to be Welsh even though it was not
at that time officially part of Wales) was indeed a crucial marker of
the distinctiveness of Wales *vis-à-vis* its larger neighbour England
with which it otherwise shared a common set and system of laws.
The Welsh had asserted their separate identity by imposing on the
individual a restriction which did not apply in England. The crucial
religious link between Welsh ethnicity and the enforcement of morality by law was Noncomformist Protestantism. The majority of the
Welsh people were Calvinistic Methodists, Wesleyan Methodists,
Baptists and Independents (Congregationalists)[7] with only an English or Anglicized minority who belonged to the established Church
of England. The Welsh asserted their collective identity by disestab-
lishing the Church of England so that there is no established Church
in Wales and by closing their public houses on Sundays, which
combined two Nonconformist Protestant themes, namely temper-
ance and sabbatarianism. The keeping of the sabbath was in Wales,
as in Scotland and in Ulster, where the Reformed Churches were
equally tied to national or ethnic identity, an expression of national
self-assertion through a display of collective religious virtue. Yet it

was achieved by restricting the freedom of choice of individual Welsh men and women to a greater extent than was true in England.

During the last quarter of a century, however, the issue of alcohol on Sunday in Wales has been decided on a different basis by the introduction of regular *local* referenda. In districts where Noncomformist chapels and national sentiment are strong, public houses have remained closed on Sundays, but in the more secular, Anglicized and cosmopolitan urban areas people voted for the laxer, more liberal opening hours on Sunday that prevail in England. Gradually the boundary between 'wet' Wales and 'dry' Wales shifted westwards from the border with England to the western sea until only Ceredigion in the far south-west and Dwyfor in the far north-west remained 'dry' on Sunday. In 1990 Ceredigion fell and only Dwyfor (the very tip of Gwynedd from which that great moral example and democrat David Lloyd George took his title when he became a lord) is left. In consequence, individuals in Wales are more free to do as they please, unregulated by the law, but the separate national and religious identity of the Welsh people has been eroded.

In the past the identity of the British people as a whole was also tied in to the keeping of the Sabbath, as we can see from the negative antithesis of this which was described pejoratively as the 'Continental Sunday'. This phrase conjured up an image of undisciplined, frivolous, hedonistic, immoral Frenchmen, Belgians, Rhinelanders, Bavarians and Italians emerging from their heretical temples on Sunday morning to spend the rest of the day in unseemly dissipation; a case of real thirst after flawed righteousness. Whenever Sunday observance in Britain was threatened, Protestant leaders would warn that if their people were not careful, they would descend to the level of 'them', the alien Europeans.[8] National identity, strength and survival and the legal enforcement of a religious sabbatarian morality were intermingled for the British as they had been for the Jews of the Old Testament. As Winston Churchill, characteristically mingling religious and patriotic rhetoric, put it in 1933: 'Sunday is a Divine and priceless institution . . . the necessary pause in the national activity; it is the birthright of every British subject . . . and above all, our great heritage and one which it is our responsibility, privilege and duty to hand on to posterity.'[9]

The Welsh, the Scots and the people of Ulster were but a more extreme version of this – more Protestant, more Calvinist, more wedded to keeping Sunday as well as themselves separate, different and special. Paradoxically, these peoples of the outer margins of Britain were thus more virtuous, more religious, more British and less 'Continental' than the English majority.

In recent years there has been a decline in Britain in religious observance, in the keeping of the sabbath and in external and internal national exclusiveness which has led to three historical ironies. Two of these have emerged as a result of attempts to repeal or avoid those clauses of the Shops Act of 1950 which prohibit and regulate Sunday trading in England and Wales. In 1986, the Conservative government's Shops Bill which sought to deregulate shop opening hours was defeated on its second reading by 279 votes to 227. Earlier private members' bills seeking to remove sabbatarian restrictions had also been defeated but this was 'only the second defeat of a government bill on second reading since 1924 and involved 72 Conservative back-benchers defying a three-line whip'.[10] The opposition of the Labour Party was to be expected given its faith in government regulations and the opposition to this particular deregulation of two of its affiliated organizations, the Union of Shop, Distributive and Allied Workers (USDAW) and the Co-operative Movement. The Conservative defections from *laissez faire* were, however, strongly influenced by pressure from church-goers in their constituencies.[11] Those Conservative MPs who spoke against the Bill consistently referred to the need to preserve and protect Britain's distinctive national religious tradition. Sir Bernard Braine said that the government had no mandate to change the traditional British Sunday.[12] Ivor Stanbrook declared: 'Conservatives are not libertarians, we are not devotees of the free market to the extreme, certainly not to the extreme that involves conflict with a deeply rooted institution in the life of the British people and a part of our Christian heritage. Woe betide any Conservative party that goes against such institutions.'[13]

However, following the failure of the 1986 Shops Bill, the term 'Continental Sunday' began to be used in an entirely new way. Those in favour of deregulation began to use it as a positive slogan to indicate

that Britain is out of step with her continental neighbours. Where British laws restrict and prohibit, European laws permit and encourage. Where Britain proscribes Sunday trading, Europe promotes it and many other forms of entertainment to boot . . . with the abolition of trade barriers within the E.E.C. set for 1992, the growing conformity of trade practices calls for a united European approach to the issue of Sunday trading.[14]

The response by the supporters of the 'Keep Sunday Special' campaign, who wanted to retain the regulations on religious grounds, was to study the laws in other European countries and to claim that in each case there are 'significant restrictions on Sunday shop opening'.[15] In consequence, in their view deregulation

would put English law out of step with West Germany, France, Italy, Holland and Belgium. Indeed it would leave our law at variance with every country in the E.E.C. (except Scotland) . . . The experience of Italy, West Germany and Holland belies the concept of the 'Continental Sunday'. Indeed, their legislation is very much in harmony with the Shops Act 1950 . . . the continental Sunday of unlimited shopping is a myth. In

> each country studied, through one means or another restrictions are placed on Sunday trading. In West Germany and Holland the legislation is more stringent. Nowhere is it noticeably more liberal . . . Sunday trading is the exception and not the rule in Europe. Deregulation of Sunday shop opening hours in Britain would put us out of step with E.E.C. practice on the brink of the unification of its markets in 1992 . . . Unfettered consumer choice is nowhere the primary principle controlling the law.[16]

The wheel of rhetoric has turned a full circle. Sunday restrictions are for the sabbatarians no longer the mark of a distinctive and separate set of British moral and religious virtues but rather a set of regulations with purportedly beneficial consequences that Britain has in common with her sensible and reasonable European partners. The alien, restless, threatening, anarchic 'continental' Sunday is no more and in its place benignly shines a diversely yet sufficiently and harmoniously regulated Eurosunday.

The opponents of restrictions have sought to evade the Shops Act (1950) ban on Sunday trading by arguing that it is in breach of European Community laws for promoting and maintaining free trade, notably article 30 of the Treaty of Rome; the so-called European defence. In 1989, Torfaen Borough Council alleged before Cwmbran magistrates' court that the do-it-yourself chain 'B & Q' had broken the 1950 law by opening on Sundays. At the magistrates' court hearing it was found that the ban on Sunday trading had the effect of reducing B & Q's total sales, about 10 per cent of which came from other members of the EEC and that there was a corresponding reduction in imports from these member states. In consequence, the case was referred to the Court of Justice of the European Community in Luxembourg for a decision. The court ruled that since the English and Welsh law prohibiting retailers from opening their premises on Sunday applied equally to domestic and imported products, there was no favouring the trade and products of one member state over another involved, and that national rules governing the opening of retail premises were a matter for national or regional political choices in the light of local socio-cultural characteristics. National rules limiting and governing working hours could be struck down only if they exceeded that which was necessary to achieve the particular social and economic goals that constituted their justification. This, however, was a question of fact to be decided by national courts.[17] What is significant here is not that the 'European defence' failed, but that such recourse to a European court was possible and that a commercial organization should have tried to overturn a restriction rooted in local religious sentiment by invoking a multi-national secular agreement.

Britain's Keep Sunday Special campaign is an alliance of religious sabbatarians, USDAW and those retail traders, such as the National Chamber of Trade, who think they would lose out if free trading on

Sundays were permitted. Most of the energy and research on the issue comes from the religious moralists but the public arguments put forward are largely secular and concerned with the welfare of shop-workers and the impact of seven-day trading on their family life. The moral, religious and national-identity arguments are now largely hidden behind mundane secular statements about welfare. The opponents of Sunday trading in the United Kingdom are a coalition who have to appeal both to trade unionists and to owners of family businesses, to a religious and to a secular constituency, to those who wish to maintain a particular national tradition and to those in favour of harmonizing Britain's laws with the laws of its European partners.

The supporters of the Charter of Fundamental Social Rights, issued by the Commission of the European Community, have also used secular justifications for keeping Sunday free from work for they have argued that in order to guarantee employees 'a reasonable quantum of leisure time, they must have the right to a weekly leisure period or to a rest period at a *regular rhythm*'.[18] This would exclude the development of other more flexible patterns of work and leisure that both employers and employees might well prefer, such as a revolving schedule of twelve-hour shifts for a stipulated time followed by an entire week away from work, or other non-traditional systems in which none the less significant stretches of work are complemented by equally significant periods of rest.[19] The use of the peculiar word 'rhythm', rather than, say, 'reasonably regular intervals', in relation to the alternation of work and leisure is one that will have an appeal both to religious traditionalists and to those of a green persuasion who see the world as a dichotomy between nature (rhythmic, organic, good) and modern modes of production (rational, technical, bad). The Keep Sunday Special campaign in a recent review of the stances taken by the British political parties shrewdly asked the rhetorical question: 'And the Greens? How does their concern for the environment and the rhythms of life (like Sunday as a day of rest) apply to Sunday trading?'[20] Both religious traditionalists and greens, though for different reasons, find the impact of technical changes and the growth of a technological consciousness threatening.[21] It is possibly for this kind of reason that no European country has ever permanently decimalized the measurement of time. Length, volume, weight and money are all metric, even in non-technical everyday life, but clocks still tick sixty, sixty, twenty-four and there are seven days in each quarter of the lunar month.

Further study of the British Sunday reveals two more ironies of history. The first is that the sabbatarian restrictions of the 1950 Shops Act do not apply to Scotland. In 1950, the fierceness of Scottish Presbyterian public opinion against Sunday trading was such that it was held to be unnecessary to enforce Sunday closing by law.[22] Indeed, the leaders of the Church of Scotland still speak with pride of the role that observation of the Sabbath has played in moulding the national character of the Scottish people. A report to the Church of Scotland's General Assembly in 1988 could still declare that 'the extent to which the Scot owes his intellectual moral and religious standing in the world to the reservation of one day in seven for religious exercises and works of necessity and mercy cannot be denied'.[23] As Basil Mitchell noted, motives and language are mixed. Sabbatarianism is a religious virtue, a way of being Scottish and the source of Scottish superiority.

However, Scotland does not stand where it did in 1950.[24] By 1975, the Church of Scotland had only 1.04 million members which had declined further to 0.87 million in 1985 and an estimated 0.78 million in 1990 (out of a total population of about 5 million).[25] In consequence, the informal pressures on retailers to remain Scots, Presbyterian and closed have declined except in areas where the stricter Free Presbyterian Church has a large membership.[26] There is now widespread Sunday trading in most of Scotland unhampered by the law or by the pressure of public opinion.[27] Today, those in favour of deregulation use deregulated Scotland as an example that ought to be followed by the English and the Welsh.[28] By contrast, those who want to keep Sunday special for religious reasons argue that new restrictions and regulations should be introduced in Scotland 'bringing it into line with European law'.[29]

The one place where a Protestant nationalism remains strong is in Northern Ireland where the Protestant majority contains a far larger proportion of active Church members than is the case in England, Wales or Scotland.[30] Many of them are Presbyterian and the fastest-growing church is the fundamentalist Free Presbyterian Church.[31] In Ulster the Protestant Unionists are opposed not only to the European Community with its Roman Catholic majority,[32] but even more strongly to the Roman Catholics of the neighbouring Republic of Ireland and to the Roman Catholic minority in their own province, many of whom have Irish Republican sympathies.

It is within this context that the Sabbath-keeping policy of the Democratic Unionist Party, for which the more strongly Ulster Unionist and Protestant citizens vote, should be viewed. In 1985 the DUP's manifesto stated: 'Recognizing the laws of God and the inherent benefits of the Ulster Sabbath as part of our heritage, the D.U.P. is opposed to the introduction or promotion of the Continental and Republican Sunday in Northern Ireland.'[33] The historical irony here is that the Britain to which the Unionists are loyal in certain respects no longer exists. They still defend their cherished heritage of the Ulster Sabbath that can be opposed to the Continental and Republican Sunday, but there is no longer a corresponding enthusiasm for the Sabbath in England where in the 1980s only 13 per cent of the population claimed any kind of church membership.[34] As Steve Bruce has noted:

> The lack of religiosity in mainland Britain also offends. A woman who had been a councillor in Bangor and a staunch Paisley supporter from the early 1960s explained what it was that she found admirable about Ulster when she moved here (from England) in the 1940s. She mentioned 'the keeping of the sabbath' as one of the things which had made Ulster 'such a great wee country', and she used the term 'republican Sunday' to describe what was threatening to become the norm in Ulster . . . Ulster loyalist views of Britain are anachronistic in that they refer to something which has all but disappeared.[35]

The Liberalization of Europe's Abortion Laws

Sunday observance is largely a Protestant issue and feelings about the issue are strongest in Ulster, the one part of Europe where an ethnic and national identity rooted in Reformed Protestantism remains very strong. Opposition to abortion by contrast is primarily, though by no means exclusively, a Roman Catholic issue and the only country in Europe where the law prohibiting abortion has recently become *more* restrictive and less liberal is the overwhelmingly Roman Catholic Republic of Ireland. When the law of England and Wales was changed in 1967 to permit abortion on reasonably liberal terms (a similar change occurred in Scotland but by different means), this did not apply to the British province of Northern Ireland and could not apply to the independent (since 1922) State of (Southern) Ireland. Both Irelands retained the older and much more restrictive English Offences against the Person Act of 1861 which permitted abortion only if the mother's life was in danger, or in practice if there was a severe threat to her health. There was far too much opposition in Ulster, mainly from the Roman Catholics, but also from some of the more militant Protestants to permit an extension to the province of the new liberal legislation.

In the Republic of Ireland, whose citizens are strongly Roman Catholic, the liberalizing of the abortion laws, not just in neighbouring Britain but in much of Europe, was regarded with such abhorrence that the Irish Constitution was amended by referendum in 1983 to make abortion unconstitutional, i.e. to make the ban on abortion part of the very definition of the country.[36] To be Irish is to be Roman Catholic is to prohibit abortion. In Ireland, religion, national identity and the legal enforcement of a particular morality are still part of a single seamless web in a way that is no longer true of most other European countries which lack Eire's ethnic and religious homogeneity. Ireland is on the very edge of Europe and the Irish emigrate rather than receive immigrants. The ease of access to Britain from Ireland ensures that most, if not all, Irish abortions take place in British clinics, beyond the bounds of Irish social pressures and legal prohibitions.[37] Within Britain the Roman Catholics, most of whom are of Irish descent, were at the forefront of the fight to stop the liberalization of the law in 1967 and of more recent attempts to make it more restrictive.[38] They failed because they are a religious minority (about 10 per cent) in a Protestant and secular society. Even in countries such as France, Germany, the Netherlands and Italy with larger Roman Catholic populations, they have been unable to prevent the enactment of permissive abortion laws, which treat abortion as a welfare issue rather than a moral one. The Roman Catholics see abortion as morally wrong *per se* but their secular and Protestant opponents argued that women will seek abortions anyway and that it is better that these be provided legally under hygienic conditions by medically qualified personnel than by unskilled back-street abortionists in whose hands the woman's life and health may be in danger.[39] The crucial European argument in favour of liberalization has been of the secular negative utilitarian kind I have termed 'causalist', i.e. the reformers argued that the harm done by prohibiting abortion is greater than the possible harm resulting from a liberalization of the law.[40]

In the Netherlands and Germany there are roughly similar numbers of Roman Catholics and Protestants and a high degree of secularization. Hence the equation of nation, people, religion and by extension morality found in the Republic of Ireland is not possible. In France and Italy there are competing secular and Roman Catholic views of the nature of the State, society and people[41] in contrast to the hegemonic Roman Catholic view found in Ireland. In France the revolutionary and anti-clerical overthrow of the *ancien régime* and in Italy the unification of the country at the expense of the Papal States has meant that it is quite possible to be an anti-clerical patriot. In the Italian referendum on abortion, it is noteworthy that only the Christian Democrats and the fascist Italian Social Movement (MSI) were anti-abortion, with the main secular parties, the liberals, republicans, radicals, social democrats, socialists and communists united around the 'causalist' argument that legal abortion was better than back-street abortion.

The most recent West European conflict over abortion occurred in 1990 in Belgium where King Baudouin, who is strongly Roman Catholic, resigned for a day so that the legislature could pass a Bill permitting abortion in his absence without his having to sign it. At the time it looked as if his action might provoke a conflict between Roman Catholics and secularists and worsen the tensions between the Flemings, who tend to be monarchist and Catholic, and the Walloons, many of whom have secular and republican sympathies of the French kind. The striking thing about the Belgian abortion law reform is how much later it was enacted than in most other European countries. As in the case of obdurate Ireland, this is probably partly because of the ease with which Belgian women can obtain abortions in neighbouring countries and partly because Roman Catholicism is a stronger component in Belgian identity than is the case with the other Catholic countries of western Europe, most of which possess stronger alternative traditions of secular and anti-clerical nationalism. Roman Catholic Belgium, by contrast, is defined in opposition to secular France and Protestant Holland, both of which have ruled Belgium in the past.[42]

The Decriminalization of Homosexuality

The prohibition and punishment of homosexual behaviour, and especially male homosexual behaviour, by law is strongly associated with the defence of revered but threatened religious, ethnic and national boundaries.[43] One of the most striking instances is to be found in the Book of Leviticus which (i) is explicitly concerned with the preservation of the separate and holy identity of the Jewish people in exile[44] and (ii) strongly condemns and calls for the drastic punishment of a linked pair of forbidden boundary- and category-breaking modes of sexual behaviour, namely sodomy, which breaks down the boundary between the separate natural categories of male and female, and bestiality, which breaks down the boundary between the equally fundamental natural categories of human and animal. As with all Jewish rules that stress the maintaining of category boundaries, the prohibition of such activities is a metaphorical reminder of the need to maintain the separation between God's chosen people, the Jews, and the heathens without the law.

The same kind of link between the enforcement of sexual taboos and the preservation of a threatened but valued religious and ethnic or national identity can be repeatedly demonstrated throughout Christian and European history.[45] An additional factor has been the fear of the disruptive effects of male homosexuality on the all-male and often de jure or de facto celibate, hierarchies of the Church and the military, which have been the very frame for preserving and administering Church and State. The formation of homosexual liaisons between those inside the hierarchy and outsiders, or between men of different rank, status and authority would be a threat to discipline and good order.[46]

The way in which these forces operated to uphold the taboo against homosexuality can be illustrated from a speech in the House of Lords opposing the decriminalization of homosexuality given by Field Marshal Lord Montgomery, which again characteristically combined religious and patriotic rhetoric:

> What is the greatest single factor making for success in battle or for efficient and well-trained armed forces in peace? It is morale. And what is the foundation of morale? It is discipline. If these unnatural practices are made legal, a blow is struck at the discipline of the British armed forces at a time when we need the very highest standards of morale and discipline with these forces serving throughout the world. Take an infantry battalion. Suppose the men know the officers are indulging in unnatural practices and nothing can be done. Take a large aircraft carrier with two thousand men cooped up in a small area. Imagine what would happen in a ship of that sort if these practices crept in . . . Far from helping these unnatural practices along, surely our task is to build a bulwark which will defy evil influences which are seeking to undermine the very foundations of our national character – defy them; do not help them. I have heard some say . . . that such practices are allowed in France and in other NATO countries. We are not French and we are not other nationals. We are British, thank God![47]

In Britain, secularization, a decline in the influence and centrality of the military, and a weakening of the sense that its people had a unique and separate national identity to be preserved at all costs enabled the British Parliament to decriminalize homosexuality in 1967 in England and Wales[48] and in 1980 in Scotland. As in the case of abortion, no attempt was made to extend the new law to Northern Ireland where it remained a criminal offence, as it did in the Republic of Ireland, Cyprus and Israel – all of which had formerly been under British rule.

However, in 1981, the European Court of Human Rights ruled in the Dudgeon case that the laws in Northern Ireland prohibiting homosexual behaviour between adults were an unjustified interference with Mr Dudgeon's right to respect for his private life in breach of Article 8 of the European Convention on Human Rights that 'Everyone has the right to respect for his private and family life, his home and his correspondence' (Clause 1). It is significant that a majority of the judges refused to accept that such interference in a homosexual's private life was justified even though Clause 2 in Article 8 allows exceptions:

> There shall be no interference by a public authority with the exercise of this right except such as is in accordance with the law and is necessary in a democratic society in the interests of national security, public safety or the economic well-being of the country, for the prevention of disorder and crime, for the protection of health or morals or for the protection of the rights and freedoms of others.

In effect the court argued that the 'protection of morals' achieved by making adult homosexual behaviour a criminal offence was insufficiently important to justify such a grave interference with so intimate an aspect of private life contrary to the rights of the individual.[49] Furthermore, the court noted that: 'in the great majority of the member states of the Council of Europe it is no longer considered to be necessary to treat homosexual practices of the kind now in question as in themselves a matter to which the sanctions of the criminal law should be applied'.[50] Here the court seems to take the view that the moral and religious sentiments of a particular individual nation or sub-nation can be overruled by appealing to the majority view of states belonging to the Council of Europe. Thus a universal right (to privacy) has been upheld because the test of protection of morals is a *European* one and not based on the moral and religious convictions of the people of a particular state or province, however strongly these may be held.

The British government accepted the ruling of the court and in October 1982 brought the law in Northern Ireland into line with the more liberal law of England and Wales by an Order in Council.[51] There was strong opposition to this in Ulster and the strongly Protestant Democratic Unionist Party launched a campaign entitled 'Save Ulster from Sodomy' to prevent the change taking place.[52] However, the British government, possibly relieved that the European Court had taken on the responsibility, declared that it had no option but to fulfil its obligations to uphold basic human rights.

The strong opposition of the Ulster Protestants can be fully understood only by taking into account their beleaguered position as a religious and ethnic group. They are strongly attached to their particular and distinctive identity and fearful that it could be destroyed if Britain were to hand Ulster over to the Republic of Ireland where the Roman Catholic Church enjoys a moral monopoly.[53] In Ulster the Protestants are in a 60 per cent majority. In a united Ireland they would be a 20 per cent minority. In 1911, there were 330,000 Protestants in the area that is today the Irish Republic, but by 1971 there were only 130,000 or 4 per cent of the population and by 1981 they were only 3.49 per cent.[54] It has proved impossible for the southern Protestants to maintain themselves as a stable separate group in so overwhelmingly Roman Catholic a country where there is but a single myth of faith and nation.[55] Given that British governments have a long record of casting aside supporters and allies on the grounds of expediency and in the name of social justice, the fears of the Ulster Protestants are not unreasonable. Their strong antipathy to the boundary-blurring sin of homosexuality is a reflection of their concern with the crucial boundary between their own people and their threatening Roman Catholic neighbour, a boundary that is of central importance to them and yet vulnerable to the unilateral political decisions of others. In addition, as the conflict between the two ethnic–religious groups has grown stronger the Protestants have become more militant and more fundamentalist, particularly with the growth of the Free Presbyterians,[56] and thus less willing to permit any departure from the morality of the Bible.

The Rev. Dr Ian Paisley's 'Save Ulster from Sodomy' campaign received a good deal of support from the Roman Catholics in Ulster, who on other issues are his key opponents.[57] Their position is the mirror-image of that of the Protestants, for as Irish Catholics they have defined themselves in opposition to the Protestant majorities in Ulster and in the United Kingdom as a whole. Many of their activities and notably their separate and sectarian schools are concerned with maintaining the boundaries of their own group and thus they too dislike the ambiguity of homosexuality.

In the Republic of Ireland, where 95 per cent of the population is Roman Catholic, religious and national identities are more secure but the fears of the past and fears for the future are also present. Until 1922, the Irish were a minority in the overwhelmingly, and at that time strongly, Protestant United Kingdom. Should the Republic of Ireland annex the six counties of Northern Ireland there could be no subsequent smooth *Gleichschaltung*. There would either be prolonged and bitter violent internal strife or else Ireland would have to become a secular, plural and, possibly, federal society in which national identity was far more loosely and ambiguously defined than it is at present. Irishness could no longer be defined *against* Britishness and Protestantism, since this would be totally unacceptable to a compact, militant and well-organized minority of a million Ulster Protestants. Thus Irish identity is both monolithic and powerful *and* fragile and contradictory, both valued *and* threatened.

It is not surprising then that the Republic of Ireland has retained the old English criminal laws of 1861 and 1885 which prohibit male homosexual behaviour,[58] nor that the Irish Supreme Court should rule in 1983 that the laws remained valid[59] despite the ratifying of the European Convention on Human Rights by the Irish government and the European Court's judgment in the Dudgeon Case.[60] The Irish judges ruled *inter alia* that 'Homosexuality has always been condemned in Christian teaching as morally wrong. It has equally been regarded by society for many centuries as an offence against nature and a very serious crime.'[61]

Senator Norris, the complainant in this case, took his case further to the European Court of Human Rights in 1988. The court ruled, as it had in the Dudgeon case, that

> such justifications as there are for retaining the law in force unamended are outweighed by the detrimental effects which the very existence of the legislative provisions in question can have on the life of a person like the applicant. Although members of the public who regard homosexuality as immoral may be shocked, offended, or disturbed by the commission by

others of homosexual acts, this cannot on its own warrant the application of penal sanctions when it is consenting adults alone who are involved.[62]

This argument based on the weighing up of the balance of harm is of the negative utilitarian kind that I have termed 'causalist'.[63] It is a universal argument concerned with minimizing the harm done to individuals, which ignores, or at least overrides, the particular collective religious identity and morality of the Irish as a people. There has been a long delay since the judgment with no action by the Irish government (in contrast to the British government's prompt response in the Dudgeon case) which probably reflects the strength of opposition to change in Eire. The most important factor will be the attitude of the Irish Roman Catholic Church which is in a triumphal mood after its victories against abortion and divorce.[64] Several prelates have already spoken out in condemnation of homosexuality, and militant homosexuals have retaliated by delaying a Roman Catholic bishop's funeral for two hours while the police searched the cathedral for an alleged bomb.

To make it possible for the Republic of Ireland to sign the UN Declaration of Human Rights, the Irish government in 1990 introduced into the Senate and the Daìl an Incitement to Hatred Bill, criminalizing any incitement to hatred against a person because of their race, colour, religion, ethnic or national origin or membership of the travelling community of tinkers.[65] In the course of the debates on the Bill, Mr Ray Burke the Fianna Fail Minister of Justice agreed to extend the provisions of the Bill to protect also lesbians and male homosexuals, an amendment supported by the main opposition parties Fine Gael and Labour. This has created an anomalous contradiction worthy of the days of the eighteenth century when Sir Boyle Roche entertained the Parliament in Dublin with his 'Irish Bulls'.[66] An Irish homosexual may not be abused or threatened, but he can be imprisoned by judges who will tell him that his behaviour has always been condemned in Christian teaching, is an offence against nature and a very serious crime.

The European Court of Human Rights' decision in the Norris case is indicative of a fundamental clash between two opposed sets of institutions. Eire is a small homogeneous society in which the Roman Catholic Church enjoys a moral monopoly. The communal solidarity of its people is based on their having the same national and religious identity and a shared morality. It is the religious and national equivalent of Durkheim's mechanical solidarity;[67] the individuals who constitute the society cohere because they are the same and their solidarity is enhanced by the use of the criminal law to repress deviance.[68] The Council of Europe by contrast is an aggregate of very diverse European nation-states, most of which are also large, cosmopolitan and heterogeneous, i.e. they have a high degree of

internal religious and ethnic diversity. Individuals appeal to its institutions such as the European Court of Human Rights against what
they regard as the oppressive legal enforcement of a local morality.
Because Europe is made up of nations and sub-nations which differ
greatly in religion no single *particular* morality can prevail or be
enforced. The court's task is to assert universal rights and to remove
obstacles to the welfare and opportunities of individuals. The loyalty
of individuals to institutions of this kind and the nature of any
solidarity they may generate may by analogy with Durkheim be
termed organic solidarity for it is based on the interdependence of
very diverse individuals.[69] The use of restitutive law[70] to uphold the
rights of others, even those regarded in their own local communities
as immoral, is the guarantee of one's own rights. In a European
context we are all heretics and aliens.

The highly plural nature of European society means that, in practice, the decisions of the Court of Human Rights will have a secularizing effect. This will be especially felt by those nations and regions
on the periphery of Europe whose isolation and lack of development
has protected them from the migrations and internal differentiation
that have produced a secular and plural society in the major
metropolitan centres of the continent. In the future this could
lend a religious dimension to the tensions between the centre and
the periphery of Europe, with the peoples of the conservatively
religious periphery seeking to resist the encroachments of the inevitably more liberal and indifferent institutions of the centre.

A Comparison with the United States

The European clash between the religious fervour of the periphery
and secularizing institutions at the centre outlined above has its
parallel in the United States where high levels of religious commitment and participation (compared with Europe) exist in a country
where there is a constitutional separation of Church and State, which
has been given an ever-stricter interpretation over time by the US
Supreme Court. However, the history of the three controversial
issues discussed here in a European context has been very different
in America, indicating the continued significance of distinctive differences in both religious tradition and secular ideology.

Many American states have long had strict laws prohibiting
Sunday trading, which in some cases date back to the middle of the
seventeenth century, before the United States existed. In 1961, these
religion-based laws were upheld by the US Supreme Court despite
the religious diversity of America and the constitutional requirement
that there should be a separation of Church and State. The US
Supreme Court ruled on 29 May 1961 that, although the laws were

religious in origin, individual states were entitled to establish and enforce a common day of rest and to restrict non-religious activities on that day.[71] As in England and Wales, the religious arguments were hidden behind secular arguments about welfare. However, in the 1980s, the supreme courts of some of the individual states declared their own local laws restricting Sunday trading to be unconstitutional and many state legislatures de-regulated Sunday trading altogether. There is now total de-regulation in thirty-seven states, local option in nine and doubtful enforcement in three, so that only Maine and North Dakota now have significant restrictions on Sunday trading.[72] This is a remarkable contrast to the situation in Europe, especially given the much higher levels of religiosity and church attendance in America.[73] The difference is in part the difference between the American ideology of free enterprise and distrust of the State and the more paternalist European tradition of compulsory welfare. In America the churches enjoy more support but in Europe they have powerful secular allies in the trade unions and in associations of vulnerable small shop-keepers. Also, America has long constituted a single market, so that once one state has de-regulated Sunday, there is considerable pressure to scrap regulations in neighbouring states because otherwise consumers simply drive across state lines to make their purchases, thus denying their custom to their local state's traders.[74]

There are also major differences between Europe and America in relation to the laws on abortion and homosexuality. Some individual American states had liberalized their law relating to abortion before the Supreme Court ordered them to do so, and others have decriminalized homosexuality, but many did not and have not, in contrast to Europe, where almost every country has enacted such reforms, in most cases without the need for the European Court of Human Rights to intervene.

In America the main battles over the issue of abortion have taken place in the US Supreme Court which has ruled that the American Constitution can be construed as containing a right to privacy and has struck down *all* state laws prohibiting abortion in the first twenty-four weeks of pregnancy as an infringement of this right. The Supreme Court ruled that abortion is a private matter, to be decided by the pregnant woman and her medical adviser.[75] It has often been argued that controversial issues such as abortion are defused by being taken out of everyday politics and handled as lofty constitutional issues by the detached and Olympian justices of the Supreme Court, who can and must exclude the partisan passions that stem from religious commitment. It has not, however, silenced the religious opponents of abortion who are greatly offended that the freedom to choose abortion is guaranteed by the same Constitution that defines the very nature and existence of their nation.

They are unable to place their religious objections to abortion before the Supreme Court[76] because of the constitutional separation of Church and State, and it is unlikely that they will be able successfully to reformulate their arguments in secular terms such as to enable them to amend the Constitution. The bitter opposition of the pro-lifers, however, is likely to remain an important force in American politics, in arguments over the funding of health and welfare and the appointment of new Supreme Court justices. The more extreme American opponents of abortion will also probably continue to attack hospitals, clinics and advisory centres associated with abortion with explosive devices, thus displaying a greater degree of hostile passion and violence than is to be found in Europe.

The Supreme Court has, however, rejected attempts to use the constitutional right to privacy to decriminalize homosexual acts committed between consenting male adults in private. In Bible-belt states such as Georgia homosexual behaviour is still strictly prohibited by law. By contrast, in more religiously heterogeneous states, such as California and New York, to which large numbers of homosexuals have migrated to avoid prosecution and harassment in their state of origin, local governments have, with an eye to the homosexual vote, outlawed discrimination against homosexuals and cut off welfare funding from religious charities such as the Salvation Army which have refused to comply with this ruling. In contrast to the nation-wide moral polarization of America that has occurred over the issue of abortion, there exists a patchwork of contrasting local ordinances, some condemning homosexual behaviour for religious reasons, others upholding the rights of homosexuals on secular grounds.

Europe: Secular Centres and Religious Peripheries

During the last forty years Britain, like most other western European societies, has become more secular and, given that religion was a key factor defining and underpinning national identity, this has contributed to the decline that has occurred in the individual's sense of belonging to a distinctive, separate nation eternally set apart from all others. In consequence there has been a decline in the willingness of the State to enforce by law moral rules of religious origin which previously would have enjoyed this support by virtue of being part of a characteristic national way of life. Those who oppose such changes have been forced to argue in the same secular and universal terms used by their opponents, such as rights and welfare, even though many of the activists were motivated by a wish to defend a particular national religious tradition. European institutions with a secular outlook, reflecting the plural and heterogeneous nature of the aggregate of nations that subscribe to them, have acquired the power to review and overturn laws enforcing a particular local religious morality and this has proved to be a further secularizing force.

At the peripheries of Europe and, indeed, of many of the nation states that make up Europe, where the religious fervour of smaller and more homogeneous communities remains strong, there is visible resistance to these trends. In the Faroe Islands and in many peripheral areas of Norway, Sweden and Finland, representatives of new Christian parties have been elected to Parliament to oppose the secular permissiveness of the metropolitan centre.[77] In Norway, similar sentiments played a part in the defeat in a referendum of the proposal that Norway should join the European Community. The most striking case is that of the two Irelands where religion and national identity are strong and reinforce each other; here alone has there been marked and at times successful resistance to the general tendency found elsewhere in Europe to revoke State laws enforcing a particular local religious morality.

It seems likely that in the long run the centre will hold and the laws upholding the morality of the periphery will fall apart, but it would be unwise to make a dogmatic prediction to this effect. The fear of a loss of communal or national identity could provoke a religious revival and an attempt to recover and recapture a revered past through the legal enforcement of morality. It is also possible that those on the periphery may find unexpected allies in the members of the stricter and more fundamentalist churches that are gaining ground in the metropolitan centres as a reaction against anonymity and anomie. Also, religious fervour is strong in some of the newly liberated and democratic countries of eastern Europe where in the past religion was one of the few permitted and potent forms of opposition to communist dictatorship. Even before the Soviets tried to impose communism and atheism on the Poles, Polish identity was strongly linked to Catholicism in opposition to the Protestantism of Prussia and Russian Orthodoxy.[78] It is hardly surprising to find that there is already bitter controversy on the subject of abortion between the Roman Catholic and the secular libertarian wings of the popular movement that overthrew communism. Sociologists committed to unilinear models of social change have been caught unawares in the past by religious resurgence and ethnic revival and it behoves us to be cautious now.

Chapter 4

Britain's Moral Majority

William Thompson

The apparent dramatic appearance of Christian political pressure groups during the 1980s took many academics by surprise. Confused by its many-faceted manifestations, scholars desperately sought an explanation within the same paradigms which had left them unprepared. These interpretations were justified by references to an erroneous American comparison. As a result, the indigenous fundamentalist religious revival upon which the political crusades rested was under-researched, and a major social movement ignored. As a result, a dominant consensus, that the Christian activists were merely an appendage of the political and economic 'New Right' emerged.

This account looks behind that consensus: first, by laying the ghost of the American model; and second, by revealing the origins, basic beliefs and activities of the groups which constitute Britain's Moral Majority.

The New Moral Right

British academics became sensitized to the existence of Christian political activism following Victoria Gillick's campaign against the British Medical Association, moral crusades against gay sex education material, and media accounts of the American Moral Majority. Political science was very dismissive: Britain's 'New Moral Right' (hereafter NMR) had neither the numbers or enough ideas of their own to transcend dependence upon the political 'right', especially the Salisbury Review group. The Christians were merely intent upon limiting personal sexual freedom by seizing a political space opened up by feminists in their own interests.[1] None of these studies, however, could name any individual beyond long-established moral crusaders such as Mary Whitehouse or Victoria Gillick, or refer to any organization other than the twenty-year-old National Viewers and Listeners Association (hereafter NVALA) or the Nationwide Festival of Light (hereafter NFOL) which no longer existed.

Radical sociology exhibited a similar weakness; reference to *The*

Sun newspaper and speeches by Enoch Powell were used to 'demonstrate' that the NMR was a temporary 'backlash' against the gay and women's movements.[2]

Apart from this lack of detailed research into the British movement, the major reason for this superficial and disingenuous analysis was the widespread acceptance of a model which asserted that the political links between the US Moral Majority and the Republican Party must be replicated in Britain, but that Britain's Moral Majority could not match the success of its American cousin. Both assumptions were incorrect.

The American Majority

The reality of the American Moral Majority belies the political and sociological indicators used to make an unfavourable assessment of the British movement's potential.

The Moral Majority was not a single group. Christian Voice had a mailing list of 150,000 laymen, and 37,000 ministers from thirty-seven denominations, including 3,000 Catholics and some Mormons.[3] It was dependent for publicity upon the '700 Club' seen on Pat Robertson's Christian Broadcasting Network. Religious Roundtable mobilized mainstream Presbyterian, Methodist and Southern Baptist Church ministers, and encouraged links with conservative Republicans like Jesse Helms. Falwell's Moral Majority drew upon the Independent Baptist Churches and claimed 4 million members.

These groups came to public prominence when political liberals sought an explanation for Ronald Reagan's unexpected 1979 election victory, and blamed Falwell's erroneous claim to have mobilized 4 to 8 million previously uninterested fundamentalists to register and then vote in Reagan's favour. As a result, the fundamentalists' moral agenda gained a high public profile, the Moral Majority became a generic term for all Christian political activists, liberals went on the defensive, and for a period the Moral Majority threatened to change the nature of American politics.

Incredibly, at the very point this Moral Majority myth was accepted in Britain, it was dismissed by American scholars who discovered that whatever political links existed at Federal level between Falwell's Moral Majority and the Republican right, the Moral Majority was religiously motivated, and its power was exaggerated.[4]

The American Moral Majority's apparent success must be placed in the context of the post-Watergate 1974 Federal Campaign Act, which reduced the major parties' spending power over candidates in favour of Political Action Committees (hereafter PACs), which were formed by interest groups which then pushed issues to the favour or detriment of particular candidates. The Christian groups which became known as the Moral Majority were seeking to become the most effective PACs on the circuit.[5] Commentators fervently stressed the Moral Majority's power in terms of money, high technology, the influence of the electronic church and size. These have all been exaggerated.

Far from collecting millions of dollars to fund campaigns, no group ever spent more than 10 million dollars in a year.[6] Though use of direct mail and the electronic church impressed many commentators, E-mail was standard political practice by the 1980s and always produced poor returns. Independent estimates of TV-church-viewers drastically cut the church leaders' claims from 130 million to a more realistic 23 million viewers, and noted that 'political' shows were the least popular.[7] The Moral Majority's membership was always over-stated both by participants to convince the politicians, and detractors to mobilize opposition. The Moral Majority deliberately associated itself with other single-issue groups in order to create the impression of a massive following it did not really control. Nor did Falwell mobilize 8 million to vote for Reagan; evangelicals were just as likely to be registered and prepared to vote as any other social group.[8]

The Moral Majority's political impact is also debatable. For every victory they secured against gay rights, 'humanistic' school textbooks, and the Equal Rights Amendment at state level, there were many defeats. At federal level, President Reagan appointed less than half a dozen fundamentalists to important political positions and refused to implement their social programme including the Family Act. Court of Appeal rulings quashing fundamentalist parental control over public school textbooks and subjects were common. The Moral Majority's one major success, the Meese Commission on Pornography, was a poor return for eight years' support of the Reagan administration.

Unfavourable comparisons between the British and American movements, therefore, tend to rely upon erroneous standards. The same cannot be said of a critique by Bruce, who provided a more sophisticated comparison. Despite being aware of the above qualifications, Bruce argued that a British Moral Majority could not exist, let alone be compared to the American group. Britain, he argued, was simply not religious enough to supply the same numbers, and Christians would be hampered by lack of the facilitating federal structure or PACs to 'impact' party candidates. Our non-elected élitist public administration structure would inhibit campaign possibilities, since we did not elect key public administrators, and British pressure groups could not exert influence on the judiciary. Unable to buy air-time and unable to lobby candidates because of the parliamentary party system, Christians were unable to make headway.

To emphasize the point, Bruce insisted that British Christians had failed to make political issues of those concerns which defined the life-style of fundamentalists, such as the content of school books.[9]

Apart from there being no reason why a political ideology, let alone theology, should have exactly the same content or take the same path in different countries, each and every point of this more astute argument, employed to dismiss the contention that Britain had a Moral Majority, can be answered by considering the real similarities between the two Moral Majorities, which offer a socio-logical means of comparison: their history, their support base, their life-style politics and the nature of their belief system.

Fundamentalism and Politics

The myth of the Moral Majority follows from the long-standing assumption that fundamentalists inevitably shun politics in favour of individual salvation. On the contrary, they have a long history in public politics. Between 1780 and 1930 evangelicals on both sides of the Atlantic, whose beliefs then corresponded very closely to those of today's fundamentalists, helped shape the nature of the family, sexuality and social norms.[10]

In Britain, their influence was felt through a series of moral cru-sades against alcohol, brothels, contraception, dancing, erotic litera-ture, ice-skating and other forms of popular entertainment; and the promotion of chastity societies, like the White Cross, and temper-ance groups. They gained numerous pieces of legislation reflecting their moral beliefs, which ensured that the State punished sin.[11] As a recent study has demonstrated, their beliefs were also seminal in other spheres, such as business and family structures.[12] This contribution should not be seen merely as a denial of pleasure: between 1780 and 1930, fundamentalists were also a major force behind the abolition of slavery, the introduction of mass education, prison reform and many other 'humanitarian' causes. America wit-nessed similar activities.[13] This history is not negated by the fact that these causes became the province of Christian modernists who defeated the fundamentalists in denominational disputes in the early decades of this century.[14]

Insular fundamentalism, therefore, is recent, and actually follows two highly symbolic defeats which did encourage a distrust of 'worldliness' in the fundamentalist camp: the repeal of Prohibition, and the ridicule following the 1925 'monkey trial', when the defence counsel, Clarence Darrow, destroyed the fundamentalist prosecut-ing attorney William Jennings Bryan's credibility.[15] To suggest, how-ever, that fundamentalism was a declining vestige of the past 'des-tined to survive only by withdrawing from active confrontation with this secular age', as sociologists did in the 1960s, reflected academic paradigms rather than reality.[16] Such a view ignored all proof to the contrary, and was an *a priori* dismissal of continued fundamentalist attacks upon 'social evils' as futile gestures against inevitable secular-ization, or as 'right-wing' extremism, without considering the origins of an anti-communistic eschatology based upon Jeremiah 4: 7.[17]

In reality, post-war fundamentalists were regrouping and waiting their turn. In Britain, as in America, this involved the creation of culturally self-sufficient communities based around local churches and fellowships, promoting 'traditional family values'.[18] The emerg-ence of British groups like the NVALA and Citizens for Decent Literature in America during the 1960s should have warned aca-demics that fundamentalists were not solely concerned with indi-vidual salvation. While some Christians do believe that political involvement is 'worldly', a distraction from worship which under-mines purity of faith, this was never true for the majority, as the rapid mobilization in the 1970s demonstrates.[19]

The Support Base

To emphasize the role of the electronic church in that mobilization is to ignore the real support base of both the American and British Moral Majorities – fundamentalist church congregations. The US Moral Majority, for example, drew upon the Seventh-day Adventists, the Church of Nazarene and Assemblies of God, which had all enjoyed growth rates of 60 to 70 per cent between 1960 and 1970. Falwell's base, the Southern Baptists, had become the largest single Protestant denomination in America by 1975.[20]

That a similar support base exists in Britain should come as no surprise. Resource mobilization theory has long since demonstrated that:

> Social movement organizations do not appear spontaneously. They are nurtured by shifts in the cultural environment which provoke changes in the mood of potential participants and by alterations in the political environment which provide opportunities for collective action. They develop through deliberate efforts to organize the participants and accumulate resources. They take shape through sustained effort of move-ment activists to effect programs of change.[21]

In other words, rapid mobilizations like the Moral Majority's can occur only when movements are able to draw on existing high-participation group networks, and can tap existing justifications for activity. These factors reduce mobilization costs, in terms of money, effort and personnel. The fundamentalist church communities also fulfil two further rapid mobilization requirements: a large number of inter-personal ties and lack of countervailing influence among potential members.

Mobilization in Britain was even easier than in America because of common Christian sub-cultural beliefs and practices. Whatever group they belong to, British fundamentalists all believe in Jesus' second coming being preceded by signs such as the increase in lawlessness (Matt. 24: 12); the reality of Heaven and Hell (Rev. 20: 11–15); the gift of the Holy Spirit to be Born Again and change personality (John 1: 12–13; Cor. 5: 17); the role of Ministry (Eph. 4: 11–12); the Virgin Birth (Isa. 7: 14; Mark 1: 1); and Jesus' atonement for our sins, which should attract sacrifice and suffering. British fundamentalists do not engage in major theological disputes.

The modern origin of this shared community of belief can be traced back to the Sunderland 'outpouring' of 1907 which later eventuated in the emergence of groups like Elim and the Assemblies of God.[22] During the 1960s, these and other independent Pentecostalists were joined by charismatics within the old line denominations encouraged by Oral Roberts's Full Gospel Businessmen's Fellowship International 1965 London convention.[23] Anglicans like the Rev. Colin Urquhart and the Rev. David Watson, who embraced the Spirit, experienced church growth in contrast to the denomination's over-all decline; so that, while the sociology of religion busied itself with obscure cults like the Children of God, it failed to note that even Anglicanism was changing as more and more churches, colleges, journals, magazines and Diocesan fellowships became not only evangelical, but more fundamentalist in approach. The third group involved in today's community is the House Church or Restoration Movement. Where the charismatic renewal was slow in coming or created inter-congregational problems, those sharing the Spirit began to break away, met in houses, and looked to the growing independent leadership of Gerald Coats and others.[24] All three tendencies share a common view of the Spirit: Spiritual gifts do not come by faith alone, or even by effort, they appear to those who pray for and desire them (1 Cor. 14: 11). Those blessed are believed to receive one or more of the Pentecost gifts: 'wisdom' – the ability to speak and act wisely beyond normal human capabilities; knowledge – about people and events that is not naturally known; faith to an exceptional level; healing through God's power; miraculous powers to change events; prophecy; the ability to distinguish good and evil spirits; speaking and/or the interpretation of tongues. Together with a stress upon an error-free Bible, and insistence upon salvation through a personal relationship with Christ, these beliefs not only separate 'fundamentalists' from 'nominal' Christians, they enable all fundamentalist tendencies to work together.

The dramatic 1,000 per cent growth-rate of fundamentalist churches – from the Bamford Chapel in Rochdale, through the New

Life Church in Worthing, to the Datchet Fellowship in East Anglia[25] – during the supposedly secular 1970s not only supplied the fundamentalists with belief-confirming evidence that they were following the Holy Spirit at work, but also produced a massive Christian sub-culture involving thousands of support services from Cornwall to Caithness.[26] These included: a Christian Introduction Agency; hundreds of bookshops; businesses supplying anything from greetings cards to second-hand cars; film and video companies producing everything from training to feature films; computer software companies; a vast array of counselling services covering marriage, divorce, homosexuality, teenage problems and God's will concerning full-time service in the faith; dance and theatre groups providing novel ways of spreading the word; double-glazing and draughtsmen; employment agencies and engineering services; furniture and flowers; hundreds of holidays, hotels and tours; missions and magazines; opticians and office equipment; publishers and property developers; musical recordings and removals; solicitors and surveyors.[27] Holiday periods can be spent at one of the many Christian festivals held each year, such as Spring Harvest, addressed by evangelical leaders and preachers such as Gerald Coats, Bryn Jones and John Noble. Greenbelt, which caters for gospel-rocking teenagers, steadily grew to become Britain's biggest rock festival.

Youth work is a high priority; for these churches are keeping their teenagers. Christian Unions are invariably the largest societies on college campuses, and have done much to inhibit feminist influence. Once committed, there are numerous means to keep youth from secular entrapments. Younger children can play religious board-games like Bible Challenge, or read *Jam*, a monthly magazine in the *Jackie* style, without the sex. Teenagers can join missions like the Dirty Hands Project, sponsored by British Youth for Christ and the Evangelical Alliance, or attend their own events and conferences such as the 1987 'Battle for the Mind' convention held at Coverley Hall, Shropshire.

In short, by the 1980s Britain contained the same type of congregations and para-church that the American Moral Majority had drawn upon. The only thing missing was the electronic church; and even here plans were prepared. Apart from the various experiments on the New World Channel on satellite, Swindon Christians have been involved in that town's cable system since 1960. More recently, Helen Penfold used the network to promote programmes influenced by the Order of Christian Unity focusing on fundamental views towards marriage, abortion and Christian standards. By 1990, the Christian community was strong enough to defeat the government's initial prohibition of religious stations in the Broadcasting Bill, and it has since been busy creating a religious radio network.[28]

It remains impossible to place a definite figure on fundamentalist numbers. According to Walker, Restoration groups amounted to some 50,000. The 1990 *UK Christian Handbook*, however, suggests 100,000, but this must be an underestimate as not all fellowships and groups record their existence with a central agency. Adding Elim and other larger groups with similar beliefs, we could treble that figure to 300,000; but still have no way of knowing how many other charismatics there are within the major denominations.[29] One thing we can be sure of, however, is that during the 1980s their numbers were growing; a point reflected in their educational facilities.

Apart from fundamentalist churches which initiated Accelerated Christian Learning Schools, the members of which withdrew their children from the State system, fundamentalists run numerous colleges and institutions which provide day schools or short courses. The Elim Bible College in Dorking, Surrey, offers everything from weekends to degrees, based on fundamentalism. The London Bible College, Northwood, Middlesex, offers correspondence and full-time courses, from GCSE to CNAA degrees. Diplomas in evangelism and MAs in biblical interpretation are also available. If you can not attend, there were several publishers producing hundreds of books, and groups issuing other material to aid spiritual growth and missionary potential.[30]

This emergent Christian sub-culture is able to support a vast array of groups which collectively make up the British Moral Majority.

Political Organizations

Formal membership of Christian political groups ranges from several hundred individuals in the NVALA, to thousands in Christian Action Research and Education (hereafter CARE). While this may not seem many by American standards, these groups' activities have convinced many British fundamentalists to support rather than avoid political intervention, so that continual church growth and common cause has produced a confidence not shared by other social movements. By reviewing the three largest groups involved, we can trace both the history and changing nature of the Moral Majority in the last two decades.

The modern movement owes its origin to Mary Whitehouse's 1964 Clean Up TV campaign which quickly became the NVALA, affectionately known as National Vala (pronounced Valour), indicating the meaning and role it had for members seeking to protect Christian values and beliefs from demonically inspired secular-humanism. Being founded in the 1960s, at the height of 'permissive' legislation and the liberal gospel decriminalizing private sin, the NVALA offered secular positivistic arguments and rationales to justify their crusades. Even their contemporary public message tends to highlight the symptoms of media secularization, rather than to spell out their religious motives which still follow those of the Clean Up TV campaign manifesto:

1   We women of Britain believe in a Christian way of life.
2   We want it for our children and country.
3   We deplore present day attempts to belittle or destroy it, and in particular we object to the propaganda of disbelief, doubt and dirt that the BBC projects into millions of homes through the television screen.[31]

The emphasis upon the BBC, which they believed should 'encourage and sustain faith in God and bring Him back to the hearts of our family and national life', was quickly abandoned to embrace all media, because the anti-communist eschatology of 1960s fundamentalism, still promoted today, required a comprehensive programme against humanist media.[32] Under Mary Whitehouse, the NVALA has always leaned heavily towards the Conservative Party despite claims of political neutrality. Crusades at national level have worked through Parliament and the courts, and these have been backed up with national petitions and media-monitoring groups. Funding comes from wealthy supporters.

It would be a mistake, however, to see NVALA with their amalgamation of religious and cultural fundamentalism setting the tone of the contemporary Moral Majority.[33]

During the 1970s as the charismatic and House Church revivals continued, NVALA was joined by the NFOL, promoting the 'regeneration of British moral standards', the Responsible Society (now Family and Youth Concern), which concentrates upon defending the institution of the monogamous family, and the Community Standards Association movement (hereafter CSAs). If NVALA represented the torch-bearers of tradition, the CSA could be seen as a transitional phase in the rise of Britain's Moral Majority, reflecting fundamentalist growth.

Initiated in Cornwall by Ms Whitaker, the CSA movement quickly expanded as single-issue campaigns developed into permanent groups: Portsmouth's CSA emerged from an anti-sex-shop campaign, and Enfield's from opposition to the alleged Thorsen film, *The Sex Life of Christ* (personal correspondence). During the 1980s, CSA groups' membership ranged from a score or so dedicated members to hundreds, sometimes including whole church congregations. CSAs promoted a mixture of both Christian and secular imperatives in their public rationales, as this Cornwall membership form demonstrates:

AIM
to promote and explain the positive value of traditional Christian Standards and warn of the consequences of permissive values and practices threatening to take over our culture . . .

The teaching of traditional Christian values and practices proven during the centuries to be supportive of a happy and secure home life have been criticised as out of date and swept aside through the influence of small minorities with extreme views about liberty. Love between husband and wife, parents and children, loyalty to God, country and neighbour, have been laughed at.

In spite of the increased material prosperity, figures of violent crime have soared in the last 20 years.

Rape, robbery and child molestation are all increasing. It has been established by nearly 750 pieces of scientific research that there is a link betwen violence on the television screen and in society. Violence, including sexual violence, on television and in the cinema, in 'girlie' magazines and now on video-cassettes is contributing to tragedy in the lives of many.

Children are being encouraged in early teenage sex by a 'you may do as you choose as soon as you can' message, sometimes reaching them through material taught in schools, certainly what they read in teenage magazines. You may be careful what your children see and hear, and the friends they make. But what is being shown and taught to other children – and adults too for that matter? Soon they will all be adults together.[34]

This attempt at a wider appeal beyond the immediate support base could also be found in Merseyside, which extended Cornwall's neo-NVALA critique into a comprehensive list of social ills, asking all new members to join a sub-group specializing in one of the following social ills:

(a) Addictions:
    Alcoholism; Drug abuse; Gambling; Pop sub-culture;
(b) Community relations:
    Housing; Education; Care of the Elderly; Social Services; Industrial Relations; Race relations; Political Extremists;
(c) Crime and Punishment:
    Juvenile delinquency; vandalism; theft; Mugging; Burglary; Rape; Assault; Manslaughter; Murder; Care of Victims; Criminal Injuries Compensation; Treatment of Offenders; Police; Judiciary; Plea Bargaining: Custodial Sentences; Release on Bail; Release on Licence; Parole Board; Football Hooliganism;
(d) Family Life:
    Marriage; Adoption; Fostering; Violence in the Home; Divorce; One-parent families; 're-marriage'; Parental Discipline; Missing Young Persons; Parental rights;
(e) Media:
    Indecent Display; Advertising Standards; Pornographic Magazines; Pornographic Books; Standards on Radio & TV, Cinema;

Theatres; Swearing; Blasphemy; Vulgarity and Obscenity; Merseyside Arts Council; The Arts Council of Great Britain;

(f)   Philosophical and Ideological opposition to traditional Christian Culture:
Atheistic Humanism; New theology; New Morality;

(g)   Science and Technology:
Responsible use of scientific and technological advances; Medical ethics (abortion, transplant surgery, artificial prolongation of life, killing deformed babies, euthanasia, genetic engineering etc.); Environmental ethics (pollution, nuclear power, conservation); Factory farming (battery hens); Animal cruelty; Blood Sports;

(h)   Sexual Morality:
Sex Education; Promiscuity; Venereal Disease; Homosexuality; Adultery; Abortion; Sex Advisory Services; The Availability and prescription of Contraceptives to children; Paedophilia; Abuse of Children; Prostitution and sex shops;

(i)   Education:
Religious Education; Educational Standards in Primary and Secondary Schools; Discipline in schools; Activities of subversive organisations in schools and colleges.[35]

Clearly, sexual permissiveness formed merely a part of a much wider social critique and programme of renewal. Although not every CSA could aspire to such a comprehensive brief aiming at the eradication of liberalism, humanism and situational ethics, they were all effective in several ways.

CSAs were very active public meetings organizers. These would include: platforms for national speakers such as Mrs Gillick and Dr Adrian Rodgers, from the Responsible Society, discussing 'The Family and Medical Ethics' for East Dorset CSA; film shows, including Francis Shaeffer's *What Ever Happened to the Human Race* in Enfield, and Dr James Dobson's *Focus on the Family* series in Portsmouth; and addressing local Christian and secular organizations such as church congregations, PTAs, the National Housewives' Register, and Women's Institutes.[36] Talks to church and social groups in Merseyside averaged one a month.[37]

Newsletters supplied information covering group activities, summaries of others' initiatives, notification of impending campaigns, recommended books, lists of campaign materials, Special Reports or Briefing sections, dates of meetings, and companies making or selling Christian materials. The Cornish group's Spring 1983 newsletter, for example, included: a resumé of the last year's activities; an article entitled 'God, Nation, Family – and in that order', justifying community action; background information and accounts of campaigns against video nasties and sex shops; extracts from the CSA's own review of the evidence concerning the effect of television violence; notes on the growth of occult shops; press extracts and comments, including St John-Stevas's report on declining religious instruction in schools, and a report of the seizure of pornography in London; quotations by a leading Christian campaigner on the need for a Christian life-style; short pieces on 'Dungeons and Dragons', a television action group poster, and a successful parent protest against a four-letter word in a school play; and a membership form. Items would frequently be followed by recommended action, such as this Cornish example, concerning a report of the contents of the film *Grease*: 'Please write to your district councillors, thank them for their interest in the films coming into the county and ask them to interest themselves also in AA and A certificate films.'[38]

Biblical references would support each initiative; for, as the Taunton group's newsletter once explained:

> We sincerely believe that the remedies to all the social evils we deplore and feel so helpless about, are to be found in the Bible, and we intend to concentrate our efforts in publicising this fact . . . In the midst of many secular opinions as to the root cause of these problems, we believe that God has something to say about them, for example, . . .
>
> Does it worry you that pornographic magazines are available to all in nearly every Newsagent in Taunton and elsewhere?
>
> 'BUT AMONG YOU THERE MUST NOT BE EVEN A HINT OF SEXUAL IMMOR-ALITY OR OF ANY KIND OF IMPURITY' (Eph. 5: 3).
>
> Is it right to regard Homosexuality as just another form of acceptable behaviour? God regards this as among the most heinous of sins.
>
> 'MEN COMMITTED INDECENT ACTS WITH OTHER MEN AND RECEIVED IN THEMSELVES THE DUE PENALTY FOR THEIR PERVERSION' (Rom. 1: 27).[39]

CSA members quickly became effective protest-letter writers to the media, councillors, MPs and organizations whose addresses were supplied in the newsletters. Effective letter-lobbying ranged from the thousand letters that convinced Portsmouth City Council to oppose sex-cinemas in 1981, to a single letter sent by a Devon CSA member leading to the removal of pin-up magazines from a local Travellers' Fare bookstall.[40] Petitions, including those backing national campaigns, were a similar device. One elderly CSA supporter in Aylesbury collected thousands for NVALA's 'StoPorn' campaign, by sending a copy of the petition to every church, Women's Institute and senior citizens' home in the town. Despite being eighty-three, she collected another 600 herself. Cornwall CSA raised 27,000 signatures for the NVALA's 1977 ABUSE campaign.[41] CSA members would frequently be heard on phone-ins, or seen in the audience during studio-participation debates on television. Leading members were given 'privileged access' in local media, providing instant sound bites and even supplying copy for news reports or features, such as the Bristol group's three-month study of the content of fourteen teenage magazines.[42]

CSA were also the obvious choice, apart from churches, to organize transport to national or local rallies. Merseyside CSA probably holds the record of 300 coaches from Liverpool to a Pro-Life rally in 1983.[43]

Members were also very effective in monitoring other organizations, institutions and business activities that broke the law or which they did not approve of. The most dramatic intervention was Charles Oxley's infiltration of the Paedophile Information Exchange, and his appearance as a witness in the trial which followed. When newsagents took no heed of a campaign by 'For A Better Bromley', involving local church congregations, police raids on shops were prompted by the publicity involved.[44] Other campaigns have covered: Dungeons and Dragons games, electric video-game violence; sex education in schools, the choice of English literature and the decline of religious instruction in schools; popular records, communist papers in public libraries; abortion, contraceptives for young girls in local authority care; and occult centres. Films refused local showings following such actions include: *The Beast, Caligula* and *The Life of Brian*.[45] Offensive advertisements have also been targeted. Letters to advertisers in *Penthouse* from Bristol led to three advertisers withdrawing. *Penthouse* were also forced to remove their own advert from the Tottenham Hotspur Football Club programme.[46] Sex-education material, from *Make It Happy* by Jane Cousins to gay-oriented material, were constant targets. Teachers were encouraged to take alternative material from organizations like Family and Youth Concern. Portsmouth CSA even produced their own audio-cassette, *Sex and Personal Relationships*, for distribution to several hundred schools. Perhaps the most novel way of promoting family values was the Family Seal of Approval, given to local newsagents who did not stock soft-core pornography. Lists of such stores have been printed in newsletters with the suggestion that members transfer their business to these shops.

CSAs also intervened in local politics. A Harrow member once stood in a local election on a moral standards platform, supporters distributed 20,000 leaflets, and forced the other candidates to comment upon the issues raised. During one campaign in 1980, Worthing CSA circulated leaflets to 47,000 homes.[47]

The most important activity, however, was and is prayer – offered for all local and national crusade initiatives and events, including specific imperatives, such as wisdom and guidance for Mrs Gillick's and Mrs Whitehouse's barristers, and the parliamentary ballot for Private Members' Bills.

All this CSA activity was justified by the concept of active democracy:

Democracy works by debate. Written or spoken faith statements, moral statements, theories and ideas, matter in democracy. They do not have to be new or original to exert their proper influence. Truth has its own authority. Old values need to be restated, supported and explained, on TV and radio, in the council chamber, in the press. Old warnings must be voiced today . . . Although all human enterprises fall far short of what they might be, it is essential to aim for the best, the right, and the good all the time if succeeding generations are not to pay the price of today's neglect in decay, disintegration and defeat . . . The Christian living in a democracy has a duty, in our opinion, to influence his community for good.[48]

To this end, the CSAs made a major contribution in the growth of the British Moral Majority during the 1980s. Yet, if NVALA represented the old order, the torch-bearers, and the CSAs the messengers, sounding the trumpet at the local level, it was the NFOL which galvanized most church groups behind a fully-fledged Moral Majority, and which introduced American-style organization.

Emerging from House Church member Peter Hill's 1971 Trafalgar Square 'Rally Against Permissiveness', the NFOL became the proof that God was working with the revivalist church groups. It enjoyed steady growth under Raymond Johnston, a member of the Church Assembly and the General Synod, but became transformed under Lyndon Bowring, a regular Restoration festival speaker and Elim Minister, as Christian Action Research and Education (CARE). Whereas NVALA tended to work through private lobbying or court cases, CSAs through the local political machinery, and the NFOL acted as an advice and co-ordinating centre, CARE developed a more comprehensive outlook.

Adopting the American organizational approach, CARE provides: educational material relating fundamentalist beliefs to politics; co-ordinates a nation-wide network of Christian welfare programmes for the casualties of the 'permissive society' – single parents, pregnant girls and drug addicts; provides the resources and expertise for Christians to be involved in politics; lobbies local and national government through its core-groups in each constituency and representation at national level; and also helps to co-ordinate the political activities of fundamentalists who have employment in the medical, teaching and social welfare professions.

Four times a year members receive a mail-shot containing a copy of the CARE Magazine (formerly CARE News), a prayer guide, a 'Parliamentary Update', appeals for donations, lists of resources and books, and copies of contemporary campaign posters and leaflets.

CARE Magazine articles cover contemporary issues such as the anti-abortion campaign, news features on subjects like pornography and AIDS, lists of fundamentalist organizations providing other services, conference notices and reports, local group news, briefings, and updates on previous initiatives.

Members' political activism is aided by the CARE Handbook and briefing papers, which rival anything ever produced by a political party or trade union. The Handbook includes theological justifications for all CARE's campaigns, the content of and background to current legislation, relevant statistics, and practical action checklists; as well as everything you would need to know about planning meetings, gaining media contacts, organizing press releases, and the best methods to lobby government representatives. It is published in a loose-leaf format so that new sections and revisions can easily be added. Briefing papers are smaller but concentrate upon one issue, such as *Opposing Your Local Sex Shops, Writing to the Media, Joining a Political Party, Monitoring Your Local Newsagent*; they enable informed and instant action.

In February 1987, following the disputes over gay sex-education material in Haringey and Ealing, attacks against their charitable status by gay activists, and fearing the Commons would not support Clause 28, CARE announced its intention to intervene directly in the British electoral system. Issuing a new briefing paper, *Becoming a Local Councillor*, CARE extolled members to stand, to quiz prospective candidates on 'vital moral issues', or to join a local political party. When it became clear a general election was imminent, core-groups were established in the vast majority of constituencies to spread 'God's Agenda'. This argued that the real purpose of government was to create a society centred on God's laws, and it rejected party loyalties in favour of the candidate's character and views on: abortion law and Obscene Publications reform; moral education in schools; Sunday trading; financial reforms affecting support for marriage and the family; embryo experimentation and surrogacy.[49]

The method and rate of growth of the core-groups varied from just two or three meetings for prayer to much larger, active groups. The centre provided contact with supporters in the constituency, a hot-line and training conferences. In this drive to establish an active group in each constituency, with roots in the local church, and para-church networks, few groups adopted the name CARE, preferring local options such as East Kilbride Christian Standards Group, Newport Christian Alert, Wyre Action for Reform, Thamesdown Family Concern and Watford CAN (Christian Action Now). Examples of early core-group activity included: monitoring local video-cassette retail stores and informing police; organizing stands at local agricultural shows; pregnancy crisis counselling; taking the *The Silent Scream* video into schools; family-fun days; and opposing sex-shop licences.

Whereas NVALA continues to be successful at private lobbying, and CSAs in local action, CARE now seeks to unite these activities with direct intervention in the traditional party political process.

Between the founding of NVALA and the mid-1980s, the three

major groups had been joined by numerous others, the most common being revamped Christian professional associations such as Christians in Education, and Caring Professions Concern involving doctors, psychiatrists, nurses, therapists and social workers, who played a major role in the recent satanic panic. The Parliamentary Scientific Advisory Committee, including scientists and medics opposed to human embryo research, co-ordinates the all-party Pro-Life group in Parliament.

For our purposes the most important group is the Cambridge-based Jubilee Centre, which promotes a biblical-based economic analysis and programme. Their 'Keep Sunday Special' campaign, with links in the trade union movement opposed to Sunday opening, was more successful than their Family Base initiative, but both demonstrated opposition to Mrs Thatcher's economic programme. The group Family Charter, launched on 12 March 1987, gaining support from churchmen, academics and eighty politicians, attacked six aspects of Thatcherism seen as undermining the family: easy credit; regional economic decline; the demand for mobile workforces; lack of support for family carers of the elderly or handicapped; the destruction of small family firms; and the threat of Sunday trading. The proposed alternatives reveal the Christian communities' independence from the so-called 'New Right': credit controls; regional policies for lending, investment and government contracts; family-oriented personnel policies in firms, with the government setting an example; more tax relief and allowances for family carers; tougher rules to govern takeovers and mergers; and minimum Sunday trading.

These groups and many others, including extensive prayer chains such as the Lydia Fellowship, are all linked to the Evangelical Alliance, which has also undergone a major transformation under its General Secretary Clive Calver, a regular Restoration festival speaker.

In 1986, the Alliance distributed *How Much Longer Must the Silent Majority Remain Silent?*, extolling members to take decision-making away from what they called the 'politicians, doubters and secularists'. Two years earlier, it funded the Leadership '84 conference to bring together religious leaders in much the same way as the American Religious Roundtable's Dallas Convention did, to plan for the next decade. The Alliance believes it has the ear of over one million people, from the ordinary members to its own affiliated groups such as the Evangelical Coalition on Sexuality, which sought to link all churches and Christian agencies involved in medicine, education, sociology and family issues to 'speak and act on sexually related issues that affect society'.

Collectively, these groups replicate the American Moral Majority, and their history demonstrates that there is nothing new about the 'New Moral Right'. Each new major organization that emerged reflected the increasing strength of the Christian sub-culture upon which it was based, and their growing confidence can be seen in the range of activities and form of organization adopted. The clear impression that they have an independent perspective is reinforced by an examination of their motivations.

Motivation

According to some sociologists, Christian activists are motivated by secular imperatives. Chief among these is the belief that fundamentalists are suffering from a loss of group or class respectability or status, which they regain through a moral crusade which affirms the 'correctness' of their values in the eyes of the public; so that the crusades are 'symbolic' acts by a declining social class, experiencing social and economic dissonance.[50] In the rare exceptions when the Christian activists' religious motives are taken into account, these are down-graded; mobilization is seen as a last hopeless swipe against secularization, or follows from the inability of 'established power structures' to control political, social and economic circumstances in a period of a 'pervasive sense of moral decay'.[51]

Such explanations effectively ignore or underestimate the independence and power of fundamentalism, its support base and the dynamics of the belief system.

Roy Wallis, by exploring how cultural and religious fundamentalism merged to inform the NVALA's beliefs – subscription to fidelity in marriage and chastity before it, authority and patriotism, and rejection of drugs, foul language, homosexuality, pornography and abortion – demonstrated the necessity of including group beliefs within explanations concerning individual motivations.[52] These beliefs ensured that fundamentalists should relate to, and would be motivated by, status indicators not deemed significant by contemporary sociologists. In the NVALA's case this would be thrift, abstemiousness, diligence, hard work, restraint and deferment of gratification.[53] As these values *were* all under attack from various economic, social and ethical forces during the 1960s, and as a rising salaried middle class embraced secularization, consumption and instrumental attitudes to work and leisure, the NVALA's interpretation of these events would clearly enhance structural explanations for mobilization.

Apart from this failure to explore current fundamentalist motivations, there are at least five weaknesses with the current sociological consensus concerning motivation. First, as British, like American, Moral Majority members tend to come from the young rising affluent middle classes, they are not economic or socially marginalized groups suffering status loss.[54] Second, the fundamentalists' strong religious sub-culture would separate them from social isolates suffering from status discontent who engage in symbolic political gestures or who, more often, simply become demoralized and do not participate in pressure-group politics.[55] Third, since history demonstrates that political–moral crusades have always been led by evangelical Christians of fundamentalist persuasion, and since reviews of recent crusade membership reveal that moral crusaders promote values inculcated during their socialization and maintained by the culture of their local fundamentalist community (whatever the secular rationale used), we need to explore this non-historically specific motive.[56] Fourth, as 'sociological' accounts assume a background of continued denominational decline and ignore recent fundamentalist growth, rationales for a sudden appearance of a Moral Majority are superfluous; there were many signs that fundamentalist political involvement was steadily growing during the period 1950–75: sociologists simply missed them.[57] Fifth, contemporary commentary cannot explain the apparent contradiction between the influence Christian crusaders have exercised in the last decade (see below) and their supposed decline in power and status. The forced closure of 500 sex-shops between 1982 and 1986, for example, cannot simply be dismissed as a symbolic act, as it halted the advance of sexually-oriented material. The rapid acceptance of the existence of satanic ritual sex allegations by secular feminists, psychiatrists and social workers also demonstrates the increasing 'cross-over' power of fundamentalist concerns.[58]

In short, as socio-economic circumstances can only induce susceptibility towards action, and an individual's motives for action invariably come from within his own belief system,[59] explanations of mobilization must include the role of belief, as well as structural factors.

Although fundamentalists' public rationales have changed over time to suit their audience, including a move away from moral to causalist justifications,[60] their personal rationale has always followed from their religious beliefs which extend beyond simple subscription to a moral code. The main rationale for mobilization between 1960 and 1990 was what I call the Ezekiel factor. In order to demonstrate the centrality of this motivation, I will first note one of its public manifestations:

> . . . by far the most significant feature of post-war Britain has been the retreat of Christianity and the advance of secular humanism; and that the great majority of the social, ethical, even economic problems facing us spring from this. An exaggerated statement? I don't believe so; . . .
>
> The collapse of the moral structure which has characterised western society throughout recorded history is the result of the gradual erosion of its very foundation – the Bible . . .

> For over a thousand years in this country, there was no serious challenge to the validity of the Christian ethic. Though people did wrong, few doubted that it was right, at least in principle, to be honest; that the authority of parents, schoolmasters and the law should be recognised and respected; that swearing, blasphemy, and obscenity were intrinsically wrong; that there could be no justification for vandalism and violence; that fornication and adultery were immoral, abortion evil, sodomy sinful, and murder a capital offence. But all that has changed. And . . . The pattern of life today is little recommendation for the 'alternative society' we have created and made commonplace . . .
>
> There is a great and understandable temptation to people today, for Christians as well as non Christians, to withdraw into smaller and smaller groups where they feel safe whether within the family or church or club. Not because they are basically unwilling to grapple with the vast social evils which surround us but because the problems seem too great even to think about let alone tackle and solve. But the truth is – it's us or no one.[61]

Such an appeal is more than a swipe at 'permissiveness', it reveals the core of the rationale for mobilization: secularization, which leads to social problems, follows from the failure to preach the true gospel; but active participation by real Christians will ensure that civilization survives by leading people back to Christ.

This is more than a contemporary variant of the Fall of Rome thesis. Although fundamentalists insist that today's moral collapse repeats the experience of twenty-seven other lost civilizations,[62] to emphasize 'Sodom watching' out of context misses the fundamentalists' determination to apply biblical standards beyond church communities, their belief that they have an understanding of social events superior to that of secularists, and that the symptoms which they identify as permissiveness extend far beyond fornication and embrace many modern trends from Women's Liberation, through rock music, to Zen Buddhism. All are unGodly.[63]

What specifically motivates politically active fundamentalists is an awe and fear of God's 'collective judgement', according to which he punishes cities and nations turning from his Grace by spreading disorder, and the further knowledge that judgement is not a single act. For:

> The Bible clearly shows that when one form of judgment fails to bring a people to repentance, God has to visit them with another judgment – of a more severe kind. And often he has to continue with another, and yet another. Each visitation takes a more serious form than the previous one, whilst all the time God is pleading with his people to return to him.
>
> When the leaders and people of a nation, such as our own stubbornly refuse to heed the warnings which have repeatedly been given and deliberately choose to ignore them, then God has to resort to far more stringent methods to bring them to their knees.[64]

In Britain, as in America, sections of the growing fundamentalist community saw permissive reform such as the legalization of abortion and homosexuality as a prelude to further judgement. The economic depression and failures in international politics during the next decade were then regarded as the fulfilment of that prophecy. This is why British fundamentalists set much store by 'Victorian standards' which God once rewarded with imperial greatness.[65] The blessings of the empire disappeared because Britain failed to keep to those standards, but a return to those values would prove that we were willing to demonstrate our collective repentance.[66] In this quest, individual Christians cannot stand aside from secular society, for Ezekiel warns them that no matter how devout they are, God's judgement doesn't fall solely upon the unrepentant:

> Son of man, speak to your countrymen and say to them: 'When I bring the sword against a land and the people of the land choose one of their men and make him their watchman, and he sees the sword coming against the land and blows the trumpet to warn the people, then if anyone hears the trumpet but does not take warning and the sword comes and takes his life, his blood will be on his own head. Since he heard the sound of the trumpet but did not take warning, his blood will be on his own head. If he had taken warning, he would have saved himself. But if the watchman sees the sword coming and does not blow the trumpet to warn the people and the sword comes and takes the life of one of them, that man will be taken away because of his sin, but I will hold the watchman accountable for his blood.' (Ezek. 33: 1–6)

It is this attempt to avoid further judgement, upon believers and non-believers alike, that constitutes the link between individual faith and public action, and explains why contemporary crusaders are blowing an ever louder trumpet on moral questions. Salvation cannot be a private concern; it has to be public, collective and national.

This imperative cannot be found in sociology's secular explanations, it must be sought in the fundamentalists' own belief system, as history reveals it always was. Three hundred years ago, Societies for the Reformation of Manners justified lobbying for State control on vice, because: 'the open and avowed Practise of Vice might provoke God to withdraw His Mercy and Blessings from Us, and instead thereof to inflict heavy and severe judgements'.[67]

Similar justifications can be found in the Victorian period, even though the Society for the Suppression of Vice also linked vice and biological disease, and the National Vigilance Association promoted eugenic justifications in their respective public rationales.[68]

Even today, when fundamentalist warnings on both sides of the Atlantic are mediated through the rallying cry of family defence, the fact that all destructive influences – pre-marital sexual experiment, adultery, prostitution and perversion and the feminist-inspired androgynous culture – are to be controlled by campaigns securing civil laws to protect 'the immature and the less well prepared in terms of economic advantage, intelligence or personality' (read: working class) who live without the 'necessary guidelines' of behaviour (read: the Bible) demonstrates that the fundamentalists have at least one eye upon God.[69] The declaratory function of the secular law (and promotion of the family through anti-permissive legislation) serves a dual purpose. It controls the moral environment, as it

> declares the mind of a community about tolerable types of behaviour. It thus contributes to social morality as well as reflecting it . . . many citizens, sadly, have little guidance available beyond the law to help them to make moral decisions, especially when they are repeatedly told that divinely sanctioned morality is either infantile or nonsensical and they are assured that it is an untenable moral position to look to God, Bible or church for sound moral principles. Under these circumstances a law relating to a moral problem becomes of great importance, with or without sanctions.[70]

It also demonstrates to God that the trumpet has sounded and been heard.

Moral Crusades

Supported by the growing Christian sub-culture and motivated by Ezekiel, the British Moral Majority sought influence in every area of society. Their major success to date, however, has been legislation in the area of sex and censorship. This includes the Child Protection Act 1978, which outlawed 'child pornography'; the Indecent Displays (Control) Act 1981, which curtailed public advertisements for sexually-orientated material; Clause 3 of the Local Government (Misc. Prov.) Act 1982, which precipitated the closure of some 500 sex-shops; the Cinematographic Acts 1982 and 1985, which eliminated the growing sex cinema industry; the Video Recordings Act 1984, which reintroduced pre-censorship; and Clause 28 of the Local Government Act 1988, which forbids the public funding of any form of communication deemed to be promoting homosexuality. Prosecutions and prohibitions under these Acts extend far beyond the 'pornographic' to rock records, computer games and women's wrestling! This legislation is complemented by the creation of a Broadcasting Standards Council to oversee the content of television programmes broadcast in Britain; which fulfils a major NVALA demand.

The effect of these campaigns is a 'chill factor' extending into mainstream media, setting a social 'standard' of acceptable behaviour and beliefs upon which to build other campaigns.[71] While the lack of consistent opposition to these measures can be explained by the influence of 'popular' feminism among potential detractors, the fact that fundamentalists rather than feminists secured this legislation, demonstrates that they can and do promote life-style issues.

To dismiss success in this area as merely evidence of the fundamentalists' obsession with sex, or, worse, a series of media-inspired moral panics,[72] demonstrates a lack of knowledge concerning the central role the fundamentalists' moral entrepreneurship played in placing these issues on the political agenda, and seeing them through Parliament.[73] In order to understand that, we must remember that the long battle against vice which was begun in the late seventeenth century by evangelical Societies for the Reformation of Manners, then continued by the Society for the Suppression of Vice and the National Vigilance Society in the Victorian period, ultimately led to public acceptance of the fundamentalist sexual perspective, especially by the British establishment. Sin was not to be aired in the media, and the wages of sin were not afforded relief, be it in the form of VD cures or divorce, which demonstrated that there was a public standard. The fundamentalists' standard-setting ability was then shaken by both the resilience of popular culture, erroneously denounced as 'American influences', and post-war structural developments which undermined the foundations and values upon which the fundamentalists had built a society free from obscenity. Between 1957 and 1968, 'traditional' standards and attitudes, based upon the secular control and punishment of sin, collapsed. Beginning with the 1957 Homicide Act, in the next eleven years prostitution, gambling, suicide, homosexuality, contraception, abortion, divorce and restrictions upon Sunday entertainments were all subject to decriminalization to varying extents. The results were far less permissive than fundamentalists allege;[74] but the role of both government and the Established Church convinced fundamentalists that the State was announcing that the Christian faith, as they understood it, was irrelevant.[75] At the very least, the State was now failing to provide the institutional and legal backing it once gave to the then fundamentalist perspective on sin.

The one major exception, to the growing cultural and political isolation, was 'obscenity'. The 1959 Obscene Publications Bill sought to exempt 'serious' fiction and educational literature, not 'pornography', from control. So it is not surprising that it was from this last barricade that the fundamentalists sought to turn back the tide of 'permissiveness' as a whole. The fundamentalists did not pick this issue; it was all that they had left. Previous reliance upon the State, however, had led to the decline of the crusaders' own organizations, and a new crusade would take time.

Between 1959 and 1970, individual fundamentalists fought numerous court cases to maintain the pre-1959 definitions of obscene material. They lost. Birth control, sex education and 'strong' literature were all freed from prosecution. After 1970, though the NVALA won a series of court cases against the political subversion of the 'underground' press, they were losing the battle against 'soft-core pornography'. An early attempt to turn the tide with *The Longford Report*, a Petition for Public Decency, and the 1972 crusade against provincial sex-shops did not succeed. Although fundamentalists convinced Portsmouth City Council to lobby the then Conservative government, the Department of the Environment rejected intervention arguing there was no support because of 'the current climate of public opinion'.[76] The fundamentalists had more success with 'X' films, and current trends in film advertising; they persuaded several local government authorities to ban films, including *Quiet Days in Clichy*.[77] But attempts to pass legislation by Mr Ironmonger MP against sex-shops, and a Sale of Offensive Literature Bill merely revealed the division in Parliament between pro- and anti-censorship lobbies. Two years later a Cinematograph and Indecent Display Bill also failed to become law.

The fundamentalists' inability to move Parliament into action was matched in the courts. Although fundamentalists gained a prosecution against a homosexual newspaper for blasphemy, the 'not guilty' verdicts against *Inside Linda Lovelace* and *Libertine* magazine led to the search for a new strategy. Together with their allies like the lawyers' group within the Conservative Party, the fundamentalists finally managed to force the Labour government into establishing the Williams Committee. To their chagrin, however, this threatened to offer legal protection to pornography,[78] and thereby threatened the last viable moral norm fundamentalists could argue was sanctioned by law.

It was the NVALA's decision to link the existence of the Paedophile Information Exchange to pornography, a move supported by Mrs Thatcher's Opposition, that led to the breakthrough in reform, in the form of fellow Christian Mr Townsend's Private Member's Bill which led to the 1978 Child Protection Act. This NVALA ABUSE campaign clearly demonstrated that moral issues could win votes: and that 'public opinion' need not be feared. Mrs Thatcher's Opposition were in agreement. At the NVALA's May 1978 conference, Mr Whitelaw insisted that both organizations had 'a duty to conserve the moral standards on which our society has been based and so preserve them for future generations'.[79]

The ABUSE campaign also radically altered the Moral Majority's discourse and tactics; the protection of children, rather than the threat of moral decline, became the major public justification for further controls; and it marked a movement away from trying to enforce existing law in the Moral Majority's favour towards gaining alternative legislation which targeted individual items and avoided court cases.

Once the Williams Report was officially shelved, following the NVALA's 'StoPorn' crusade, the 1980s saw a continual battle by the CSAs against newsagent stocks, the growing number of provincial sex-shops, and videos, in what amounted to a permanent crusade against any and every new form of distribution, and a determined effort to reverse the legacy of the 1959 Act. Though the Churchill Bill, controlling newsagents' magazine stocks, was lost, television programmes became subject to the 1959 Act, and a new crusade outlawing pin-up magazines from newsagents was underway in 1991.

Although each crusade is different, the 1981 campaign against sex-shops and the 1984 Video Nasties panic were representative of how such gains are made.

In 1981, when David Sullivan attempted to establish a chain of over one hundred sex-shops, the fundamentalist community organized a nation-wide series of pickets and protests. This public pressure led the government to suggest a licensing experiment in Soho. The fundamentalists objected, and the Portsmouth CSA convinced Portsmouth Council to promote a Private Bill in the House of Lords containing planning controls enabling councils to ban the shops outright. When the government realized that Portsmouth would not drop its proposal, they introduced nation-wide licensing powers in the Local Government (Miscellaneous Provisions) Act 1982. Once the Act was secured, the fundamentalists systematically lobbied every council to adopt these enabling provisions, and then close the sex-shops in their area.[80]

Whereas sex-shops were closed by lobbying within the system and open argument, pre-censorship of video-cassettes (a procedure which avoided acquittals in the courts) came through the promotion of a public panic, promoted through sympathetic media, concerning forty horror videos which allegedly normalized violence for child viewers. But the media campaign could not have succeeded without local and national fundamentalist campaigns. In Portsmouth, for example, the CSA lobbied the council and local MPs, including Bonner-Pink who eventually chaired the committee stage of the Bill, to put pressure on the government. They also registered numerous complaints with the police which led to raids on fifteen stores between September 1982 and April 1983. Meetings were held in schools with teachers, letters sent to local media, and a local Christian film-maker sold a documentary on the subject to Southern TV. The CSA pressed home the advantage by compiling a list of videos subject to prosecution and pressed dealers to withdraw them from stock. As a result, video nasties were impossible to obtain in Portsmouth long before they became subject to national debate.[81] This and similar local initiatives were paralleled at national level by the NVALA and the Parliamentary Video Inquiry. Having secured a ruling that video-cassettes could be designated an obscene article in the London courts, Mary Whitehouse then took her campaign to sixteen marginal constituencies, sent letters to 150 provincial papers, and held a 'Video Nasty' film show at the Conservative Party Conference to gain more support.[82] Meanwhile, a group of parliamentarians and academics – Lord Nugent with his history of promoting moral legislation; Raymond Johnston, Director of CARE; Lady Watherston of Christian Unity and soon to become President of the National Council for Christian Standards in Society; Lord Swinfen, a veteran anti-porn campaigner; and Tim Sainsbury who promoted the 1981 Indecent Display Act – established the Parliamentary Video Inquiry, led by fundamentalist prophet Dr Clifford Hill, who ran an evangelical mission in London. The Inquiry's sensational Report, accepted uncritically by sympathetic newspapers, merely repeated Hill's previous thesis and prophecies about adverse media effects, justifying parliamentary intervention to protect children's moral welfare; yet it had a dramatic impact on national debate, and was used to justify legislation.[83]

It is by these means – direct access to power through sympathetic councils or by raising fears in the media that gain some measure of public support – that the fundamentalists are able to 'cross-over' into the public domain. To enlist the aid of MPs who win the right to present Private Members' Bills each year, CARE now employ a full-time parliamentary secretary. Fundamentalists have also become very skilled at manipulating the media, not only through feature-writers like Butt and Holbrook, but also providing sensational copy that appears to justify drastic action. More recently, the NVALA's friendly relations with the Scotland Yard Obscene Publications Squad has developed into an open alliance.[84]

To explain how the strategy and tactics of the Christian fundamentalists had such a powerful effect upon the public debate would take too long to cover here. A major factor in that success, however, has obviously been a willing government. Scholars' attempts to link the fundamentalists' pro-family strategy with the New Right's assault on the welfare state, however, is to confuse a symptom with the cause.

As early as 1971, Ian Lloyd and the Conservative Lawyers group promoted the possibility that an assault on pornography could secure votes. It was the NVALA's 1977 ABUSE campaign that convinced the party to take 'a tougher line on what was permissible', and appeal to 'Victorian standards'.[85] Since then the Conservatives have offered the fundamentalists several concessions in this area, and the party's last three election manifestos promised to enact a major fundamentalist demand for media reform: 1979 – sex cinema/shop controls; 1983 – video controls; 1987 – broadcasting controls. These have secured the fundamentalist vote, despite their growing reservations regarding the effects of the government's economic policy. Unlike the American Moral Majority, British fundamentalists do not believe the free market automatically promotes moral responsibility, and they are actively seeking alternatives.[86] Concessions covering media censorship are obviously easier to make than other demands such as restrictions upon company mergers; for while a complete overhaul of the Obscene Publications Act at that stage may have divided the Conservative Party, step by step legislation keeps the moderately moral happy, and removes obscenity cases from the courts where numerous acquittals demonstrate that the public do not necessarily share the fundamentalists' standards. By giving way on these issues, the party was able to avoid bringing into the open the growing contradictions between its own and the fundamentalists' wider philosophies.

That groups like CARE finally lost patience, and began to explore the possibility of promoting their own parliamentary strategy, demonstrates rather than negates the fact that such a balancing act existed. When the fundamentalists complained that sections of the Williams Committee Report, officially rejected by the government when taking office, were steadily being introduced by Willie Whitelaw, Leon Brittan and Mrs Thatcher gave their personal support for the Video Bill, and convinced the NVALA to stay with the Conservatives despite the 'libertarians in the Home Office'.[87]

Fundamentalist pressure groups are, therefore, clearly engaged in life-style political campaigns, and the history of that crusade demonstrates that they are not seizing a political space opened by feminists. Media censorship is merely the first step in their attempt to stem permissiveness.

This review also demonstrates that the British Moral Majority not only exist and that they can be effective, it also questions the viability of Bruce's disqualifications.

The ability of British charismatics, Pentecostalists and fundamentalists to unite within the Christian sub-culture, against the common cause of permissiveness, more than makes up for lack of numbers. By securing access to power through the media, local councils and Private Members' Bills, they do not need to influence either the judiciary and/or the civil service. These groups are forced to respond to 'moral panics' promoted by the fundamentalists through willing media. As British fundamentalists are not hampered by First Amendment considerations, they have easily placed life-style issues including abortion and embryo research on to the political agenda. They have also secured far more legislative success than their American counterparts.

Following the adverse public reaction surrounding the Bakker and Swaggart scandals, the American Moral Majority officially disbanded in 1989. Though they secured local state victories banning various 'humanist' school books, defeating the Equal Rights Amendment for women, and preventing various states adopting special provisions for homosexual rights, the Moral Majority were a failure. Not one piece of federal legislation based upon their beliefs was secured, because they never succeeded in moving beyond their own support base, in what is clearly a pluralistic society. The high media profile that aided their initial impact upon American society was also their undoing: opponents were able to exaggerate their threat to pluralism and mobilize opposition. Whether or not Don Wildmon's Family Association can gain greater success remains to be seen.

In contrast, the British Moral Majority continue to gather strength, reflecting their deliberate decision to keep a lower profile, and their policy of backing issues which enjoy wider public support, such as anti-pornography crusades. In this way, they are slowly but steadily altering the public discourses concerning moral issues.

The long-term prospects, however, are in the balance. As Britain becomes more integrated into the European Community the relative legislative power of the British fundamentalists will decline.

The Future

The real issue is whether the fundamentalists can be successful without Mrs Thatcher's tacit support, and if they can gain success beyond sexually-oriented issues. Though individual MEPs, notably NVALA member Richard Simmonds, have been attempting to export fundamentalist media standards to the EC with efforts such as the 1987 'Television Without Frontiers' directive, the collapse of the Conservative Family Campaign within the parliamentary party is an important setback. Are the fundamentalist organizations strong enough to continue on their own?

CARE are determined that they will be. To this end they have made great efforts to emphasize the caring nature of their campaigns over the need to avoid collective judgement. They have also promoted books and educational material that cover a much wider range of issues from a Christian perspective, including: poverty, multi-racialism, human rights and the environment.[88] New alliances are also being forged in older campaigns, as the co-operation between radical feminists like Catherine Itzin and Clare Short within the Labour Party in the contemporary assault on soft-core pornography demonstrates.[89]

There can be no doubt, however, that the experience of Britain's Moral Majority demonstrates that social–moral issues are still open to debate in the western world, and, like any other political issue, can mobilize people. As more and more norms and values are determined by the interaction between highly organized sub-cultural pressure groups,[90] academics need to pay far more attention to Christian social movements than they have thus far.

Chapter 5

The Distinctiveness and Effectiveness of Church Schools

Leslie J. Francis

This chapter begins by charting the historical development of the church school system in England and Wales, by summarizing the contemporary debate regarding the character and future of church schools, and by arguing that this debate focuses issues which are properly a matter for empirical inquiry. The following sections then review a series of empirical studies designed to address some of these issues over the past two decades. These studies examine the influence of church primary schools on pupil attitudes towards Christianity, describe the attitudes of teachers working in church primary schools, compare the religious curriculum and ethos of church and county primary schools, chart the impact of church primary schools on local church life in rural and urban parishes, unravel the influence of Anglican secondary schools on pupil religious development, and model the relationship between Catholic secondary schools, church and home on the religious attitudes of pupils in England, Wales, Scotland, the USA and Australia. Cumulatively these separate studies begin to answer fundamental questions regarding the contemporary distinctiveness and effectiveness of church schools. It is argued that such empirical data need to be taken fully into account in developing a realistic theology of education for church schools into the twenty-first century.

The Historical Context

Church schools are an integral part of the state-maintained system of education in England and Wales as a direct consequence of the accidents of history.[1] Long before the State established the machinery to build Board Schools through the 1870 Education Act,[2] the churches had taken their own major initiatives through voluntary enterprise. The main antecedents of the present system, therefore, were two voluntary societies founded at the beginning of the nineteenth century. Both were inspired by religious principles and it was religion which kept them apart.

The British and Foreign School Society emerged in 1814 from the Royal Lancasterian Society and was supported primarily by Nonconformists and liberal Anglicans.[3] Religious instruction in British schools was confined to 'general Christian principles' and the society explicitly proscribed the teaching of 'catechism or peculiar religious tenets'.

The National Society was founded in 1811 as a direct challenge to the Royal Lancasterian Society and had the backing of the great body of Anglicans.[4] National schools were founded to promote 'the education of the poor in the principles of the established church'. Religious instruction in National schools was to include the doctrines, catechism and liturgy of the Church of England. For a time National schools even insisted on attendance at an Anglican church or Sunday school as a condition of entry.

After government grants became available to these voluntary societies in 1833 to assist with school building, other church-sponsored societies entered the field as well. In 1843 the Methodist Conference decided to provide voluntary day schools and accepted its first state grant in 1847. In 1847 the Catholic Poor School Committee was established and, after some delay, was recognized as an authority able to receive grants from the State.[5]

The problem with leaving the development of a national system of schools to voluntary initiative was that provision was erratic over the country as a whole. The 1870 Elementary Education Act recognized that compromise was essential and made provision for two different types of school. On the one hand, the schools founded by the voluntary societies were permitted to continue and given official entitlement to grants-in-aid. On the other hand, local school boards were established to build schools in areas where voluntary provision was inadequate. Board schools were intended to make good the gaps in the voluntary system, not to replace that system. Indeed, the possibility of competition from board schools spurred the voluntary societies to increase their own initiatives.

While the 1870 Education Act enabled voluntary schools and board schools to develop side by side, the financial provisions of the act favoured the board schools. The churches found it increasingly difficult to keep pace with the board schools and to maintain educational standards. The 1902 Education Act established greater parity between voluntary and board schools, under the newly-created local education authorities.[6] Board schools were renamed 'provided' schools and voluntary schools were renamed 'non-provided' schools. The significant feature of this Act is that both provided and non-provided schools were to receive aid from the local rates. It was this rate aid for Catholic as well as for British and National schools which provoked a violent opposition from some members of the Free Churches.

Between 1902 and 1944 the dual system of provided and non-provided schools continued, in spite of the churches' increasing financial difficulty in maintaining their commitment to schools and in spite of the Fisher Education Bill's abortive attempt to introduce a unitary system in 1921.

1944 Education Act

The partnership between Church and State as experienced today in England and Wales is a direct result of the 1944 Education Act which set out to reconstruct the educational system after the Second World War.[7] At the heart of its thinking was provision of secondary education for all. To make this possible a large number of existing schools required extension, modernization and re-equipment. New senior schools were needed. On the one hand, the churches could not afford to maintain their voluntary schools and to bring them up to the new standards required. On the other hand, the State could not afford to buy up the church schools and was reluctant to annex them. In short, the church schools presented a major political problem.[8]

At the same time, the churches were themselves divided on their understanding of the future of voluntary schools. Catholic opinion insisted on retaining the full denominational character of their schools and remained clearly in favour of separate Catholic schools for Catholic children. A Catholic lobby pressed for a solution similar to that achieved by the 1918 Education Act in Scotland, according to which the secular authorities covered the whole cost of denominational schools.[9] The main body of Free Church opinion advocated the replacement of the dual system by a unified state system. They argued that the Christian presence in education could best be preserved through non-denominational religious education in provided schools. Church of England opinion was clearly divided on the issue. Some Anglicans tended to agree with the Free Church view. Bishop Brook of St Edmundsbury and Ipswich, for example, argued that 'it is neither buildings, syllabuses, nor timetables that matter most. What matters is that the teachers in all the schools whether voluntary or county shall be Christian men and women.'[10] Other Anglicans tended to agree more with the Catholic view. Bishop Kirk of Oxford, for example, argued that 'our church schools are essential means towards making our witness effective; we must not let them go'.[11]

Prolonged negotiations resulted in another compromise between Church and State. By the 1944 Education Act, voluntary schools were individually given the choice between 'aided' or 'controlled' status. This choice enabled schools which could afford to retain a high level of independence to do so, while those that either could not afford or did not desire to retain such a high level of independence could nevertheless retain something of their church-related character.

Voluntary controlled status absolved the Church from on-going financial responsibility for the maintenance of the school, although the Church retained the right to appoint a minority of the governors, provide denominational worship throughout the school, offer denominational religious education on parental request, and, in schools of more than two teachers, appoint 'reserved teachers' competent to give denominational religious instruction. Voluntary aided status gave the churches additional rights, including the appointment of the majority of governors and the provision of denominational instruction, as well as worship, throughout the school, but also involved them in continued financial liability for certain capital expenditures.[12] Government grant aid was made available to meet 50 per cent of these costs. Subsequent legislation raised the grant to 75 per cent in 1959, 80 per cent in 1967 and 85 per cent in 1974.

A third category of voluntary school, 'special agreement schools', was created to honour arrangements negotiated between local education authorities and the churches as a result of the 1936 Education Act. For most practical purposes the provisions are the same as for aided status, except in relation to the appointment of staff.[13]

The basic intention of the provisions distinguishing aided and controlled schools have remained essentially unaltered by the 1980 and 1988 Education Acts.

Current Provision
Following the 1944 Education Act, the Catholic Church rejected controlled status completely. Just two small Catholic schools accepted the irreversible designation of controlled status. Murphy accounts for these two anomalies 'as the result of administrative oversight'.[14] The Catholic community continued to feel that the financial arrangements of aided status were unfair, but worked hard to finance a national network of aided schools. In 1949 the Catholic Church provided 8.8 per cent of state-maintained primary places in England and Wales. The proportion expanded to 9.7 per cent in 1959 and 10.2 per cent in 1969. In 1989 it stood at 9.6 per cent. In 1949 the Catholic Church provided 2.9 per cent of state-maintained secondary places in England and Wales. The proportion expanded to 4.4 per cent in 1959 and 7.9 per cent in 1969. In 1989 it stood at 9.2 per cent.[15]

As far as Church of England schools were concerned, the choice between aided and controlled status was left in the hands of the individual governors or managers. While Church of England schools are autonomous, the diocese is in the position to offer advice, guidance and financial aid. In the absence of an agreed central policy, each diocese formulated its own recommendations. Some dioceses, like London, Southwark and Blackburn, opted heavily for aided status. Other dioceses, like Bristol, York, Coventry and Lichfield, opted mainly for controlled status. In 1949 the Anglican Church provided 22.5 per cent of state-maintained primary places in England and Wales. The proportion contracted to 18.8 per cent in 1959 and 17.0 per cent in 1969. In 1989 it stood at 16.8 per cent. In 1949 the Anglican Church provided 3.8 per cent of state-maintained second-ary places in England and Wales. The proportion contracted to 3.1 per cent in 1959 and to 3.0 per cent in 1969. Subsequently it has expanded to 4.6 per cent in 1989.[16]

Within this overall pattern, Church of England school provision now varies greatly from one area to another. In some areas, like Oxfordshire, Shropshire, Somerset and Wiltshire, as many as half of the primary schools are Church of England voluntary schools. In Cleveland and County Durham the proportion falls to one in ten.

The Catholic View

Historically, the aim of Catholic schools in England and Wales was to provide an alternative educational system to make it possible for 'every Catholic child from a Catholic home to be taught by Catholic teachers in a Catholic school'.[17] In 1929 Pope Pius IX's encyclical letter 'Divini Illius Magistri' confirmed 'the prescriptions of canon law which forbid Catholic children on any pretext whatsoever to attend . . . schools open indiscriminately to Catholics and non-Catholics alike'. Insistence on this basic view is now couched in far less assertive terms. The 'Declaration on Christian Education' issued by the Second Vatican Council reminded parents of 'their duty to entrust their children to Catholic schools, when and where this is possible, to support such schools to the extent of their ability, and to work along with them for the welfare of their children'.[18] In their document, *The Catholic School*, the Sacred Congregation for Catholic Education replaces the note of command with that of reasoned argument in favour of Catholic schools.[19]

More recently, the 1981 report to the Bishops of England and Wales, *Signposts and Homecomings*, recognized that Catholic edu-cation should be confined neither to the years of compulsory school-ing, nor to the Catholic school.[20] Nevertheless, the report reaffirmed the identity of the Catholic school as 'a believing and integrated Christian community'. It argued that:

> Within a Catholic school the ultimate distinctive element is that its life is based on the vision of Christ in which all learning, growing, service, freedom and relationships are seen as part of a growth in the knowledge, love and experience of God. In other words there is a deliberate hope that the experience of belonging to this school will encourage personal commitment to Jesus Christ.

This statement provides a clear indication regarding the expectations of distinctiveness and effectiveness associated with Catholic schools in England and Wales.

The Anglican View

Although historically the aim of National schools was to promote education 'in the principles of the established church', the Anglican Church has, in theory and in practice, taken a much broader view of its involvement in education. The Durham Report, a key statement on the Anglican philosophy of church schools, published in 1970, sharpened a distinction between the Church of England's *domestic* and *general* functions in education.[21] The report argues that:

> It is extremely important to recognize at the outset that the Church of England voluntary school today is an institution whose roots go back into a past where its role was seen as two-fold. It was general to serve the nation through its children, and domestic, to equip the children of the church to take their places in the Christian community.

After recognizing that historically these two roles were 'indistinguishable, for nation and church were, theoretically, one, and the domestic task was seen as including the general', the Durham Report argues that 'nowadays no one would pretend to claim that nation and church are co-extensive' and draws the logical conclusion that the domestic and general functions of church schools can no longer be confused. The report's recommendation is that the Anglican Church should 'see its continued involvement in the dual system principally as a way of expressing its concern for the general education of all children and young people rather than as a means for giving "denominational instruction" '. This emphasis is reaffirmed in the more recent green paper, *A Future in Partnership*, published in 1984, which argues that the idea of *partnership* should be stressed in preference to the *dual system* and that the *voluntary* aspects of church schools should be stressed in preference to *denominationalism*.[22] At the same time, the green paper is careful to support the distinctiveness of church schools by cataloguing an inventory of ten distinctive features characterized by the following labels: a safe place, an ecumenical nursery, a place of distinctive excellence, stepping stones to and from the community, a house of the gospel, a place of revelation and disclosure, a foster home of enduring values and relationships, a beacon signalling the transcendent, a place where you can see the wood from the trees, a creative workshop. These characteristics are reaffirmed by subsequent National Society documents.[23]

While the Church of England has made this recent pronouncement regarding the distinctiveness of church schools, it has remained comparatively reticent regarding its expectations concerning the impact of these schools on the pupils who attend them.

Growing Criticism

The case against church schools within the state-maintained system has been argued increasingly in recent decades on secular, political, educational and multi-cultural grounds. Voices within the churches, too, have shared in this criticism.

The British Humanist Association's pamphlet, *Religion in Schools*, published in 1967, argued strongly on secular grounds that the dual system had become an anachronism, and accused the churches of abusing their privileged position by indoctrination.[24] The report argues that the State should not be involved in financing and recognizing the religious teaching of individual churches or religious bodies.

The Socialist Education Association's discussion document, *The Dual System of Voluntary and County Schools*, published in 1981, argued strongly on political grounds that 'the continuing existence of the segregated voluntary sector will frustrate the achievement of the truly comprehensive system'.[25] The discussion document makes the secondary case that, if certain churches are permitted to operate voluntary schools, every sect and faith should be allowed the same privilege. The document envisages that this would lead to 'divisive sectarianism and some of the difficulties already evident in places like Northern Ireland'.

In a paper entitled 'Education, Catechesis and the Church School', published in 1981, Professor Paul Hirst argued strongly on educational grounds that education and catechesis are two very difficult activities which obey different rules and are logically incompatible.[26] He maintained that a school undertaking both activities would find itself at one and the same time committed to trying to develop commitment to reason and commitment to a particular faith, 'leading to confusion for both pupils and teachers'. The logical conclusion of this argument is that 'church school', like 'Christian education', is necessarily a contradiction in terms.[27]

In the Swann Report, *Education for All*, the committee of inquiry into the education of children from ethnic minority groups gave particularly close scrutiny to the church school question.[28] After reviewing the arguments for and against voluntary schools for other ethnic and religious groups, the majority voice of the committee stresses 'misgivings about the implications and consequences of "separate" provision of any kind'. Having come to this view, the majority voice of the committee faces the consequence that 'our conclusions about the desirability of denominational voluntary aided schools for Muslims or other groups, by extension seriously call into question the long established dual system of educational provision in this country and particularly the role of the churches in the provision of education'.

This debate concerning the role of denominational schools within a multi-cultural society has also been pursued within the churches by Catholic[29] and Anglican[30] reports.

A Research Agenda

The very existence of church schools within the state-maintained sector of education poses a number of empirical questions of interest and relevance to educational policy, practical theology and the sociology of religion. The importance of these questions is heightened by political debate regarding the role of voluntary initiative within state-maintained schools,[31] by theological debate regarding the churches' responsibility towards the young,[32] and by political and sociological debate regarding the contemporary relationship between Church and State.[33] The key questions can be grouped into two main categories, concerned with the distinctiveness and with the effectiveness of church schools. The first group of questions compares the situation in church schools with that in non-denominational state-maintained schools and examines the relationship between these findings and church policy statements. The second group of questions explores the impact of church schools on the pupils who attend them.

The present author's research agenda over the past two decades has consistently addressed these two groups of questions. The following discussion describes the studies stimulated by this agenda and attempts to integrate their findings.

Primary Pupils in East Anglia

The first study was set up in a sample of East Anglian primary schools in 1974 with the express intention of assessing the influence of church schools on aspects of pupil religious development.[34] Thirty comparable primary schools participated in the study, including fifteen county, ten Church of England aided and five Catholic aided schools. The number of schools from each sector reflected that sector's relative contribution to the state-maintained system.

The definition and assessment of religious development is itself a complex problem within the psychology of religion.[35] This study opted for a psychometric solution to the problem and proposed a measure of attitude towards Christianity as the primary index of pupil religiosity. The instrument employed was the twenty-four-item Likert scale[36] developed by Francis in an earlier study[37] and subsequently employed widely in a range of studies.[38] The scale is known to function reliably and validly among eight- to sixteen-year-olds.[39] It contains items concerned with the child's attitude towards God, Jesus, the Bible, prayer, the Church and religion in school. Each item is assessed on a five-point scale, ranging from 'agree strongly', through 'not certain' to 'disagree strongly'.

While the simple comparison of the overall mean attitude scores recorded in the three types of school would adequately reflect any significant difference in the overall religious climate among the pupils, such analysis would not permit the cause of any detected difference to be attributed to school influence. It was known from earlier research, for example, that factors like sex and age,[40] intelligence,[41] religious behaviour,[42] parental religious behaviour[43] and socio-economic background[44] may also influence pupil attitudes towards religion.

The survey questionnaire, therefore, took these other factors into account as well. Socio-economic background was assessed in terms of the scale proposed by the Office of Population, Censuses and Surveys[45] used in association with information about parental employment. Intelligence was assessed in terms of IQ ratings made available from school records and collapsed into a scale of five categories.

The questionnaire was administered to all third- and fourth-year junior pupils within the participating schools by the class teachers. This method has been shown to produce minimal response falsification.[46] Completed responses were received from 2,272 pupils.

The data were analysed by means of linear multiple regression and path analysis,[47] using the SPSS package,[48] in order to control for the influence of age, sex, social class, parental church attendance, IQ and religious behaviour, before testing for the influence of church schools on pupil attitudes. Two key conclusions emerged from this path model: Catholic schools appear to be exerting a positive influence on the development of pupil attitudes, while some Church of England schools appear to be exerting a negative influence.

In view of the potentially controversial nature of these findings, the Social Science Research Council sponsored a replication of the study four years later in 1978.[49] The replication involved going to the next generation of pupils occupying the same school places. Contrary to the author's hopes, path analysis confirmed the earlier findings.

A further replication was funded in 1982,[50] after another period of four years, returning to the third generation of pupils occupying the same school desks. For the third time path analysis identified the positive influence of Catholic schools and the negative influence of Anglican schools on pupil attitudes towards Christianity. Unfortunately it proved impossible to raise sponsorship for a further replication in 1986.

In the paper which reported the simultaneous analysis of the data from the 1974, 1988 and 1982 surveys, I formulated the following tentative conclusion.

> Since the stated aims of the Church of England's continued involvement in education do not necessarily concentrate on emphasizing the religious distinctiveness of church schools, these findings are not necessarily a criticism of the success of Church of England voluntary aided schools. However, irrespective of the educational philosophy underlying the Church of England's involvement in church schools, I suspect that these findings might leave a theological problem for the Church of England to account for operating schools which actually lead to *less* favourable pupil attitudes towards Christianity than county schools.

Primary Pupils in Gloucestershire

Although the East Anglian study[51] had been conducted among three generations of pupils, the generalizability of the findings remained limited in three serious ways. All the participating schools were located within the same part of England, each sector was represented by a small number of individual schools and these particular schools may not necessarily have been representative of East Anglian schools in general.

The next study, therefore, was established to make an in-depth study of the situation throughout one entire local education authority, namely Gloucestershire.[52] The study, initiated with the support of the county, Anglican and Catholic education authorities, approached every primary and junior school within the county, inviting each school to administer the attitude survey to all fourth-year junior pupils. This included 111 county schools, forty-one Church of England aided, seventy-three Church of England controlled and eight Catholic schools. Co-operation was given by 87 per cent of county schools, 83 per cent of Church of England aided, 78 per cent of Church of England controlled and 63 per cent of Catholic schools. All told, 4,948 pupils completed questionnaires.

Once again path analysis was employed to control for sex, mother's social class, father's social class, mother's church attendance, father's church attendance, the pupil's personal church attendance, and differences between rural, urban and suburban environments, before testing for the influence of church schools on pupil attitudes. These data reaffirm the positive influence of Catholic aided schools on pupil attitudes, even after controlling for the effects of home and Church. The Gloucestershire data, however, do not confirm the view that Church of England aided schools exert a negative influence on pupil attitudes. In Gloucestershire attendance at a Church of England aided school makes no difference in one direction or the other to pupil attitude towards Christianity. Unlike the East Anglian study, however, the Gloucestershire study also included Church of England controlled schools in the sample. This time path analysis demonstrates that Church of England controlled schools exert a small but significant negative influence on pupil attitudes towards Christianity.

The generalizability of findings from the Gloucestershire study is still limited by three factors. Only one local education authority was involved in the survey. Only one outcome measure of pupil religiosity was employed. In the case of Church of England aided schools some conflict has clearly emerged between the East Anglian and the Gloucestershire findings. Further research, therefore, is now needed to clarity these issues.

Teacher Attitudes in Suffolk
Both the East Anglian and the Gloucestershire study raise, in a slightly different way, a question regarding why it is that Church of England schools may exert a negative rather than a positive attitude on pupil attitudes. The next study, therefore, turns attention away from the pupils to the teachers who work in church schools, in order to assess their understanding of, commitment to and attitude towards the church school system.[53]

This project was sponsored by the Saint Edmundsbury and Ipswich Diocesan Education Committee and managed by a committee involving teachers from church schools in the diocese.

It was decided to invite every teacher working in the twenty aided and ninety-one controlled church schools in the diocese to complete a questionnaire, a total of 519 full-time teachers. The questionnaires were distributed personally by the diocesan religious education adviser or by another member of the working party. Replies were returned anonymously by post by 76 per cent of the teachers in aided schools and 60 per cent of the teachers in controlled schools.

The questionnaire considered four main sections. Part one concentrated on the personal background of the teachers, including their religious involvement. Part two contained a Likert scale assessing their overall attitude towards the church school system. Part three examined their understanding of the characteristics of a church school. Part four explored their views on the distinctiveness of church schools.

A major finding from this survey indicated that only a small proportion of those who teach in church schools specifically chose to be working in the church school system, just 10 per cent of the teachers in controlled schools and 37 per cent of teachers in aided schools. More than half of the teachers working in the church school sector expressed no particular preference for that sector and a further one in eight would actually prefer not to be working in a church school.

While many teachers who did not specifically opt to work in the church school system still show considerable good-will towards that system, path analysis demonstrated that this good-will is clearly associated with good-will towards the church in general and with age.

The statistical model concerned with exploring over-all attitude towards church schools suggested that the younger teachers are less likely to be church-goers and that the teachers who are not church-goers are less likely to be favourably disposed towards the church school system. This model suggests that the next generation of teachers in church schools is likely to be less favourably disposed towards the church school system than the present generation. The puzzle with which the Churches will be left is making sense of retaining an investment in school sites after the commitment of the teaching staff to the Church's involvement in education has worn thin.

The second statistical model, concerned with exploring individual differences in teachers' attitudes towards the distinctiveness of church schools, shows an even stronger relationship with age. This model suggests that the belief that church schools should be different is likely to disappear more rapidly, as the next generation of teachers emerges, than their general good-will towards the Churches' continued involvement in education. The puzzle with which the Churches will be left is making sense of operating schools which are indistinguishable from comparable neighbourhood county schools.

The data suggest that the Churches will have to face this problem soonest in the controlled sector.

School Ethos in Gloucestershire
The study conducted in Suffolk suffers from two main limitations. By concentrating entirely on church schools, the findings do not permit comparability with the situation in county schools. By concentrating entirely on teacher attitudes, the findings do not permit firm inferences to be made regarding actual practice. The next study, therefore, addresses these issues by turning attention to curriculum provision and school ethos throughout the state-maintained primary sector in Gloucestershire.[54]

Alongside the study of pupil attitudes described above, the head teachers of the 111 county schools, forty-one Church of England aided, seventy-three Church of England controlled and eight Catholic schools were invited to complete a detailed questionnaire. Replies were received from all the Catholic and Church of England aided schools, 96 per cent of the county schools and 93 per cent of the Church of England controlled schools.

The questionnaire was designed to discover what was currently happening in the religious life and curriculum of primary schools and to enable comparison to be made between different types of school. Seven main areas were surveyed, namely religious education, assemblies, worship, church contact, resources, staff qualifications and the head teachers' personal religious commitment.

Initial analyses of the data made it clear that considerable variation exists both among county schools and among church schools. Some schools within both sectors consider it appropriate for state-maintained schools to function as an extension of the Christian Churches, while some schools within both sectors consider it inappropriate to act in this way. In order to explore these differences further, factor analyses and other exploratory correlational techniques were applied to identify the key pieces of information which most clearly differentiate between schools which adopt a church-related approach and those which do not. Twenty-two pieces of information cohered to produce a cumulative scale of church-related education.

According to this scale, the most church-related schools receive regular visits from clergy who contribute to assemblies and religious education. They arrange for pupils to visit and study the local church. They hold a school service in church from time to time, display pupil work in the church building and prepare drama, music or dance to contribute to the service. Assemblies set out to be explicitly Christian acts of worship and reflect closely the shape of the Church's year. They regularly make use of readings from the Bible and stories from a Christian background. The pupils regularly recite the Lord's Prayer and sing hymns used in local churches. Religious education makes regular use of the Bible and studies church-related topics.

Path analysis demonstrated that the personal religious beliefs of the head teachers are crucial in determining the church-related character of primary schools. In some cases a church-going head teacher of a county school may exert more Christian influence in his or her school than a non-church-going head teacher of a church school. At the same time path analysis demonstrated that the school's foundation exerts two forms of influence on the church-related character of the school. First, there is an indirect influence through the Church's role in the appointment of head teachers. Thus 42 per cent of heads of county schools are regular church-goers, compared with 51 per cent in Church of England controlled, 71 per cent in Church of England aided and 100 per cent in Catholic schools in the sample. Second, there is a direct influence according to which controlled schools are more church-related than county schools and aided schools are more church-related than controlled schools, even after controlling for differences in the head teachers' religiosity.

These data clearly confirm the distinctiveness of church schools within the primary sector and illustrate the considerable influence of the Church over the religious character of local neighbourhood schools. This influence is exercised both directly through the ownership of schools and indirectly through the Christian commitment of head teachers. Christian people may rejoice that the Church's influence can still be so strong in a secular educational system. Secular educationalists may be suspicious of such pervasive religious influence.

At the same time, path analysis demonstrates that the church-related character of both county and church schools is closely related to the head teachers' ages. Young head teachers are less likely to be regular church-goers and less likely to promote church-related education in their schools. If this trend between head teachers' age and church-related character of schools persists, it is likely that the Christian character of schools will decrease as the older head teachers are replaced by a younger, more secular generation of head teachers.

Local Church Life
Another group of studies has attempted to evaluate the impact of Church of England primary schools on local church life. The first of these studies[55] was based on a detailed survey of church attendance and activities throughout one anonymous Anglican diocese.[56] The data were furnished by a 92 per cent response rate among the 185 clergy in the diocese.

Path analysis was employed to assess whether the presence of a church school in a benefice increased the number of six- to nine-year-olds who come into contact with the local church during the course of a week. The results of this analysis indicated that, while the presence of a church school makes no difference to the number of six- to nine-year-olds who attend church services or children's groups on Sunday, it does increase the likelihood of the local clergy having contact with this age group during the course of the week, usually by visiting the school.

Although this study provides an interesting example of data analysis, there are five significant limitations to it. The survey was based on data from just one diocese. The path analysis was conducted on benefice units, rather than individual parishes. Although the response rate was high, the number of benefices involved is comparatively small. The data include both rural and town situations and church schools often function differently in these two environments. The outcome variables included in the study are limited simply to Sunday and weekday contact with six- to nine-year-olds.

In order to address these limitations, Francis and Lankshear undertook two further re-analyses of the detailed data collected on 7,129 Anglican churches to inform the study *Children in the Way*.[57]

This represents a 72 per cent response from the churches throughout twenty-four dioceses and one additional archdeaconry.

In their first study, Francis and Lankshear[58] examined the impact of church schools on a number of indices of village church life in a sample of 1,637 communities, ranging in size from 250 to 1,250 inhabitants. After controlling for the influence of population, electoral roll, the amalgamation of churches within multi-parish benefices, the age of the clergyman and whether or not there is an occupied parsonage within the area served by the church, the presence of a church school is shown to augment slightly the village church's usual Sunday contact with six- to nine-year-olds and with adults. The presence of a church school is also shown to have a small positive influence on the number of infant baptisms, the number of six- to thirteen-year-olds in the village church choir and the number of young confirmands under the age of fourteen years.

In their second study, Francis and Lankshear[59] examined the same questions among a sample of 1,316 urban parishes. After controlling for the same variables as the previous study, the presence of a church school was shown to augment slightly the urban church's contact with under-fourteen-year-olds through membership of the choir and team of servers. The presence of a church school also increased slightly the number of young confirmands under the age of fourteen and the number of fourteen- to seventeen-year-olds contacted through church youth groups. There is also a higher number of infant baptisms in urban parishes which contain a church school.

Both of these studies, therefore, demonstrate the beneficial nature of the impact of Church of England voluntary secondary schools on local church life.

Anglican Secondary Schools
Considerably less is known about the impact of Anglican secondary schools on pupil religious development than is known about the impact of Anglican primary schools. Three comparatively small studies have explored aspects of this question.

The first study, by Francis and Carter,[60] administered the Francis scale of attitude towards Christianity[61] to a sample of 802 fifth-year secondary pupils within twenty-one Church of England, Catholic and county schools. Path analysis indicated that Church of England secondary schools exerted neither a positive nor a negative influence on their pupils' attitudes towards Christianity.

The second study, by Francis and Brown,[62] employed path analysis to model the influence of home, church and school on an attitudinal predisposition to pray and the practice of prayer among 711 sixteen-year-old adolescents attending Catholic, Church of England and county schools. In comparison with Francis and Brown's earlier findings among eleven-year-olds,[63] the influence of church is stronger and the influence of parents is weaker among sixteen-year-olds than among the younger age group. After controlling for the influence of home and church, Church of England secondary schools were shown to exert a small but significant negative influence on attitude towards prayer.

The third study, by Francis and Jewell,[64] examined the religious beliefs, practices and attitudes of 546 fourth-year pupils attending the four county and one Church of England voluntary school within the same town. The data demonstrated that the Church of England school recruited a higher proportion of pupils from church-going homes and that church-going homes tend to represent the higher social classes. After taking into account the influence of sex, social class and parental religiosity, path analysis indicated that the Church of England school exerted neither a positive nor a negative influence on its pupils' religious practice, belief or attitude.

The findings from these small-scale studies clearly indicate the considerable need for more sustained research into the distinctiveness and effectiveness of Anglican secondary schools.

Catholic Secondary Schools
During the past decade a series of interrelated studies has explored different aspects of the relationship between Catholic secondary schools and pupil attitudes.

To begin with, surveys in England,[65] Scotland[66] and Northern Ireland[67] have employed the Francis scale of attitude towards Christianity to profile the attitudes of pupils in Catholic schools and to compare these profiles with comparable data collected in county schools in England,[68] non-denominational schools in Scotland[69] and Protestant schools in Northern Ireland.[70] Data from all three cultures confirm that there is a more positive pupil attitude towards Christianity among pupils in Catholic schools.

In Scotland the Catholic Church both provides separate schools within the state-maintained system and offers separate religious education courses within some non-denominational schools. Rhymer employed the Francis scale of attitude towards Christianity to compare the attitudes of 1,113 Catholic pupils attending three different types of school: 882 pupils were drawn from Catholic schools, 121 from non-denominational schools receiving Catholic religious education and 110 from non-denominational schools not receiving Catholic religious education.[71] Rhymer describes this as a stratified sample representing the distribution of Scottish Catholic pupils between Catholic and non-denominational secondary schools, and drawn from areas of Strathclyde region typical of geographical and economic conditions in Scotland as a whole. In the re-analysis of these data, the path model demonstrated that both the separate school system and the provision of Catholic religious education in non-denominational schools contributes to the development of positive pupil attitudes.[72]

In parts of England the development of middle schools involved the Catholic Church in restructuring its educational system.[73] Boyle employed the Francis scale of attitude towards Christianity to assess the implications of such restructuring for pupil religiosity.[74] He administered the scale to 1,205 twelve- and thirteen-year-old pupils drawn from six Catholic schools within two northern metropolitan districts, one of which had developed a three-tier system of schools and the other had not. In the re-analysis of these data the path model demonstrated that there was no difference in attitude scores between comparable pupils attending middle and secondary schools.[75]

Demographic shifts in the Catholic population in England led during the 1980s to a growing proportion of non-Catholic pupils being admitted to Catholic schools, generally recruited from other denominational church-going backgrounds. The Francis scale of attitude towards Christianity was employed in a study designed to examine the implications of this change in pupil recruitment both for the non-Catholic pupils admitted and for the general religious ethos of the Catholic school.[76] All the pupils from the first through to the fifth years in five Catholic comprehensive schools in two Midland conurbations were invited to take part in the survey in 1981. Completed questionnaires were received from 2,895 pupils, representing 88.9 per cent of the total school population. The data indicated a significant increase in the proportion of non-Catholic pupils admitted in the first year, 17 per cent compared with 7 per cent in the fifth year. The path model indicated that non-Catholic pupils, even from church-going backgrounds, in Catholic schools show a less positive attitude towards Christianity than Catholic pupils. On the basis of these findings the recommendation is made that, if Catholic schools recruit a higher proportion of non-Catholic pupils, the doctrinal, liturgical and catechetical assumptions of the school need to be modified in order to preserve the good-will and enhance the religious development of the pupils from other denominational backgrounds.

These findings open to scrutiny the whole assumption that Catholic schools function as an extension of the faith community. This assumption was tested by Egan in a large-scale study of the fifth-year pupils attending fifteen of the sixteen Catholic state-maintained secondary schools in Wales during the academic year 1983–4.[77] Completed questionnaires were returned by 1,638 pupils. In the re-analysis of these data, the path model identified three clear groups of pupils: practising Catholics, non-practising Catholics and non-Catholics.[78] By looking in closer detail at possible aspects of pupil disaffection from the Catholic school, this study suggested that the real problem lies not only through the recruitment of non-Catholic pupils, but also through the recruitment of Catholic pupils from non-Catholic backgrounds. This is a much larger problem for the Catholic Church in Wales. While less than 9 per cent of Egan's sample of pupils claimed themselves to be non-Catholics, less than half of the girls and only slightly more than two-fifths of the boys were weekly mass attenders themselves, while about two-fifths of both sexes were supported by weekly mass-attending mothers and only one-quarter by weekly mass-attending fathers.

Given the significance of these findings for the underlying philosophy regarding Catholic schools as an extension of the faith community, Egan replicated the Welsh study in both the USA[79] and Australia.[80] In both cases the basic conclusions of the Welsh study were reinforced.

On the basis of the findings from England, Wales, the USA and Australia, Francis and Egan formulate the following conclusion.

> This incompatibility between the theory and practice of Catholic schools can be resolved in two different ways. On the one hand, Catholic schools could attempt to re-define enrolment policies to ensure that they more truly represent the kind of faith community which would fully satisfy the assumptions underlying the socialization or inculturation model. This would involve radically reducing the number of places in Catholic schools and denying the opportunity of a Catholic education to a number of people who could in many ways benefit from such provision. On the other hand, the theory underpinning the Catholic school system could take into account the presence of non-Catholic pupils from non-practising Catholic backgrounds and non-practising pupils. This would involve recognizing the needs of these non-practising Catholic pupils when structuring the doctrinal, catechetical, liturgical and educational goals of the school. Far from weakening the distinctiveness of Catholic schools, such a strategy could help to secure a significant and appropriate Catholic presence in education in a fast changing secular world.[81]

Postscript

This chapter began by charting the historical development of the church school system in England and Wales, by summarizing the contemporary debate regarding the character and future of church schools, and by arguing that this debate focuses issues which are properly a matter for empirical inquiry. A series of empirical studies designed to address some of these issues over the past two decades were then reviewed. Other similar studies are still in process in order to add further pieces to the complex jigsaw puzzle, as each completed project raises fresh perspectives and poses fresh questions. The empirical picture inevitably remains imperfect and incomplete. Nevertheless, it might be unwise for future educational and theological debate to ignore entirely the reality described by empirical research into the distinctiveness and effectiveness of church schools. In particular, the theology of education, like other branches of applied theology, has a responsibility to be fully open to empirical data.[82]

Chapter 6

Roman Catholicism: Function versus Performance, Universalism versus Particularism[1]

Karel Dobbelaere

The Impact of Contextual Factors on 'Performance' and 'Function'

A reader of the recent book, *World Catholicism in Transition*,[2] is likely to be struck by the way in which contextual factors define both the position of the Catholic Church within nation states, and also its relationship to sub-systems of society. Two major problems confront the Church: secularization and acculturation. The process of secularization which is pre-eminent in western Europe and America is a consequence of functional or structural differentiation and of the process of societalization following from it. Religion is becoming more and more a sub-system among other social systems (education, policy, economy) and its over-arching claims are denied as useless, irrelevant and even dysfunctional by those people involved in other sub-systems. Communal relations persist only in the private sphere – in the family, some neighbourhoods and in social networks. Even here, however, changes are paramount: in the past the community was given – the extended family, the local neighbourhood and the village – now we talk of private networks, niches, which are built up, achieved, and discontinued as people come and go, geographically and socially.

Religion, being socially less and less important, has also lost its impact on the people. Except for rites of passage, most western Europeans no longer find their way to the Church. I have tried to explain the effect on the personal level of what is happening at the societal level, by referring to the decline of the belief in God, more specifically in a 'personal' God.[3] What do people do with a notion of God when they increasingly think themselves capable of controlling the physical, psychological and social environment, and when they or the experts whom they trust, in effect, altered a traditional gospel song to read '*we* have the whole world in *our* hands'? And if the notion of God lingers on, it is none the less difficult to conceive of him as a personal God since societal relations have become so impersonal, administrative and role-related. Indeed as Durkheim,

Swanson and other sociologists and anthropologists have convincingly demonstrated, people's conception of their God(s) depends to a large extent on the structure of their society. Consequently, the Church's impact is largely reduced to its primary 'function': expressing the tension between immanence and transcendence, and ritualizing it, and even in this, the Church seems no longer to be heard, or only on special occasions.

Has the Church then lost all impact on the other sub-systems of society? Performances[4] are still possible if the Church can motivate its members: remedial teaching (USA), Third and Fourth World programmes, are examples. A typical structure which emerged at the end of the last century and early in this century, was the Catholic pillar, as found in Austria, Belgium, Italy, the Netherlands and Switzerland, constituting an integrated Catholic network of ancillary organizations. Today, however, these pillars are collapsing or, under the pressure of functional differentiation and secularization, are changing drastically from being specifically Catholic organizations into more general Christian organizations, shedding their typical Catholic collective consciousness and re-formulating it in a more general and universal language anchored in the Gospels.[5] These are all indicators of how contextual factors have changed the functions and performances of the Church in western Europe. The fact that church practice remains higher in the USA than in Europe depends, to a large extent, on historical and contextual factors. The pillars offer substitutes for communal life in Europe: in the USA, on the other hand, it is rather the parishes that perform this function.

Another example of what Luhmann calls 'performances' was to be found in eastern Europe. It was the Christian churches that offered an open area to the opposition in which they could express criticism of the communist regimes. On the ninetieth *Katholikentag* in Berlin, E. Epler, President of the Protestant *Kirchentag*, stated that: 'The peaceful revolution in Eastern Germany was the result of the Christian peace movement: the communist regime could not withstand its weekly candlelight procession.'[6] In Poland, as Barbara Strassberg points out, the Catholic Church was involved

> in the postwar struggle for freedom and social justice . . . On the political level, the church functions as a surrogate for the state; on the social level, the ethics of solidarity developed by church intellectuals supports current social programs and activities, and religious myths remain an integral part of Poland's national myths. Moreover, religion and the church act strongly on behalf of the oppressed.[7]

In Latin America, 'performance' was also high on the Church's agenda. As in Europe, the Church built a complex of services, associations and organizations – not only to help people, but also to protect the faithful from the secularizing tendencies that were evident in the wake of industrialization and urbanization. The object was to restore the influence of the Church over the masses.[8] However, the local Latin American churches were not then, and are not now, united in their approach to the social, economic and political problems. The Church did not speak with one voice: there were divisions between and within the hierarchy, the laity and the clergy. In the second half of the 1960s and the 1970s, after Vatican II, internal conflicts were aggravated, and the Latin American Bishops' conference in Medellín (1968) offered religious legitimation to those engaged in the struggle for socio-economic justice, human rights and peace, by identifying the Church increasingly with these causes. The extension of basic ecclesiastical communities – which pre-date the Medellín conference[9] – as a means of both evangelization and social action was encouraged, and a typical Latin American theology, liberation theology, emerged.[10] These are further examples of how pastoral responses and theological thinking have been influenced by the societal context and how some within the Church promote social action or 'performance' rather than evangelization or 'function', the latter being the primary concern of the bishops. The last example also shows that not only 'performance' but also 'function' (e.g. liberation theology) adjusts to the particular societal context in which the local church is situated.

This effort of adaptation or acculturation is not new, nor is Rome's reaction to it, as evidence of which we need only to recall the problems which Rome experienced with 'Gallicanism', or the problems which Father Lebbe had with Rome when he wanted to acculturate Catholicism into Chinese culture. However, more recently, Rome has seemed to take more account of the local situation. Did Pope Paul VI not say in his papal visit to Africa in 1969: 'You may, and you must have an African Christianity.' Acculturation, then, is the second problem that the Church is facing. The two problems are, however, related: acculturation to the new structure of society appears to be a much-needed church approach to secularization,[11] and, consequently, it is not limited to the so-called Third World. But let us examine the problems of acculturation which the Church faces in Africa.

Under the influence of Vatican II, an openness towards the world developed that was embodied 'in the key conciliar decrees on religious liberty, the church in the modern world, and dialogue with other Christian churches and with non-Christian religions'.[12] The development of an African Christianity was also demanded by the new situation created in Africa in the 1960s: the political revolution or the de-colonization of Africa, and the cultural revolution: the re-writing by Africans of their own history; African novels and plays were published; and African philosophies of society were produced.[13] Adrian Hastings pointed out: 'The mood of the council, its optimistic image of *aggiornamento* and the opening of windows, fitted extraordinarily well with the wider mood of Africa.'[14]

Hastings and Heba describe many forms of acculturation that occurred in Africa, albeit in different degrees in different regions.[15] Thus there were liturgical changes; a massive rediscovery of the catechist and a series of studies on the practice, and even a theology, of this form of ministry; the creation of new regional pastoral institutes in which every aspect of a new pastoral policy was worked on; Bible Societies arose in which Catholics joined Protestants to translate the Bible; and ecumenism. Not only was religious 'function' changed, but so also were aspects of religious 'performance', such as development work. Nevertheless, aspects of the African family structure such as polygamy appeared to be a major obstacle for acculturation.[16] The Church also obliged people to contract marriage three times: a ritual ceremony before a priest after the customary marriage in front of the two families (a procedure that can take years), and a matrimonial contract before a government official.[17]

By the mid-1970s, the logic of reform had given way to the logic of conservation which was imposed by Rome's selection for the African Church of leaders who were African bishops trained in Rome, and who identified almost entirely with the Roman view of things. Papal nuncios ensured that bishops should conform to policies preferred by Rome. Independently-minded African bishops were obliged to resign. Rome imposed Thomism in the major seminaries to the exclusion of any contemporary approaches: 'The seminary directors [of Cameroon] were called to Rome to be told again that Thomism was exclusively to be taught; if this was not done, all financial subsidy would be withdrawn from their schools.'[18] All this occurred in a period of political turmoil and economic crisis, which restricted the organization of conferences, the buying of books and journals, the development of regional pastoral institutes, and international exchanges. Local isolation again set in, bringing the African Church back to the pre-Vatican II conditions. In this situation, the bishops needed the moral and financial support of Rome. They were cautiously anxious lest they displease either the Roman curia or local politicians.[19] Consequently, the Africanization of the Church, its acculturation, was blocked by internal church policies supported by contextual factors. Hastings suggests that, 'In comparison with the African church of the 1960s, that of the late 1970s and 1980s has become a Church of Silence.'[20] Indeed, Roman officials did silence the African churches and did not allow them to organize a regional pastoral council, since they considered them to be 'immature churches'.[21]

The foregoing discussion illustrates the limitations on pluralism in 'performance' and 'function'. On the level of *'performance'*, Rome appeared to accept particularism, i.e. a religious policy adapted to contextual factors. However, there were restrictions. In politics, the Church sought a secure place that allowed it to operate without constraint. To this effect, it has sometimes promoted the founding of Christian parties, as in Chile.[22] This also explains its compromises with conservative governments as in Latin America,[23] while it has generally perceived Marxist governments as a threat to its existence. However, if the political situation demanded it, the Church might be forced to a kind of rapprochement with such governments (as in eastern Europe and Cuba). This conclusion extends Margaret E. Crahan's suggestion 'while the initial reaction of the Catholic church to revolution may be determined largely by general institutional characteristics, external reality will eventually determine its specific stance'.[24]

In the field of education, the missionary church has built schools to evangelize the population as in India.[25] Consequently, it had to 'defend' pluralism. In formerly traditional Catholic regions, the Church has fought and continues to fight secular education as in Belgium and France,[26] and it has especially opposed Marxist indoctrination, as in Nicaragua.[27] The Church, then, has affirmed the 'absolute right for parents to choose the type of education they desire for their children and for confessional schools and teachers to freely discharge their responsibilities'.[28] To guarantee this, the Church has defended its right to build and extend its own Catholic school system and reluctantly has 'accepted' pluralism for others.[29]

Thus, if need be, in these areas the Church has accepted and has even defended pluralism. This is, however, not the case in respect of the family, as was pointed out in regard to the African Church. On the level of 'performance', the relationship of the Church to the family has not been open to pluralism. How is this to be explained? In a recent allocution, Joseph Cardinal Ratzinger, addressing the presidents of the Commissions for the Doctrine of the Faith of the different European Bishops' Conferences, linked the opposition of modern people to the Church's sexual morality and the quest for a revision of the unequal treatment of women and men in the Church to a vision of faith.[30] As in the case of acculturation in Africa, the Holy See does not accept pluralism in matters of faith or in the philosophical grounding of the faith. However, the majority of Catholics have separated their faith from their attitudes towards contraception, pre-marital sex, divorce, etc. In a period of increasing secularization, the Magisterium has lagged behind both its constituency and those progressive Catholic theologians who have been trying to re-formulate the relationship between ethics and faith and the basic tenets of the faith (men such as Hans Küng and Edward Schillebeeckx).

On the level of *'function'*, the Church seemed at first to allow for some pluralism in Africa, but this did not last long, and contextual factors helped Rome to regain its power. As far as secularization is concerned, the answer of Rome to the European situation seems to be clear: to confirm the tradition and fight back through evangelization,[31] consequently, it takes Berger's 'deductive response'.[32]

The situation in the Catholic Church seems to express the following oppositions between centre and periphery: uniformity versus pluriformity, universalism versus particularism, centripetal versus centrifugal forces, centralization versus decentralization, institutional versus individual authority.

The Vatican: Centralization, Uniformity and Universalism

Analysing the Roman strategies in times of crisis, Leo Laeyendecker suggests that the following have been used: centralization; regimentation of ministerial conduct; the politics of piety combined with the politics of heresy; the creation of a distinct Catholic ghetto (pillarization); and the accentuation of the special position of the Pope.[33] I take up three of these items: centralization and the accentuation of the special position of priests and the Pope.[34]

Centralization
The centralizing forces in the Catholic Church have always been strong, especially in times of crisis as defined by Rome. The nomination of the local bishops by the Pope – selected on criteria of obedience, conformity and preferably Roman training – is an element in this policy. The African, Dutch and other churches testify to this: the 'Cologne Declaration', in which a number of European theologians manifested their concern about Roman centralism, is further evidence. However, this is manifested not only in the appointment or dismissal of bishops, but also of professors of theology and editors of periodicals, and in the authoritarian imposition of responses on matters of faith and morals. Let it suffice here to refer to the *Catechism for the Universal Church* that is in the making.[35] Other centralizing policy elements are the nuntii and the financial dependency of poor dioceses on Rome. Modern means of communication promote greater visibility and allow for better control. As Franz-Xaver Kaufmann affirms:

> Centralizing claims remain rather harmless as long as the means of real hierarchical control remain quite limited. The expansion of the means of control was the historical reason why it was just and necessary to formulate the principle of subsidiarity with regard to the state. The church has to keep in mind that the very secular means of control today are growing so fast that it cannot consider them indifferent to its spiritual and social task.[36]

Vatican II had, of course, encouraged the development of Episcopal Conferences, which is a factor of decentralization. However, as
Liliane Voyé states, these conferences

> today engender the distrust of Rome, and, in particular, of Cardinal Ratz-
> inger. In his *Entretien sur la foi*, he has more or less explicitly expressed
> his misgivings about them: the national level should not be an ecclesial
> dimension; they blur positions and give power to enterprising minorities;
> they undermine the personal responsibility of each bishop and the direct
> link of the bishop with the Pope. This mistrust is also expressed just as
> clearly in the Code of Canon Law of 1983, which situates the attributions
> of the Episcopal Conferences short of that which the Council allowed one
> to expect.[37]

It is clear that the Roman Curia found power-sharing with regional
(local) churches frightening and fought back. By stressing the personal responsibility of each bishop the Vatican ensured subservi-
ence. To guarantee the power of the centre it also combated the idea
of collegiality advanced by Vatican II.

A Charismatic Pope
The centralization of the Church also implies the accentuation of the
special position of the Pope. He is presented to Church members
and the world as a leader of extraordinary capacities, charismatic in
the Weberian sense.[38] However, facts indicate that the conduct of
the enthusiastic crowds is in flagrant contradiction of the precepts
he voices. This shocks the hierarchy of the Church and a minority
of the faithful. To explain this contradiction, Voyé suggests that the
legitimacy that is socially granted to the Pope does not derive from
the functionality of the discourse, its usefulness for daily life, but
from the symbolic register, that is, its imaginary dimension.[39] His
discourse offers a frame of principles, ideals, that people hear and
read in the enunciation of his precepts, such as sanctity of life,
sacredness of marriage bonds, love of one's neighbours, respect for
nature, esteem for labour, the need for justice, etc. However, these
principles are accorded different substance by those same people
when confronted with the contradictory demands of everyday life.

> Implicitly for the crowd, to applaud the Pope is to recognize him as the
> bearer of a rationality other than that which controls the functional in
> everyday reality. It is a rationality that liberates the crowd from the contra-
> dictions of everyday reality. The crowd adopts the Pope as the enunciator
> of the principles of reference in relation to which the contradictions take
> meaning.[40]

The Segregation of Priests and Laity
Finally, the organization is also staffed with consecrated celibate
men, whose life-style is controlled by the bishops to ensure that they
have a well-disciplined and loyal 'army'.[41] The declining number of

vocations and a high number of departures has caused a greying of the clergy, especially in western countries.[42] In Africa too, the need became apparent for a more diversified ministry including the ordination of married men.[43] During the Synod of the Laity (1987), however, Rome reaffirmed the fundamental difference between priests and lay people, and the supremacy of the former over the latter. Ordination to the priesthood remained open only to unmarried men; married men might have a lesser ordination: become deacons, but they were not allowed to remarry if widowed. Consequently, priests were more and more confined to strictly sacramental tasks; the other traditional priestly tasks, like the teaching of religion and catechesis, were now being done by volunteers, especially women. The 'professional' church is a church of unmarried men, and, in many parts of the world, of older men, that survives thanks to the dedication of many women who do volunteer work for the church, but who are not considered sufficiently worthy for sacerdotal work.

The 'presentation of self' of priests in social life reflects their social status. Some walk with a bowed head, bashfully, and their attire is outmoded in style and shows bad taste in the combination of colours. Indeed, they seem to have lost their pride, their status and their power. This is especially apparent in the decline of private confessions, a decline which has occurred even in the Irish Republic, where traditional Catholicism has remained very much alive.[44] Their power to secure salvation has depreciated: on the one hand, because there has been a decline in belief in the traditional Catholic eschatology[45] – it became rather a vague hope; on the other hand, many Catholics appear not to believe in the need for an intermediary between themselves and God. To use Bryan Wilson's terms, we may say that 'magical intercession is questioned', and the 'magical interpretation of sacraments abrogated'.[46] The eucharist, for example, is seen more as a symbolic commemorative ritual rather than the magical re-enactment of the 'primary' salvation by Christ. Consequently, many Catholics have rejected 'sacerdotalism and the mystical claims that had come to characterize the style and performances of the Roman clergy'. The priesthood and its function have been 'demystified' and put on a par with the Protestant ministry. Consequently, many Catholics have become ready to abolish clerical celibacy and to open the 'priesthood' to women.

Organizational Weaknesses, Marginalization and Tensions

From the outside, the Catholic Church seems to be a strong, hierarchically centralized organization with a 'charismatic' leader that has a universal message and appeal. However, appearances are deceptive: the Church has increasingly encountered organizational problems, disintegration, tensions and exodus.

Organizational Problems
First, there is the problem of recruitment to the priesthood in many parts of the world, and then there are the financial problems which the Vatican is facing. Even if the Church has still been recruiting the same number of priests globally, is a redistribution – as was done in the missionary period – possible? Is it possible to reshuffle an excess of priests, for example in India and Poland, to other parts of the world? The question is not the possible negative reactions of haughty westerners to people from the 'east' or the 'south', or the non-religious cultural differences; the problem is how would people in the West react to conservative priests, trained according to the traditional doctrine of the Church, who were unprepared to face the theological and ethical problems that engage westerners? Of course, in a universalistic mood, convinced that it already possesses all the answers, the Church might decide to redistribute its 'professionals' and that process has indeed already started. In this vein, the Church defines other points of view as 'heretical' or as expressions of nega-tive forms of individualism that reduce 'conscience' to individual self-definition and which no longer equate it with 'co-science', the higher form of knowledge, of which, of course, only the Church is the true interpreter.[47] It is, of course, also possible that the Church might take a 'sectarian' option: the theology of a 'minority church' suggests this alternative. In that case, the Church would be implying that the time of 'Christendom' was over and that the truly Catholic minority might become a better 'beacon of hope' for the world. As a minority, the local church might then demonstrate that religion was not a separate dimension of life (typical of a secularized world) but an 'over-arching canopy' informing all aspects of life.[48] The final option for the Church in this matter will ultimately depend upon its self-understanding. Is the Church to be a professing church or a popular church?[49] A third option, linked to the vision of a 'popular church', would be to broaden the basis of recruitment for the 'priest-hood'. This option appears, for the present, to be the least likely one.

Exodus and Disintegration
The 'universal church' has not only a staffing problem, but the problem of losing many members, especially in the western world, while, simultaneously, the degree of involvement of the members that it has retained has greatly declined. This is the case not only in the western church but in other places as well.[50] This development indicates how remote popular Catholic life has become from the

formally prescribed doctrinal, ritual and ethical prescriptions.[51] This situation is, of course, most apparent in the western world and has been variously described by sociologists as a 'pick and choose' Catholicism, a 'Catholicism *à la carte*', 'diffused religion', and 'selective' Catholicism. It reveals the individualization of religion,[52] which is linked to the individuation of choices (this being a structural characteristic of a functionally differentiated society); the destruction of collective identities and the growth of 'private niches' in postmodernity, and the deconstruction of 'the grand narratives' or '*métarécits*' (J.-F. Lyotard) such as socialism, communism, catholicism and scientism.[53] The process is also promoted by the refusal of the Magisterium to take seriously the ethical and doctrinal problems which engage Catholics. One of these problems is the vision of God: many modern people, according to the data of the European Value Study, find it difficult to conceive of a 'personal' God. Inasmuch as this depiction is expressed in the rituals, doctrine and ethics of the Church, people distance themselves from the Church and its teachings.[54]

Tensions
In reaction to liberal or critical Catholics, there are, of course, groups that express loyalty to papal authority and the Catholic tradition. *Communione e Liberazione*, which is attractive to the more affluent Catholic youth, also supports traditional social policy.[55] *Opus Dei* accepts the modern world 'as the real arena of human beings' sanctification' and has 'a genuine appreciation of the values of professional and ordinary life'. Thousands of executives and professionals joined *Opus Dei* 'linking the traditional religious values of private prayer, religious devotion, spiritual direction, and high moral standards with successful professional dedication'.[56] Some refer to it as the 'Catholic mafia'. The *Cursilo*, another movement, 'departs from anonymous, external, and massive expressions of orthodoxy, stressing instead individual assertiveness, commitment, and the relevance of the faith to everyday life'. It 'embodies a search for the true Christian lifestyle and a reaction against the folksy, gregarious religious experience'.[57] These movements combat secularization and stress the relevance of Catholicism for everyday life, private as well as public.

Another type of attack came from the *Charismatic Movement*, which stresses the joyful personal experience of meeting God in public and private prayer. It reacts against the Church which, after Vatican II, adapting to modernity, insisted on the intellectual dimension of faith, and eliminated some of the festive and magical elements that had existed in its rites and practices. Charismatics stress emotions, gestures, songs and glossolalia, and receptiveness and openness to God's action within oneself. As such, they oppose Catholic Action, which was primarily oriented to social action for others.[58] There are also emotions, feelings, songs and gestures that still draw 'dormant' and 'marginal' Catholics to rites of passage and 'popular' Catholicism (pilgrimages, devotions to the saints, etc.). These Catholics look for concrete reassurance related to changes in their social position and to the tensions, problems and sorrows that crop up in their everyday lives. Certain magical aspects of Catholicism still appeal to some people, especially to a large number of marginal Catholics. This, perhaps, is one of the aspects of Catholicism that enables the Church to retain a large number of nominal members.[59] Apart from large-scale movements, there are also many small-scale movements with low visibility which generally want to remain so. They assemble mostly upper-middle-class people in late middle age. Even when they identify themselves as Catholics they are situated on the fringes of the institutional Church. Indeed, such movements reflect a concern for independence with respect to the enclosure of the sacred in a definition imposed by the Church.[60]

> It expresses a quest for meaning that is emancipated from the universal and more or less mechanical institutional responses proposed by the Church and whose results are not postponed to the beyond. Moreover, some offer the hypothesis, and we agree with them, that the rise of such groups and movements (the charismatics and the small-scale movements) reflects the fulfilment of secularization. Already eliminated economically, politically, and socially by the general process of secularization, the Church is now also seeing its symbolic apparatus losing relevance: collective significations, individual identification, and the quest for meaning no longer find a satisfactory expression in the Church and in its language. Thus, people search outside the Church for the foundations of plausibility suited to the modern world.[61]

Conclusions

Developing in a European context, the Church's culture and structure is not adapted to the particularities of foreign cultures. Although the universality of the Church has given the young, small, local churches a strong foundation, problems of acculturation have, sooner or later, emerged, as in Japan.[62] Since modernization and the deconstruction of the 'grand narratives', the Church is also faced with problems of adaptation in the western world. The low number of vocations, the decline of membership, the decreased involvement of a large number of the still faithful, and the tensions between factions all attest to this.

In his study of the 'principle of subsidiarity' that emerged in the context of the social teaching of the Catholic Church (Quadragesimo anno, 1931) and the 'Episcopal Conferences' as a factor of

decentralization, Kaufmann formulated a point of view that con-
verges with our analysis:

> It is quite clear that a central administration will always be more insensitive
> to regional particularities. From a sociological point of view, however, it
> is quite obvious that effective evangelization requires a variety of social
> forms to express and experience the faith, and that the conditions of their
> plausibility and their practicability are linked to particular circumstances.
> The more an organization is centralized, the less it is flexible and adaptable
> to changing circumstances . . . It is clear enough that centralization of
> competence is often harmful to the commitment and above all to the
> initiative of those who are nearer to the base and that it is often experi-
> enced as a lack of confidence.[63]

This posits the problem of the extent to which the Magisterium is
willing to accept particularism in questions of 'performance' and
also of 'function' without fearing that the Church is losing its distinctiveness. This, of course, is very much related to the vision one has
of the local church and also to the theological options that inspire
one's vision of the world. These visions may be classified, according
to L. de Vaucelles, as the 'Augustinian heritage' and the 'pagano-
christian heritage'. The Augustinian theological orientation is the
answer of the Christian community confronted with a crisis of marginalization (as in the period following the end of the Roman Empire;
during the French Revolution and the subsequent laicization; and
in the age of secularization). Contemporary civilization is seen
as ignoring and undermining spiritual values, and pluralism is seen as
provoking an absence of beacons and norms, which leads to extreme
individualism and social fragmentation with repercussions even in
church life. Consequently, according to this vision, the present time
does not demand openness towards the world but rather a confrontation with it. The 'pagano-christian heritage' in theology, in contrast, has a positive vision of the evolution of western history
towards democracy and of its corollary, the secularity of the civil
institutions and culture. It accepts the pluralism of our civilization,
promotes dialogue with the world and stimulates its followers to
engage themselves in the world. Such a theology does not impose
its answers to the problems of the world but is convinced that it may
learn from the world and from other points of view. Consequently,
instead of seeing man as an already universally constituted reality,
it sees him as an historic identity.[64]

The Magisterium has changed from reading the 'signs of the times'
(Vatican II) to defining them as 'countervalues' secreting 'toxins'
(the Sixth Symposium of the European Bishops' Conferences, 1985)
and it now applies to European culture and its intellectuals its policy
on heresy.[65] The prevalent theological mood of the Magisterium
reflects the 'Augustinian heritage'. Consequently, the Church is

opting for confrontation with the world, stressing centralization and institutional authority and defying particularism and the so-called centripetal forces.

From a sociological perspective, however, the question may be asked why the Magisterium's point of view should be defined as 'universal'. It is after all also a 'particular' interpretation of the gospel and can be defined as 'universal' only because the Magisterium's intentions are to impose it 'universally'. Of course, Rome's policy has always been to stress tradition, the Church Fathers, and the right and the obligation of the Magisterium to have the final word in matters of faith and morals. It has also used and developed such notions as 'natural law' in order to impose its views, reading into nature the will of God. However, in the last resort is Catholicism not lived locally?

Is not the local church the 'living church'? Despite its pronouncements – e.g. on morals; women in the sanctuary; styles of liturgy; lay involvement; parish organization; dogmas and the sacraments – or punitive actions, e.g. against theologians, what can Rome really do? *'Sind die Gedanken nicht Frei?'* and also their applications? No matter what the pronouncements from Rome, or even those from the local bishop, the local pastor's orientation might be more critical on questions relating to the everyday lives of hard-core Catholics. However, since the parishes have become open places, hard-core Catholics do not much care about even the orientations of the pastors of the parish within the boundaries of which they live. Indeed, in this case 'ascription' is also gone: there is a 'pick and choose' attitude with respect to the churches in which people worship. They more and more choose to worship in a church of their liking and, consequently, active lay people also exert an influence on the orientation of the pastors. Parishes are like 'shops': the clients also influence what brand of Catholicism is sold.

Rome, however, now has a powerful weapon at hand to implement its views: the shortage of priests in those countries that are most secularized! In a 'universalistic mood' – convinced that the Church already possesses all the answers, i.e. the 'Augustinian heritage' – Rome might decide to enforce a policy of redistributing its priests, trained according to the traditional doctrine of the Church. According to Godfried Cardinal Danneels, the Eighth Synod of Bishops recommended a redistribution of available priests to overcome the lack of priests particularly in western Europe.[66] In his yearly letter on the occasion of Holy Week (1991), the Pope reaffirmed commitment to this solution.[67] This operation might bring the local churches more into tune with the 'universal' Church, and, consequently, augment the chance that liberal Catholics, who until now had attended churches of their own choosing, might quit. Such a

course might well be the end of the 'popular Church' and the beginning of the implementation of the theological 'minority Church' view
of a 'professing Church'.

Chapter 7

Believing without Belonging? The Case of Roman Catholics in England

Michael P. Hornsby-Smith

In recent work, Grace Davie has suggested that in recent decades a peculiar mismatch between religious belief and belonging has emerged in contemporary Britain.[1] Since this trend is particularly apparent among the younger generations and appears to be new and more permanent rather than a life-cycle phenomenon, it is likely to have serious consequences for the Churches and for the transmission of traditional Christian doctrine. This chapter aims to respond to this claim in the light of recent research into post-war social and religious transformations in Roman Catholicism in England. Three questions are addressed. First, some reservations about Davie's claims are presented. Second, the relevance of Davie's typology in the light of the patterns of heterodoxy among English Catholics revealed by survey data is examined. Third, the relationship between the 'customary' religion of English Catholics and the religious phenomena described by Davie is considered.

Davie's Typology: a Critique

The core of Davie's claim is that 'a large majority of people in contemporary Britain continue to believe but have ceased to belong to their religious institutions in any meaningful sense . . . More and more people within British society are, it appears, wanting to believe but without putting this belief into practice.'[2]

There are a number of reasons why caution is appropriate before accepting Davie's formulation. In the first place, does the evidence from recent surveys support her claim? For England in 1985, she reports that 11 per cent of the adult population could be regarded as 'belonging' in the sense that they could be counted as members of a Christian Church.[3] At the same time, the European Value Systems survey data reported that only 31 per cent of the adult population of Great Britain believed in a personal God.[4] These figures suggest that only around 28 per cent of the population can be found in the 'believing not belonging' cell. By comparison, three-fifths of the population are to be found in the completely heterodox cell of those who neither believe nor belong. In terms of the two indicators which have been chosen, quite legitimately, it is therefore statistically incorrect to make the claim above.

A second and related point is that of definitions and corresponding indicators. In her review of the European Values data, Davie reports twelve indicators of orthodox belief. The proportions affirming these various beliefs range from 25 per cent personally fully accepting the commandment regarding the Holy Sabbath to 76 per cent believing in God. Clearly there is a considerable diversity of beliefs. The religious situation is extremely complex and multifarious so that no clear demonstration (or falsification) of what constitutes 'belief' for Davie's purposes is possible without more explication than she has so far given. She admits this when she contrasts 'nominal belief in God' with low levels of 'creedal awareness'.[5] In our research into 'progressivism' among the delegates to the National Pastoral Congress in 1980 we were able to identify seven types of respondents with characteristics defined by six discriminant functions which were found to be theoretically meaningful.[6] In other words, belief is an extremely complex religious variable and it is necessary to distinguish creedal beliefs from other doctrinal beliefs and from social and personal morality. In her proposed typology of belief[7] Davie suggests that the Roman Catholic Church is characterized by 'belief expressed' without defining what this implies.

Similar problems arise with the 'belonging' variable. Davie uses church membership data but recognizes that there are difficulties in obtaining comparable definitions between different Christian churches. She also recognizes that there are distinct types of belonging in the inner city, the suburbs and rural areas, in the Roman Catholic, the black and other immigrant churches, and, indeed, even in religious broadcasting which she regards as 'an almost pure case of believing without belonging'.[8] The concept 'belonging' covers a multitude of sins and is almost as slippery a concept as 'community'. Among relevant considerations are questions of 'identity'. Members of a low status and oppressed religio-ethnic immigrant group in a hostile environment (such as was the case to some extent for the Irish Catholic working class in inner-city parishes in England up to the 1950s or 1960s) have what Hammond calls a 'collective-expressive' view of the Church and identity.[9] This type of involuntary 'belonging' was well expressed in an interview in the mid-1970s with George Woodcock, the retired General Secretary of the Trades Union Congress, who was a traditional Lancashire Catholic: 'I couldn't leave the Catholic Church just as I couldn't leave my family . . . I've never been ashamed of it . . . never kept it in the dark . . . I never say "as a Catholic"; it is just part of what I am . . . but what I am is because I was born a Catholic.' According to Hammond, this type of identity is being replaced by a largely voluntary 'individual-expressive' view under the impact of social change such as upward group mobility and the assimilation of immigrant groups and the decline of hostility towards them. In addition, the sense of 'belonging' can vary considerably. There can be a sense of belonging to a local parish such as is frequently referred to in the rhetoric about parish community. I have argued elsewhere that the reality is often very different, and that at least three criteria must be met for a sense of community belonging to be sociologically meaningful: shared beliefs and values, frequent interaction, and reciprocal social support and mutual aid.[10] But other forms of belonging with a more cosmopolitan orientation are also important. These might, for example, include a sense of belonging to a 'special purpose group' such as a justice and peace network of activists with either a national or, indeed, an international concern.[11] Thus the concept of 'belonging' also presents problems for analysis. One final point here: in my view Davie is making ideological assertions and is being insufficiently critical sociologically when she makes exaggerated claims for the parochial system of the Established Church in Britain 'that everyone "belongs" somewhere, whether they choose to acknowledge this or not'.[12] Indeed, it also contradicts her main claim that believing and *not* belonging characterize the British religious scene.

My third reservation about Davie's thesis concerns the historical dimension and the implication that there has only recently emerged the phenomenon of 'believing without belonging'. This is an issue which clearly needs to be addressed by historians. But there are at least some grounds for doubting that what Davie notes is either particularly new or remarkable. I have reviewed elsewhere[13] some of the historical evidence which suggests, in the words of the Rev. Winnington-Ingram a century ago, that 'it is not that the Church of God has lost the great towns; it never had them'. Indeed we can trace the alienation (or absence of 'belonging') from institutional Christianity of the labouring poor and working classes from the sixteenth and seventeenth centuries[14] and the evidence of an 'older, half-pagan popular culture' before the nineteenth century,[15] through to the Victorian age,[16] the early years of this century[17] and the contemporary inner city.[18] Thus, although she admits that 'this situation of alienation is nothing new',[19] her claims that the religious pattern has changed radically since the Second World War, based largely on the analysis of cross-sectional data on age differences, must be regarded as speculative.

The Heterodoxy of English Catholics

In her suggested typology of belief, Davie refers to the 'belief expressed' in the Roman Catholic Church[20] though she goes on to point to markedly higher practice in this country compared to Latin countries. This can be explained in terms of the concept of 'cultural defence'.[21] Davie does not define her term but merely asserts: 'But quite apart from the context, Roman Catholic obligation requires a degree of practice absent from the Protestant Churches. In consequence, the relationship between believing and belonging is bound to be different for Catholics whether they are a minority or not. The typology needs to reflect such differences.'[22]

However, even this claim depends on who is counted as a member of a church. If one takes 'total community' members the generalization holds.[23] But if one takes a more restricted figure of church membership such as is taken by Brierley,[24] then Protestant churches in 1979 reported an attendance rate of 81 per cent of membership compared to 37 per cent for the Roman Catholics in England. Furthermore, when the Protestant churches are disaggregated, it is clear that some have attendances much higher than memberships (e.g. the Baptist, Independent, African/West Indian, and Pentecostal/ Holiness Churches).

Empirically, far from being highly constrained by the obligation to attend mass at weekends, Catholic practice and beliefs are remarkably heterodox. The evidence from the 1978 national survey[25] was that only 31 per cent of adult Catholics could be regarded as orthodox both in terms of weekly mass attendance and in terms of a measure of orthodox belief. (The measure used was a 'certainly true' response to the statement 'at the consecration the bread and wine are really changed into the Body and Blood of Christ'.) Ten distinct types of Catholics, in terms of the five variables – religious identity, belief, practice, institutional involvement and sexual morality – were identified.[26] Neglecting the 8 per cent of Catholics who could not be adequately classified yields the following distribution of English Catholics in terms of the two dimensions of belief and belonging:

	%
Believing and belonging	34
Believing without belonging	23
Belonging without believing	5
Neither believing nor belonging	38

Such figures indicate clearly that Davie's categorization of religion in Britain does not hold for English Catholics in terms of our two measures of orthodoxy.

The above distribution needs some interpretation. Elsewhere I have argued that in the decades since the end of the Second World

War, and more especially since the 1960s, there has been a steady dissolution of the boundary walls which once defended the 'fortress' Church against a hostile society.[27] As Mary Douglas has said, 'Now the English Catholics are like everyone else' as a result of the expansion of secondary and higher education opportunities and general processes of embourgeoisement in the boom years of the post-war world.[28] The warmer ecumenical climate since the Second Vatican Council has been reflected in a decline of hostility and the need for the social policy of 'cultural defence'. This has been reflected in a considerable increase in the proportion of Catholics marrying outside their own religious community.[29] At the same time there has been a shift of theological emphasis from a more authoritarian Church of rules imposed downwards towards a more participative and gentler Church. The novelist David Lodge has characterized this shift in terms of the loss of 'the fear of hell'.[30] This, in turn, has led to increasing numbers of Catholics 'making up their own minds' over an ever-broadening range of issues, from the personal morality of contraception, to the response to the disciplinary rules of the Church, to the authority of the pope and priest in the post-Vatican Church, and to non-creedal doctrines such as that of papal authority.[31]

In sum, the results of survey research indicate that the label 'believing without belonging' is highly misleading as far as English Catholics are concerned. In the first place, far from there being a tightly structured belief system (as is sometimes supposed), Catholics' beliefs and attitudes are highly differentiated (between creedal and non-creedal beliefs, personal and social morality, and responses towards the disciplinary rules of the Church and deference towards the clerical leadership).[32] Secondly, English Catholics are also highly differentiated as regards their institutional involvement, used as an indicator of 'belonging'. At the very least it is necessary to distinguish between weekly mass attendance (currently below one-third of identified Catholics) and other indicators of belonging, such as membership of parish organizations (around one in eight Catholics). In spite of the rhetoric of parish 'communities', the reality is that around two-thirds of self-identified Catholics do not attend mass weekly and only a fraction of those who do participate to any meaningful extent in the social activities of the parish. Those who do are disproportionately middle-aged and middle-class and, paradoxically, the reforms of the Second Vatican Council appear to have marginalized working-class Catholics for whom the old inner-city parish performed vital functions of social support and identity-affirmation.[33]

As the data reported above indicate, the modal Catholic form of religion, reported by around two-fifths of English Catholics, is a residual 'communal' form of identity without belief or belonging.

Around one-third can be regarded as a 'faithful remnant' of those who both believe and belong, and only one-quarter fit the categorization of 'believing without belonging'. Looking to the future, it seems likely that social change will continue to erode the 'communal' form of identity typical of the 'fortress' Church period in its emerging history. Increasingly it seems likely that Catholics will select a more individually-chosen form of religious identity.[34] Far from being distinctive, therefore, as Davie argues, the evidence suggests there may be a considerable measure of normative convergence between the Catholics and members of the other mainline churches.

Customary Catholicism

In a recent work I have reviewed the results of focused interviews with a wide range of English Catholics from those 'core' Catholics, actively involved in the institutional Church and members of the former advisory commissions to the Bishops' Conference, to 'ordinary' Catholics, both at the parish level and among those attending the public events during the Pope's visit to Britain in 1982.[35] These interviews were, in the main, tape-recorded for subsequent analysis. Our aim was to explore further the range of meanings encapsulated in the heterogeneity of beliefs and practices demonstrated by social survey methods.

In the first place we found that there was no simple contrast between the orthodoxy, conformity and deference to clerical authority of 'core' Catholics and the heterodoxy, deviance and resistance to authority of 'ordinary' Catholics. The former group showed no deviation from creedal beliefs but they did express a strong awareness of a hierarchy of truths with differential claims to adherence. Thus, the further they moved from creedal beliefs, the stronger became their acceptance of private judgement and 'making up one's own mind' regardless of any official teaching. When questions of ecclesiastical discipline were addressed, it became clear that lay compliance was highly problematic, especially among the younger members. In the areas of sexual morality, too, there were substantial disagreements with the official teaching of the Church, and core Catholics demonstrated clearly a search for less rule-bound, absolutist and deductive forms of moral teaching.

Our early studies of 'ordinary' Catholics attempted to relate their responses to post-war social changes and to the reforms and shifts of theological orientation arising from the Second Vatican Council. We concluded that

> there has been very little coherent ideological opposition to that renewal. This is not to say, however, that its absence betokens a widespread

commitment to renewal. We suspect that the official functionaries within the official Church have too often assumed that lay Catholics have been effectively socialised, are ideologically committed, have a coherent belief structure, and are responsive to direction by the institutional leadership and that they have interpreted the absence of a widespread and coherent negative reaction to the post-Vatican changes as a sign that they have been substantially accepted.[36]

It was quite clear from our interview data that all of these assumptions were problematic. In the first place, recent changes in the Church were unlikely to have much impact on the majority of self-identified Roman Catholics with little institutional involvement. Secondly, the changes were unlikely to produce passionate opposition where the involvement in the institutional Church was of an essentially conventional kind. Many of our 'ordinary' Catholics failed to see the liturgical changes of the past two or three decades and the increase of lay participation as anything other than a 'nice idea'. They demonstrated no awareness that these changes might signify a fundamental new self-awareness of the Church as the 'people of God' and a dynamic religious community on pilgrimage rather than as a static, hierarchically structured religious organization with a subordinate laity deferential towards clerical officials.

The evidence from our interviews with ordinary Catholics suggested that their previous experiences of religious socialization had inclined many to judge the various changes selectively. For example, some who stressed such notions as the universality of the Church disliked the emergent forms of liturgical pluralism, while others recalled, uncritically, catechism answers learned in childhood. It seems that the religious involvement of many Catholics is coloured by apathy and self-interest so that changes which tended to make religion easier or less unconventional in a pluralist society were welcomed. Such passive or negative reasons were found, for example, in the approval given to the ending of Friday abstinence; the eased fasting regulations; the eliminations of sanctions against, and the relaxation of the granting of dispensations for, religiously mixed marriages; and the vague and unreflexive approval of ecumenism. The widespread disbelief in evil or in hell might also be interpreted as an aspect of apathy and self-interest which characterized much of the religiosity of ordinary Catholics.

It was the accumulation of such evidence that led us to distinguish between the 'official' religion of the clerical leadership in the Church and the 'customary' religion of ordinary Catholics. Our qualitative interview data showed many of the characteristics of the 'common' religion noted by Towler.[37] Towler's analysis, however, included not only a definition but also a description of 'the religion of common people' as well as a theory of its transmission through childhood peer-groups prior to any 'systematizing influence of official religion'.

These additional elements created unnecessary ambiguities and we argued that magic and superstition should not be seen as all of a piece with the sorts of beliefs and practices which have tenuous links with institutional religion and which were described both by our own respondents and by those interviewed by Towler and Chamberlain.[38]

It was for these reasons that we proposed the term 'customary' religion for those beliefs and practices which were derived from official religion, normally through the processes of religious socialization in the home, school and parish, but which were no longer subject to the control of the clerical leadership. We then suggested that the term 'common religion' be restricted to non-institutionally contexted religious beliefs and practices, particularly of a magical or superstitious nature. We saw customary religion as resulting where there was a breakdown in the processes of formal socialization, particularly in the post-school years. Current expressions of customary religion resulted from processes of trivialization, conventionality, apathy, convenience and self-interest, which had eroded and modified the formally prescribed beliefs and practices of official Roman Catholicism.

Examples of customary religion have recently been reported.[39] Thus, for example, the *trivialization* of Catholicism was demonstrated by the picturing of God as an Arab with a beard, or the devil with a tail, or heaven as a place of peace and contentment and hell as a 'fiery furnace'. Other examples include prayer to saints, primarily to assist in the finding of lost objects.

Conventionality was manifested in unreflective references to the three persons of the Trinity, or to God as a holy man, and catechism notions of mortal sin, conscience and will. It could also be discerned in references to routinized and habitual forms of prayer, such as the morning offering and examination of conscience at night, and in references to such slogans as 'the family that prays together stays together'.

Apathy seems to be indicated by the absence of personal prayer, or the assertion that you can get on with religion if you like it, or the admission that church attendance is contingent on feeling in the mood.

Finally, we argued that, for many Catholics, teachings about the final judgement, hell and eternal damnation, and the devil are uncomfortable, unpleasant and inconvenient. In many cases it seems that such teachings are either rejected or modified to suit the *convenience* and *self-interest* of the ordinary Catholic. Other examples seem to be the approval of many of the recent changes in the disciplinary rules of the Church in a rather vague, uncritical and passive way. Other interview data suggested that changes in the regulations regarding Friday abstinence from meat, or the length of the period of fasting prior to the reception of Holy Communion, or the easing of ecumenical relationships, have resulted in approval not so much because of any ideological awareness of the new religious insights and possibilities, but mainly on grounds of convenience and self-interest. What the data from our 500 hours of interviews demonstrate, therefore, is evidence of a residual form of Catholicism which has been filtered through personal interpretative processes.

Apart from the evidence of customary Catholicism, these data also point to the existence of what might better be called 'popular Catholicism', with its close links with 'implicit' religion.[40] In our interviews there are numerous instances of superstitious beliefs in luck, good fortune, fate, and the power of charms and rituals. Respondents 'touched wood', were unwilling to walk under ladders, regarded having their house blessed or their grandchildren baptized as important sources of protection, and used prayers, holy pictures and holy water as lucky charms. Other examples might be the wearing of 'miraculous medals' or the fixing of a St Christopher medallion in the car, the making of pilgrimages, the saying of prayers of indulgence and the wide range of almost magical insurance policies employed by Catholics to 'save our souls' and guarantee salvation. There also seems to be an area of 'popular Catholicism' where the borderline between official religion and its customary forms, on the one hand, and instances of 'implicit' or 'folk' religion, on the other hand, become quite blurred. Thus there is the suspicion in our data that flirtations with reincarnation are derived not only from folk religion but also from the search for more convenient and comfortable versions of what are perceived as unacceptably harsh official doctrines of the final judgement, hell and eternal damnation.

The burden of our research findings is that English Catholics in the 1970s and 1980s differentiated significantly between creedal or core beliefs (which continue to attract very high levels of assent), non-creedal or more peripheral beliefs (including papal infallibility), personal and social morality (where many Catholics considered the clerical leadership to lack both credibility and legitimacy), and institutional rules and regulations (which were regarded as no longer incurring effective religious sanctions, and to which conformity was largely dependent on such pragmatic considerations as convenience and self-interest). Increasingly Catholics, most especially the younger generations, made up their own minds on a growing range of issues.

Concluding Reflections

This chapter has demonstrated that Davie's charcterization of religion in Britain as 'believing without belonging' does not hold for

English Catholics. In their case there is evidence of considerable variability of both belief and practice or belonging, and of customary forms of religion reflecting the breakdown of processes of religious socialization. Rather than assuming that 'customary religion' is a peculiarity of English Catholicism,[41] it seems likely that where the structural context is similar in terms of weak religious socialization and parochial support, the religious outcomes are also likely to be similar. What appears to make customary forms of religion more evident in the Catholic case is the generally stronger religious socialization in maintained Catholic schools as compared to local authority or Church of England schools, especially where these are strongly supported by close parochial links.

The specific historical context is an important variable here. Thus up to the 1960s, the Catholic Church practised a policy of 'cultural defence'[42] and generated a 'collective-expressive' form of religious identity.[43] A strong religious socialization was an essential part of that policy. With the softening of religious hostility, the dissolution of the distinctive Catholic sub-culture, the uncertainties of the post-Vatican religious scene so that processes of religious socialization are likely to have been less effective than in previous decades, and the evidence of a strong process of normative convergence as indicated by the fact that Catholics increasingly make up their own minds especially in matters of personal and social morality, the differences between Anglicanism and Catholicism are likely to have declined. The religious situation in Britain is therefore far more complex than the slogan 'believing without belonging' suggests.

The reflections offered here point to the need for comparative research, not only between Catholic and Anglican beliefs in England, but also Catholic beliefs in England (where there is no serious anti-clericalism) and France (where there has been), and between the customary religion of the minority Catholic community in England and the minority Protestant population in France. Comparisons between the older Irish immigrant groups and newer black churches might also be instructive in pointing to the impact of assimilation processes. Finally, the influence of religious education in schools at a time when the State is becoming increasingly interventionist requires close attention.

Chapter 8

The Demise of Liberal Christianity?

P. J. Gee

The pronouncements of senior clergy of the Established Church of England on matters of politics and morality are clearly still of considerable interest to the press and broadcast media in Britain today, as are internal debates within that church which are often simplistically presented as conflicts between 'liberals' and 'conservatives'. Thus the appointment by the former prime minister of an evangelical bishop, Dr George Carey, to the See of Canterbury was widely viewed as setting the seal on the demise of Anglican liberalism, as represented by the previous Archbishop Robert Runcie. But, of course, predictions of the demise of liberal Christianity are not solely based on recent senior appointments in the Church of England. There have been a number of authoritative sociological predictions of the demise of non-conservative religion. This chapter addresses the broader theme of the survival of that strand of modern Christianity open to engagement with 'secular' forms of knowledge in contemporary science, the arts and humanities, prepared to reflect critically on its own history and practice, and concerned to stress the ethical implications of Christianity for wider culture. This has been most strongly identified with Protestantism, but particularly in the years since the Second Vatican Council, it has also been present within contemporary Roman Catholicism, albeit assuming different institutional forms. Donald E. Miller gives the following forward-looking description of this tendency:

> I foresee an emerging membership in Christian churches of those for whom theological interpretations are undergoing important transformations. These are persons who recognise the ultimate emptiness of individualism, who seek membership in a community united by a common symbolic paradigm. They are those who want roots that can be celebrated collectively. They are those who have not given up the search for ultimate Truth, but who in all likelihood have concluded that the truth is embodied only in community and expressed and made available to individuals in the collectively celebrated rites, acts and service of the community.[1]

The term 'liberal' is not always accepted by Christians who would identify with this description. For some 'progressive' Christians the 'L' word is almost as unacceptable as it was to George Bush when he was campaigning for the presidency of the United States. But other labels are equally problematic.

Where is liberal Christianity to be found in England today? As a tendency rather than a movement one cannot always point to specific institutions. However, there are pressure groups or associations within the churches which adopt a predominantly liberal stance. Within the Church of England, examples are the Modern Churchman's Union, the William Temple Foundation, and the Open Synod Group. The single-issue 'Movement for the Ordination of Women' is not exclusively liberal, but most liberal Anglicans would support its aims. In English Roman Catholicism the issues are different, but there is the Catholic Renewal Movement, and in the Free Churches there are the Alliance of Radical Methodists, the Baptist Renewal Group and a strong tradition within the United Reformed Church.

There is still an influential group of Oxbridge-based, mainly Anglican 'liberal' theologians, for example Maurice Wiles, John Fenton, Stephen Sykes and Don Cupitt. And many of their books are published by the liberal religious publishing house, the SCM Press (now merged with the New York-based Trinity Press).

Liberals are still well represented on the Church of England's bench of bishops with, for example, the Archbishop of York, Dr John Habgood, the Bishop of Durham, Dr David Jenkins, the Bishop of Manchester, Stanley Booth-Clibborn and the Bishop elect of Bath and Wells, Jim Thompson. And there are high-profile liberal churches, for example St James's Church Piccadilly, with its Rector Donald Reeves. There are a number of broadly-based interdenominational liberal organizations – for example the Student Christian Movement, the Christian Education Movement, and many 'single-issue' groups are predominantly liberal, e.g. Christian CND, Pax Christi,[2] the Lesbian and Gay Christian Movement, and various loosely-knit Christian feminist networks. Finally, of course, individual liberal Christians can be found in congregations throughout Britain, although they cannot always be easily identified.

If liberal Christianity has no clearly defined programme it does have an implicit agenda: pro-ecumenism, pro-women's ministry, pro-liturgical reform, pro-critical theology. Is this strand of Christianity sustainable today? Or is it the case, as the leading article in a new liberal theological newsletter recently claimed, that: 'If present trends continue, as far as Christianity is concerned, we could be on the verge of a new dark ages, and this time with fewer resources to carry through a precious intellectual heritage to brighter times.'[3]

Let me begin in the realms of popular perception. Conservative religion of all kinds is apparently growing, in Christianity and most noticeably too in Islam. Groups, churches and tendencies which place an overriding emphasis on faithful and close adherence to revealed supernatural religion are in the ascendency, in this country, but perhaps even more so elsewhere in Europe, in North America and Latin America. In England, the fastest growing communities of Christianity in the past two decades have been conservative evangelical or charismatic, whether within the boundaries of the denominations, or outside them in the burgeoning House Church movement. It is this trend which has apparently been given recognition within the Church of England by the appointment as Archbishop of one who clearly represents this tradition. In North America the religious right may have suffered a few moral setbacks recently, and under the Bush presidency it has had less direct access to power, but it, together with broader, less-politicized conservative denominations exercises an important influence.

So one factor is that liberal Christianity is being 'crowded out' by the expanding forces of religious conservatism. Church decision-makers and leaders are increasingly being drawn from the conservative evangelical or charismatic sector. Popular debate about this trend has often been characterized by the drawing of political parallels. In the English context, in the aftermath of the Falklands War, the *Faith in the City* report,[4] and the widely reported comments of the Bishop of Durham, many senior church leaders have been identified with political liberalism, with a defence of the old political ascendency challenged by the Conservative Party politics of the 1980s. But these parallels are superficial and misleading. With a Conservative Party dominated by an economic policy traditionally associated with classical liberalism, it may be argued that senior 'liberals' in the churches have only been filling the vacuum left by the eclipse of 'High Toryism'. And why could not liberal Christianity prove to be compatible with liberal, *laissez-faire* economics?

There has been some truth in popular perceptions of a liberal dominance in Anglican church leadership during the past decade. Even now 'liberals' do hold key positions, and exercise an influence arguably disproportionate to their numbers in the wider church. This is partly because the theological colleges at which they were trained – mainly Cuddesdon, Oxford, or Westcott House, Cambridge – were liberal and partly a tribute to the effectiveness of liberal movements in earlier decades. The ecumenical movement, and particularly the Student Christian Movement in the 1940s and 1950s, was very effective in promoting the liberal cause. But these channels have withered away in the intervening years and fewer liberals have been appointed to senior church posts in the past two decades.[5]

Why has conservative religion grown so much and why does this threaten the persistence of liberal Christianity? We begin at the level of ideology, in terms of the logic of belief. As Dean Kelley argued way back in 1972, conservative churches tend to have succeeded because they articulate a well-defined system of objective beliefs which give meaning to the lives of their members, offering them the certainty of salvation, while maintaining strong boundaries between believers and non-believers.[6] Kelley emphasized that conservative religion makes demands on its members both in terms of belief and life-style. By contrast, liberal denominations have been less successful because they do not offer a comparable certainty. They are pluralistic and open-minded, and do not demand great conformity. On many issues their theology cannot easily be distinguished from alternative secular philosophies.

Developing this argument with relation to British society during the 1980s, given the widely noted end of the post-war value-consensus, one might have predicted an increasing interest in more privatized forms of religious expression, paralleling the corporate privatization programme of the government.

On the liberal side, there is also considerable evidence to suggest that, if carried too far, some liberalizing tendencies may prove fatal for the survival of a religious group. In her studies of humanist societies in Britain during the 1960s, Susan Budd discussed the dangers posed by a diffuse belief system.[7] The argument is that a theology that takes on board the insights of (for example) Marxist analysis and then relativizes its own claims to objective truth and an exclusive path to salvation might end up by offering little more than straightforward Marxism unencumbered by theological baggage.

These analyses clearly have some validity, but they cannot adequately justify predictions of liberalism's demise. They raise as many questions as they resolve, with their implicit assumptions of an inevitably conservative religious dynamic. Empirically, liberal Christianity is not as open-minded as Kelley's description would suggest. 'Core' members of liberal congregations do have considerable demands made on them. If there is scope for diversity on certain matters of faith, there are pressures for conformity on others: to join action groups and campaigns on issues like Third World development, environmental preservation, peace and disarmament, as well as all the more usual church meetings and discussion groups.

The more serious underlying problems are structural and institutional and of particular interest from a sociological perspective. To make sense of them it is necessary to reflect on the manner in which English Christianity has adapted in the course of social and cultural change over the period since the eighteenth century. This is the familiar ground of the secularization thesis. There have been many criticisms of the strong version of that thesis, as originally propounded by Bryan Wilson during the 1960s,[8] and viewed from the perspective of the post-modernist 1990s, that straightforward analysis of a declining traditional religion, as a concomitant of an ever-more rational modern society seems difficult to uphold. A simple model of irreversible decline does not fit the contemporary religious scene very well. On the other hand, there has been a long-term decline in the numerical strength of the mainstream churches, however it is to be interpreted and whatever reasons are given.[9] This has been an uneven process, overlaid by regional and sub-cultural influences, and there are signs that the rate and character of the decline has slowed in the last decade. It is important to emphasize that this is not simply a process peculiar to religious institutions. There has been a decline in the popularity of many secular commitments too – in political parties, and other public activities.[10] Perhaps the image of fragmentation is now more appropriate, as the religious culture splits into diverse groupings, most, in religious terms, of a conservative disposition. In any case, the sociology of religion in Britain does seem to have moved beyond the sometimes sterile terms of the secularization debate of the late 1960s and early '70s. There is much more of a theoretical consensus on this now.

As important for my theme as the numerical decline is the response of the Christian community to social and cultural change over the past few decades. In the 1960s, Peter Berger presented in ideal typical form the options facing contemporary religion as a choice between *defence* and *accommodation*.[11] To maintain the objectivity of orthodox formulations of faith in the often hostile environment of a pluralistic society, the defensive strategy involves building a well 'insulated' sub-culture – a ghetto of traditional religion within secular society. The social engineering involved can be very expensive – for example, the very high cost of the Roman Catholic school system in this country, borne by the Catholic community – and there can be no guarantee of success. The alternative of accommodation, generally the path taken by liberals, involves adapting the shape and content of Christian belief and practice to make it more compatible with the reality presuppositions of contemporary society. This is also potentially hazardous. Writing in 1967, Berger warned of the dangers of theologians and clergy getting caught up in a process of compromise in which traditional formulations of faith begin to lose plausibility for them too: 'When this point is reached, the floodgates are opened to a veritable onslaught of relativising challenges to the tradition.'[12]

This typology can be useful in analysing some of the social consequences of responses to secularization by religious organizations, but it is inadequate for interpreting contemporary liberal Christianity. It presupposes a static view of the corpus of Christian doctrine, subsequently diluted or adjusted to be consistent with secular beliefs and practices. Yet the history of the development of Christianity from Constantine onwards is a history of many accommodations with alien, or potentially alien, cultures and movements.

It is ironic that sociologists of religion often seem to end up implicitly advocating or defending conservative religion – this seems to be particularly true in the field of liturgy[13] while liberal theologians expect us to be on their side.[14] This is partly because some liberal Christians are ignorant of social and cultural factors and are often insensitive in introducing change. But there is a more fundamental reason: sociological definitions of religion tend to favour conservative forms with their explicit references to the supernatural.

To return to my main argument, I want to put forward a different model to wrap up several centuries of theological ferment in a few lines. I am sure it does violence to the historical reality, but it may make my point.

Until the Enlightenment, religion and culture were more or less co-terminous in Europe; no clear distinction could be made between the realms of the religious and the secular. There was some conflict between the Church and science (Galileo) but the Church had the upper hand. Since then, the huge social shifts brought about by industrialization and economic growth have advanced a process of differentiation moving religion into a much more distinctively separate sector.

During this period most clergy and church leaders have resisted the marginalization this has brought about, partly because they have feared losing their social power and influence, but also because they foresaw the difficulties for the survival of mass Christianity posed by the separation of Church and State.[15] To retain cultural power and influence, the Christian intellectuals embarked on a process of accommodation, engaging with newly emergent scientific and philosophical traditions. The classical Protestant liberal theologians – Kant, Schleiermacher, with his addresses to religion's 'cultured despisers', and Ritschl – were very much in this vein. Their attempts to reconcile Christianity with contemporary culture may have been potentially more corrosive of their own tradition in that the rationalist emphasis of the Enlightenment challenged orthodox Christianity in ways that earlier philosophies had not. But they were only doing what earlier generations of religious intellectuals had done, searching for truth as they perceived it. Or, to put it differently, they were striving to keep Christian thought and practice within the core culture, to retain a place for religion in mainstream understandings of the world. And to some extent they succeeded, although of course the powerful forces of social change could not be arrested by such purely intellectual reappraisals and reconciliations. Theologians and moralists have probably always been in the position of producing *post hoc* legitimations for cultural trends which were likely to happen anyway.

Thus, as the Christian churches have increasingly become marginal social institutions with diminished social functions, theologians have sought to maintain the intellectual respectability of Christian faith in terms consistent with contemporary culture, so that even if the objective of retaining control over the total society has been lost, it has remained possible for Christians to be part of the mainstream culture while retaining their intellectual integrity.

I am not therefore convinced by arguments put forward by sociologists and others that complex diffuse systems of belief cannot be sustained in the contemporary era. Difficulties certainly face those who attempt to popularize the more sophisticated and abstract intellectualized theologies. But there are many layers of belief in all Christian denominations. A survey of many supposedly 'liberal' congregations would reveal a wide diversity of perspectives from the extreme conservative to the incoherent radical. In reality, liberal Christianity has often been the preserve of intellectuals, and it has always been parasitic upon orthodox 'conservative' Christianity. It emerges whenever religious people encounter secular belief systems and political perspectives and endeavour to achieve some degree of synthesis between them. In so far as they consider it to be necessary, individuals will always be able to construct their own idiosyncratic modes of reconciling their religious commitment with secular philosophies.

As long as Christianity retains a significant cultural base in England, pressures for the articulation and development of liberal Christianities will continue. New kinds of liberal Christianity may emerge, although certain historically contingent, if familiar, English manifestations may be doomed, as their institutional base in certain Anglican theological colleges, cathedrals and movements withers away.

But in another respect the prognosis is not so good. However well the churches have adapted institutionally to marginalization and pluralization, they have not done so very effectively at the level of core belief. So much of Christian theology, and this applies even more to 'liberal' theology, was fashioned in a context in which Christian social power and influence could be taken for granted. So, for example, the recommendations of reports like the Church of England's *Faith in the City* are dependent on precisely the types of power and influence that changes in British society are sweeping away. And Christian radicals who feel compelled to apply the insights of their faith to the national and international political scene are increasingly coming up against this problem.[16] Religious change and fragmentation make politicized interpretations of the gospel easier, but there are fewer people ready to be influenced by it.

Tied up with this, in England at least, has been the impact of establishment. While many senior Anglican clergy still apparently regard their Church's established status as an asset, there is evidence to suggest that it may have actually hindered the ability of the churches to respond to social change. As David Martin has put it recently:

the effect of establishment and religious monopoly such as existed in Europe has been to inhibit the adaptability of religion to social change, above all to the industrial city. However the North American paradigm seems to show that once religion is no longer a matter of a relation of a particular body to the elite and to the state, religion adapts quite successfully to a changing world. In all the proper senses of the word it becomes popular. Indeed it shows itself endlessly inventive and actually succeeds in assuaging the anomie and combating the chaos of the megacity.[17]

Since the Established Church of England has been the home of many liberal Christians, this factor has been of considerable importance. Indeed, many Anglican liberals resist the implications of marginalization. A new liberal theological newsletter, launched in 1990, offered this interesting analysis:

> To [] an observer, 'believing' can virtually amount to adopting an ideology . . . and once this assumption gains ground, it is not long before all groups of religious believers, including Christians, are regarded as groupings apart from 'the world', opting for their own conventions of behaviour and beliefs. Each of these systems of belief and behaviour is seen as valid for a particular religious group in its own right but relative to other belief systems (the Christian community is active in one way, the Jewish in another).
>   However once this kind of relativity is accepted, the quest for meaning, for making sense of one world under one God, the search for truth, is abandoned. Christian belief, in particular, severs the links with the wider world which it has had from the start and retreats into a ghetto. Given all this, the odds against the survival of a form of Christian belief which carries on the breadth, intellectual commitment and generosity of the best of past tradition are high.[18]

This expresses the dilemma which haunts many contemporary liberal Christians but also gives the game away. There is a clear implication in the notion of 'making sense of one world under one God' of continuing to strive for cultural centrality for their religious perspective. It assumes that theologians in one tradition are capable of exercising a legitimated role of ethical interpretation for the whole of a multi-cultural society, rather than simply for a small segment of a minority religious sub-culture. In England this is likely to become increasingly problematic, as the maintenance of that degree of engagement with the wider world will become increasingly difficult.

The real challenge facing liberal Christianity will be to find a creative and effective response to marginalization, and the progressive severing of its former effective links to social power. Instead of looking nostalgically for ways to re-create lost social and cultural power, will liberal Christians find new ways to respond to the religious needs of a post-modern culture and the imperatives of their faith? If not, the fate of liberal Christianity may be sealed, in England at least.

Chapter 9

Does the Social Gospel Involve the Collapse of Christianity?

Kenneth Minogue

My central question concerns the identity of a Christian Church. Churches are institutions, and as the generations change so the institution may be transformed, as medieval guilds became merely ceremonial, or friendly societies became trade unions, and trade unions changed their character in the course of this century. A Christian Church, however, is the custodian of what it takes to be a truth and a set of practices having divine sanction. There is no doubt it can change and perhaps develop, but its self-determination depends on its being able to respond to a changing world in its own terms. Otherwise it loses its identity.

We might well diagnose such a loss of identity in the response of the Rev. William Hybels of Chicago who designed his liturgy on the basis of a consumer survey. 'He found', it is reported, 'that people wanted "higher take-home value", "entertainment" and a "convenience-oriented gospel". Now boasting the second largest congregation of any Protestant church in America, he believes his methods bring to God hundreds of people who find ordinary services too boring.'[1] This is a form of Christianity, if such it is, distinctly removed from that of the followers of *Opus Dei*, some of whom scourge themselves with a cord called a 'discipline' and wear round the thigh for an hour or so a day a spiked chain called a 'cilice'.[2] A church is above all an institution which is likely to be damaged by more than a superficial response to a changing world because its very claim to our attention lies in being the still centre of a changing world. None the less, in practice, religions do sometimes develop in small ways that culminate in contrasts, such as the one mentioned, the terms of which seem so great as to have lost touch with their foundations.

The charge that a church has lost its way is a common one in the history of Christianity, and in rhetoric may be formally rebutted by the claim to be emphasizing some part of the message which has fallen into the background, or which requires to be given a special prominence in current circumstances. A formal rebuttal, however, leaves everything to play for. What concerns me in this paper is the distribution of emphasis in Christian practice between the social and what we may broadly describe as the mystical. Indeed, in this area, all descriptions are pretty broad, for that term 'social' certainly incorporates the political, and may indeed often be used by way of semantic disguise as a respectable cloak for a basically political impulse. Until quite recently, churches were keen to guard their religious character as rendering them politically neutral. This is why a political commitment might well require presentation under some different rubric such as the 'social'. An act can only ever be justified under a description, and we are here dealing with an area which can plausibly be described in various ways.

Before moving to the centre of my argument however, I want to note what I take to be a vital feature of the rhetorical situation of the Christian Churches in the twentieth century. I refer to the sense in which they have seemed to be alienated from the two most powerful intellectual tendencies of the modern world: science and progress. Like most religions, Christianity affirms the reality of entities which cannot be observed, and of causal connections which cannot be tested. To be a Christian in modern times was thus to be on the defensive against the charge of merely succumbing to wishful thinking. Christians were sociologized by Marx and psychologized by Freud. The history of Christianity in recent centuries has been a history of retreat from doctrines which conflicted with the march of science, from Copernicus to Darwin. To be an educated Christian was thus to be intellectually on the defensive. No less important in some places was the fact that in a critical and rebellious time, Christianity seemed to be politically aligned with the established order, and in some cases some rather unpleasant political orders at that. In these circumstances, to be a Christian was to be, in a sense, politically and intellectually out of the mainstream, and, in an increasingly conformist time, this constituted a distinct disadvantage. In the jargon which reflects this conformist tendency, Christians were 'marginalized'. Much of the development of contemporary Christianity may, in these terms, be explained by the powerful impulse to demonstrate that Christians were neither superstitious nor reactionary. Like desperate sailors shedding cargo in a storm, theologians were to be found rationalizing the supernatural elements of their religion and theorizing God as metaphysical grounding. A corresponding dissociation from established authority (in liberal democracies no less than in authoritarian states) led churches to repudiate the past image of cannon-blessing bishops and take up pacifism and the cause of the poor.

It was this general background which no doubt made it easier for the churches to be infiltrated by a new generation which found in Marx's derision of Christianity not an entrenched and gnostic hostility to the Christian religion, but the marks of a higher spiritual sensibility responding to the human suffering of the proletariat in a manner that was a model to Christians everywhere. Nor should we forget that many churches were ripe for takeover: they were rich in both money and prestige, and they were feeble. Their image was the gothic or neo-gothic building at the heart of a community attracting the merest handful of worshippers. Let us turn to those who have entered into the churchly inheritance.

The most conspicuous inheritors are those who identify the Church with the social gospel, and the social gospel with left-wing politics. This sequence of intellectual steps corresponds to the life experience of many a priest or clergyman, some of whom in some cases have secularized themselves completely. Edward Norman has described the politicization of religion as 'the internal transformation of the faith itself, so that it comes to be defined in terms of political values'.[3] Those attracted into the churches by this process are political activists in a familiar idiom. In January 1980, thirty of them formed a 'campaigning network' called 'Christian Organizations for Social, Political and Economic Change', which, following the conventional taste again typical for acronyms goes by the familiar designation of COSPEC.[4] These groups co-operate in the Synod and find international influence through the World Council of Churches, set up in 1948. In the 1980s, one focus of these priestly endeavours was support for liberation movements in Southern Africa, which eventually led to embarrassing commitments of loyalty.

> When it was revealed that SWAPO has tortured 2,500 of its own members the Churches' commitment to 'opposing repression in all forms' appeared slightly hollow. The Council of Churches in Namibia finally issued a statement stating that it is 'totally opposed to the abuse of human rights by whoever and for whatever reason' but added, 'we also condemn the use of this suffering as a weapon to be exploited for party political aims'.[5]

'Without in any way condoning these atrocities', affirmed the Bishop of Manchester boldly, 'it is a fact that war always produces them.'[6] In this, as in many other cases, a political commitment (and especially this kind of ideological political commitment) leads spokesmen for the churches into the sleaziest kind of moral evasiveness.

The liberation theology of the Catholic Church, emanating it is said from South America, is a subject in itself, but it is one which reminds us that Christian churches have often suffered from the kind of sectarian enthusiasm which results from one aspect of a complex doctrine coming to dominate thought. The medieval Church oscillated between rich orders becoming corrupted by their wealth, and new orders being formed on the basis of a poverty which could often become an end in itself. The meek were all right, as the joke has it, until they inherited the earth. Certainly some prelates of the Church in the middle ages regarded themselves as having complete authority by virtue of a sanctity which they contrasted with the sinfulness of the fighting estates of the time. In the contemporary world, the effect of this perennial religious response is to inject an intransigent moral righteousness into straightforward modern left-wing enthusiasms. It is this combination which has led to the 1980s version of the quarrel between *regnum* (alias Margaret Thatcher) and *sacerdotium*. The Dominican Order in Britain is a notable exponent of this kind of enthusiasm. 'In some senses,' declared Father Herbert McCabe, a prominent member of the Dominican Order, 'Mrs Thatcher has the same mind-set as the fascists.' He attributed to her the view that 'organized greed is the best way of running a society'. Asked about the difference between religion and politics, he replied: 'Is there a difference?'[7]

These examples merely demonstrate the fact that most church opinion, in Britain and throughout the western world, has become socialist at the very moment when socialist governments have been shown to fail. It might be argued, of course, that such an orientation is natural for a church based on the divine mission of a crucified carpenter, and indeed the parable of the good Samaritan has become one of the battlegrounds of interpretation in the encounter between Church and State. But there are two considerations which should give one pause in any identification of the Welfare State with Christian charity.

The first is that the arcane bureaucracy of the social service state does not express the heartfelt love of the British for their less fortunate brethren. It results rather from a desire to unburden ourselves of these responsibilities and to load them on to the State where they are carried out automatically, without most of us having to be bothered about them. It results, in other words, from that culture of indifference which is so profoundly hostile to Christianity. I have heard one academic social democrat (not at all Christian) remark that the benefit of an efficient Welfare State is that he could walk down the street without having to worry whether the beggars he sees are in real need or not.

The second point follows from this: charity is the business of the Church which, in fact, as locally based, would be able to make better judgements of local service in distributing help to the poor. It alone can unite material benefits and a charitable spirit. At the beginning of the modern era, the State took over most of the secular responsibilities of the churches; for the churches not only to acquiesce but enthusiastically to endorse the continuation of this process into the field of charity is merely to declare a fatal collapse of vocation. It is true, of course, that the contemporary rhetoric for the distribution of such benefits is that of rights, and that charity has a bad name

as something condescending, but this truth merely reflects a secularization of attitudes which is destructive of Christianity itself. Having
opinions and expressing grievances is something endemic in modern
democratic societies, and it is clear that most clergymen prefer pontification without responsibility to actual power to influence the
world.

These tendencies exhibit the way in which the churches have in
many cases abandoned their moral and spiritual basis in favour of
behaving like one more left-of-centre political party. But the spirit
abhors a vacuum no less than nature, and with the collapse of
the spiritual vocation has come the intrusion of many strange and
wonderful phenomena, like weeds growing in an untended garden.

One is the revival of the natural religions which were superseded
millennia ago by the great religions of the East. Every religious
decline is, of course, a relapse into idolatry, and the body is one of
the new idols, nature or 'the environment' another. The Rev. Ian
Bradley (author of *God is Green*) describes green theology as something which must be advanced

> not as some aberrant departure or some opportunistic attempt to grab the
> headlines but as the very core of our faith in God the Father who knows
> and cares about one sparrow falling from heaven, the Son who was born
> among the animals and who spoke to the winds and waves and the Holy
> Spirit who moves over the face of the waters as she animates our souls.[8]

Bradley even discovers some elements of pantheism in the later
prophets; he will certainly find it in many of his environmental
associates. The point here, of course, is not that it is foolish to be
concerned about the effects of modern human life on nature, but
that such greening can have no central place in the spiritual vocation
of a church.

The most spectacular case of secular intrusion into Christianity is
no doubt the feminist campaign for the ordination of women.
Women have always played a vital role in the Church, often among
congregations a central role. They have often been instinctively
pious, perhaps in recognition of their situation in a social order
which the Church has always sustained. The power of women has
commonly been exercised through the family, and the family has
been sustained above all by the sacrament of marriage. The collapse
of that sacrament and the increasing ease of divorce has left many
women alone and vulnerable, a situation secularly described by the
self-contradictory rubric of the 'one-parent family'. A family requires
two committed parents, and while misfortune may reduce this to
one, the term cannot legitimately be used for single adventures in
procreation.

The movement for women's rights in the Church is unmistakably secular, and in secular terms there can be no reason for resisting it. What is there in the duties of a priest which could not be done with equal competence by many women? Nor need we doubt that there are women who sincerely experience a sense of pastoral vocation. But much of the impetus for this movement comes from a feeling right across the social spectrum that all pleasant occupations, especially those giving a certain degree of automatic respect, should justly be open to women. All that stands in the way is the tradition of the Church and the practices of its founder. But on what else is a church based? If Jesus, who was remarkable for his propensity to overturn the conventional judgements of his time, is understood to have appointed only male disciples because he was a creature of his time, what is left of divine revelation? The whole proposal points a deadly dagger of relativism at the heart of Christianity itself. We may go further, to suggest that while sincerity may fuel some of this demand, vanity and ambition cannot be ignored. Further, the demand is parasitic in a way typical of feminism as a whole. A creative feminism could create and develop women's movements of its own. In fact, all that is at issue is the power to share in what has already been created.

Similar considerations apply to the place of homosexual priests in the Church. There must always have been a lot of it around, and a Christian church must be the last organization to be surprised at human peccadillos. Except in an age of protest and liberation, such things could be discreetly accommodated, giving rise to scandal only when the occasional vicar was caught out with a choir boy. Now, however, the Church finds itself split on a variety of homosexual issues. Bishops spoke in the House of Lords against Clause 28 of the Act of Parliament which prohibits the 'promotion' of homo-sexuality by local authorities as nothing more than a legitimate sexual preference, an alternative to heterosexuality. In the rush to be up-to-date, some clergymen have preached against celibacy and monogamy, though primarily in the United States where these mat-ters are more advanced. 'If you are asking me whether Mother Theresa would be better off if she got laid,' memorably remarked the Rev. Robert Williams in New Jersey, 'the answer is yes.' Admit-tedly he was sacked, but his bishop did so 'with a heavy heart'.[9] There is a campaign for the recognition of homosexual marriage, and it is unlikely to go away in a hurry.

To treat the ecumenical movement as further evidence of a col-lapse of Christianity raises complicated questions, for the original impulse of this movement arises not from creeping secularization but from an endogenous sense that many of the divisions between the followers of Christ are absurd. The search for common ground is reinforced by a sense that a united Church would be better placed to meet the evident weakening of Christianity in a secular world.

This may be good institutional strategy, or it may not. Empires are not always stronger than their components. But what ecumenism means, in the first instance, is that beliefs and practices for which earlier Christians were prepared to die are now negotiable. But where might this negotiation then stop? Ecumenism can hardly help getting tangled up with the modern defensive propensity of theologians to retreat back into symbolism, and with liberal affirmations about tolerating all faiths. This is potentially a slide towards relativism, and to a concession to the secular belief that all but a tiny core of moral belief in religion is irrational anyway. The combination of these factors means that some in the churches become prepared to trade off not merely what Hooker, following the Stoics, called 'things indifferent' but (on a severe reckoning) Christianity itself. What has emerged in practice from this tendency is belief in a kind of 'perennial philosophy' by which Christians recognize believers in all faiths as co-religionists, all worshipping God, as they say, in their own way. Search for a bit of decent bigotry in religion these days, and you will find it only in small groups like the Free Presbyterians, prepared to expel Lord Mackay for merely attending a Roman Catholic funeral service for a brother judge, or in Islam. No one has a good word to say for bigotry these days, and no doubt we would generally find it intolerable, but it is certainly one measure of the vitality of a belief.

My purpose is to explore the doctrinal erosion of Christianity, and before I go further, I should perhaps specify what I take to be essential to that belief. The philosopher Hobbes had a brisk way with this problem, at a time when one's life might depend on it. He thought it consisted purely in the belief that Jesus was the Christ. The rest could be whatever the sovereign thought fitting. But basing myself on the tradition of political philosophy, I should go a little further.

It is impossible to be a Christian without believing in original sin. The fall of man is inescapably the central subject of meditation of a religious imagination. The story is found in Genesis and like all the other narratives in the Bible can never be exhausted by any theoretical attempt to state what it means. Yet in our intellectual age, there is a temptation always to discover a meaning and worship the meaning, as being rather more theoretical and defensible than the simple narrative. I take the story to be an account of individual self-consciousness, which generates the sin of pride, and that sin is the model of all others. This is the Augustinian view, but for religious purposes, the story must be treated as inexhaustible.

The second basic doctrine is that of the immortality of the soul, which is the basis of Christian individuality, and the necessary theological condition of the current vogue for rights. This is an important doctrine because it is a recognition of the fact that accounts cannot be tidily squared in this necessarily imperfect world. Marx recognizes the importance of this in his denunciation of Christianity as wish fulfilment, because unless this belief is destroyed, the conception of a modern society as a zero-sum contest between classes loses its sharpness. You cannot promote a really ferocious class struggle without persuading people that this is all there is. Correspondingly, religious belief has the effect of facilitating social peace because many people much of the time think in terms of some ultimate reconciliation. As with all religious doctrines, immortality is situated far beyond any possible evidence, and in different cultural environments many people will find it either virtually self-evident, or else patently absurd. But the role it has played in the creation of our civilization depends crucially on its being literally believed.

Most of what is important in Christianity can be elicited from these doctrines, but I should like to add a third which is perhaps a corollary. The Tower of Babel story is that of sinful men trying to take steps to secure themselves against their dependence on the accidents of nature and the will of God. This was, significantly for our purposes, a collective project, conceived under the charismatic leadership of a revolutionary called Nimrod. This is a story which warns us against expecting too much from human arrangements.

These and other doctrines combine to warn us that human life is not a bed of roses, and that our basic business during the adventure of mortality is to accept this with a good grace. Yet the essence of Christianity is to encourage in us a sense of gratitude for the blessings of the world in which we find ourselves, and of gladness that it is all so much better than we deserve. This is the key by which we may understand what it is that is eroding the core of Christianity. For it is invariably true of the components of the social gospel that they deal in grievances and indignation as they characterize a world which is unworthy of the human beings who inhabit it. Just such a reversal is characteristic of the gnostic heresy, which has plausibly been seen as at the root of modern ideologies.[10]

These modern ideologies (communism, fascism, feminism, nationalism, sundry liberations, etc.) all share with religion the character of being salvationist, but the salvation they promise is, in a sense, in the here and now. One must say 'in a sense' because what is promised is a form of collective salvation which the individual could enjoy only by losing himself or herself in some grander collective. Whereas religion (like philosophy according to Socrates) is a kind of meditation on and preparation for death, ideologies take death to be (as Marx describes it) merely a 'biological accident', for reality inheres in the human collective.[11] It is along these lines that Marx declares religion to be the opium of the people. The puzzling question, then, is why anyone should take Marx to be anything else except an enemy of religion, and of everything spiritual involved. Yet in liberation theology, he has been virtually canonized.

The solution to this problem follows the line that 'my enemy's enemy is my friend'. Marx is above all hostile to individualist liberal democracy, alias capitalism, while one strain in Christianity is deeply hostile to the same thing, alias *materialism*. If we shuffle these categories around a little, we come up with the discovery that Marx's hostility to religion is really to be taken as hostility to the apologetics of capitalist materialism, and may thus be taken as a version of the higher spirituality. The same conclusion can be reached by tracing Marx's view of religion back via Feuerbach to Hegel, where we do indeed find a genuine insight into spirituality. It is an old observation that the generation of socialists of the middle of the twentieth century (such as Pandit Nehru) admired the Soviet Union precisely because it had *failed* to produce a consumer paradise. The emphasis on struggle and the evidently austere commitment of revolutionaries had a similar appeal to one strain of Christian believer – a discovery which long ago led the Vatican to suspend the experiment of the worker-priest. Many of them soon went native.

The social gospel in Christianity is not merely a matter of taking up left-wing political positions, but of absorbing a certain style of discourse. It consists in sociologizing every problem, and thus unmasking all competing doctrines as nothing more than ways of sustaining the evils of an established order of things. The local variant of this move tends to turn clergymen into down-market sociologists. A contemporary version would be: 'Churches reflect the dominant values of society.'[12] Such a statement is, of course, the end of Christianity, because it denies that the Church is the custodian of a universal and transcendent truth. But it is not what it seems. It insinuates into any discussion a distinction between those discovered to be reflecting the supposed moral values of society and those others who are critical of such values. In other words, the speaker of such an utterance seems to be including only himself within the range of his universal sociological generalization. What he is actually doing is dehumanizing a position he seeks to attack by presenting it not as the result of thought, but as a mechanical implication of something non-rational. He then advances his own position as a critical rejection of those dominant social values, which turn out not to be as dominant as they seemed. We thus see that the apparent sociological fundamentalism of this ideological rhetoric is deceptive. It quickly turns into an exploitation of the academic propensity for critical analysis. The critical analysis is of a fairly simple kind. In Britain in the 1980s, which is my pool of experience for this argument, it usually amounted to the heroic discovery, overcoming all those dominant social values, that Thatcherite society was inspired by greed and self-interest. But the move from the sociological to the academic is also incomplete. The ultimate foundation for this kind of argument, taken to be beyond critical cavil, is a posture of moral righteousness, usually focused on injustice to the poor.

Such a new model clergyman, once launched, can easily master the critical patter of the ideological world. A writer in the *Tablet* promises to tell us things called 'unwelcome truths' and sneers at our 'pious complacency'.[13] In this world, clergymen are everywhere to be found popping up asking what they themselves describe as 'awkward questions'. These postures of heroism might well be condoned as harmless vanities were it not that the rhetoric here assumes the level of discomfort to be an index of truth. It helps us to keep our bearings in this confusing world to remember that the whole basis of the atheist attack on Christianity in the last three centuries has been in terms of the rhetoric of courage, the atheist presenting himself as someone willing to reject wishful thinking and face up to the reality of human mortality.

It is not merely the rhetoric of courage which has been appropriated by liberal churchmen from their enemies, but also the rhetoric of the open mind. This parody of academic inquiry is merely self-flattering, and an experienced controversialist knows, when he hears someone boasting an open mind, that he must stand by for unargued waves of dogmatic passion. Opponents are characterized as neurotically fixed in some shell of irrational belief, and real sensitivity to problems has shrunk to a few shibboleths.[14]

The outcome of this capitulation to ideological modes of talking is an abandonment of the language of Christianity in favour of contemporary political cliché. And where locutions lure, can belief be far behind? As the Dominican Father McCabe, whom we have already met, put it: 'What we have in this country is a conservative society based on capitalism, so to have no politics is to be Conservative.' It is all nostalgically reminiscent of a 1960s undergraduate.

My argument, then, is that Christianity in Britain (and in many places elsewhere) is a largely abandoned building given over to political squatters. Some of these squatters are deliberately trying to make the building over, others are merely relieved at no longer having to hold out against what they have always half-believed to be the truths of the modern world, and no doubt there are a lot of real Christians wondering what to do. One question we may ask is whether this situation is entirely new.

Evidently not. We have mentioned the spiritual Franciscans of the fourteenth century, and we might also invoke the antinomians of the sixteenth and after. They also brought spirituality down from the skies and invested it in some social or political cause. To do this is the basic error of moving from symbolism to idolatry, the error from which an abstract monotheism protects us.

It was the seventeenth-century case which haunted the imagination of Edmund Burke as he contemplated the Rev. Richard Price's sermon at Old Jewry in 1790. The signal for revolutions, he observed, has often been given from pulpits.[15] And he goes on to quote Dr Price's raptures:

> What an eventful period is this! I am *thankful* that I have lived *in peace, for mine eyes have seen thy salvation* – I have lived to see a *diffusion* of knowledge which has undermined superstition and error. – I have lived to see the *rights* of *men* better understood than ever; and nations panting for liberty which seemed to have lost the idea of it. – I have lived to see *Thirty Millions of People*, indignant and resolute, spurning at slavery, and demanding liberty with an irresistible voice. *Their King led in triumph, and an arbitrary monarch surrendering himself to his subjects.*[16]

Burke goes on to quote from the *State Trials* the deposition of a witness who saw, in the previous century, the Rev. Hugh Peters riding before King Charles I, who was being brought back to London to face trial, and expressing an attitude which the witness called 'triumphing'. Peters it was who also concluded a long prayer in the royal chapel by invoking, as Price did, the *nunc dimittis*. Burke is eloquent in his horror of these vulgarities.

These developments, then, are by no means without precedent, though we may well say that the churches today have fewer resources for regeneration than in the days when Hannah More was creating the Sunday School movement.

It might be suggested, however, that while the present direction of the churches may not be grandly spiritual, it is at least better than it was in the days of burning heretics and blessing artillery. But to believe this would be to accept things at their face value. The rhetoric of our time is what Nietzsche characterized as 'sickly' – it is full of hypocritical asseverations of compassion and guilt. But this kind of righteousness is no guarantee of intellectual honesty. This may be illustrated by the way in which Mrs Thatcher had become a hate figure in clerical discourse. She must herself be recognized as a traditional Christian of a somewhat Low Church kind, and it would be quite wrong to underestimate her moral seriousness. Yet when she remarked that 'there is no such thing as society' she was interpreted by many churchmen as saying that every individual should try to get as much money as possible without consideration for anyone else. There is quite simply no doubt at all that this is precisely what she did *not* mean, but she was ruthlessly attacked as if she had. The Rev. Leach, whom we have already quoted, ended his attack on her with the words: ' . . . in the crude materialism of Thatcherite values, we are all prostitutes. It is therefore unsurprising and deeply symbolic that the Good Samaritan is only remembered for his money.' This is not only ugly, it is unmistakably distorted. And when the Rev. Brendan Callaghan[17] characterizes fundamentalists as victims of neurosis, he is certainly dehumanizing them. It is perhaps only the fact that clergymen have no leverage on the punitive institutions of the country which prevents a severer fate being meted out to them.

We live, to be sure, in milder times, but the contestation for power and place would seem to be no less ferocious than in earlier times. The events leading to the suicide of Gary Bennett suggest that the spirit of gentle compassion is not entirely universal in the Church, and is sometimes least evident in those who talk most about it. There are sharks swimming round in the spiritual unction. Sometimes this even emerges into political comment. The Rev. Dr Mervyn Stockwood is reported as writing in the *Evening Standard* about Enoch Powell of whose speech he disapproved: 'Enoch's evil speech last summer was the equivalent of a foul smell. Until Powell let off his fart white and coloured lived happily together.' In revolutionary assemblies, verbal violence has often preceded the real thing.

Does all this matter very much? After all, the Church is but one among the set of institutions of a civil society, and relatively few people these days actively participate in its doings. I think it is important, for many reasons. One of them is that the Church's loss of interest in religion is similar to the way in which women have lost interest in the feminine, judges in merely declaring what the law is, and journalists in merely reporting events. In all these and many other cases, the dominant passion is to engage in the kind of politics which gives the pleasure of pontification.

The abandonment of the spiritual dimension of British society will do more than threaten the existence of buildings which are integral to the British skyline. It will affect morality as well, leading increasingly to the replacement of manners and morals by rationalized codes against sexual harassment, against racial discrimination, etc. It will leave modern Britons even more than ever before merely creatures entirely absorbed in work and distracting pleasures, without any sense of mystery and the boundaries between different elements of the self. We are on the move from a society in which eating a meal begins as a ritual preceded by grace and ends in the informalities of the television supper. A vital dimension of human experience is being abandoned by a politicized Church. There is as yet no sign of what it is that will fill this emptiness, but whatever it will be may not be greatly to our liking.

Chapter 10

Discourse on Women in the Clerical Profession: the Diaconate and Language-games in the Church of England[*]

Alan Aldridge

In 1986 the Church of England permitted women to enter the lowest rank of the clerical profession, the diaconate, while reserving to men the offices of priest and bishop. For male clergy, the period served as a deacon is normally a one-year probation before ordination to the priesthood, whereas for women it is a terminus. This limited incorporation of women into the clerical profession has been accompanied by a prolific discourse on the need for an enriched diaconate. Although the focus of debate is ostensibly the diaconate, the discourse is a power struggle over the ordination of women to the priesthood. For those who oppose women's entry into the priesthood, the discourse of enriched distinctive diaconate legitimizes women's subordinate and marginal position in the clerical profession. For women deacons, on the other hand, in so far as the metaphor of *diakonia* has salience, it is typically mobilized in a critique of authoritarianism among the male clergy. Evidence gathered from women serving as deacons shows that the great majority find the diaconate frustrating, support the ordination of women priests and have themselves felt a calling to priesthood. Drawing on Wittgenstein's concept of language-games embedded in forms of life, an analysis is presented of the grounding of this gendered discourse in the occupational culture of the clerical profession.

Introduction

Central to the problematic of the contemporary sociology of religion is the analysis of power. This involves, as Beckford has argued, 'the practical processes whereby religion is actually lived out at both the individual and collective levels in a struggle for power. The struggle

[*] Thanks are due to the editors of *Sociology* for permission to reprint this article, which first appeared in *Sociology*, 26, 1, 1992.

is over the power to define situations, to affect the course of events, and, above all, to gain a hearing for religious testimony, declarations, and direction.'[1]

These conflicts take place not only in secular settings such as courts of law[2] – where religious testimony may be a contested element in adversarial proceedings – but also within religious organizations themselves. Here, too, the religious dimension is contested: in pursuit of their own objectives, rival interest groups seek the authority to define and the power to mobilize sacred symbols and the charismatic legacy.

The object of analysis in this article is current discourse within the Church of England on women's subordinate position in the clerical profession. This subordination is legitimated by appeal to the concept of *diakonia*, service. The ultimate role model for Christian ministry, Jesus Christ himself, is portrayed as a suffering servant who repudiated secular models of authoritarian leadership; he washed his disciples' feet. This symbolic portrayal of Christ has deep roots in the contemporary situation of the mainstream churches, which have suffered severe institutional decline. *Diakonia* as a metaphor for ministry is therefore hard to challenge; what is in dispute is its operationalization. Evidence from women serving as deacons shows that they are discontented with their current role and career prospects, and reject the rhetoric of *diakonia* as a device for their continued subordination. Denied full access to theological discourse even when they are its objects, women deacons have been forced to be non-participant observers of language-games devised, played and refereed by clergymen.

Mobilizing Latent Charisma: *Diakonia* and Legitimation

The clerical profession in its Anglican variant is divided into three Holy Orders: deacons, priests and bishops. Hitherto, the Church's attention has focused almost exclusively on the priesthood and on its relation to the laity. Thus, guides written for prospective and trainee clergymen have concentrated on the questions, what is it to be a priest, and how should the priest discharge his responsibilities? Little effort has been devoted to answering these same questions for deacons. The reason is plain: for men, diaconate is seldom more than a one-year probation before ordination to the priesthood. It was only when women's entry into the clerical profession became imminent that attention switched to the diaconate. In 1986, the Church took the decision to open the diaconate to women. The first ordinations took place in February 1987. Very rapidly, the great majority of deaconesses were ordained deacon.[3] This influx of women into the profession has prompted a burgeoning discourse on diaconate. One strand in the discourse is the call for an enriched diaconate, designed to retain men who may progress to priesthood and to satisfy women who may not.

The theological basis of diaconate, *diakonia*, is usually translated 'service'. It has an unchallenged position as a core value of Christian ministry. This centrality of *diakonia* is derived from twentieth-century understandings of Jesus, which emphasize his humility and ostensible powerlessness. Jesus, 'man of sorrows', is equated with the 'suffering servant' of Israel. Jesus reversed worldly hierarchies by washing his disciples' feet, overcoming their offended sensibilities with the message: 'I am among you as one who serves.'

The practice of *diakonia* is thus heavily invested with the charisma of the Church's founder. Following Hill's suggestion, the charisma of *diakonia* may be seen as latent in the Church of England. Hill argues that 'any institution that claims a charismatic pedigree will retain in its structure of roles a latent form of charisma which is always available as a source of legitimacy for office-holders who are involved in the process of innovation'.[4] Even in bureaucratized religious institutions, where heroic personal charisma has long been displaced by routinized charisma of office, the founder's historic imprint remains.

Latent charisma is a resource to be mobilized by interest groups which seek to establish a link between the charisma of the founder and their own desired *praxis*. Revival movements within churches base themselves on appeals to latent charisma. Although their visions of the charismatic heritage vary, they are at one in seeking to recapture in the present the charismatic fervour of the institution's origins. For example, the Tractarian revival of the nineteenth century stressed 'apostolic succession' as the means by which, through laying-on of hands by a bishop, charisma had been transmitted down the centuries in an unbroken lineage from Jesus to the contemporary priesthood. Similarly, this century's charismatic renewal movement has sought to revive and re-enact within the Church the ecstatic experience and miraculous charismata of the first Pentecost.

'Suffering servant' is not the only available image of Jesus; others include political activist, Jewish prophet, worker of miracles, incarnation of the Divine, Christ the King, and *pantocrator* – ruler of the universe. Why, then, does the particular image of Christ the suffering servant have such deep resonance among Anglican clergy? The answer, I shall argue, is twofold. First, because 'feminine' traits are typically repressed in Protestant churches, they tend to find an outlet in projection on to the figure of Christ. Second, the ravages of secularization have called forth a more overtly humble iconography of priesthood, depicting pastoral service to the community as the core activity of the cleric.

One sign of the repression of feminine symbolism in the Church of England is the atrophy of the cult of the Virgin Mary. Only in the Anglo-Catholic wing of the Church is cultic devotion to the Virgin a potent force; but Anglo-Catholicism has been in long-term decline.[5] The dominant central tendency is embarrassed by what it sees as excesses of Marian devotion; Evangelicals are concerned at unbiblical Roman doctrines and practices; while liberals regard Anglo-Catholicism as a stronghold of superstition, reaction and misogyny.

Accompanying the theological objections is revulsion, expressed from the nineteenth century onwards, at the 'effeminate' qualities allegedly sponsored by Anglo-Catholicism.[6] Protestant heirs of strenuous muscular Christianity find themselves repelled by the outward show of sartorial fastidiousness and camp self-parody running through Anglo-Catholic ritualism. Among Evangelicals, straightforward unquestioned masculinity is the model for men. Evangelical thought operates with 'a stereotyped scheme of psychological dynamics',[7] in which complexity, ambiguity and anomaly cannot easily be accommodated. It offers no incentive to recognize the Jungian shadow. Unsurprisingly, Evangelicals have been prominent in the campaign to expose and condemn gay clergymen.

Marian devotions are not just unmanly; they are un-English.[8] Anglo-Catholics are aware of this, and even relish it; they see themselves as 'against the stream' of English social life.[9] One of their prime targets has been the shallow religiosity of the boys' public schools. This antipathy was heartily reciprocated by the schools themselves, which rejected the ethos and practice of Anglican Catholicism. In the rare instances when they were encouraged, neither auricular confession nor regular fasting proved popular with the boys. The masters sought to cultivate not the spiritual path of asceticism and introspective piety but an active, manly conquest of weakness and adversity.[10] The cult of the Virgin may have an elective affinity with Latin *machismo*,[11] but not with Anglo-Saxon stoicism.[12] Leach's jibe is acute: 'God and Jesus fit well enough into the English Public School ethos; the Virgin-Mother has no place at all.'[13]

What, though, of the doctrine of the Virgin Birth, which remains an indispensable article of conservative Protestant faith? Does this not show the continuing power of feminine symbols? The point here is that the doctrine of the Virgin Birth is totally disconnected from the use of feminine symbolism in public ritual or private devotion. It focuses not on Mary but on Jesus; all that matters about Mary is her voluntary submission and her unbroken hymen. In the context of power struggles within mainstream Protestantism, insistence on the Virgin Birth does not challenge the dominance of masculine symbolism. Its function is as a formal creedal test of orthodoxy, a sign of correct conservatism. It is a polemical weapon in the war against theological liberals. As Barr points out in his extended analysis of Protestant fundamentalism, the doctrine of the Virgin

Birth is a radical challenge both to rational scientific materialism and to everyday commonsense. Were it not for its scriptural warrant, who would believe it? Within the confines of Christian fundamentalism it has become 'an emptied and formalized doctrine, emphasized not for its own content but because it furnishes the best test case for the authority of scripture on fundamentalist terms'.[14]

As feminine symbols have been repressed, so feminine traits have been projected on to the figure of Christ. He is seen to embody the virtues of compassion, mercy, gentleness and humility – precisely those qualities which popular Catholic devotion pours into the cult of the Virgin. This feminization of Christ is an unintended consequence of the dynamic of Protestantism. Whenever it comes to the attention of Protestant thinkers it is likely to be condemned. Thus the great Swiss theologian Karl Barth, in his monumental *Church Dogmatics*, denounced the feminizing strand of Christian iconography:

> one of the worst accusations we can bring against Christian art (so-called) is that it has had a fatal tendency brazenly to represent the figure of Christ, when it lays violent hands upon it, with that well-known and frightful mixture of masculine and feminine traits (for which there is no foundation whatever in the biblical tradition) instead of honourably at least in the form of a man.[15]

A second factor accounting for the appeal of the image of the suffering servant is the impact of institutional decline. *Christos Pantocrator* – the awesome image of Christ as stern judge and omnipotent Lord – was a powerful icon when Byzantium was at its height, but hardly serves as a role model for the beleaguered Anglican clergy today. This is not the Christ whom they seek to imitate. Faced with a society in which the authority and expertise of the religious profession are increasingly under threat, the clergy have redefined their role to emphasize the element of service to the community. The suffering, humble Christ is symbolically congruent with a clerical profession which has been, in Martin's phrase, 'winkled out of the structure of legitimation' nationally and locally.[16] The feminization of Christ, as Rosemary Radford Ruether has argued,[17] reflects the churches' differentiation from secular institutions and relocation in a more private, domestic sphere. As industrial societies move into a post-industrial phase, this trend is likely to be reinforced.[18]

The symbol of Christ the suffering servant, the supreme deacon, has a contemporary impact and deep historical roots. This does not mean, however, that the interpretation of the symbol, and the uses to which it is put, are unequivocal and unproblematic. Quite the contrary. It is a cultural resource[19] on which conflicting interest groups draw in order to legitimize their conception of appropriate gender roles and relationships. As with the Virgin Mary so with

Jesus Christ: the symbol of the servant may be a warrant for submission or an emblem of liberation.

Operationalizing *Diakonia*: from Charisma to Job
Specification

Diakonia is not a concept but a metaphor. The relationship of the
metaphor to the structure of the Church considered as a hierarchy
of bureaucratic offices, is complex and negotiable. Operationalizing
diakonia – deriving from the metaphor a set of working practices,
appropriate terms and conditions of employment, and a career structure – is heavily contested by men and women who have a vested
interest in the outcome.

Advocates of a permanent diaconate typically assert or assume
that the diaconate has declined or degenerated into a mere probation, the bottom rung of the professional *cursus honorum*. This
they represent as a betrayal of the charismatically charged ideal of
diakonia.

On rational–legal grounds, however, a probationary diaconate
is unproblematic. It is common practice in organizations to have
probationary periods built into the career structure. One obvious
function of probation is to enable senior management to identify
inefficient and unsuitable personnel; even if rarely invoked, this is
a powerful sanction. Conversely, probation is a trial period during
which the potential recruit may review his or her career goals.
Probation thus serves the twin functions of social control over and
socialization of clerical personnel. It is also appropriate to the characteristically threefold structure of rites of passage: the probationer is
in a liminal state between status of origin and status of destination,
an experience which both generates and symbolizes commitment to
the new status.[20] The fact that all the Church's priests have served
their time as deacons is one of the psychological bonds between
them.

The history of the diaconate from the Middle Ages shows that it
has been the lowest in the hierarchy of three Holy Orders. Cranmer's
Book of Common Prayer proclaimed this robustly. In the Prayer
Book service for the ordination of deacons, the bishop explains their
duties to the candidates: to assist the priest liturgically, to catechize
young people, to baptize infants when the priest is absent, and to
seek out 'the sick, poor, and impotent people of the Parish', reporting back to the incumbent so that he may organize the distribution
of alms. Towards the end of the ordination service, the bishop prays
that the deacons 'may so well behave themselves in this inferior
Office, that they may be found worthy to be called unto the higher
Ministries in thy Church'. In the ecclesiology of the Prayer Book,

the deacon is clearly identified as both assistant and apprentice to the priest.

The Alternative Service Book of 1980, in contrast, reflects the contemporary attempt to redefine diaconate as a worthwhile order in its own right, one to which people will feel a specific vocation. Diaconate is to be not a mere staging-post to priesthood but an autonomous order possessing its own theological rationale and distinctive range of duties. The vocabulary of apprenticeship and inferiority has therefore been erased from the discourse of the ASB. In the list of the deacon's duties, the task of assisting the parish priest remains, but has been relegated to the end. First place is given to the deacon's vocation 'to serve the Church of God, and to work with its members in caring for the poor, the needy, the sick, and all who are in trouble'.

The Church as a sacred institution has especial difficulty in confronting rational–legal demands.[21] Theological, not economistic, discourse is given supreme value. Thus the debate on diaconate has often been detached from any hard economic analysis of the problems of deployment and remuneration of clerical personnel. Rational organizational analysis gives way to its theological counterpart, ecclesiology, in which the Church's sacred character is paramount.

Attempts to describe a distinctively diaconal ministry are, then, invariably abstract and visionary. For example, in his report on the role of deacons in the USA, Brother Victor commends an 'organic' view of the Church in which the three Holy Orders neither compete with one another nor detract from the role of the laity, but 'focus' particular elements of the Church's mission: 'the individual orders and ministries are not, then, to be understood as part of the body as such, as its heart or its hands, but rather as those who focus and encourage those vital characteristics of the ministry of Christ which the whole body is called to reflect and which they represent and focus as ministers'.[22] Discourse of this kind, though typical of in-house church debates, does not generate anything that an organization operating on entirely rational–legal principles would recognize as a job description.

The modern quest for a distinctive diaconate has become entangled in a double problem of defining the deacon's role. First, the Church of England has been unable to differentiate the role of deacon from that of lay person. One response to church decline has been to encourage active lay participation in church work. There is an obvious problem that an expanded and enhanced diaconate would encroach on activities that are increasingly undertaken by the laity; would lay people then be shepherded unwillingly into the Holy Order of deacons? If so, would not the blurring of the distinction between professional practitioners and their lay clients seriously threaten the profession itself? Second, the only way the Church has been able to differentiate the diaconal from the priestly role has been in negative terms: deacons have exactly the same duties as priests except, crucially, that they are not permitted to consecrate the eucharistic elements of bread and wine, nor may they pronounce absolution or blessings.

Given the operational limitations of the diaconal role, it seems unlikely that any management consultant would recommend a move to permanent salaried diaconate as a rational financial strategy for the hard-pressed Church. It would be economically viable only if permanent deacons were substantially less well remunerated than priests. This is, in fact, the current national situation with regard to women. A survey carried out at the end of 1989 showed that, of the Church's 999 licensed women deacons, only 51.2 per cent were in receipt of a full stipened paid by the Church; 8.7 per cent had a part stipend, and 8.3 per cent received a part or all of their salary from secular authorities such as the Home Office or the National Health Service.[23] The remaining 31.8 per cent were not in receipt of a stipened from any source. This survey documented one unsung characteristic of diaconal service: its inferior remuneration.

Contested Terrain: Women's Experience of the Diaconate

How do women respond to the discourse of enriched diaconate, and what part have they played in shaping it? Does the conception of a distinctive diaconate offer to women the hope of a satisfying career?

Evidence I have gathered from a postal questionnaire sent in the summer of 1989 to all the women serving as deacons in four dioceses of the Church of England shows that the problems of the diaconal role are of high salience.[24] Their everyday experience of ministry, career prospects and sense of their own worth are all profoundly affected by the inherent limitations of the diaconate.

Women deacons do not regard the diaconate as the terminus of women's ministry. Strikingly, 98.6 per cent of my respondents were in favour of the ordination of women to the priesthood; only one person was uncertain. There was 100 per cent agreement with the statement that 'there are no valid theological objections to the ordination of women to the priesthood'; a remarkable result given that the theological debate is sharply contested. On the question of timing, 83.1 per cent disagreed with the frequently entertained proposition that 'the time is not ripe to ordain women to the priesthood'.

Turning to their personal aspirations, 85.9 per cent said that they felt called to the priesthood, and 81.7 per cent that they would seek to go forward as a candidate if the Church opened the priesthood to women in the near future. However, only a bare majority, 50.7 per cent, thought that the Church of England was likely to ordain women priests before the end of this century.

Some of the frustrations of the diaconate are shown in the responses to the question, 'Have you raised any complaints with fellow clergy about aspects of your current position?' 54.9 per cent indicated that they had complained, and among these the ratio of resolved to unresolved complaints was 1 to 2. The complaints that had been successfully settled were of three kinds: that tasks and responsibilities were too restricted, that the workload was excessive, and that some clergymen were unsupportive. These are problems which can normally be solved within existing organizational structures, given good-will. Twelve of these thirteen women had complained to their immediate superior in the Church hierarchy, who had sorted it out. Unresolved complaints, in contrast, involved other problems: pay, resources, housing, job insecurity, career blockage. These are structural problems of the deacon's career and its resourcing. Significantly, these issues had been taken up with a far wider range of people: rural dean, post-ordination training officer, diocesan adviser on women's ministry, archdeacon and bishop. Women deacons evidently experience a range of material and career-related problems which cannot be resolved by good-will alone.

The problem of gaining a hearing for women's experience, frustrations and sense of vocation is compounded by the passive 'waiting' role that many women are constrained to adopt. The attractions to women ministers of this role are many. It gives them a working rationale for their day-to-day professional practice. It achieves some success: doubters are won over by the example of a woman competently discharging ministerial duties. The enactment of a humble role does not cause overt trouble in the sacred organization.

The manifest disadvantage of a waiting role is that it leaves intact the gulf between women's private experience of ministry and the public debate on the ontology of diaconate and priesthood. Persuading through uncomplaining example rests on the assumption that observers will draw the correct inferences. Some of the clergymen I interviewed[25] deduced different but superficially plausible conclusions: that women were well-suited to diaconal roles; that diaconate is not a surrogate priesthood but the heart of all ministry; and that women have found true fulfilment in the permanent diaconate.[26]

From Exclusion to Accommodation: Language-games and Forms of Life

Because they occupy subordinate positions in a male-dominated authority structure, women deacons have difficulty in gaining a hearing for their experiences and aspirations. They are subject, as Jill Robson has argued, to the gendered inequalities of clerical discourse.[27] Drawing on Wittgenstein's concept of the language-game embedded in a form of life, Robson distinguishes two language-games, one concerned with 'ministry' and the other with 'profession'.

The language-game of ministry contains a cluster of interrelated terms including *diakonia*, service, sacrifice, selflessness, humility, relative poverty and unconcern for material rewards. This language-game is highly and explicitly theological: it draws on the symbol, discussed above, of Christ the suffering servant.

The second language-game, more overtly secular in tenor, concerns the Church as a profession offering a career structure to its practitioners. The reference group is professional colleagues. Informal networks are acknowledged to be important – who knows or is related to whom, where a man trained, and so forth. There is much talk of clerical careers, of appointments and promotions. Terms and conditions of employment are openly discussed – salaries, pensions, housing, job descriptions, days off, holiday entitlements.

A number of points are made in Robson's analysis. First, the language-game of ministry is often played in such a way that it legitimates women's subordination to men. Second, when clergymen play the language-game of professionalism, women have been typically absent, ignored or marginalized. This has meant, evidently, that career rewards have been more frequently distributed to men than to women. Third, the rules of the game – and even which game is being played – are determined by men.

Wittgenstein's own approach to the study of language became gradually more sociological in its implications. Abandoning his early conceptualization of language as a propositional calculus, he developed the analogy between language and games, an analogy which reached fruition in his *Philosophical Investigations*.[28] Initially, chess served as the paradigm case of the game. As his thinking developed he came to see that chess, a zero-sum contest with precise and invariant rules, is simply one member of the extended family of games.

For all the emphasis which Wittgenstein's later work placed on the grounding of language-games in what he called 'forms of life', neither he nor his philosophical followers have offered a systematic analysis of the relationship between language-games and social context. This challenge has been taken up by Bloor,[29] who has advanced a comparative theory of language-games derived from the work of Mary Douglas.[30]

In this approach, Wittgenstein's forms of life are interpreted as socially sustained boundaries. The boundary around a community, separating it from outsiders, corresponds to Douglas's concept of 'group'. The boundaries within a community – demarcations of roles, status and authority – correspond to Douglas's 'grid'. These boundaries, as with any classificatory scheme, generate anomalous cases which do not fit neatly. As Douglas argues, there is a limited repertoire of social responses to anomaly; these are set out in the figure below.

Typology of Responses to Anomaly

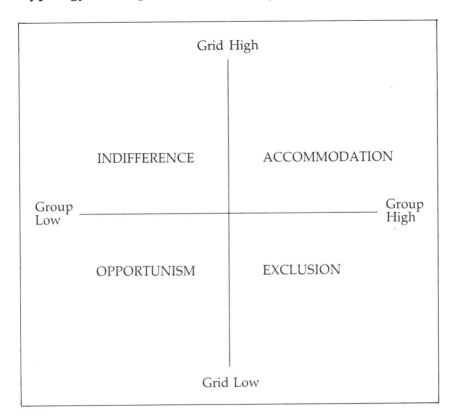

Each of these responses to the 'anomaly' of women ministers is to be found in the Church of England, though at different levels in the organization and with unequal chances of mobilizing support.

Indifference   Even though debate over ordination of women to the priesthood is often acrimonious and potentially divisive, it is greeted with relative unconcern among some sectors of the clergy and laity. This reflects, as I have argued elsewhere,[31] the autonomy enjoyed by many parish clergymen and their ability to insulate themselves from the 'problem' of women's ministry. Indifference is widespread at the individual level, but would lack plausibility as the dominant corporate response of the Church.

Opportunism   This is the least common response to women's ministry. It implies a selective welcome to any anomalies which are calculated to be advantageous. The situation where both grid and group are low is 'individualistic, pluralistic, competitive and pragmatic'.[32] Its ethos is secular. The Church's corporate response cannot be seen to take the form of opportunism; theological legitimation has to be supplied.

Exclusion   This response is fostered by social structures with a strong group boundary against outsiders, but a low degree of internal demarcation. Anomalies are a potent threat to such pollution-conscious cultures. The social bond between insiders is strong, though it may be periodically disrupted by internal conflict allegedly imported from the world outside.

Accommodation   Social structures which score highly on both the grid and the group dimensions are not markedly pollution-conscious.[33] The group boundary between insiders and outsiders is not the only divide of significance; internal demarcations may be equally salient. Extended and complex gradations of rank are defined and sacralized. This is the home of the legal fiction, and of experts skilled in subtle classification and re-classification.

Discourse on *diakonia* is a dialectic between corporate strategies of exclusion and accommodation. Those who seek to exclude women from full and equal membership of the clerical profession typically draw a sharp Durkheimian distinction between the sacred office of priest and the profane status of lay person. The ontology of the sacred priesthood is defended against pollution from the profane realm. Discourse is highly and explicitly theological; the Church is the Body of Christ, not a complex bureaucratic organization. Hence the discourse on *diakonia*. The rediscovery of the diaconate as a distinctive order, legitimated by the charismatic foundation of the faith, is an attempt to reaffirm traditional group boundaries.

Douglas's theory does not imply denial of human agency. Grid and group do not determine responses to anomaly. Within the Church of England, a diversity of response to women's ministry is displayed. The point is, as Bloor argues,[34] that any given response to anomaly will tend to lose credibility if the conditions are not propitious to mobilize support for it. So it is in the Church of England. Women's incorporation into the diaconate has signalled a shift from exclusion to accommodation. Pressure for accommodation had built up to the point where it proved impossible to resist, so that the majority even of opponents of the ordination of women to the priesthood voted in 1986 for women's incorporation into the diaconate. The attempt to marry the rhetoric of exclusion to social processes of accommodation is a mismatch that is likely to appear increasingly implausible within the Church, let alone outside it.

The move from exclusion to accommodation is demonstrated in two reports prepared for the Church of England. *Deacons in the Ministry of the Church*[35] is an attempt to construct a theological rationale for a distinctive diaconate; the language-game of ministry is dominant. In contrast, *Deacons Now*[36] addresses the challenge of women's career development; here, it is the language-game of professionalism which prevails.

The language-game of diaconal ministry has little attraction for the overwhelming majority of women serving as deacons. In so far as they participate in this language-game, it is to use *diakonia* as a resource not to legitimize their own subordination but to challenge male clerical authoritarianism and the accompanying conception of the Church as high group low grid.

Hitherto, women have been excluded from the language-game of professionalism, which has the potential to accommodate them, and included in the language-game of ministry, which is designed to exclude them. Women's incorporation into the lower ranks of the profession has made this pattern more difficult to sustain. If women are ordained to the priesthood, the language-game of enriched diaconal ministry will become a game with no players.

Chapter 11

Television, the 'Bartered Bride'; Broadcasting, Commerce and Religion: Transatlantic Perspectives

Kenneth M. Wolfe

On returning from America, Oscar Wilde thought it the noisiest country that ever existed. Those old enough to remember their childhood may recall a party game of finding one's partner by making the appropriate animal noise loud enough to be heard above the racket of the others doing the same. The bigger the room, the more the people and thus the more deafening the clamour. So with broadcasting in America: radio and television stations can be counted by thousands whereas in Britain they are rather in tens. There are four times as many people in a country with a history of broadcasting which was pluralist from the start. In the 1920s, American radio stations sprang up like crocuses: but like voices themselves, there were limits to the range of transmission distances. Smaller, myriad stations could develop locally beneath the canopy of the growing networks now famous as NBC, CBS and ABC. The American public was an aggregate of distinct ethnic groups, emerging states and religious bodies all seeking protection for their individual identities under the stars and stripes. Since 1920, broadcasting in America has reaffirmed and exported the values of the pioneer, explorer and nation-builder.

In Britain, by contrast, following the disaster of the First World War, the public was exhausted, was still mourning and was looking for a change, and certainly a diversion.

By 1922, the commercial endeavours of British radio manufacturers were under the public eye of the Post-Master General who was already well established as the custodian of the air-waves. John Reith's British Broadcasting Company had only four years to live before the commercial interests of the wireless manufacturers were subdued by a powerful concept of public service. His British Broadcasting *Company* was turned into a public Corporation by parliament.[1]

The key perspectives in this chapter focus on broadcast religion and contrast two notions: American minority enterprise in the public interest and British public service broadcasting in the interest of minorities. These issues are subtle and one is well advised by H. L. Mencken, the Americal columnist, who pointed out that for every complicated question there is an answer that is simple, easily understood, and wrong!

There are, I believe, four aspects of transatlantic religious broadcasting which repay examination: commerce, technology, education and populism.

First, *commerce*. The whole history of broadcasting took a commercial turn when the Peacock Committee (inquiring into the future financing of the BBC) reported in July 1986 and introduced new concepts for funding which, sooner or later, may have to run an advertising gauntlet. The Cable Act of 1984, two years earlier, marked the end of an era: the second age of broadcasting was over.

Long ago, Sir Ian Jacob, the Director-General from 1952 to 1959, coined probably the most compelling definition of public service broadcasting: it was, he said:

> a compound of a system of control, an attitude of mind, and an aim, which if successfully achieved, results in a service which cannot be given by any other means. *The system of control* is full independence, or the maximum degree of independence that parliament will accord. *The attitude of mind* is an intelligent one capable of attracting to the service the highest quality of character and intellect. *The aim* is to give the best and the most comprehensive service of broadcasting to the public that is possible. The motive that underlies the whole operation is a vital factor; it must not be vitiated by political or commercial consideration.[2]

This was not merely a pipe-dream but stood at the roots of a democratic culture and enshrined a philosophy which understood history and destiny in terms of freedom – the freedom to question and to debate both eternal and temporal verities in public, whatever the consensus; and to make editorial decisions in all areas in the interests of the public. It took initiatives or operated as an élite – whichever you prefer. In either case, it was and remains, for the time being at any rate, 'a delicate estate of the realm', as Simon Jenkins has neatly observed,[3] 'in an intensely privileged position'.

By the same token, independent television shared similar aspirations, albeit nearer to the edges of their philosophy than the BBC. We should not forget that it was on independent television in 1985 that debates about the Virgin Birth and about the truth of the creeds were given wide coverage by the Bishop of Durham, and on the BBC, Don Cupitt examined other creedal statements in another controversial series 'The Sea of Faith'.

Mrs Whitehouse of the National Viewers and Listeners Association struck at the stem of Ian Jacob's convictions by demanding the right to reply on behalf of 'simple believers', reckoned by her to be in the majority. Adjacent to this lobby is the more alarming prospect of advertising on the BBC and therefore a deep threat to independence and with it originality.

Second, *technology* and specifically satellite television. A satellite TV channel promoting 'the Christian message' and 'a sense of hope' has begun broadcasts to Britain and is seeking outlets on cable stations. The European Broadcasting Network (with headquarters in Norway) was launched here in 1986 and its British director outlined the basic idea 'to promote a wholesome family alternative to violent and immoral material'[4]. It failed! The material envisaged for the Sunday provision was American, and by that is meant the so-called 'electronic church'.[5] Robert Schuller's 'Hour of Power' is now on Sky weekly. William Fore, in charge of communications for the ecumenical National Council of Churches in the USA, in 1983 told an IBA religious symposium quite bluntly that, 'American evangelists are eagerly awaiting the chance to buy into [British] audiences'.[6] He expects that homegrown copies and direct US imports will be legion. Dr. Morris Cerullo, an American Evangelist, is about to launch his *European Family Christian Network* on Satellite, 24 hours a day.

Thirdly, *education*. The British churches are usually optimistic in their assessments of numbers of adherents. Their own figures for congregational commitment and membership have (with the exception of a slight upturn in 1947) shown a steady decline since 1922, ironically the year broadcasting began in Britain.[7]

There are several indicators which suggest that this seemingly inexorable decline continues: a drastic shortage of clergy, a rising number of co-operative endeavours among Protestant congregations and, of course, the loss of revenue. The theological crisis goes hand in hand: religion, and particularly Christianity, struggles to make itself intelligible to a culture increasingly untutored in the basic rudiments of Christian belief. Religious education struggles to maintain its integrity and relevance within the maintained schools' curriculum. In doing so, plurality and relativity have inevitably laid the schools open to the charge by believers that Christianity is no longer being properly taught.

In 1985, the Church of England published *The Theology of Laity*[8] which upset the elements of the leadership with the suggestion that the clergy operate a sort of conspiracy against the rank and file to keep them at a safe arm's length from biblical criticism, the formation of the creed, and the complexity of church history; all for fear that the democratization of knowledge will destroy the faith or create widespread uncertainty.[9] Clifford Longley, commenting in *The Times*, feared that only a minority of the laity could recognize any religious currents below the secular surface of our culture and were desperate for a religious utterance which would engender both optimism and social commitment.[10] The controversy begun by the

Bishop of Durham in 1984 on television made clear just how profoundly lay people are untaught and how little is being demanded
of the clergy that his remarks be put into a broader context. Of those
responsible for teaching religion in British schools, more than half
have no qualification whatever in the subject; the TES survey in
autumn 1989 indicated over 68 per cent – not very different from a
DES/BCC report twenty years earlier.[11] A broad theological scholarship is as remote from most of the committed rank and file as
computer technology. In both, the future depends on it. After the
remarks from Durham, which recalled comparable remarks from
Woolwich in 1963, several clergymen resigned their orders.

Fourth, *populism*. Since the late 1950s British Christianity, increasingly cognisant of profound social change and the re-examination
of traditional cultural values and the fact that the churches are in
decline, has sought both popularity and intelligibility. To many, the
spectre of thousands assembling to hear the American evangelist
Billy Graham was impressive, positive and productive – or so it
seemed to many churchmen whose optimism had been shaken by
the failure of so much post-war missionary endeavour. In the 1960s,
Mrs Whitehouse raised evangelical alarm at the public exposure of
private behaviour on Hugh Greene's BBC. She rallied the churches
to proclaim the gospel of certainty and simplicity and the evangelicals and fundamentalists were happy to co-operate with Catholics
in the Nationwide Festival of Light. Cliff Richard was the star then,
and his picture appeared in London's underground stations pro-
claiming the virtues of the 'plain truth' for the World Wide Church
of God. In the 1970s, grave dissatisfaction with dull services, staid
leadership and with cold churches among large numbers of British
Christians led to the cultivation of a more enthusiastic and youth-
oriented upbeat Christian life-style. In the run-up to the 1980s, the
Church of England laboured with intermittent agonies to give birth
to an alternative service book which would capture the rising generation either unmoved by or unfamiliar with the use of the Book of
Common Prayer.[12] The charismatic movement in the House Church
movement of late has managed to cross both cultural and class
boundaries and appeal to those who have had little connection with
formal and traditional Christian life-styles. It is positive, optimistic
and a reminder of nineteenth-century American sectarian Protestantism. Biblical text is inerrant and axiomatic for all issues of life and
death. To make matters more complex, the charismatic style operates
successfully both in new sectarian break-away communities as well
as among Anglicans, Nonconformists and Roman Catholics.

Thus, *four features of concern*: the commercial threat to the BBC;
deregulated cable and satellite technology; the mainstream church
decline; and the increasing coalition among evangelicals, both Protestant and Roman Catholic, in pursuit of certainty.[13] The electronic

church and commercial religion are being exported; Christianity will be packaged as entertainment for all classes with a superficial and inelegant sophistication that will fill some British churchmen with despair and others with hope. In the 1970s we did it here with 'Stars on Sunday' for ten years with audiences of 11 to 15 millions. Religion, like other features of British culture, will increasingly reflect the cruder elements of American television. Professor Neil Postman of New York University believes that American television simply 'serves a nation of consumers rather than citizens and delivers them to the advertisers'.[14] That's the idea – citizens or consumers: the polarity between these two concepts is seen as a serious threat to Christian citizenship, democratic culture and European liberal traditions, particularly when religion is no less commercial than candy.[15] Not surprisingly, the architects of British broadcasting philosophy at its 1960 high watermark saw commerce as a real danger to PSB.

Public Service Broadcasting has 'the duty' said the Pilkington Report, 'of providing a service of broadcasting, and the responsibility for what is broadcast is vested in public corporations – the BBC and the ITA – since the purposes and effects of broadcasting are such that the duty and responsibility should not be left to the ordinary processes of commerce'.[16] The BBC's endeavour was defined as 'one which will use the medium with an acute awareness of its power to influence values and moral standards; will respect the public right to choose from amongst the widest possible range of subject matter, purposefully treated; it will watch for and be ready to try the new and the unusual'. Satellite technology, American commercial religion and a public thirst for secure identities may threaten these objectives as never before, and the Christian religion may parade as wolf in sheep's clothing, cosy outside but longing to bite hard into the succulent gullibility of vulnerable mass audiences clinging tight to conservative values, religious and otherwise, and surrounded at home by familiar cherished trinkets.

Public Service Broadcasting and Religion

There are five features: establishment, independence, protection, conservation and competition.

In a 1931 *Punch* cartoon, a smart lady interviewed her prospective maid: 'Are you a member of the Church of England?' she asked. 'Well, Ma'am, father went to chapel, but personally I'm wireless.' From the beginning, British broadcasting was committed exclusively to the Christian faith, not the least because the first Director-General, John Reith, was himself a son of a Presbyterian manse with a fearsome father who was once Moderator of the Church of Scotland.

Reith respected the authority of his own ecclesial hierarchs but particularly liked Anglicans because of their connection with the Crown: that was the real Establishment!

Reith also admired the breed of military chaplains he had seen only a few years before in the trenches; some of them had never seen the common man dead or alive before! In 1919 the church leadership had got the surviving chaplains together and asked just how religion had appealed to the common soldier. Not much, they said, and it was the mainstream churches and, notably, some eminent Anglican bishops who were courageous enough to admit that rigid ecclesiastic structures were 'no longer adequate for the necessities of our spiritual life'.[17]

First, the mainstream *establishment*. Reith believed that broadcasting could get true religion – the sort he had seen on Flanders' fields – over to the common people in an intelligible and straightforward style; his Christianity was masculine and just as much about Christian nationhood as Christian manhood. He took advice from Lambeth Palace and created a Religious Advisory Committee – the first such authority outside the BBC. It was set up to organize Sunday preachers. Thus, from the start, the BBC was committed to serving the mainstream churches among whom the Church of England naturally had the lion's share of the increasing time allotted to religion. Reith's religious policy was also shaped by his impatience with the churches for not recognizing the importance of the new medium for religion and for a society becoming much less interested in Christianity.[18] In 1923, when the Duke of York was to marry Elizabeth Bowes Lyon – later King and Queen – Reith thought it would be beneficial to have the wedding broadcast. No, said the Chapter of Westminster Abbey, men may be listening in public houses with their hats on![19] He thought rightly or wrongly that much in what he called 'organized Christianity' was a barrier between the ordinary man and the Jesus of the gospel story.

Although serving the mainstream churches, Reith's BBC searched out the padre class up and down the country. The most famous was Dick Sheppard at St Martin's-in-the-Fields; he too was impatient with the churches. Sheppard believed that: 'a lack of interest in church affairs may be perfectly compatible with a sincere enthusiasm for Christianity. It is here that broadcasting has an opportunity which none of us yet recognizes.'[20] It was not very long before both the church press and leadership complained about 'BBC religion': 'I'm wireless!'

Sooner or later Reith ran out of padres and anyway the rank-and-file clergy were demanding their right to a turn at the microphone. The BBC had to find a man who knew this business to run a religious broadcasting department with its own staff, budget and facilities and to see that the denominations had their fair share and that fringe groups like Christian Scientists, Jehovah's Witnesses and other American imports were kept out – not to mention Unitarians and the MRA and, of course, dull preachers! Public revenue from the licence money was thus committed to the mainstream churches in general who naturally symbolized the notion of a Christian Britain; and naturally the Church of England in particular.

Secondly, *independence*. As is well known, Reith's BBC – then and now – has jealously guarded its freedom. In the 1926 General Strike Churchill and Reith fell out over radio access to the nation when there were no newspapers. Reith said no to any political propaganda and to government exploitation of the air-waves. Likewise with religion: the BBC would be advised but the mainstream churches had no executive control. The BBC's constant endeavour was to reflect the life of the churches and to encourage Christian commitment. But it also wanted to educate both believer and unbeliever alike in the rudiments and, indeed, the complexities of Christian belief, theology, ecclesiology and creed: to challenge as well as to comfort. It maintained this aim more or less intact until 1977 (when the Annan Committee decided that both authorities now had a commitment to religions other than Christianity).[21] Radio was the supreme instrument of literary enfranchisement.

In its religious output, the BBC imposed a discreet ecumenism and forbade any one denomination to attack another. Protestants could criticize the Catholics in the press, but not on the air: conversely, when a Roman priest prayed for the conversion of England, he was seriously ticked off. There were constraints upon the exposure of some controversial religious issues and upon the dullness of so much preaching Sunday by Sunday. Although Roman Catholics most particularly complained at this 'secular' authority interfering with the broadcast utterance, the BBC maintained its control over who was invited to the microphone and to some extent what was said, especially from the studios (as against straight church services where priest or minister had more freedom).

At no time was this control more authoritative than during the Second World War. In Germany after 1933 Goebbels gradually tightened his hold on broadcasting and brought the German rank and file into submission.[22] In Britain, broadcasting was under the watchful eye of government through the Ministry of Information at Senate House. Every word was censored, including sermons, and most of the talk was naturally of supporting the war effort.

But not, however, if you were a pacifist as were many notable clergy, not the least Donald, later Lord, Soper.[23] He, with others, was soon banned from broadcasting: they suffered from what the Board of Governors defined as a 'civil disability' and were not to use their privileged position to undermine the war effort. Naturally the churches and others protested. The Glasgow Orpheus Choir was also dropped because its conductor was a pacifist. Vaughan Williams withheld a symphony from the BBC in protest and Winston Churchill was consequently asked in the House if being a pacifist made a musician play flat. He replied that the distinction was not worth making – his endeavour was that he should play up! The ban on pacifists was not lifted until 1945.

Third, *protection*. The BBC and several church leaders maintained that, like pacifism, other controversial issues were capable of conflicting conclusions. William Temple, Archbishop of Canterbury, said loudly that when he spoke on political matters, he did so as an educated citizen. That he was archbishop added no necessary wisdom to his political or theoretical analysis.[24] Others, moreover, said that because the BBC was a public utility its business was to uphold the basic doctrines of the Christian churches, and that the Christian faith should not be subject to attack by humanists or scientists or even radical churchmen. We were, after all, a Christian country.

After the war, Director-General William Haley (later editor of *The Times*) committed the BBC to 'the search for truth' and, in a Christian country, to Christian moral values. But it was *not* the business of the BBC in *all* its output to promote or even defend the Christian faith.[25] That was rather the task of the religion department. Moreover, with myriad voices clamouring for a hearing in the post-war years, the BBC was naturally obliged to initiate more rapport between belief and unbelief – between established creed and new movements in theological, philosophical and religious thinking. Such open-ended endeavour was embedded in the soil of public service broadcasting. It was to prepare the ground for the later debate which exploded on the publication in 1963 of John Robinson's (then the Bishop of Woolwich) *Honest to God*. It was an explosion indeed: fuming churchmen lobbied both broadcasting authorities to ensure the affirmation of religious certainties and to prevent the authorization and aggrandisement of the doubters.

In that year, 1963, the National Viewers and Listeners Association and Mary Whitehouse began the campaign against the BBC's Sir Hugh Greene. The BBC, she said, then and now had a duty not only to search for the truth, certainly, but in so doing must at least maintain both Christian moral values and the essence of the Christian message as proclaimed by the mainstream churches. In 1984, Don Cupitt's 'Sea of Faith' series had a similar effect to *Honest to God* – simple faith had to be affirmed, said Mrs Whitehouse. Most viewers could not grasp these complexities anyway, but if the BBC insisted on the series, then it had a duty to screen an alternative view and refute Cupitt's agnosticism. She cried for balance as the BBC had always done, and the BBC took the unbalanced view that programme content simply could not always be balanced.

Thus, for fifty years or more, Christian utterance on the air has run the gauntlet of the clergy on the ground who have always resisted the implications of the broadcast exposure of the techniques of theological and religious method. The rank and file were readily patronized by an academically robust clerical middle-management which kept the faithful well away from the philosophical and hermeneutic revolutions about which Cupitt and many others were so positive. For many, the broadcasters committed a sin because they authorized doubt just when the churches, in their palpable decline in secular society, so patently needed certainty and simplicity.

What was said against William Temple in the 1940s, was also said against Mervyn Stockwood in the 1950s, John Robinson in the 1960s; in the 1970s, they talked of God Incarnate being myth; in the 1980s, the Bishop of Durham talked similarly of the Virgin Birth. In private among consenting adults you may speak of convictions; on television, however, be sure they will be seen as opinions!

Fourth, *conservatism*. Mary Whitehouse and plenty of churchmen said again and again that since broadcasting was about the sensational and readily understandable, attempts to refine public conviction by theological documentary and investigative, journalistic television could have only negative results. Religious producers at the BBC – from the beginning, all clergy – and those few churchmen attracted by the idea of enfranchising the rank and file, predictably did not agree.

Their opponents insisted that broadcasting should affirm and do it simply. Repetition, certainty and directness were the hallmarks of the best programmes. The professionals had heard this somewhere before from another world-famous broadcaster: 'Only he will achieve results in influencing public opinion who is able to reduce problems to the simplest terms and who has the courage to keep forever repeating them in this simplified form despite the objections of intellectuals.' This was said not by Billy Graham, although he said exactly this in Manchester in 1988; it was Joseph Goebbels in 1942.[26] Once the Second World War had begun, the BBC, much to the irritation of some in its own ranks, was forced to give the public more of what it wanted rather than what it believed was good for it. If it had to be popular, it naturally had to be simple; and religion too. This was fine for some but not for others.

By 1948, the BBC had stratified the audiences into Home, Light and Third. The Corporation did well but Radios Luxembourg and Normandie had caught the popular ear; then as now the BBC was forced to compete. Otherwise, why should we pay the licence fee, people asked, and why should Parliament make it a crime not to?

Goebbels was right: intellectuals, i.e. theologians – mostly dons (there were not too many amid the rank and file) – only made life complicated for those who, in their daily routines, would never meet one anyway, not even among the clergy. They were best shunted on to the Third Programme to which the rank and file, including church people, by and large do not listen. The Central Religious Advisory Committee which the BBC met twice a year did not much like trouble on the Third either! They need not have worried: in 1967, for example, half the population tuned into 'Five to Ten' – 'A Story, a Hymn and a Prayer' as they called it – a daily service for the Light Programme listener. Choral Evensong was on the Third with an audience of 100,000. One in every two for something simple; one in every 1,500 for something sublime! In between, church services, talks, documentaries about religious life and belief, together with so-called religious 'current affairs', all clamoured for a slice of prime time if they were lucky. All clung to the regular spots associated with the times of church-going: evensong and epilogues. Because of these two profile-times in the daily ecclesial discipline, religion was either in the Sunday 'God-slot' or shunted to the very late evening. Now, with all-night television, the epilogue is more or less Breakfast TV!

The religious broadcasters, at some times more than others to be sure, have consistently tried hard to educate their constituency – notwithstanding the wrangles over who exactly that comprises – towards a more intelligent grasp of religious faith and its origins. Broadcast religion must be popular said the constituency and its leaders for fear of censure by the planners on the one hand and from the church advisers on the other. The BBC in its wisdom, from the beginning had called upon the churches to provide advice and was not really surprised when they tried very hard indeed to dictate policy. This went back to 1922 when Reith himself asked the mainstream church establishment to advise on preachers for the Sunday-evening concert interval. Eventually, he had his own opinions.

Other churchmen saw broadcast religion quaintly as the 'hand-maid of the churches' – an evangelical endeavour preparatory to their local endeavours. When this harmony seemed out of tune, the producers responsible for religion in the two authorities believed their task to be educative and even pastoral. Some wanted to be rid of the protected times for religious television on Sundays to let religion float in the schedules and take its chance with the rest. Others said that it had to be protected or there simply would not be the finance.

Since the mid-1970s, 'Everyman' and 'Heart of the Matter' in prime Sunday time have set themselves to investigate the beliefs, passions and values that shape our society against the background of the Christian repository.[27] In even better prime time, 'Songs of Praise' appeals to millions through hymns and biography. The erstwhile LWT 'Credo' series gave time to the Bishop of Durham before the York Minster fire. Harry Secombe's 'Highway' is rather more down-market and reaches those parts of the audience that the others do not.

Finally, *competition*. In the 1950s, there was widespread disquiet and indignation over the BBC's monopoly, with cries for more choice; competition was the key to a better public service; a species of marketing ideology would in the end, they said, make for better programmes. Opponents asked if that simply meant that more people were watching. For forty years, competition has animated the two authorities in the UK as well as the churches themselves eager for a place in the schedules and for the programme funding to go with it.[28]

The Independent Broadcasting Authority (now the ITC) was a little more ready to do the churches' bidding as ITV was desperate to be acceptable to the Establishment. Moreover, the independent companies decided from the beginning that they would not use clerics; they might come as advisers but it was the increasingly self-conscious professional television producers who would make the programmes, governed first by the craft of television production in the service of good programmes rather than unashamed propaganda – the political term for preaching.[29] Everyone knew that the statutory 'Party Political Programme', then as now, was not taken seriously but perhaps propaganda or preaching might make good television. Both authorities were battling for audiences and the importance of the 'hand-over' factor on Sunday evenings remains crucially important. Churchmen tend not to mind this combative element; after all, must the task of religious broadcasting be to reach the greatest number, almost at any cost? ask the producers, and the churchmen tend to say, Yes. Most realize that the audience cannot switch off only metaphorically, but literally.

Drawing these five features of British broadcast religion together, namely, establishment independence, protection, conservatism and competition, it is clear that practice has favoured the mainstream religious bodies. Consensus Christianity has been protected provided that the utterance is popular and that churchmen take due notice of the importance of the ratings. The broadcasters have fought to take the initiative and not to be dictated to by their advisers whom, latterly, they wished they could have done without; the Controllers feared the public furore and letters from Lambeth Palace. Between the Corporation and the independent companies there remains the most vigorous and diverting competition. Every so often, one side or the other falls from grace: the BBC with Don Cupitt, and ITV with David Jenkins. Others would say that the BBC never fell so far as did Yorkshire Television with its decade of 'Stars on Sunday'. Observers thought it was the nearest thing to the style of 'commercial religion' in America, rather brash but without the cash. 'Stars on Sunday' attracted huge audiences which enjoyed all the razzmatazz of a star-studded show-biz television programme. It was adored and hated; and the nearest thing to the 'electronic church' in the USA, to which we now turn.

'Bartered Brides': the Electronic Church

I borrow the title from Alistair Cooke: 'the inconceivable has happened', he wrote in 1959, 'the mismating of the salesman and the artist; an alliance [has occurred] which suggests that American television may not be entertainment at all. It has been ruinous to all free experiment in the arts, to free discussion and to the display of American scholarship and American learning. All have been sold to the highest bidder; cash is the criterion.' Cooke had obviously spent far too long in his native land where the BBC looked so innocent that money would not melt in its mouth.

In Britain, a broadcasting élite gave the public what it thought was good for it; but in America it had to be democratic, as the *New York Times* once noted: 'it is the first culture available to everybody and entirely governed by what the people want. The most terrifying thing is what people *do* want.' Not the least, game shows, as British audiences have discovered since the 1950s. This is not the place to search for nobility in the character of American television. Our concern is that species of remarkable entertainers drawn from the ranks of congregational, participant Christianity whose churches have become studios where the alchemy of television has turned liturgy into entertainment; consolation into solicitation – for Bakker and Swaggart – solicitation into litigation! They are the erstwhile Elmer Gantrys no longer campaigning under canvas but now sweating under studio lighting fighting for their audiences, their incomes and their integrities. They still have a good deal of all three, in spite of a broadside last year from the Moody Institute in Chicago accusing every one of them of distorting that vibrating concept of original sin so beloved of evangelicals.[30]

From the mainstream churches, William Fore and Neil Postman of the National Council of Churches in New York's Riverside Drive are the most outspoken critics of television's one-man healing preacher shows: 'Televangelists have bought popularity at the expense of integrity. The whole weight of Christian history, thought and teaching stands diametrically opposed to the media and its values.' It is a peculiarly American observation. But the top ten evangelists are still exposed to some 40 per cent of the American people although Hadden and Swann, the leading American analysts, say that it is simply not possible to be precise about how many people are watching religious television. The audience probably is somewhere between 13 and 25 million: a recent study held that it could be about 8 per cent of the total viewing population.[31]

Televangelists spend astronomical amounts of money – perhaps up to 2,000 million dollars – buying time on some 1,200 local television stations for syndicated programmes designed to entertain, entice and embalm substantial audiences with a larding of popular religious imagery and the aesthetics of a soft-soap operetta. The electronic preachers exploit, with all the flair of a millionaire pied-piper, a deep-bosomed yearning for personal religion, the pioneering spirit and the security of traditional American values authorized by traditional American Christianity. Above all, they neither speculate nor argue. Televangelists do not discuss, they disclose; they do not educate, they enjoin; they do not explore, they excite. They also rise and fall as we have seen: Bakker has a lifetime in prison before him. But there are always others to take their place. In Britain we see only the few; there are many others.[32] Meanwhile, all the resources and television know-how of modern marketing are employed on a staggering scale in order to convince the rank and file that complexities can be simplified and that political ideologies can be fused, honed and packed for mass consumption, disguised as a species of biblical Christianity.

The televangelists have an elegant pedigree: Elmer Gantry is fiction; not so Aimée Semple McPherson, Billy Graham and before him Billy Sunday, forever in combat with the liberal theologians of his day; they were 'hog-jowled, weasel-eyed, sponge-columned, jelly-spined, pussyfooting Charlotte-russed Christians'.[33] Dwight L. Moody, it was said, 'made the business of revivals, business-like'.[34] Looking at the televangelists against a broader background of American television, there are three mutually focusing perspectives which display co-ordinates between our two cultures: first, centrality; second, funding; and third, personality. Or more neatly, control, cash and charisma.

First, *centrality*. Broadcast religion was already nation-wide in America in the 1920s; there was frequency space. There was so much space that no one feared being elbowed out by another. Thus today in Denver, Colorado, there are fourteen radio stations devoted wholly to religion. Diversity, locality and federation are key-words. In Britain, by contrast, the BBC soon had the technology to speak to the whole nation and London thus held control over the whole output. The history of British broadcasting, among other things, is a battle of the regions. There has always been a tension between the centre and those identifiable areas marked by existing regional characteristics including language, landscape and even diet![35] Thus the mainstream churches were more or less brought to heel by the London-based BBC executive.

In post-war America, the mainstream churches began their decline at the very time when – as here – the leadership sought greater intelligence, competence and insight in the rank and file, particularly as the same leadership, mainly the clergy, saw increasing signs of secularization and a growing gulf between the worlds of academic theological exploration and the local worshipping communities. The heresy trials of Charles Augustus Briggs[36] at Union Theological Seminary which reverberated across the nation at the turn of the century illustrate this tension.[37] Since the First World War, the churches have seemed reticent about having their flocks exposed to contemporary theological debates and, as in the UK, increasing numbers became more and more disenchanted with the seemingly unbending traditions.

Television as we all know developed rapidly after the Second World War, and the American 'revivalist tent campaigner' looked to the air-waves; television was, however, very expensive. Opinions in post-war Britain as television started up again regarded it as of little consequence for religion; after all, television was designed for entertainment. Religion, however, would be entertaining soon enough. Then the god-father of television evangelism came to London and churchmen heard about reaching the masses. Many thought with Goebbels that Billy Graham was right: repetition and simplicity would restore the congregations as once they thought religion in broadcasting would 're-Christianize the nation' as one priest put it. Billy Graham was a deal better than all these South Bank theologians called in by the BBC to air their doubts in public.

In America, the mainstream churches for their part developed a notable track record. The Federal Communications Commission in Washington decreed that there should be religion, and the major networks carried programmes made not only by themselves but also by the mainstream churches with impressive albeit modest technical facilities.[38] The Roman Catholic Fulton Sheen in the 1950s commanded huge audiences for his acclaimed religious programmes which were both intelligent and popular. While he was head and shoulders above the rest, there was a clear commitment by individual networks and stations to fund and produce good religious programmes, and they still do. The mainstream churches, however, are no match for the televangelists.

The problem was control: it became increasingly difficult for the FCC to legislate the policies of the increasing number of local stations financed by sponsorship, and they were less and less able to remain committed to the idea of public service broadcasting. In the 1960s it all changed. The Federal Communications Commission skewed the whole pattern of religious utterance on television which had a serious knock-on effect upon the rest of the English-speaking world. The reason is straightforward: the FCC decided in principle that the public interest could just as well be served in the religious field by those who broadcast free as by those who bought time for their broadcasts from the station or networks. Television moguls thus found it more profitable to air religious programmes that paid them money rather than programmes which cost them money to make as well as transmit.[39] It was as simple as that.

In Britain, as we have seen, the 1962 Pilkington Report had said a very firm no to any such endeavour and, of course, it had the weight of law. In the USA control over the indulgences of the electronic fundamentalist-cum-evangelical preacher is now not held in any such manner and is finally subject only to the market, by which we mean the audience. Jerry Falwell, once the focus of the Moral Majority, reached some 34 million homes and endorsed Ronald Reagan's policies on South Africa, homosexuals, abortion, etc. The televangelists were free on television to venture firmly into party politics. They brought together previously diffuse elements in American culture under a flag of star-studded fundamentalism and national identity. Television reinforced the status quo from the secure broadcasting base in which – unlike the UK – there were no public service watchdog boards of governors such as the BBC has still; and since 1 January 1991 the Independent Television Commission, with rather fewer teeth than its predecessor, the IBA.

Television in America, on the other hand, has for a generation promoted consumer attitudes towards social issues and human relationships. Religion must above all be private. Robert Bellah at Berkeley has put it neatly: 'Privatization is the story of American religion.'[40] Harvey Cox too: 'Americans don't want their churches; they want their gods.'[41] Bellah believes that the crisis of authority in the American churches lies in their preoccupation with social adaptation and their theological inertia: the young are not animated by internecine squabbles among clerics who represent strong sectarian or sectional interests. This was the case in Britain too: Reith and those he employed, then and later, thought that broadcasting was free to reach the unchurched and those parts of society to which mainstream clerics could not preach. In America after the 1966 FCC decision, television was the way to do it.

It is no surprise, therefore, that the mainstream churches have not been able to cope with the competition of the more vigorous forms of radical individualism now compelled by television. Claims of dramatic self-realization and a go-getting conservatism spell out clear and simple answers and advice in an increasingly bewildering world to the untutored and unsuspecting rank and file. Depressing world-wide realities are brought to their hearthrugs by sophisticated news-gathering technologies: no wonder there is an audience desperate for the safe hideaway.[42] Televangelists bring assurances of renewal and an escape with God – all free of charge, more or less. Never mind that they undock people from their communities. William Fore thinks this the most serious flaw.[43]

In effect, the televangelists are not under anyone's control – neither the mainstream churches nor the federal broadcasting authorities. In the UK, the churches always tried to keep some control and to be firmly represented in the councils. Both authorities resisted this – and they remain vigilant still. As in the 1990 drama over politics in 'Thought for the Day', the BBC made very clear that it could well justify its editorial decision over the script of an eminent, respected, albeit socialist, churchman who resigned his place in the BBC's 'Thought for the Day' team.[44] Canon Eric James could not, with Robert Schuller of the Crystal Cathedral, croon his favourite argument that he was 'doing it my way'.

Almost without restraint, television increasingly dictates patterns in religious fundamentalist and evangelical utterance-styles: the televangelists have become the affirmers, and the mainstream churches the mavericks. They have long since parted company and nothing will bring them together. For the televangelists, quite rightly in a commercial television environment, the ends justify the means and they stop at almost nothing in their television 'missions', just at the time when the mainstream churches loudly affirm that television itself, and all that it betokens, should actually be the target of that mission.[45] Moreover, public broadcasting is shaped in the commercial mould and increasingly must find more and yet more money so as to compete with any degree of success. The televangelist prodigal has the cash and he's on his way.

Second, *finance*. He who pays the piper calls the tune; it is a precise figure that highlights the differences between our two broadcasting ideologies. In Britain there are always those who watch only ITV and ask why they should pay the licence fee. In the late 1950s, this was even more the case as commercial (or independent) television began. There is here a certain fiscal and consumer logic: why should I pay for something provided but not required? It must all be paid for, and the BBC, as it anticipates the renewal of the Charter in 1996, is worried about the funding of its commitment to a broad range of programmes in tune with definitions of public service: it must do darts and Bruce Forsyth as well as Wagner's Ring Cycle and 'Timewatch' – although usually not nowadays for the same audience. Reith had hopes that the nation could rise from the pit of light entertainment to the pinnacle of erudition, but Hugh Greene changed all that. Perhaps, they keep saying, the BBC should advertise or even consider sponsorship. Co-production is a much cleaner word.

In the late 1970s it began in earnest and was well established by the mid-1980s with the dramas of C. S. Lewis, the 'Everyman' series, together with hugely expensive documentary series in the tradition of Ronald Eyre's 'The Long Search', looking at world religions, Bamber Gascoigne's 'The Christians', 'The Sea of Faith' – a stab at philosophy by Don Cupitt – and John Romer's Channel Four 'Testament'. Moreover, 'Heart of the Matter' now alternates with 'Everyman', not on the edges of the schedules but in prime time. Who pays? The BBC and the licence fee contributor; if he does not pay, he commits a crime.

The astonishing feature of the electronic church is the willingness of the audience to pay for a service for which they are cleverly encouraged to feel directly responsible. Recent research has located the supporters of the televangelists as being mostly middle-aged and upwards; they are women with less education than most and committed to conservative political affiliations. Moreover, the more politically conservative the preacher, the more they are likely to attract the menfolk, especially those dissatisfied with what they see as the collapse of moral standards. They are ready to support simple solutions which fundamentalist religion offers in all its diversity from Pentecostal to Baptist. The most frequent on-air refrain is simple: 'By supporting this mission, God will bless you. Without your gift, it may not be possible to bring this message to those who need it most.'[46]

It is ingeniously simple: audience solicitation is allowed in the USA but not in Britain. Televangelists have enormous expenses for universities, hospitals, leisure parks and complete broadcasting networks. Computer technology is the means by which it is all achieved. Rex Humbard, Jerry Falwell and Pat Robertson are just three who need to spend up to a third of their income on fund-raising and at least 10 per cent of their air-time on making their appeals. Robert Schuller in the Crystal Cathedral gives away trinkets, and Falwell enlists his Prayer Partners who in other contexts would be called shareholders. Junk mail is in the air. Jim Bakker raised something akin to 100 million dollars to fund his personal alternative to Disneyland. Oral Roberts and the rest simply must raise money in huge quantities to pay the bills for the high-tech communications facilities and the life-style to which they have become accustomed. The *New Yorker* astutely observed that they need to match their corporeal media empires with an equivalent presence in space; they tend to build 'symbolic representations' of their theology in expensive architectural styles: artless, unrestrained and lavish depending upon the income and their aesthetic sense – if they have any. Robert Schuller's Crystal Cathedral – ten years ago, the largest glass structure in the world – cost a mere 12 million pounds.[47]

Pat Robertson's '700 Club' outruns the lot: he has some 3 million subscribers and the high-tech means to keep tabs on them all in order to sustain the contributions. His Christian Broadcasting Network (CBN) not only buys time but comprises a whole network making not only religious programmes but television entertainment for the whole family for the whole day, including news and comment. Its charity operations spread faith, fundamentalism and foods. The computer helps the rank and file to feel hugged and participant. It encourages them above all to pay and to pay again.

A standard computerized so-called 'personal letter' from Pat Robertson has the names of the donors in four places and it speaks of Pat Robertson's missionary work in Latin America and Africa 'both struggling with poverty and the sinister forces of Marxism'.[48] His organization can handle some 20,000 pieces of mail per day following a particular broadcast appeal. The greatest scandal of all this to the mainstream churches is clearly the vast sums of money elicited from audiences affected by the specious propaganda drawn from the repository of religious language and imagery about changing the world in general and America in particular: 'The Lord is getting ready to change America,' says Pat Robertson, 'I have found a remarkable spirit of unity in the Body of Christ about America's future under God.' In fact the American body ecclesial is as diverse as ever. Whatever else, the mainstream churches are certain that the cause of Christian, even religious, truth is not served by what they call the 'commercial' preachers.[49] The trouble is that they simply do not have the money to compete and, moreover, have never demeaned themselves to ask for it over the air; it is an option forbidden by an amalgam of Protestant theology, public service and good taste. The televangelists have little of all three. The fundamentalist poetry is beguiling: 'God blesses those who succeed and we can help you do just that.' It is the litany of positive thinking; or as Douglas Kennedy in his 1989 excursion around the Bible belt called it 're-invention'. Conversion is a logical need in a rootless society.

The solicitation of funds is, of course, neither immoral nor criminal; in broadcasting terms it is simply distasteful and the consequence of giving the public what it wants. Democracy, said Clement Attlee, depends upon the voice of the people, but succeeds only when you stop them talking. Soliciting the audience for money is enormously effective and only to those outside these money-spinning galaxies does it offend all the canons of the broadcaster committed to serving the public before himself. We have seen how excess has led the weaker ones astray: Bakker and Swaggart knew the truth of it. Huge sums of money perhaps have created extravagance not only in life-style but in the abuse of religious tradition, language and consolation. The healing of sickness is the most obvious and the televangelists are not the only ones to lead people astray. The restoration of the ailing self and the revitalizing of the nation's morals are signals which open up all manner of pockets.

Robert Schuller's television budget, for example, is 37 million dollars; he is in business to promote hyper-optimism with revenues from such books as he has time to have his speech-writers produce. In 1985 he published a re-write of the Beatitudes under the title *The Be-Happy Attitudes.*[50] 'Blessed are those that mourn, for they shall be comforted' is now, 'I'm really hurting – but I'm going to bounce back.' He is the cultural descendant of Norman Vincent Peale whose *Power of Positive Thinking* sold millions in the 1950s: 'The core of sin', said Peale, 'is a lack of self-esteem.' Schuller is happy to sell you a replica of the glass segments which make up the cathedral with your name inscribed. Pat Robertson opened his new multi-million broadcasting HQ in Virginia and suggested to viewers that for 100 dollars they could send in their 'Seven Lifetime Prayer Requests' which would be microfilmed and interred in a pillar inside the Prayer Chapel. They would be 'surrounded by prayer twenty-four hours a day until Jesus came back.'[51] For 120 dollars, your name could go inside the altar itself!

Such endeavours are totally alien to broadcasting traditions in Britain. Serving charitable causes in pre-Telethon days, the BBC, in 1924, mounted and refined an 'appeals' policy which originally sprang from the urge of grateful listeners to church services to put something in the plate. The Appeals Advisory Committee then as now deliberates from the centre over who is eligible to use the airwaves to raise money for good causes. The BBC decides – as indeed, it always did. As in America, the best talkers tend to elicit the best response, all the more if they are well-known figures in the media galaxy themselves. Jimmy Savile was knighted by television. But then so was Huw Wheldon, both for contrasting good causes![52]

Which idea leads thirdly to *charisma and personality*. Whatever the exaggerations of the televangelists and their value to vast audiences, and however absurd their claims to be in the vanguard of moral renewal or at one with all Christians world-wide, these men are the stagecraft masters of entertainment. They have their ears to the ground, where most of their audience are at home and for whom the elevated, poetic language at the heart of serious religion designed to console and inspire remains unintelligible. However preposterous their aesthetic television pageantry, razzmatazz and kitsch, men such as Roberts, Falwell and the erstwhile Swaggart and his successors front their operations and can change with the fashions. Faith, hope and love may abide but that's all: we must ever be up-front with new styles lest we become yesterday's men like the heroes of 'Dynasty' or 'Dallas'. They front their operations like comic field-marshals and if they fail, it all fails. However, the ideology always has an answer: Forgiveness. One of Kennedy's characters believes that 'guys like Bakker and Swaggert are, at heart good men with the right intentions thwarted by a satanic attack which ravaged such godly men'.

The commercial preachers need high cash-flows to generate and sustain the interest of an audience which has the ability to concentrate for not much more than three minutes. They must create charisma as artificially as television creates illusion – above all, it must be recognizable by the bulk of the audience and its religious perceptions. Steve Bruce rightly notes that it is unlikely that ideas conveyed by these evangelists are 'drastically at variance with the notions and practices in other parts of the typical viewer's religious world'.[53] These are beautiful people, especially to the lower income respondents, who aspire to the glamour of nouveau riche preachers who themselves came from a similar, modest social stratum. They might once have preached against the excesses and the sins of leisure, but now embody high fashions to undergird the theology of positive thinking, self-approbation, achievement and reward: give to this cause and God will give to yours. And never mind the sins of leisure because televised preaching sanctifies an essentially leisure-time pursuit. In Britain some worried about this from the start. Broadcast religion makes demands only upon the concentration – unless it is entertaining; then it can raise money in huge quantities as we have seen. Showbiz Christianity is a success; in the churches, it is another story – in America as in Europe.

The televangelists hog the religious limelight and the common view of religion is increasingly defined by these entrepreneurs. Louis Palau from Oregon, who once came to convert London, is quoted in *Time* Magazine: 'When you talk about Jesus in America, they immediately think you want their name and zip code.'[54] However false the impression of a true relationship that millions get from the personalized letters from the sleek administrative machines, these men command attention with their use of dynamic language and discreetly coercive television artefacts. The whole operation exists to sustain the ego of the evangelist who remains free to pursue his angels and demons – as we have seen with Bakker and Swaggart.[55]

The televangelists do little for the local churches; they do little for theology, moral philosophy or church history. They talk about God as their friend and about their private calling. They talk of what Jesus wants from you and me. They recite the traditional moral jargon and about good and evil behaviour; they fashion traditional values like potters at their wheels. Worldliness has now lost its intrinsic harm.

In Britain, broadcast religion always resisted the grooming of personalities; why else do we robe our priests? Surely, to sustain a theology of anonymous mediation. Television, unlike the altar rail, cultivates personality and then scrutinizes it very carefully. The charismatic movement in the UK throws up not only hands but personalities. Broadcasting focuses upon heroes and heretics alike. A remarkable chunk of the British audience now recognizes the

Bishop of Durham whose theology on television brought down the fires of heaven upon York Minster (now happily repaired). People actually believed it! The theologically unfranchised were led by their instincts to make superstitious connections from which the clergy might have protected them.[56]

Nevertheless, substantial sectors of the British church-going population remain dissatisfied with broadcast religion in the UK simply because it is prosaic, egg-head and dull, except for high audience-rating dramas and popular hymn-singing programmes. Why not have some real entertainment? After all, Jesus was a lively human being, was he not? This is television and not the local church, they rightly say. British evangelical believers – as in the USA – are as much in search of something successful and positive; an affirmative Christian faith and vibrant, popular liturgical aesthetics. In the UK they tend not to find it in the broadcast output. Evangelicals are irked because they have been more or less excluded from policy-making. The programmes here tend to be balanced and all colours of the British ecclesial mainstream have been shown. This will all slowly change with deregulation, and evangelicals in touch with substantial monies will perhaps now have their day, but the divide will remain: they will speak to the converted; or as seen by their opponents, the blind will lead the blind. Hence the worship styles of combative charismatic simplicity, on one side, and radical politics and theological exploration, on the other side – both in the name of the historical Jesus still regarded as faithfully 'reported' in the four canonical Gospels. Modern translations of the Bible endeavour to put the record even straighter. In American television religion, biblical criticism as ever is Public Enemy No. 1 and has no place in the evangelical positivism of the prime-time preachers; and, oddly enough, little it seems in the mainstream churches.[57]

Robert Runcie has rightly observed that if the US experience is repeated here, the mainstream churches will lose the balanced diet of public service broadcasting so long cherished for its comprehensiveness.[58] In the USA, comprehensiveness has for some time been the objective of the televangelists: to create their own networks as Pat Robertson has done most successfully. His '700 Club' provides religion atomized in entertainment, current affairs (i.e. republican politics) 'Wagon Train' and 'The Flying Nun'; more of the old-time religion and less sex and violence – all designed to alleviate the guilty feelings that come with positive thinking and social mobility among the bulk of the less privileged audience.[59] Dr. Cerullo will probably do the same.

This wholesome diversion is funded on a monumental scale and at the apex stand the charismatic and beautifully-groomed megastars of commercial religion each competing for his share of the old-time-religion market and waging a sort of friendly holy war on others in the field. When the finances drop, it took an audacious Oral Roberts to raise money by claiming that unless he received 8 million dollars for his university, hospital and the rest of his empire, the Lord would take him home. Money came from the owner of a dog-track.[60] Such men are purveyors of belief without belonging, healing without wholeness, success without achievement. They are the most eloquent, televised alchemists who combine the trivial and artless with the language of attenuated religion just enough to convince an untutored mass audience long since disenchanted with its priests but beguiled by pedlars.

It all changed in the 1950s. Billy Graham was deeply irked that he could not buy time from the BBC! Today satellite opportunities, as we all know, make the equation more complex. The market for religious television is hardly less cut-throat than the personalities from the USA who might provide the inspiration and the funding not only at home but among those odd conservative British (as one Ernest Aingley put it as he contemplated the expansion of his markets) 'ready for the simple gospel', whatever its source.[61] Dr. Cerullo on his wall-to-wall satellite religion network may prove him right.

T. S. Eliot in his 'Notes Towards the Definition of a Christian Culture' lamented that 'no security against cultural deterioration is offered by any of the three chief types of religious organisation: the international church with a central government, the national church and thirdly, the separated sect'. As Haddon and Swann, and later observers, have shown, the televangelists in the USA have undermined all three and now taken the cultural high ground and somewhat saturated their markets.[62] Whether they will do the same in Britain is a question still not easily answered. But we have no ground to be culturally high-minded: for ten years, 'Stars on Sunday' thrived. A keen mainstream churchman may harbour a lurking preoccupation with numbers, especially as the baptism figures drop.

From the outset of broadcasting in Britain, there was substantial pressure on the BBC and later on the independent companies from clergy who believed that the recital of Christian belief through broadcasting could re-establish Christendom as never before. No matter how drastic the attenuation of religious utterance for popular consumption, if it was said simply and often enough, popular faith was sure one way or another to be seeded. The broadcasting élite – drawn mostly from maverick churchmen – was not so sure and their controllers were absolutely certain. This was not public service broadcasting: it must be made intelligible to a general audience. Broadcasting was about audiences, they said, not congregations!

In America, Tom Lehrer in the introduction to his cheeky 'Vatican Rag' thought that the liturgical changes following Vatican II were an endeavour to 'make the church more commercial'. He was right:

ten years later, the electronic church was a force to be reckoned with politically, culturally and ecclesially. The Moral Majority banded together in an alliance between Protestant fundamentalists of various kinds to do battle in the name of a home-spun DIY gospel against Freud, Marx and sociologists.

Ecclesially, it is a force against theological renewal and biblical scholarship; culturally, it streamlined its efforts to lead the masses by their emotions up a short garden path to eventual disillusionment – and leave them to find their own way back. The television and computer technology gathers its responses, however tenuous and superficial, from good people prepared to pay for the televangelists' special entertainment; it produces 'participants' in millions. They give people simply what they want and they give it simply. The BBC said from the start that they never would. The televangelists reject ecclesial mainstream authority and exploit Holy Writ with consummate skill and thus put the clock back in their appeal to the vulnerable, the lonely, the chronically ill and the vast successful majority amenable to the sacralization of the American dream machine.

In Britain, sectarian energies are more than ever questioning the authority of the mainstream leadership, and many observe that forty years of ecumenical endeavour has not come to much nor has exposure to new theological movements done much for the rank and file. Against this background, the adaptable and market-oriented organizations of the electronic preachers may well find the untutored and unprepared in British mainstream Christianity an attractive target. Bryan Wilson has illuminated this question, remarking that the UK, like the rest of Europe, has provided 'the most congenial climate for American sects'.[63]

Whatever the resistance here to high-tech or hard-sell religion, there is little doubt that the prime-time preachers will detect the philistine shadows cast by the growing shapes of British evangelical, charismatic and anti-mainstream activity, not to mention the accompanying political conservatism. British broadcasting has fought hard and long against evangelicals or anyone else having control in their own interests. It fought against gross over-simplification; and, indeed, developed new national channels both in radio and television to go deeper. American television went into the shallows: the televangelists provide what the BBC always feared: an attractive, well-packaged alternative experience of public religion not to be found in their local churches. How could they? It was a fundamentally different product. Elements in contemporary British Christianity, however, now seem bent on a comparable product which will raise morale, pay the bills, and even appeal to those outside to whom all comes by way of cathode tubing.

This growing energy becomes increasingly impatient with the

religious output provided for two generations in a public service ambience by the two UK authorities. Religious broadcasting, it laments, teeters on the edges of the schedules to cater only for a fringe audience. The electronic preachers, they note, reach huge audiences with the gospel. Let them come here. Indeed, Sky has brought the first – from California.

But their package will not embrace the minority endeavour of historical religion sweating it out still between belief and ideology; between scientific method and religious truth; between an instant, cliché-theology and one which takes centuries to cultivate. It is so much easier to side-step history and suspend the intelligence. For millions across the Atlantic, Jesus is always ready for the taking, and fits neatly into imagery of the television commercial – no longer for enchantment in the sacred ritual but entertainment in a secular routine.

We have green and pleasant lands with a fertile mixture of artless religion, theological illiteracy and high television audiences all thriving in the British cultural soil. Seeds wafted across the Atlantic, therefore, could take root and bear a rich fruit which is sure to be harvested. While the combined expenditure of the BBC and independent system is larger than any other commercial operation in the world, satellite reception and de-regulated transmission may nevertheless feed and water such seedlings. There are now 7 million satellite dishes and this figure is rising rapidly. There is moreover, a rich mulch around our popular religious broadcasting traditions which might well encourage a remarkable growth which may not be stopped.

Chapter 12

Some Recent Developments in Seventh-day Adventism

D. S. Porter

Despite having a world membership of around 7 million and one of
the largest foreign mission programmes – particularly in the realm
of medical care – of any Protestant denomination, the Seventh-day
Adventist (SdA) Church is much less well known than some other
religious movements of comparable size. This ignorance was well
illustrated a few years ago in the celebrated Dingo-Baby case in
Australia, which of all the 'developed' countries has the highest
ratio of Adventists to population. Morning after morning, Australi-
ans reading their daily papers over their bowls of breakfast cereals
(as likely as not to have been manufactured by Adventists, who run
the largest cereal-producing company in that country) were induced
to believe that the religionists responsible for that harmless, even
perhaps beneficial, product regularly cut the throats of their infants
in acts of ritual sacrifice in secluded desert places.

The reality is mercifully a good deal more prosaic. SdAism was
one of several movements to emerge from the Millerite revival in
the north-east of the United States in the 1830s and 1840s. Its earliest
adherents had survived the so-called Great Disappointment when
Christ did not return, as the Millerites had predicted, in 1844 and
were later to take over seventh-day observance under the influence
of Seventh-day Baptists. In 1863 the SdA church was formally organized. It is trinitarian and not fundamentalist in the strict sense of
the word as it does not espouse verbal inspiration. Its thelogy is
mortalist, but neither this nor its sabbatarianism makes it unique.

Two beliefs do, however, set it apart from all other Christian
churches. One is the doctrine of the Investigative Judgement; the
other is what the more conservative Adventists term 'the Spirit of
Prophecy'. The latter, in connection with Sabbath observance, is
thought by official Adventism to mark out the movement as 'the
Remnant Church', with a special role to play in last-day events.
Significantly, in our present context, it is these two beliefs that have
come under particular scrutiny in the last decade or so.

The doctrine of the Investigative Judgement is said to have originated in a special revelation to one of the disappointed Millerites

in 1844. It teaches that God began a work of looking into the records of all who have ever lived on the very day (22 October 1844) when the Millerites had expected the Second Advent (thus fulfilling the prophecies on which they had based their hopes, but in a different way) and that when that work is completed Christ will return. Connecting this with the ancient sanctuary ritual of the Israelites, Adventists teach that Christ, as High Priest, was in the 'first apartment' of the heavenly sanctuary until 1844, when he moved into the 'second' (corresponding to the holy of holies in the wilderness sanctuary) to begin the investigation. No other Christian body accepts this doctrine, and, as we shall see, it has been much questioned within the SdA Church itself.

By the 'Spirit of Prophecy' conservative Adventists mean a special gift bestowed upon Ellen Gould Harmon (1827–1915), later Mrs James White, manifesting itself first in waking visions and later in dreams, by which she was enabled to substantiate SdA doctrines (the movement is careful to point out that these had already been formulated as a result of study of the Bible), and later guide the Church into its extensive publishing, medical, educational and overseas missionary work.

Until the 1950s these beliefs were enough to cause SdAism to be considered a non-Christian cult. Then, in that decade, an American researcher, Walter Martin, who had already written books on other cults, turned his attention to SdAs. He did what most others who had written about SdAs had not done: he went to the headquarters of the denomination to find out for himself what its beliefs were. The result of his inquiries were two books. One, written by Martin himself, was entitled *The Truth about Seventh-day Adventism* (1959). In it he expressed his opinion that the SdAs were truly Christian and evangelical although with some aberrations. The two which he considered most serious were the Investigative Judgement and the acceptance of an alternative source of inspiration in the writings of Mrs White. The other book was compiled by those Adventists with whom Martin had had his series of discussions; it was called *Questions on Doctrine* (1957) and, as its title suggests, consists of the questions asked by Martin and the detailed answers, with sources, given by the Adventists he met with. This is easily the most 'liberal' or 'evangelical' (the terms in the Adventist – unlike the Anglican – context are virtually synonymous) statement of SdA belief ever published and a good many conservatives were unhappy with it.

From 1966, when Robert H. Pierson was elected President of the General Conference (in other words, world leader of the SdA Church), there was a gradual, although unacknowledged, retreat from the position taken in the book, back towards something more akin to what had characterized Adventism in its early days: a stress upon imparted, rather than imputed, righteousness, veiled suggestions that possibly works have some part to play in salvation, leading to perfectionism and exemplarism, together with a once-for-all justification and an emphasis upon sanctification. Along with this went a greater assertion of the role of Mrs White (who, ironically, might have been shocked by some of the current doctrinal emphases), culminating in the publication of a multi-volume biography (some said hagiography) of her by her grandson, Arthur White.

Indeed, except during the late 1950s and early 1960s honeymoon with Martin and his evangelical backers, Mrs White had never been far from the top of the Adventist agenda since the early years of the twentieth century. When one reads the history of Adventism in the nineteenth century one is forced to the conclusion that her position then was rather different from what it later became. She was respected and usually listened to, but by no means always agreed with, and indeed on some occasions not listened to at all. There was even a period in the 1860s when her 'visions' ceased altogether because, she claimed, the Church was taking no notice of them. She and the elected leaders were often at loggerheads, most notably over the controversy about righteousness by faith which came to a head in 1888 when Mrs White took what today would be described as the more evangelical side. Her contemporaries knew that in the early days of the movement she participated in extremely 'charismatic' episodes, such as that at Atkinson, Maine, in February 1845, although she was later inclined to condemn such manifestations. They knew, too, that a lot of her writing was not original, because it was 'borrowed' (to use the current euphemism) from some of theirs, although they may not have been aware of the extent to which she borrowed from sources outside the movement.

Her position changed between 1902 and 1907. Those years witnessed what can only be described as a struggle for power in the denomination. On one side of this conflict was perhaps the best-known Adventist of his day, Dr John Harvey Kellogg, the head of the Battle Creek Sanitarium, the Church's largest medical facility. Kellogg, who had invented the breakfast cereal exploited by his brother, Will K. Kellogg, a direct outcome of the Adventist emphasis upon health reform, felt that the Church was not as serious about this so-called 'right arm of the message' as it should be, and also that the growing numbers of medical personnel in the movement were made more subordinate to the ministry than they ought to be. Mrs White, who had written a good deal on the subject of health reform, at first was inclined to favour Kellogg. Gradually, however, she was won over to the side of his antagonist, A. G. Daniells, President of the General Conference from 1902 to 1922.[1] Daniells was concerned to assert the supremacy of the General Conference over all branches of the work and viewed with suspicion the ambitions of Kellogg for the medical work. A great deal of what happened is clouded in mystery, but it seems clear that Daniells used W. W. Prescott, a minister close to Mrs White, and, even more, her younger son, W. C. White, whom Kellogg believed wrote at least some of the 'testimonies' sent to him under the name of Willie White's mother, to win the prophet to his side. In order to destroy Kellogg, Daniells created a belief in the infallibility of Mrs White's pronouncements. He achieved his object; Kellogg was driven out of the denomination, although he took the Battle Creek Sanitarium with him, a loss which changed for ever the arrangements for holding property in the denomination.

After Mrs White's death in 1915, Willie White lost all influence and it seems likely that Daniells deliberately isolated him. Prescott had already become disillusioned and in that same year had written to Willie complaining of the way in which the leadership allowed the members to entertain misconceptions about the way Mrs White's books had been written. In 1919, Daniells himself somewhat cynically disavowed the image of the prophet which he himself had done much to create. So powerful a hold had that image taken upon the denomination, however, that this disavowal was probably a key reason why in 1922, at the next General Conference session, Daniells was denied the re-election he so much wanted.

Its creator had gone, but his creation lived on, and, apart from the low-key treatment of Mrs White's position and authority in *Questions on Doctrine*, the Daniells-made concept of Mrs White held the field until the 1970s. An illustration of the power her words had over the thinking of many Adventists – and, indeed, still have for conservative members of the Church – was provided by the very case with which this chapter began. When the search for the missing child proved fruitless, Lindy Chamberlain, the mother of the baby in the Dingo-Baby case, was alleged to have said: 'It says angels will bear the little children back to their mothers' arms.' The 'it' in this case is not the Bible, but the writings of Mrs White.

In the early 1970s, a series of articles[2] began to appear in *Spectrum*, the journal of the Association of Adventist Forums, an academic organization in America, which demonstrated that in her treatment of certain historical subjects such as the French Revolution, Mrs White had copied extensively without acknowledgement from nineteenth-century Protestant historians. It emerged eventually that she had in fact copied from another Adventist author, Uriah Smith, who had copied from the historians. Then, towards the end of that decade, tapes began to circulate from one Walter Rea, a pastor in California. Rea had been what might be called an Ellen White fundamentalist, memorizing and publishing extensive extracts from her books. In the course of this work, he had begun to read others who had written on similar subjects. He claimed to have discovered not merely similarities between the treatment of identical subjects by Mrs White on the one hand and earlier writers (especially English clergymen) on the other, but in many cases identical or near-identical wording. A committee was set up by the General Conference to investigate Rea's allegations of widespread plagiarism in her writings, and its 1980 report spoke of 'alarming proportions'. Despite this, Rea was told to get back to his pastoring and the committee's proposals for further investigations were ignored. Rea, however, went on circulating his findings and before the end of 1980 he had been defrocked amid a blaze of newspaper publicity.

Only then was an investigation set on foot, and this concerned only a few chapters of one book. Its results, published in 1990,[3] went far to justify Rea's position, although it is doubtful if more will be heard of the matter. Long before that, in 1982, Rea had published his findings in book form under the title *The White Lie*.[4] As one reviewer said, there can have been few books in which style so completely overwhelmed content. The tapes on the whole had been soberly presented and factual: the book screamed. Over and over, clergy (not just Adventist clergy) were denounced as 'super salesmen of the psychic'; the early Adventists were in a conspiracy 'to steal the lot' (that is, to put out as Mrs White's inspired writings wholesale plagiarisms); their successors were 'magicians', 'conning the innocent' and interested only in extracting their money; 'there are', according to Rea, 'few, if any, saints in religion'. Even the liberal Adventist journal *Spectrum* could find nothing good to say of the book, but Rea was unrepentant, accusing his reviewers of 'bleeding on the rug because of the style'. Not only is the book appallingly badly written, but also part of it is completely irrelevant to its subject, because during its gestation a financial scandal had erupted in the Church in the United States and Rea was anxious to assert his part in uncovering it.

There is great need for a really scholarly book about Mrs White, but it is difficult to see how such can ever come into being. The White Estate controls her manuscripts; no non-Adventist scholar is likely to be allowed access, except perhaps under conditions that would be refused by any academic historian. One Adventist layman has produced a book on one aspect of Ellen White's work – health reform – without access to the papers. Ronald Numbers' *Prophetess of Health* (New York, 1976) showed that, far from being an innovator in the field of health, Mrs White had taken ideas (mostly good, it should be said) from medical reformers of her day. The wrath that that had called down from the White Estate was not likely to encourage other laity to do likewise.

There remain Adventist church workers. One such, indeed, has tried, and paid the penalty. In 1983, Ronald Graybill, an employee of the White Estate, submitted a thesis for the degree of PhD to Johns Hopkins University, Baltimore. It was entitled 'The Power of

Prophecy: Ellen G. White and the Women Religious Founders of the Nineteenth Century'. He dealt with three other woman founders, but it is hard to see why they were included, unless to sugar the pill, as his treatment of them owed nothing to original sources. The case with his treatment of Ellen White was far different. Being employed where he was he had had the run of the archives. He had not, however, requested 'clearance', that is, had not submitted to censorship. Had he done so it is difficult to believe that the thesis would ever have seen the light of day, for the picture that emerges of the prophet is very different from that of Adventist tradition and much more credible. There is, for example, a good deal in the thesis about Ellen White's own home life (domestic relations being something she wrote much about). In this context it is not perhaps her poor relations with her husband and older son, Edson, that are important, but the proof that Graybill advances that by the 1890s Willie White was controlling what went to his mother and what supposedly emanated from her, just as Kellogg had complained. Graybill also demonstrates that up to the 1860s 'walking visions' were very much a part of American Protestantism and by no means unique to Mrs White. He shows, too, that early Adventists accepted other visionaries, whom later they denounced. Graybill had requested that the company which microfilms most American doctoral theses and markets the films should not make his available. However, when the editor of *Adventist Currents*, a journal further to the 'left' than *Spectrum*, requested a copy, the company sold him one. In a short time copies were circulating widely. Shortly after this the *Adventist Review* carried a Soviet-style confession of guilt by Graybill, together with the news that he had been reassigned to other work. It is unlikely that the archives will ever be made so freely available again.

One interesting passage in Graybill's work is that in which he showed how Mrs White, contrary to her usual practice, intervened in a doctrinal dispute when, in 1905, one A. A. Ballenger challenged the doctrine of the Investigative Judgement. She asserted its correctness on the basis of her own revelations. Coincidentally, beginning in 1979 that doctrine had once again been called into question and in a much more public and widespread way, thanks to modern communications technology, than Ballenger or any of the several others who had challenged it had been able to do. Two years before that, an Australian Anglican, Geoffrey Paxton, had published a book (derived from a thesis) called *The Shaking of Adventism*.[5] Paxton's book was an investigation of the treatment of the doctrine of righteousness by faith in the SdA Church throughout its history, with special reference to the movement's oft-repeated claim to be the rightful heir of the Protestant reformers on this subject. Paxton, in short, did not think highly of that claim, but there was one

Adventist, who, in his view, was reasonably near the truth on the matter. This was Dr Desmond Ford, an Australian who had studied at Manchester under F. F. Bruce. Paxton had a lot to say about Ford's battles with the perfectionists in the Church in his native country in the 1970s. However, as the Church at large under Pierson from 1966 onwards silently drifted back towards perfectionism, legalism, sanctification as part of righteousness by faith, a belief in Christ having had a sinful human nature, and the positions of *Questions on Doctrine* had been discarded and even – privately – denounced, Ford's opponents began to get the upper hand and were even preparing to bring heresy charges against him. Ford was therefore transferred from the Adventist college in Australia, where he had taught large numbers of those now in the ministry there, to Pacific Union College in California. There on 27 October 1979 he gave what came to be viewed as perhaps the most famous address in SdA history. In this he questioned the doctrine of the Investigative Judgement as contrary to the teaching of the Epistle to the Hebrews. He declared that judgement took place at the cross, and that, far from waiting in some outer chamber of the heavenly sanctuary until 1844, Christ on his ascension had gone straight into the presence of the Father. Ford's rejection of the Investigative Judgement followed naturally from his view of righteousness by faith, which, he felt, must have assurance as a vital element: the doctrine of the Investigative Judgement gave no assurance.

Ford was given a leave of absence, taken to Washington, DC, where the General Conference was situated, given secretarial help and six months in which to expound his views on paper. He made good use of the opportunity and the end-product was over 900 pages long. By far the most interesting part was that in which Ford tried to reconcile his rejection of the Investigative Judgement with Mrs White's acceptance of it. Thus, once again, the battlefield in recent Adventist history was the authority of Mrs White. Eventually, in August 1980, 114 Adventist administrators and scholars assembled at Glacier View, Colorado to deliberate on the issues. This was said not to be a trial of Ford (indeed, at first he was not even going to be invited), and the majority of the scholars drew up two documents (on the Investigative Judgement and the position of the Ellen White writings in the Church) which Ford claimed he could have signed with a clear conscience. The administrators, however, drew up a third document, called the 'Ten Point Critique', apparently after most of the scholars had left. This Ford refused to sign and the following month he was defrocked. Ford is on record as saying that he believes that his stress on the primacy of justification in righteousness by faith was the real reason for his unpopularity with the leadership, which could not, however, expel him on that alone. That may be part of the truth, but it seems certain that it was the incompatibility of his views with those of the prophet that sealed his fate. Conservative Adventists were soon finding clues in recent events to the identity of the mysterious 'Omega of apostasy' spoken of by Ellen White when she denounced Kellogg as the 'Alpha' of the same. Ford's dismissal was followed by large numbers of secessions or sackings of ministers, who were believed to share his views, 200 of them in Australia alone.

It might be thought that the administration of the Church had, in these events, proved itself conservative enough, but not so for some. Since 1980 various organizations have sprung up, called in the official Adventist press 'independent ministries', with the avowed aim of calling Adventism back to the 'pillars of the faith'. Perhaps the most influential of these is that known as Hope for Today, or the Firm Foundation, after the title of its widely-circulated journal. As well as its publishing ventures, which include reprints of Mrs White books, it runs a college to train missionaries to the SdA Church. The adherents of that church are to be called out of 'apostasy' or the 'new theology' back into the 'truth', for the official Church seems to supporters of these ministries to have become, or to be in danger of becoming, part of 'Babylon'. This writer does not know how many adherents the Firm Foundation and similar movements have (the fact that, unless expelled, its supporters tend to retain their membership of the official Church, presumably on the ground that their mission can better be accomplished thus, makes it difficult to ascertain how many there are), but, judging from the frequency of official warnings against them, there is probably a fair number. In 1989, it was even thought worthwhile to send the editor of the *Adventist Review* to Britain to sound the warning in view of increasing numbers in this country.

As the 1980s came to an end, along with the growth of ultra-conservatism in doctrine, the administration had another developing problem with which to contend, and, indeed, a development which may in the long run foster even more conservatism. In the corridors of SdA power in its heartland, the USA, the talk is now less of doctrinal deviance, worrying though that is, than of Third World dominance. The Americans, who have hitherto ruled the Church and who still provide something like 90 per cent of its finance, see their position being challenged. The last two General Conference sessions (1985 and 1990) have seen considerable increases in the number of Third World appointees to the governing bodies of the Church, not only in the world at large but in the General Conference also. Indeed, at the 1990 session a West Indian might have been elected General Conference President had he been willing to stand, and, as it was, the eventual appointment went to an American who had spent a large part of his working life in Latin America. So fearful have some North Americans become of a General Conference dominated by non-Americans that considerable impetus has been given to the movement to divorce the North American Division (the SdA Church world-wide is divided into twelve divisions), and, by implication, its money, from the uniquely close relationship that it has had hitherto with the General Conference.

In this context what has happened to the Adventist Church in Britain over the last thirty years or so has special relevance, for during that period the Third World has come to dominate the movement. What may happen to the Adventist Church world-wide tomorrow happened to its British branch yesterday. Some figures may help to set the scene. In 1953, the membership of the SdA Church in the British Isles (which includes the tiny membership in the Irish Republic) was 7,257. From 1889 on the average annual membership increase had been about 100. In 1990, the membership stood at 17,609, an average annual increase since 1953 of 280. Where had this comparatively large increase come from? The answer is: immigration from the West Indies. Today it is acknowledged that the membership of the Adventist Church in Britain is 80 per cent black, the white membership having fallen in numbers to where it was in the early 1920s. The impact has been greatest in the larger cities, for that is where most Adventist evangelism had been carried on before and after the Second World War and where later the majority of immigrants settled. In London, for example, in 1953 there were 1,215 members, almost certainly all white; today there are 6,612 members in London, and although the denomination no longer publishes ethnic statistics, it may be confidently asserted that no more than 100 are indigenous. In an ideal world without prejudice or national or cultural differences, or even in a denomination not primarily evangelistically-orientated as the Adventists are, these statistics would have little relevance. However, as the Adventists believe that they have a mission to present their distinctive doctrines to everyone who will listen, what these figures mean is that a population overwhelmingly white (the 1991 Census figures are not yet available, but conservative estimates put the indigenous population at at least 95 per cent, with half or more of the remainder Indian or Pakistani, not West Indian) has to be evangelized in Adventist terms by a Church membership 80 per cent black, with a different culture and style of worship.

The reasons for, and course of, the immigration of large numbers of West Indians into Britain in the later 1950s and early 1960s are well known, as is the fact that although many were Christians when they left their homelands, the pressures upon them in the new environment and the differences they found in churches in Britain from those with the same names 'back home', caused a large-scale abandonment of church-going.[6] What is less well known is that, by and large, the Adventist immigrants proved an exception to this rule. This is highly creditable to the West Indian Adventists, for, observing the Sabbath from sunset on Friday – very early in the winter – to sunset on Saturday, it was probably more difficult for them to obtain employment than it was for Sunday-observing Christians. Perhaps, however, the Adventists were better equipped spiritually to withstand the prevailing atmosphere of irreligion in Britain. They had been taught to regard themselves as part of a 'remnant' in an apostate world and to expect persecution in the 'last days' considerably more severe than either unemployment or the sneers of workmates when they whistled hymns at work or read the Bible in the tea-break. Moreover, while it is likely that the Adventists, like their erstwhile fellow Christians, found their Church in Britain rather different, especially in style of worship, from what it was in their home islands, there was one aspect which was completely familiar – doctrine.

The SdA Church has always stressed the importance of correct beliefs in contrast to many other Christian bodies which emphasize certain ritual observances while allowing considerable latitude in belief. One of the major institutions for ensuring uniformity of belief in the Adventist Church is the Sabbath School (for adults as well as children) which meets immediately before the main worship service on Saturday morning. In all Sabbath Schools all over the world the same passages of scripture are studied at the same time each week. Thus the immigrant found the same Sabbath School lessons being taught in Manchester, England, as in Manchester, Jamaica. In this connection it is interesting that Rex and Moore found that in the south Birmingham area which they investigated in the middle 1960s, only the Adventists and the Jehovah's Witnesses had large immigrant memberships (60 per cent and 30 per cent respectively).[7] On this they commented that both of these are movements in which 'a sense of the rightness of their beliefs binds people together'. In this context it is probably true that not many of the old-established white Adventists have been lost through the influx of black believers, although as they have died they have certainly not been replaced, for reasons which, of course, it is impossible to determine.

Given the comparatively large numbers of Adventists in the West Indies (it has been estimated that out of about 260,000 Christians in Jamaica in the early 1950s, some 40,000 were Adventists, second in number only to Roman Catholics and easily the fastest-growing denomination) and a greater propensity to retain their faith during the migration than was evinced by other Christians, it may easily be imagined that their impact upon the existing SdA Church in Britain was considerable. Clifford Hill gives a figure of 2,563 West Indians attending church in London in the early 1960s in the six denominations he investigated.[8] As the West Indian population of Britain was reckoned at that time to be around two-and-a-half times that of London, the six denominations may have had an immigrant attendance of about 7,000 or so. Hill does not mention Seventh-day Adventists, but a little later than his investigation 1,843 West Indians were attending church in the South England Conference alone (almost all in London), so a total figure for the whole country of about 3,000 may not be wide of the mark by very much. One does not know how many West Indians were in other churches, but, apart from the Jehovah's Witnesses, there were probably few, as the growth of autonomous West Indian sects had not yet begun. Allowing for some distortion, it is probably safe to say that in the early 1960s one in four West Indians in Britain who wished to engage in Christian worship passed by the imposing edifices of the Anglican, Methodist, Baptist and other churches and sought out the usually humble – and often rented – meeting-places of the small SdA denomination. Not without reason, therefore, did Roswith Gerloff call the Adventist Church in Britain 'the only functioning multi-racial community in a well-established body'.[9]

The early immigrants received a warm welcome from the British Adventists. Adventism has always had a large overseas mission programme, and every week in the Sabbath School mission news is read and an offering taken up which is devoted exclusively to financing that programme. To the British Adventist, who had probably never seen a black man in his life, here was evidence of the effectiveness of missions. Writers of the 1960s commented favourably on the attitude of the host Adventists. Malcolm Calley wrote: 'Seventh-day Adventist congregations strive to make the stranger, whether white or coloured, feel at home and the welcome they extend goes far beyond the conventional clerical handshake at the door.'[10] Sheila Patterson in her *Dark Strangers* refers to 'the warm welcome extended to newcomers not only by the pastor but by members of the congregation'.[11] In 1965, one of the earliest Adventist immigrants to Britain from the West Indies, Hymers Wilson of the Holloway church, testified to the welcome he had received in a national television programme about Adventists called 'The Saturday People'. This point is worth stressing because later a myth was to grow up to the effect that Black Adventists in Britain had experienced rejection and prejudice from their arrival. Calley and Patterson also refer to the fact that in most British Adventist churches where they settled the West Indians were soon inducted into church office, something which helped to lessen the feeling of rejection by society at large.

The progress of the black membership towards majority status is not easy to trace, as at first no ethnic statistics were kept; then, when they were, they were kept in different ways in the various organizations which comprise the SdA Church in Britain, and counts were made at different times. In 1970, the percentage of black members to white in the South England Conference was given officially as fifty-three to forty-seven. In 1972, a census of attendance (a more reliable indicator than membership, as many 'members' are simply names on books) in the North British Conference recorded 1,528 black adults and 1,315 children as attending on one Sabbath compared with 1,330 white adults and 368 children. In 1973, a similar census in the South England Conference recorded a black attendance of 2,942 adults and 1,467 children, and 2,352 white adults and 841 children. Throughout the 1970s there was an average of two black baptisms to one white. Exactly when the black membership (and it is important to remember that black membership and black attendance were probably about the same whereas white membership was considerably larger than white attendance) overtook white has been a matter of some dispute,[12] but it had certainly happened by the end of the 1970s. Today, as we have seen, total membership approaches 18,000, and, unofficially, it is estimated that of these members about 80 per cent are black.

It may well be asked whether the increase in the black membership and the decline in the white are related. This is a question which it is impossible to answer with any certainty. On the one hand it can be argued that there has been a general decline in church-going in Britain since the Second World War and that Adventism has shared in this. Certainly there was only very small growth (and in some years no growth at all) in the post-war years. On this assumption, black immigration has saved the Adventist Church in Britain from possible extinction. On the other hand, it has been pointed out that in the 1940s the Adventist Church, then all white, may have been static but it was not declining; and that the Mormons (a body which to the general public may – although erroneously – seem more akin to the Adventists than, say, the Anglicans and other declining churches) have increased their membership in Britain very considerably during this period, for much of which they were a racially discriminatory body which attracted few blacks. It has also been suggested that the church-growth principle that like attracts like may be relevant, a statement that appears to receive some support from the fact that in a few places some white Adventists who found themselves in a church in which blacks had become a majority either migrated to another church where whites still predominated, or founded a new group themselves.

Little research has been done in this area. One SdA minister did survey the growth-rate in two all-white areas of the South England Conference for 1953–78 and found that it continued at the former national average of around 2 per cent per annum.[13] During this same period the white membership in London, also part of the South England Conference, declined by over 80 per cent. This may have nothing to do with the fact that in the former case there was no black immigration into the district while in London large numbers of black immigrants settled during that period, but it does indicate that the decline in London cannot be attributed only to a decline in interest in religion on the part of whites in Britain. Some writers on the subject claim a connection between black immigration and white decline. Rex and Moore say that in the Birmingham church they studied, West Indians 'have come to predominate in the organiz-ation and the English have become a minority group . . . We suspect that the beliefs of this sect and its predominant membership are so alien to the ordinary Englishman that it will not attract any more English members.'[14] An immigrant author, Dilip Hiro in his *Black British, White British*, details the large percentages of black members in several big-city Adventist churches and goes on to remark that 'one of the reasons for this was the white members' propensity to leave as West Indians joined in numbers'.[15] Among the immigrant Adventists themselves a connection has also been noticed. We shall return to an organization of black Adventist laity in London called the London Laymen's Forum, which played a significant role in events yet to be narrated, but suffice it to say here that in its journal *Comment*, Vol. 4, No. 1 (January 1977), one of its leaders, G. S. Escoffery, had this to say: 'The Adventist Church experienced a similar "impact of immigration", e.g. in the 1940s Holloway Church had over 300 members, 99 per cent of whom were indigenous. Today there are over 500 members, 99 per cent of whom are immigrants. This applies to dozens of other Churches around Britain; this is known as the "white flight".'

If there was, indeed, a connection between growth in black num-bers and diminution in white, one is led to ask why it was so hard to establish integrated churches in those places (largely the great cities) where by 1980 at the latest white congregations had largely given way to black. Undoubtedly racial prejudice played a part once the numbers of blacks had increased beyond the small group of 'black brothers from the mission-field' situation. To the present writer's knowledge, only one small piece of research has tried to probe beyond the blanket assertion of prejudice in the Adventist context.[16] The author, writing in 1968, speaks of the embarrassment caused to whites by the black image presented to the world at large by the Adventist churches in the larger cities (in this context it is interesting that the SdA church in Oxford, when its membership was only 25 per cent black, was known in its area as 'the Jamaican church'). The 1968 researcher also found that there were difficulties in communication between the races, even though both were sup-posed to speak the same language, and she quotes 'an experienced minister' as saying of churches with a preponderance of black mem-bers: 'In such a case, all outlook, planning and systems of work and worship become geared to the West Indian outlook and custom. Not unnaturally this becomes offensive to the more sensitive of English worshippers and they drop out from church attendance or move their membership to another church which conducts the type of service to which they are accustomed.' The writer also refers to 'the educational and cultural differences of the West Indians' *vis-à-vis* the English. They are, she says, 'quick and willing to render items which to British ears may lack polish, practice or suitability . . . Also their eagerness to hold office, although commendable, is often felt to be wrongly timed or misplaced.'

Clifford Hill, although not referring to Adventists, mentions another problem, from which the Adventist Church was by no means immune, and which tended to alienate white members. He says:

> Local English people are often shocked by differences in behaviour patterns that they observe between immigrants and themselves. They notice, for example, that West Indians have different attitudes towards marriage and consequently different sex mores. The absence of any attempt to hide what are considered deviant sex patterns has often been an affront to local white people . . . Local English people who have little or no knowledge of the West Indian background see the sex practices of these immigrants as deviant and potentially morally corrupting.[17]

To Adventists, with their rigid insistence upon observance of all Ten Commandments, this was a particular difficulty, and most white Adventist office-holders in local churches which contained numbers of black members can tell stories of stormy church board meetings which wrestled with this problem in the 1950s, '60s and '70s, and the accusations of prejudice against blacks which were occasioned by attempts 'to keep the church pure from moral defilement'. With time and greater integration the problem has diminished.

Whatever problems may have been posed for the existing white members, they were soon overshadowed by those perceived by the immigrants themselves. Although, as has been remarked already, there were sufficient similarities betwen the SdA Church in Britain and that in the West Indies for the immigrants to feel at home in a not unfamiliar environment, there were also differences which, with time, made themselves felt and led to discontent.

When the West Indians arrived there was room and to spare in the existing British churches. No need was felt to establish churches of their own. The ministers, of course, were white and it was upon their functions and their perception of them that dissatisfaction eventually began to develop. As Gerloff remarks: 'In Jamaica the pastor still serves as the real social worker.'[18] Most British ministers did not see themselves in a role which for many years they or their predecessors had not been called upon to perform for their compatriots, and even those few who did found the problems presented by the immigrants' situation intractable. Thus the newcomers, needing certain kinds of help in a strange land, turned to those whose position they felt qualified them to give it, but found them ill-equipped to do so. This is no criticism of either ministers or immigrants. The former were doing the job they had been trained to do and which their indigenous congregations expected them to do; the latter wanted something which their own ministers could give, in both pastoral care and style of worship, but none of their own ministers had come over with them.

Soon requests for black ministers to be brought over began to be heard and they grew louder as church after church in the cities became black, until in some cases only the minister was white. The answer given to such requests was always that the SdA Church in Britain could not afford to call black ministers. The reason given for this was that, under Adventist church policy, a minister called from an overseas country is entitled to regular furloughs there with all expenses paid and, if a higher salary is paid in the country from which he comes, the difference is invested for him to draw upon later. With hindsight it is easy to say that this was a mistake which was to have far-reaching consequences. It is possible that if black ministers had been placed in certain churches in the 1950s and early '60s, each community – black and white – would have gone where it found the style of worship to which it was accustomed and a *de facto* 'regional' system on American lines would have developed.[19] That course was not taken, and the penalties for not taking it became apparent as early as 1959 in an incident which was to become a sort of touchstone in racial relationships in the Adventist Church in Britain.

In 1953, the Adventists had purchased the lease of the former New Gallery cinema in Regent Street in the west end of London and had transformed it into a well-appointed evangelistic centre. This was a new departure in SdA thinking in Britain, where for long many churches had been located in obscure and often not very attractive suburban areas, frequently in halls rented from such bodies as the Oddfellows and the British Legion. The idea behind the New Gallery was that with a more intellectual approach to evangelism in pleasant surroundings the 'upper classes' of London might be induced to listen to Adventist preaching. Although the original plan was that converts made at the New Gallery should be fed into the existing London churches (it was hoped that they would survive the shock of the transfer from one set of premises to the other), a church meeting on Sabbaths had, in fact, been started there in addition to the public evangelistic activities. By 1959 large numbers of West Indian Adventists were attending both the Sabbath services and the Sunday evangelistic meetings. There is, of course, no way of determining whether this caused a decline in white attendance at the public meetings. There was such a decline, but it may have been coincidental. The important point, however, in this context is that the church administrators of the day believed that there was a connection and this belief governed their actions.

In 1959, a circular was sent to black members asking them not to frequent the New Gallery on Sundays. At the same time plans were set in motion to find an alternative home for the church which met there on Sabbaths (a redundant church at Chalk Farm was eventually purchased). Those actions have been looked upon as pieces of blatant racial discrimination, and in the later political agitation in the church they were cited extensively. It would perhaps be nearer the truth to say that it was a course of desperation which might never have been necessary had there been even a small corps of black ministers in London who could have handled the problem. A problem there undoubtedly was: the reading-room at the New Gallery, furnished rather luxuriously and equipped with Adventist literature to attract the general public was, for example, being used on Sabbaths as a place to eat sandwiches and attend to babies. There had also been complaints from the police about large numbers of people standing around and blocking the pavement after services. However, there was all the difference in the world between having the matter dealt with by a wholly white administration and what might have resulted from its being handled by black ministers, who would have been in a position to enforce a discipline which would have been accepted.

The New Gallery incident induced not only anger but also a feeling of powerlessness on the part of black members, and this was enhanced as at conference session after conference session (local conference sessions are held every three years, and Union sessions – for the whole of the British Isles – every five) they voiced requests for black ministers and even more insistently for schools for their children. In many parts of the world the SdA Church conducts an extensive school system (indeed, in the US it is said to have a system second only in extent to that of the Roman Catholics) where children may be taught in harmony with what Adventists consider biblical principles without the admixture of theories such as that of evolution. In Britain, the SdA Church had only a handful of schools, most of which were not located in places convenient for the majority of the immigrants. Nor was it easy to bring more into existence, given the comparative poverty of the British Church, the price of land and buildings, government regulations, and the shortage of trained Adventist teachers (it is noteworthy that when a highly successful black school was eventually started in North London, the debt incurred was enormous). The West Indians probably did not realize that white Adventists had been voicing those same demands for church schools – with equally barren results – for many years. What, however, the white laity had never done, the blacks began to do:

organize a pressure group. Thus began what Robin Theobald has called the 'politicization' of British Adventism.[20]

On 23 November 1973, a group of blacks in the London area founded the London Laymen's Forum, the stated aim of which was 'to encourage the progress of the Church in Great Britain'. This, according to the Forum, would be achieved by the appointment of coloured ministers 'because cultural differences make it difficult for many ministers to understand our coloured members'; by 'proportional representation on the executive committees of conferences and Union'; and by 'more expenditure in immigrant areas'. Other goals were 'a regional' (i.e. black) 'representative at the conference office'; 'coloured office staff'; and 'immigrant-orientated articles in church papers'.

In June 1974, the LLF began to publish a duplicated paper called *Comment*. The third issue of this (September/October 1974) carried a summary of a document recently sent by the Forum to the General Conference, the governing body of the world Church in Washington, DC. This commenced with the exclusion of blacks from the New Gallery and went on to make specific complaints of discrimination in the locating of public evangelistic campaigns, the small number of black ministers in Britain, the lack of black representation on various denominational committees, and the alleged encouragement by the church administrators of the 'hiving off of white members into strictly white enclaves', etc. It was further said that large numbers of black young people were leaving the Church because they were denied church school education and black leadership. The same issue of the paper contained the remark that 'our administrators must sit up soon and take notice of the stream of justifiable discontent in the mainly immigrant churches. They must not let it become a raging torrent which could tear apart the unity in our beloved Church.' (It should perhaps be remarked that the LLF was probably a minority of the black Adventists even in London, but it was a very vocal and well-organized minority.) At the very time when this article appeared, the President of the British Union, E. H. Foster, was in Washington with a detailed memorandum to the General Conference about the situation in Britain, what might be done to remedy it, and an appeal for funds to do it. With a fine sense of impartiality the General Conference turned a deaf ear to both Foster and the LLF.

At the 1975 session of the South England Conference held at Plymouth, a venue which gave rise to further suspicions of discrimination, the administration tried to appease the LLF by having two of its leaders put on the conference executive committee for the ensuing three years. Also, at this session, the Plans Committee (usually a harmless exercise to allow the laity to believe that they have some part in denominational decision-making) produced a resolution entitled 'Integration and Growth' and referred it to the incoming executive committee. What happened next is complicated and tedious to describe. Suffice it to say that the resolution was passed from body to body up the Adventist hierarchy. Along the way, the idea of a 'regional' conference on American lines was taken up. Eventually a study group was established to go into the feasibility of this in Britain, with special reference to the financial aspect. The biggest source of finance in the SdA Church is the tithe, which every member is supposed to pay (although many do not). The study group looked at the tithe income in South England, or rather it looked at the respective black and white membership figures and then jumped to the unjustified conclusion that payment of tithe was in the same proportion.[21] On this basis the group recommended that a black conference was feasible. It should be remarked that its idea of a 'regional' conference was a highly circumscribed one, including only nine churches currently in the South England Conference, with a total membership of well under 2,000 (97 per cent black), while leaving under the jurisdiction of the South England Conference nearly 6,000 members (42 per cent black and 58 per cent white). The study group suggested that the British Union should hold a referendum on the matter, although, strictly speaking, this should have been confined to the South England Conference. In October 1976, the church paper *Messenger* carried an article by E. H. Foster on the referendum and voting papers.

The January 1977 issue of *Comment* roundly condemned the referendum. It complained about 'the rejection of the Forum's suggestion for an Integrated London Conference and the Administration's imposition of a Referendum about Regional Conference'. The referendum was, apparently, a conspiracy by the administration: 'The leaders calculated that if the idea of Regional Conference is [*sic*] put to the membership in such a way that it appears to have been the request of a few black agitators and it is based on the principle of separation or segregation between blacks and whites, then the constituency is sure to object to such a Conference.' The same issue contained the text of a protest sent to the British Union by one of the LLF leaders, which, *inter alia*, questioned 'the right whereby the future of black British Seventh-day Adventists should be determined by the vote of the indigenous community'. Neither the Forum nor anyone else knew how the 'indigenous community' had voted, for the make-up of the vote has never been revealed. There is a belief that most of the whites who voted were in favour of a regional system, seeing it, perhaps, as the only hope of preserving a white SdA Church in Britain. If that was so, their votes were completely outweighed by what must have been a very large black vote against a regional conference (which showed, incidentally, how unrepresentative of most of the black members the Forum was), for the figures showed over 4,000 opposed and only 800 in favour. As far as the administration was concerned that was the end of the matter. The status quo would be maintained.

The Forum, however, had other ideas. In the issue last alluded to, it had given some hint of its intentions. In two separate articles it had said that it would refuse to accept a 'no' vote in the referendum and also that there was a 'powerful weapon' in the hands of black members to bring about a change. In its March/April 1977 issue, *Comment* again attacked the referendum and urged the case for a 'regional' conference which would offer 'a future in which blacks and whites can worship in harmony and work together for the good of the church', as against the 'present system' which was 'rife with injustices, unequal opportunities, racial discrimination and exploitation'. The 'powerful weapon', too, was being brought into the open with the statement that the study group had been doubtful whether the rest of the British Union could operate without the money that would have been hived off by a regional conference. An undated publication (probably late 1977 or early 1978) by the Forum entitled *Towards Regional Conference* was even more outspoken: 'Have our brethren suddenly learned to love us as equals?' it asked. 'Their refusal to share responsibility in the Church with us suggests, not love of us, but love of something we have which is necessary for their well-being.'

As early as June 1976 one of the LLF leaders, Michael Kellawan, had been interviewed by the *Observer* and in the resultant article on 27 June appeared the words: 'Most of the 23 churches in London, for example, are now predominantly black and there is resentment that their sacrificial tithe payments go into largely white hands . . . Mr. Kellawan is withholding his tithe and paying the money into a special bank account.' In 1977, three London churches withheld tithe completely and were estimated to have kept back some £18,000. This was only for the latter part of the year and did not take into account tithe withheld by individuals in other churches. Kellawan had done more than withhold tithe: he had demonstrated that the LLF could get a hearing in the national press for its grievances. Adventists have always set great store by having a favourable public image and this adverse publicity may well have played as great a part as the financial factor in inducing compromise.

The compromise (some disgruntled whites saw it as a sell-out to militancy) came into being on 8 March 1978. A high-level delegation from the General Conference, led by the President, Robert H. Pierson, together with officers of the Northern Europe–West Africa Division (the arm of the General Conference within whose jurisdiction Britain falls) and of the British Union stood before a gathering of London ministers and laity in – ironically – the New Gallery, to unveil peace proposals to end the 'tithe war'. Most of the laity present were black, simply because there were not many white laity left in the London Adventist churches. Those withholding tithe were allowed in but not allowed to speak. This included most of the LLF leaders, but it was obvious that they did not lack well-drilled spokesmen. Much of the day was spent in speech-making from which it became apparent that there was considerable – although by no means unanimous – support for a 'regional' conference on the part of the black London laity. It was equally apparent that the General Conference representatives would allow no such thing. The reason for this, although set forth publicly in spiritual terms, was rooted in the American situation. As we have seen, black conferences had been established there in the 1940s. For some time there had been considerable agitation to take the next step and organize those 'regional' conferences into 'regional' unions. The General Conference retort to this was that what was appropriate in the segregationist 1940s was no longer so in the integrationist 1970s. That argument would have been stultified had a new black conference been established in Britain in 1978–79. Thus, not only did the General Conference misread the situation in Britain by reading it in American terms, whereas the situation in the Church in the two countries was vastly different largely by reason of the fact that in the US blacks formed only a small minority of Adventists, but also, sadly, it was prepared to use the plight of the British Union as a sacrificial pawn in a larger game of denominational power politics.

Eventually the moment was judged right to unveil the plan which 'the brethren' had brought with them to the meeting. This came to be known as the 'Pierson Package', although, in fact, it had been drawn up in the Division office and Pierson was merely its mouthpiece. The 'Package', as subsequently printed in the *Messenger*, began with a series of quotations from Mrs White about the relations between Americans and Europeans taken out of context and made to apply to those between black and white.[22] It then went on to set forth a series of proposals for 'more meaningful racial representation' in the Church, ranging from black typists in offices to black officers and departmental directors in conferences and Union. All committees and boards were to have greater black representation. There were to be human relations workshops to teach the church members how to get on with one another, a black youth centre in London, better educational facilities for blacks and so on, all, apparently (and it turned out to be only apparent) to be financed by the General Conference. The meeting, although having no constitutional status, was urged to accept this (which it did) and to promote it back in the local churches. Then, at the ensuing conference sessions that year and at the Union session three years hence, the proposals would be voted and implemented in the respective territories.

Apparently the LLF decided to accept the 'Package' and drop its demand for a 'regional' conference. After all, as one of its leaders said at the ensuing South England Conference session, it was obviously a first step on the road to eventual black control of the conferences and Union, a goal which was fully achieved only thirteen years later. At the South England session there was opposition from a group which had thus far not been heard from in the controversy – the white laity. Some of them felt that the full implementation of the 'Package' proposals regarding black representation (which would inevitably be mostly lay) on committees would diminish, or even abolish altogether, the already small white lay representation. This was met by an amendment increasing the size of the conference executive committee. The white protesters also felt that to put straight into office blacks brought in from overseas with no experience of conditions in Britain would not be in the best interests of the Church. At an unofficial meeting with Division officers some of them believed that they had been told that blacks from overseas would serve first in pastoral roles for a while so that their suitability for office could be assessed.

On the last day of the session, the 'Package' was forced through under an arbitrarily-introduced rule limiting debate, with no motion moved and no adherence to the rules of parliamentary procedure. A secret ballot had been promised, but in the event those opposing the 'Package' were required not merely to raise their hands but to stand in their places. All in all the picture presented was one of panic on the part of the white administrators, with fear of adverse publicity (the LLF leaders had alerted the *Guardian*, which carried a major story the next day) prevailing over even elementary fair play. As to the supposed promise that no blacks should be brought into the country and put straight into administrative office, later that day one such, who knew nothing of Britain, was elected to the post of Conference Secretary, the second post in the organization. To emphasize the administration's determination that nothing should hinder the first step on the road to black control of the Church, those white lay people who had objected to certain aspects of the 'Package' were excluded from consideration for membership of the executive committee while LLF members were put on it. The second step on the road was taken in 1981 when the man elected as Secretary of the Conference was elevated to the position of President. That position has ever since been held by a black. In the smaller and poorer North British Conference (so named because until 1991 it included Scotland) the presidency has been allowed to remain in white hands, although, as we shall see, in 1990 it remained so only by courtesy of certain black members who objected to the manoeuvres engaged in to elect an unpopular black candidate.

It may be that those who presided over the adoption of the 'Pierson package' in 1978 at the two conference sessions believed that it would be a final solution to a vexing and long-drawn-out problem, and in so believing felt justified in forcing it through at all costs. If so, events have proved them wrong. Those blacks who had campaigned for a 'regional' conference, but had, in the 'Package', achieved something potentially more significant, were thereby encouraged to press ahead to all-out control. This might be thought to be only a matter of justice, given the large black majority in the Adventist Church in Britain. However, it should be remembered that the politically-minded black members were probably only a minority; many blacks were as non-political as the white laity had traditionally been and felt, as Theobald says, that politics were of 'the world' and should have no place in the church.[23] Such black members genuinely wish to see white people joining the Adventist Church and are disturbed by the massive decline in white membership. It is believed by some in the movement that such members would willingly sacrifice black power if it would aid the evangelization of the indigenous population: these, however, are not the people who are active and articulate at conference sessions. Also it should be borne in mind that the Adventist Church has never been, or claimed to be, a democratic movement in which the majority rules. It has always been described as having a 'representative' form of government, in which local churches select delegates to a local conference session, local conference executive committees select delegates to a Union session, and Unions select delegates to a General (World) Conference session. Critics have sometimes described this as a means of maintaining tight clerical control. Whether this was its deliberate aim or not, there is no doubt that this has been its effect. Of all the Protestant denominations the SdA Church is probably the one in which the laity have the least influence on government. Indeed, it was not until after the Second World War that any lay representatives were allowed on British Adventist committees. All large issues (such as the ordination of women – consistently rejected in the SdA Church) are determined by bodies and gatherings dominated by the clergy. It may be remarked in passing that as far as Britain was concerned, the triumph of the lay-led campaign for black power was unique.

Now that large numbers of black ministers are present in Britain, it has become comparatively easy to assert and maintain black control of the movement, provided that black ministers and laity maintain a united front and – since the façade of equal representation on some committees is maintained – can rely on the support of one or two strategically-placed complaisant whites. What happened at the North British Conference session in 1990 and the British Union Conference session in 1991 is instructive in different ways. At a local conference session, such as the North British, the delegates sent by the constituent churches choose some of their number in proportion to membership to serve on a recommendations committee. This, in turn, recommends delegates to serve on the standing committees of the session, the most important of which is the nominating committee which suggests to the whole session the names of individuals to fill the offices and executive committee of the territory for the ensuing three years. A majority of the whole delegation must endorse the recommendations for the standing committees, and the eventual nominations from the nominating committee.

Apparently, before the North British session of 1990, private caucuses were held which suggested to certain churches which of their delegates should be put on the recommendations committee.[24] These people, in turn, were pledged to recommend certain delegates for the nominating committee, and those delegates were committed to nominate a certain man for the presidency of the conference (up to then held by a white). At the session a nominating committee (with two-thirds black membership, the first time since the adoption of the 'Package' that there had not been equal representation of the races on such a committee) was selected and voted by the session.

Overnight, however, second thoughts began to prevail and on the next day disquiet was voiced by a leading black pastor, supported by several other delegates. The account in the church paper refers to 'caucus meetings . . . in advance of the session' and goes on to say that 'the only specific point' made by these objectors 'was that certain churches had received disproportionate representation on the nominating committee'. 'Nevertheless', it goes on, 'it was clear that there was much more to be said.' When the composition of the nominating committee was referred back to the recommendations committee, 'a number of pastors took the opportunity of presenting evidence' to that committee 'to substantiate the more general allegations made from the floor'. Subsequently a new nominating committee was formed and eventually the existing administration was re-elected.

The outcome of this particular piece of political manoeuvring may have been due in part to the less than universal popularity – even with his fellow blacks – of the man for whose benefit it was believed to have been organized. Given a popular candidate and minimal support from whites (it is believed one vote in this case), the result could be very different as was demonstrated the following year at the British Union session.[25] In that case, the incumbent white president had been in office for only fifteen months, serving out the unexpired term of his predecessor who had moved to another post. The nominating committee was equally divided between white and black, but it is perhaps not too difficult to find whites who feel that black administration is in the best interests, at least internally, of the Church. This had, in fact, been the case in 1981 when the black secretary of the South England Conference was nominated for the presidency. Exactly the same happened in 1991; the name of a black candidate for the presidency was put to the session by the nominating committee and quickly voted through by 205 votes to 163, with 'about 100' abstentions. For the first time in British Adventist history, a Union president able and willing to be re-elected had been rejected, significantly in favour of the first black to hold the premier position in the Adventist Church in this country.

Thus have both Theobald's prediction of the increasing politicization of the Adventist Church in Britain and the prophecy of the member of the LLF, who said that what happened in 1978 made it only a matter of time before blacks were in full control of the Church, been fulfilled. Black politics, which were aimed originally at the redress of what were perceived as inequalities, have become an instrument of control, with white influence in the Church reduced to mere tokenism, a complete reversal of what is sometimes said to be the situation in the wider society.

Even though the white membership still appears to provide an amount of financial support disproportionate to its size, its numbers are declining and its average age appears to be high. Even in some areas where the SdA churches are still all-white a knock-on effect is being felt. For example, in some of the resorts of the south coast, where Adventist evangelism has never been very successful in the religiously-conservative senior citizen environment, the churches were, nevertheless, maintained in being by retirements of existing members from London and other large cities. Now there are no white Adventists in those cities to retire to the south coast (black Adventists, when they retire, tend either to stay where they are or return to the West Indies). It appears that soon many of these churches will become extinct. As things stand, it will not be very far into the next century when the SdA Church in Britain will be categorized as a black sect; and where Britain is going, the rest of the Adventist world seems likely to follow. Even in its place of origin, the United States, the bulk of the baptisms are now of blacks and Hispanics, and while, for example, in the countries of continental Europe growth rates are static or at best small, the membership in Africa and Latin America is burgeoning.

To end where we began. Increasing Third World dominance in the Church is likely to be reflected in a marked right-ward shift in theology (just as it has already been reflected in policy, such as the rejection of the ordination of women), for if black theology in Britain is anything to go by, it appears to incline towards perfectionism and works-based salvation, which will move Adventists even further away from the evangelical wing of Protestantism with which in the late 1950s it seemed likely to align itself. It is not a situation in which Mrs White would have taken much comfort.

Chapter 13

New Zealand's Cultic Milieu: Individualism and the Logic of Consumerism

Michael Hill

A number of significant attempts have been made in the past decade to locate the sociological study of religion in the mainstream of more recent developments in sociological theory but all of them acknowledge the importance of the classical groundwork.[1] All these recent accounts demonstrate that a close reading of these seminal theorists – especially one which bypasses the subsequent exegesis of such interpreters as Talcott Parsons[2] – underscores the validity of the agenda they established around the turn of the century.

The last decade of the nineteenth century was pivotal in the sociological interpretation of religion. As part of a broadly-based 'revolt against positivism' social scientists adopted a stance towards religion which gave it a markedly enhanced authenticity compared with its treatment by Enlightenment thinkers and their successors.[3] Instead of viewing religious belief systems as various species of mistaken science or flawed rationality, the belief systems of the world religions were studied in their own right, as statements which were not empirically verifiable but which nevertheless bore close relationship to the social environment of those who maintained them. This is the meaning of Durkheim's statement that 'there are no religions that are false. All are true in their own fashion'[4] and the principle behind Weber's intense concern with the theodicies of the world religions.[5]

A concern to incorporate belief systems within a sociological account of religion implied no necessary 'religious' position on the part of the sociologist. It was compatible with the rationalism of Durkheim, for example, and equally it accommodated the agnosticism of Weber (who described himself as being religiously 'tone-deaf'), and the liberal Protestantism of Weber's colleague Ernst Troeltsch. If any religious position was more fertile for the development of a sociological approach, however, it was that of the latter (which would also include such figures as H. R. Niebuhr[6] and Joachim Wach[7]) – one of the reasons being that liberal Protestantism regarded

Christianity's organizational forms as being conditioned by variable social environments rather than located in divine *fiat*.

Even though, as sociologists, they attributed a central role to variations in the *social* environment, it is noteworthy that Durkheim, Weber and Troeltsch gave prominence to the role played by the *internal* dynamic of the belief systems themselves: expressed more formally, they saw theology as an independent variable. This paper examines in some detail one aspect of this relationship as presented by Durkheim and Troeltsch. Both of them, it will be shown, regarded the prevailing emphasis on individualism in western religion as originating *within* Christianity and as having as much relevance for the wider legitimation of modern complex societies as for the organizational viability of contemporary Christianity itself. The chapter examines aspects of the 'cultic milieu'[8] in contemporary New Zealand, showing that some of its features conform remarkably closely to the earlier predictions while others remain problematic. Finally, the context of modern consumerism will be seen as a congenial locus for the growth of world-affirming, market-oriented movements of a religious and therapeutic kind.

Durkheim and the Problem of Individualism

One of the most remarkable features of Durkheim's work is its consistency. Within the first few years of his academic career he had already established the central concern of his subsequent writing – the issue of social solidarity and its maintenance in modern complex societies – and while he expanded some aspects of his work in the light of new empirical evidence, he never modified its major direction. We can therefore find in his earliest diagnoses elements that persisted until one of his last major contributions, *The Elementary Forms of the Religious Life* (1912).[9] These include analyses of, and predictions about, religion in complex societies.

In his first important published work *The Division of Labor in Society* (1893),[10] Durkheim established the proposition that while in simple societies the basis of social solidarity could be found in moral consensus (or a strong collective conscience), in modern societies the same *degree* of moral consensus was not required because social solidarity was based more on the mutual interdependence between people brought about by the division of labour. The heart of the problem was expressed by Durkheim as follows: 'What explains the fact that, while becoming more autonomous, the individual becomes more closely dependent on society?'[11] Durkheim thought that the collective conscience formed only a very restricted part of the belief systems of advanced societies, and that it became weaker and vaguer as the division of labour developed. Its contents became increasingly secular, and human-oriented rather than oriented towards other-worldly concerns, and it became correspondingly more rational. The domain of religion would greatly contract, and there would be a decrease in the number of beliefs that are strong enough, and sufficiently collectively held, to take on a religious character.

What *would* become a stronger part of shared values was the way in which the *individual* was regarded. The supreme value placed on the rights and dignity of the individual would take on a religious form, so that there would emerge a 'cult of the individual' which, because it was shared by all the members of an advanced society, would become a 'cult of humanity'.

To his earlier treatment in *The Division of Labor* he appended a more detailed statement in *Suicide* which contained a prediction of the form religion would take in complex societies:

> As societies become larger and more densely populated, they become more complex, labour is differentiated, individual differences multiply and one can foresee the moment when there will be nothing in common between all the members of the same human group except that they are all human beings. In these conditions, it is inevitable that collective feeling will attach itself very strongly to the single aim that it shares and to which it attributes by that very fact an incomparable value. Since the individual human being is the only entity which appeals without exception to all hearts, since its exaltation is the only goal which can be collectively pursued, it cannot but acquire an exceptional importance in all eyes. It thus rises far above all human objectives and takes on a religious character. (My translation)[12]

The outcome was a 'cult of humanity', and in a subsequent paper published the following year, which incorporated the passage quoted above, he depicted it in greater detail, setting it in an historical context.[13]

The occasion of Durkheim's 1898 paper is important because it shows him defending firmly-held convictions which remained at the heart of his entire work. In response to an attack by the anti-Dreyfusards on 'atheistic intellectuals' whose undermining of Catholicism and traditional social institutions would, they claimed, eventually lead to anarchy, Durkheim neatly turned the tables by claiming that the principles of individualism were the true heirs of Christianity. It was Christianity, he maintained, which transferred the centre of the moral life from outside to within through its emphasis on individual conscience and in the process it opened the way for the development of individualism and for the progress of scientific thought. Thus 'the originality of Christianity has consisted precisely in a remarkable development of the individualist spirit'.[14] The symbolic focus of belief and ritual in a modern society would become the idealized individual personality. Nor was this merely an egoistic pursuit since the idealized personality provided social integration through a common cause:

> The religion of the individual can therefore allow itself to be flouted without resistance, only on penalty of ruining its credit; since it is the sole link which binds us one to another, such a weakening cannot take place without the onset of social dissolution. Thus the individualist, who defends the rights of the individual, defends at the same time the vital interests of society; for he is preventing the criminal impoverishment of that final reserve of collective ideas and sentiments that constitutes the very soul of the nation.[15]

In presenting this view of the form which the 'collective conscience' would take in complex society, Durkheim identified 'an ideology sanctifying the values of liberalism and pointing towards Socialism'.[16] In a real sense, humanity itself became sacred:

> This is why man has become a god for man, and it is why he can no longer turn to other gods without being untrue to himself. And just as each of us embodies something of humanity, so each individual mind has within it something of the divine, and thereby finds itself marked by a characteristic which renders it sacred and inviolable to others.[17]

There are three noteworthy features of the 1898 paper which deserve comment in the present context. The first is Durkheim's use, in the passage in which he depicts the process by which the 'religion of humanity' will arise, of identical phrasing to that of the account in *Suicide*: the passage from the latter quoted above simply reappears in its entirety. Second is his polemical technique of claiming the 'normality' of his interpretation of Christianity against the conventional view of its function in embodying tradition and stability (in much the same way that he labelled complex societies as 'organic' when this epithet appeared more appropriate to communally-based societies). Third is Durkheim's emphasis on the internal dynamics of religious beliefs in the process of social change rather than their emergence as a product of such change.

Further implications of Durkheim's prediction are that the 'cult of humanity' will appeal especially to those who are most acutely aware of having 'nothing in common', i.e. to those who occupy specialist roles in the occupational structure and lack primary group membership as a source of identity – in other words the environment of the skilled and the mobile. There will be a variety of groups within the over-all 'cult of humanity', appealing to specific social constituencies through the special emphasis of their beliefs but united in their elevation of human personality to an absolute goal. Contemporary scientific thought, rather than being rejected, would be incorporated in the belief systems of such groups, though possibly in a transmuted form. A useful summary of these components is given by Westley:

Durkheim's predictions concerning religion in the future allow for the possible coexistence of a variety of different religions (and certainly cover the possibility of an increasingly specialized and differentiated society). The theme running through these various movements will be the sacredness of the ideal human. People will still feel a need to join in groups to dramatize these beliefs and the social realities which underlie them, and to be empowered and 'morally remade' by this group interaction.[18]

Westley's reading of Durkheim thus recognizes that despite the individualistic mode of religion in complex societies there will still be a felt need collectively to dramatize beliefs and to empower participants. This provides a link with the more familiar reading of Durkheim which emphasizes the concept of 'civil religion'. The latter derives more directly from a concluding passage of *The Elementary Forms of the Religious Life* published in 1912 and arguably influenced by the nationalism which preceded the First World War (in which Durkheim himself became involved as part of France's propaganda effort). Durkheim tried to envisage the future forms of religion and concluded:

> Thus there is something eternal in religion which is destined to survive all the particular symbols in which religious thought has successively enveloped itself. There can be no society which does not feel the need of upholding and reaffirming at regular intervals the collective sentiments and the collective ideas which make its unity and its personality. Now this moral remaking cannot be achieved except by the means of reunions, assemblies and meetings where the individuals, being closely united to one another, reaffirm in common their common sentiments; hence come ceremonies which do not differ from regular religious ceremonies, either in their object, the results which they produce, or the processes employed to attain these results. What essential difference is there between an assembly of Christians celebrating the principal dates of the life of Christ, or of Jews remembering the exodus from Egypt or the promulgation of the decalogue, and a reunion of citizens commemorating the promulgation of a new moral or legal system or some great event in the national life?
>
> If we find a little difficulty today in imagining what these feasts and ceremonies of the future could consist in, it is because we are going through a stage of transition and moral mediocrity. The great things of the past which filled our fathers with enthusiasm do not excite the same ardour in us, either because they have come into common usage to such an extent that we are unconscious of them, or else because they no longer answer to our actual aspirations; but as yet there is nothing to replace them . . . But this state of incertitude and confused agitation cannot last for ever. A day will come when our societies will know once again those hours of creative effervescence, in the course of which new ideas arise and new formulae are found which serve for a while as a guide to humanity . . . As to the question of what symbols this new faith will express itself with, whether they will resemble those of the past or not, and whether or not they will be more adequate for the reality which they seek to translate, that is something which surpasses the human faculty of foresight and which does not appertain to the principal question.[19]

On the one hand Durkheim says there can be no society that does not feel the need to reaffirm collective ideas; but on the other he says it is difficult to envisage what the collective consciousness would look like in a complex society. This is because – as spelled out in *The Division of Labor in Society* – the collective conscience in complex societies *is* vague, indeterminate, and lacking in intensity and volume. It is therefore an appropriate gloss on Durkheim to point out that: 'The substitutes for religion which sociologists have discovered in football, coronations, independence day celebrations and civic flag-waving are indeed weak substitutes for the dense, dynamic, all-embracing *conscience collective*. Empirically, modern societies do not have . . . common cultures which embrace all classes and segments of society.'[20]

Nevertheless, particularly among sociologists influenced by Talcott Parsons' interpretation of Durkheim and his view that normative consensus is a central concern of every social system, there has been a persistent search for evidence of 'civil religion'. In particular Robert Bellah, initially in 1967 and subsequently as part of an ongoing debate, has argued that an American civil religion exists and can be identified in such locations as presidential inaugurals and myths of origin celebrated on such occasions as Thanksgiving Day and the Fourth of July. There has been considerable debate over the viability of the concept *within* the USA,[21] but attempts to generalize it further have met with even more scepticism.[22]

Troeltsch on Church–Sect and Emergent Individualism

A second prediction about the future of religion was made in the first decade of the present century. As far as is known, it was made independently and without awareness of Durkheim's prediction,[23] but it is remarkable in providing an almost identical scenario for the future of western religion. In *The Social Teaching of the Christian Churches*, first published in 1911, Ernst Troeltsch was concerned to encapsulate the development of Christianity within a framework of two competing models of organization.[24] Like Durkheim, he saw the internal dynamics of belief systems as a key variable in the social forms taken by different religious groups, and his particular concern was with the gospel ethic of Christianity and its realization in social organization. On the one hand, he identified the Church – large, conservative, socially dominant and allied with the ruling class in any society – while, on the other, was the sect: small, radical, socially marginal and representing a religion of the oppressed. It is important to note that Troeltsch regarded both radical and conservative forms of Christianity as legitimate developments of the gospel blueprint, albeit co-existing in a state of tension: there was a tendency for subsequent writers such as Niebuhr to regard sectarian forms of religion as 'authentic' and their more institutional church-type outgrowths as in some sense 'compromised'.

Out of the dialectical conflict between these two types of organization, which Troeltsch argued had characterized most of Christian history, he traced the emergence of a third, more recent type of religious response which he saw as having its origin in the late-medieval urban centres and which he described as 'a foreshadowing of coming developments in this interplay of Church and Sect'[25] – in other words, this is his prediction of the future of religion and can be seen as a dialectical synthesis emerging out of church–sect tension.

He labels the emergent form as mysticism, and depicts it in terms of a growing individualism. Lacking the institutional authority of the Church or the radicalism of the sect, this form of western religion combines with modern scientific thought, though it does so in a flexible, free-floating way. Adherents to mystical forms of religion, he suggests, have little desire for organized fellowship and place more emphasis on the importance of freedom for the interchange of ideas. He continues:

> Gradually, in the modern world of educated people, the third type has come to predominate. This means, then, that all that is left is voluntary association with like-minded people, which is equally remote from Church and Sect . . . It is neither Church nor Sect, and has neither the concrete sanctity of the institution nor the radical connection with the Bible. Combining Christian ideas with a wealth of modern views, deducing social institutions, not from the Fall but from a process of natural development, it has not the fixed limit for concessions and the social power which the Church possesses, but it also does not possess the radicalism and the exclusiveness with which the sect can set aside the State and economics, art and science.[26]

Mysticism would prosper at the expense of other forms of religion because its values were more resonant with those of a secular, scientific culture. 'The characteristics which give mystical religion its adaptive advantage in this sense are its monism, relativism, tolerance, syncretism, and above all, its individualism.'[27] Troeltsch came close to Durkheim's formulation when he argued that in this form of religion: 'The isolated individual, and psychological abstraction and analysis become everything.'[28] Graf's account further highlights the parallels between Durkheim and Troeltsch when he encapsulates the latter's treatment of mysticism in the following way:

> [In mysticism] the opposites of religion and society are reconciled within the pious subject himself, to the extent that he knows himself to be a participant in the divine spirit and he glimpses the true reality of the kingdom of God in a purely spiritual and universal brotherhood of those gifted by God . . . [Troeltsch] understood the Christian tradition primarily

as a force for the strengthening of individual autonomy over against the depersonalizing tendencies of modern capitalism. Moreover, the church's tradition had to be provided with a new cultural credibility; that is, 'religious individualism,' inspired by the mystical tradition, which had been forced out of the evangelical church, had to be again given a right to exist within a 'flexible church of the people'.[29]

Self-perfection and self-deification are the ethical absolutes which emerge from modern individualism: coupled with a strong valuation on tolerance, these goals are highly congruent with the pluralist environment of a modern, complex society. Pluralism is also related to syncretism, whereby consumers of mystical religion 'mix and match' their beliefs from a variety of sources, both secular and spiritual – the latter also involving non-Christian sources of beliefs. Finally, Troeltsch saw the appeal which Romanticism – both because of its idealization of the individual and its pantheistic notion of an all-pervasive spiritual quality within the world – might have for liberal, educated Protestants. The end product is 'simply a parallelism of religious personalities'.[30] 'This', he said, 'is the secret religion of the educated classes.'[31]

As the above account clearly demonstrates, Troeltsch's characterization of mysticism located its influence within the mainstream of liberal Protestantism, and to that extent his ideas have remarkable resonance with some of the recent writing of Don Cupitt.[32] Cupitt never acknowledges any debt to Troeltsch, and his understanding of Durkheim seems confined to the Durkheim of the *Elementary Forms*,[33] but his scenario for the future of Christianity would repay comparison with these earlier predictions. Certainly some of Cupitt's critics have rounded on precisely those elements in his thought which approximate Durkheim and Troeltsch most closely: Cowdell, for example, complains of Cupitt's 'self-religion' and suggests that it is too demanding for 'ordinary people'[34] – precisely the sort of complaint one might make of a 'religion of the educated classes'.

However, although Troeltsch located mysticism within the mainstream, his ideas have entered the sociological literature largely as a result of Becker's use of the term 'cult' to depict the end-point of Christian individualism.[35] Becker drew attention to the way in which the 'I' became the centre of the believer's cosmos, and thought that only a highly atomistic and secular social order could give rise to cults, and he gave as examples Spiritualism, Theosophy, New Thought, Christian Science, Buchmanism and a variety of 'pseudo-Hinduisms' associated with 'Swamis and Yogis who consent, for a consideration, to carry their messages to the materialistic Western World'.[36] As well as anticipating the element of consumerism in the individualistic forms of contemporary religion, Becker also anticipated some of the conceptual confusion which has increasingly surrounded the concepts of sect and cult when he pointed out that the dividing line between them was difficult to draw. By the late 1970s use of the term 'cult' in sociology had become sufficiently confused – not least because it had become increasingly invaded by popular usage, especially in the media – that alternative formulations of a more neutral kind had become essential. Though Beckford appropriately titled his book *Cult Controversies* he argued for a replacement of the terms 'sect' and 'cult' by the lable New Religious Movement (NRM),[37] and the task of re-labelling has been largely accepted in subsequent treatments.

The Cult of Humanity and the Secret Religion of the Educated Classes

By incorporating the insights of Westley and Campbell we can merge the predictions of Durkheim and Troeltsch on the future of western religion into a single inventory and identify the following six features as typifying the religion of modern, complex societies:

1   It is *individualistic*. In a society with an increasing division of labour there is a demand for beliefs and life-styles which permit individual choice and expression. There is considerable variety in religion of this sort, but a second feature provides its common thread:

2   It emphasizes an *idealized human personality*. The ideal personality takes on a sacred quality as adherents pursue the goal of self-perfection and a realization of their human potential. This will not lead to mere egoism, however, since an awareness of others in pursuit of similar goals will lead to a third feature:

3   It maintains a degree of *tolerance*. Though different elements in this humanized religion appeal to different social constituencies, with a prevailing emphasis on occupational specialists lacking intense primary group membership, there is a free exchange of ideas and a relativistic acceptance of alternative views and versions (though see the following discussion which emphasizes the limits of tolerance). As a result:

4   It is *syncretistic*. A range of ideas – from the beliefs of different world religions, philosophies, esoteric and scientific traditions – is shaped into a relatively plastic amalgam by adherents and adepts. As well as an emphasis on idealized human personality, this set of ideas has in common a fifth feature:

5   It is *monistic*. Humanized religion rejects the dichotomy of body and mind, matter and spirit in favour of a world-view which sees spiritual power as diffuse and all-pervasive. In therapeutic groups, the conception of the human being in relation to the

natural environment is holistic. From this follows an important feature of the ritual of humanized religion:

6 It emphasizes a process whereby individuals are *'morally re-made'* or *empowered*. Though ritual may be minimal in this associational milieu – sometimes involving only a guru/practitioner–client relationship – when it does exist it dramatizes the release of inner power from a newly-enabled personality.

An important implication of predictions about this future religion of humanity is that, far from being seen as a deviant and socially peripheral phenomenon, it will increasingly come to express aspects of the dominant culture.[38] This is because its beliefs and symbols are highly resonant with the life experiences of mobile, educated individuals in a modern society. We should therefore expect to find a significant and growing proportion of the populations of western societies having some contact with, or at the very least knowledge of the area of new religions and – what I shall argue is a closely related phenomenon – complementary therapies. As a means of putting this into an over-all perspective, Beckford suggests that it is likely that western participants in Human Potential groups – the characteristics of which appear to place them in the category we are considering – outnumber those in the four more visible and 'notorious' 'youth cults', namely the Unification Church, the International Society for Krishna Consciousness, Scientology and the Children of God/Family of Love (note that Beckford here excludes Scientology from the broader Human Potential grouping).[39] The four groups adopt a more monopolistic and authoritarian stance in relation to membership boundaries and practice than is common among groups of the Human Potential type.

The characteristic of tolerance deserves closer attention since it has occupied a central position in conceptual debates about the boundaries of sectarian and cultic groups[40] as well as in competing theories of change in new religious movements.[41] In a variety of ways, sociologists have found it important to distinguish between those movements – traditionally labelled sects – which insist on some form of exclusive and monopolistic closure on the part of their members, and other movements – 'cults' – which expect a more amorphous and free-floating association among their clientele. Movements of the second type, however, seem to espouse a tendency to discard tolerance in favour of a more authoritarian demarcation of belief and membership boundaries: Scientology and Synanon have been seen as exemplifying this process. Wallis explains the tendency as a response to the basic precariousness of such movements.[42] Because they frequently offer techniques and services of a therapeutic kind they face market precariousness in the face of a range of competitors. Product diversification is one response to such competition, but a stricter insistence on the spiritual equivalent of service contracts and franchises is another. Similarly, charismatic leadership, which is often a feature of new religious movements, is inherently precarious and one of the strategies for handling the resulting instability is to amplify the leader's charismatic credentials in order to ensure compliance: this seems to have been a tactic of Jim Jones and the People's Temple; though the Jonestown community, of course, was very different from the type of group with which this paper is concerned.[43] We might express the elaboration succinctly by suggesting that the basic precariousness of new religious movements in the 'cultic milieu' – meaning those of the world-affirming, therapeutic variety – also extends to their tolerance, which can give way to totalism.

In her recent analysis of 'self-religions' in Australia, Rachael Kohn assessed the extent to which the individualistic component of the cult of humanity was compatible with the maintenance of authority in religious movements with a charismatic basis and concluded that 'self-religions', based as they were on the suppression of the conscious, analytical mind on the one hand, and the unification with, or the approximation to, the Divine Self (which in some movements is embodied only in the leader and in no other human or conceptual form) on the other hand, constituted a situation in which 'authority does not reside in the self, but absolutely and unquestionably in the leader'.[44] In the three groups she studied – the Da Free John movement, Scientology, and est – such a conclusion is undeniable, and very effectively emphasizes a dilemma faced by movements which oscillate between individualistic precariousness and authoritarian closure. However, these are three among a wide range of movements within the general category of the Human Potential movement (from which Beckford, as we have seen, would exclude Scientology): other groups may therefore have a less focused locus of authority. Even when charismatic authority *is* the characteristic mode, it is also possible to envisage a range of possible internal relationships within the group: Beckford's distinction between devotees, adepts, clients and patrons, for instance, is intended to point to a spectrum of possible linkages within NRMs.[45] Thus, while such movements may sometimes contain a core relationship of the guru–disciple kind, it may simultaneously attract a broad penumbra of associates with more individualistic concerns.

New Zealand's Cultic Milieu

Here, I transpose discussion to the contemporary New Zealand context. The six components identified as typical of new individualistic religious movements outlined above are first of all examined in relation to a range of complementary therapies which were the subject of an official report by the Health Services Research and Development Unit of the New Zealand Department of Health.[46] McGuire has provided a succinct rationale for incorporating alternative – or complementary – therapies within the category of new religions by noting that they 'do appear to function as religions for many adherents – providing cosmologies, rituals, a language for the interpretation of believers' worlds, a social context for belief and practice and a group of fellow believers'.[47] After a consideration of the milieu of complementary therapy I briefly examine one imported movement – Transcendental Meditation – and one indigenous movement – Centrepoint – together with some comments on the networking of groups in one New Zealand city, before turning to an interpretation of, and the popularity of such movements, and in this way testing the utility of Durkheim's and Troeltsch's predictions.

The Health Department report on complementary therapies contains extensive and detailed empirical data.[48] It shows that the level of usage of complementary therapies in western society is increasing, along with public interest in and awareness of the therapies available. European estimates suggest that at least 10 per cent of the population use such therapies and up to one-third is interested in them.[49] While there is no reliable national estimate of provision and use in New Zealand, the regional survey of Wellington and Hutt health districts gives some extent of the variety available with ninety-four separately listed therapies.[50] Questions about user motivation found repeated evidence of individualistic concerns – a dissatisfaction with the impersonality, discontinuity and brevity of consultation with orthodox practitioners and a search for fuller interaction with the therapist which would serve the individual needs of the client.[51] The theme of idealized human personality was especially well represented in advertisements for therapies, which contained such phrases as 'inner peace, sustained happiness', 'deepen self understanding in life purpose', 'increase your efficiency and productivity' and 'keep in touch with yourself on a deeper level'.[52] Clients of complementary therapists themselves tended to place great importance on the goal of taking responsibility for oneself, gaining control over one's own life and future, and taking an active role in improving maintaining health.[53] Tolerance was shown by the characteristic approach of 'mixing and matching' or shopping around for suitable therapy, with a prevailing philosophy of 'No one has all the answers'[54] while syncretism was shown by the common tendency of practitioners to offer more than one therapy and for therapies to appear in clusters. Examples of three such clusters were:

1 Massage, Touch for Health, Iridology, Nutrition, Naturopathy;
2 Rebirthing, Bach Flower Remedies, Massage (Deep Tissues),

Touch for Health, Herbalism, Homeopathy, Nutrition (Allergies), Aura Therapy, Polarity Therapy;
3   Nutrition, Iridology, Orthobionomy, Massage, Tissue Salts Therapy, Bach Flower Remedies, Homeopathy, Herbalism.[55]

The monistic/holistic conception of therapy was strongly represented among practitioners and their clients, as well as evidence consistently suggesting a higher than average educational level among users of complementary therapies. Clients, who tended to be well-informed about the variety of therapies available, were frequently seeking a more 'natural', drug-free form of therapy than that offered by orthodox practitioners, and tended to emphasize the need for over-all well-being, including preventative aspects of health care.[56] In the words of the report: 'Concepts are changing – most significantly in the vision of health as total well-being rather than just the absence of disease. There are many different models of what well-being actually is, but most usually incorporate ideas of physical and emotional health and social and spiritual ease.'[57]

Finally, the response of users of complementary therapies was very much of the 'morally re-made' or 'empowered' variety. Most clients felt that complementary therapy worked and, the report emphasized: 'In the many anecdotes of successful experiences, people mentioned feeling more powerful after a therapy.'[58] To cite the words of one young woman who visited an astrologer:

> I went away feeling great. In the two year progression [the astrologer] talked about being happy in a relationship and things working out and so I felt there is no need to be really worried . . . He gave me a sense of me that I knew, that I felt was right and that maybe other people don't pick up. He could see I had potential in a lot of ways. So it was kind of personally affirming.

It has been suggested by Westley, expanding on Durkheim's concept of the cult of humanity, that where ritual elements were present they would be of the empowering kind, dramatizing the inner potential of human personality. Analysing the complementary therapies offered, the report found that 270 individuals offered 376 different services, of which 126 were consultations, 201 courses or workshops and forty-nine public meetings. A wide variety of group activities was included in the set of services called 'courses and workshops' – class, course, workshop, retreat, experience, celebration and fair were some of the descriptions used by therapists. Selected titles emphasizing the self-enhancing aspect of complementary therapy were: 'Meditation's the Way', 'Delving into the Unknown', 'Everyone Has an Aura', 'Wellness Comes by Learning How to Transform Negative Feelings', 'Optimum Health Through Self Awareness' and 'Organics – Key to Health'.[59] Thus, while the popular image of complementary therapy sees it as being centred on the dyad of practitioner–client, group participation played a significant role in the therapeutic offerings studied by the report. The individualistic milieu of contemporary therapy is clearly one in which, supporting Westley's view, people will still feel the need to join in groups.

Transcendental Meditation (TM) is a movement which is more commonly accorded the status of a minority religion. It has much in common with a number of complementary therapies, however; its self-presentation contains a large input of scientific ideas, and its meditation programme can sometimes be found advertised – for example, in management magazines – alongside those of more overtly 'secular' organizations. Had Durkheim and Troeltsch been seeking a concrete example of their future religion, they would surely have been impressed by the beliefs and structure of TM, for it meets all the features on the combined inventory. Its individualism is evident in the promised benefits for those who practise (in isolation) their two fifteen- to twenty-minute daily sessions of meditation. The list of benefits is too long to give in a comprehensive form but includes: improvement in job performance and satisfaction, in athletic performance and in sensory-motor tasks; decrease in anxiety, neuroticism, depression and aggression. A more recent claim has been advanced that TM can actually reverse the ageing process.[60] The idealized human personality of TM can be described as a person who has 'enlightenment' and a 'higher state of consciousness', and egoism is avoided by the claim that the presence of a sufficient proportion of TM adepts in a population will lead to 'invincibility' for the whole society by triggering the so-called 'Maharishi Effect' (World Government of the Age of Enlightenment: WGAE). Of particular interest in the light of Kohn's treatment of the problematics of authority in self-religions is the contrast between TM's individualistic orientation and the more totalistic and authoritarian features of another movement which owes part of its inspiration to the ideas of the Maharishi, the School of Economic Science.[61]

When the 'Ideal Wellington Campaign' was conducted by the TM organization in 1978 as part of a 'global research programme' its purpose was to show that Wellington, with a claimed 0.98 per cent of TM meditators (the 'Maharishi Effect' is triggered at 1 per cent of a city's population) was enjoying many social effects not apparent in Auckland, where the percentage of meditators was 0.24 and a rival technique was popular. The improved quality of life in Wellington was measured by such indices as: fewer sickness and domestic purpose beneficiaries, fewer paternity orders and divorces, lower prices, better employment opportunities, fewer road deaths, hospital admissions and civil court cases. More cargo was moved in the port of Wellington and – according to a TM representative – the incidence of sexually-transmitted diseases was lower in Wellington than in Auckland. An emphasis on the social benefits of this individualistic technique has been strongly maintained through TM's international organization, which has been characterized as both utopian and millennial.[62]

Although tolerant to the extent of claiming that the practice of TM is compatible with membership of other religious bodies, the movement is certainly competitive and claims that its own form of meditation is superior to others – as indicated, Auckland's lack of 'invincibility' was attributed to rival meditation techniques. The movement is market-oriented, charging a graduated scale of fees as adepts progress through the TM/Sidhi (or 'superman') yoga programme, and seeking sponsors and credentials for its product: both the Psychology and Sociology Departments at the Victoria University of Wellington were approached for credentials during the Ideal Wellington campaign. It is worth adding that, in line with TM's marketing orientation, after the campaign in Wellington had reached a plateau, the organizers turned their attention to a then relatively wealthy section of the population, the farming community. Syncretism is most clearly evident in the combining of the Maharishi Mahesh Yogi's interpretation of the *Bhagavad Gita* with a range of scientific interpretation and support. The collected papers of scientific research on the Transcendental Meditation programme contain sections on physiology (metabolic change, electro-physiological and electro-encephalographic change), psychology (intelligence, learning, academic performance and personality development), sociology (rehabilitation and crime prevention), quantum physics and neurophysiology.[63]

TM can be typified as a one-level, technical, monistic group.[64] By this is meant that enlightenment is attained immediately or rapidly on adherence to the group, is based on standardized techniques rather than on veneration of a charismatic guru, and conveys a vision of the universe in which there is ultimate 'oneness'. The emphasis on this monistic conception has if anything strengthened with the development of TM, particularly in its attempt to locate the meditation technique within the basic laws of physics. By use of the technique, adepts are claimed to be empowered in an impressive variety of ways, a number of which have already been itemized. They may be summed up in the following account: 'Maharishi has described this state of [transcendental] consciousness as nothing less than the fundamental constituent of creation, unbounded in nature and functioning as the "ground state of all the laws of nature". He describes it as the source of all order and growth in the individual and his surrounding.'[65]

An indigenous New Zealand self-religion – albeit one with distinct international links – is Centrepoint. Its origins lie in the Human Potential movement and especially in the growth centre known as Esalen in California, where in the late 1960s a group of innovative therapists including Fritz Perls and Bill Schutz were working.[66] Centrepoint's guru, Bert Potter, who had earlier found success as a businessman using Dale Carnegie principles, visited Esalen in 1971 and over a three-month period underwent a personal transformation before returning to New Zealand. The change had been dramatic: 'The deep massage technique of Rolfing changed his posture so much that when he stepped off the plane at Auckland on his return, [his wife] hardly recognized him, so much had his walk changed.'[67]

At this stage he became involved in counselling, working with a group of sympathetic mental health professionals and gradually building up a reputation as a powerful if controversial therapist.

By 1977, several thousand people had experienced Bert Potter's groups and he had attracted a number of people who wanted to form a community: this was the nucleus of the present Albany community, which numbers over a hundred people. In analysing the growth of the community against the inventory of characteristics of cultic religion, there are some apparent parallels together with some points of divergence, the latter arising from the group's *communal* base.

It is first necessary to examine the extent to which Centrepoint is individualistic. On initial analysis, the community organization would seem to run counter to this feature of contemporary religious groups, having such firm charismatic and communal characteristics, though a closer scrutiny identifies a number of individualistic themes. First, allowance is made within the group for the exercise of a range of individual activities on the part of members: these range from highly skilled craft work to a variety of trained counselling roles within and professional occupations outside the community. Members have been encouraged to undertake training in counselling (sometimes in response to internal exigencies, such as problems with the adolescent children of members) and the presence of professionals in the group has provided a source of outside income. Second, since Centrepoint offers numerous workshops and therapy sessions on a fee-paying basis it has attracted a penumbra of associates – Beckford's adepts, clients and patrons – whose association with the group is necessarily of a temporary and more individualistic nature. In this respect, there is an interesting parallel between some organizational features of wider Christianity and Centrepoint which highlights the paradox of individualism. It has been pointed out that in places where religious sociation is individualistic and tangential – at shrines, in places of pilgrimage and, it might be added, on retreats – there is often a permanent community to service the needs of the temporary clientele.[68] In exactly the same way, the community nucleus at Centrepoint offers services on a drop-in, workshop or weekend basis for individuals who will not become permanent members.

The range of therapeutic techniques employed by the group have as their goal the realization of an idealized human personality in the sense already defined. As the authoritative account of Centrepoint puts it: 'The "technology" of the spiritual life is insight into process, the Delphic command to "know thyself".'[69] By way of illustration, the brochure for a creativity workshop promises: 'In Creativity workshops, laughter and insight combine to open your senses and reconnect you with your spontaneous, ever creative child.' The ultimate purpose of therapy is seen as reaching the 'centre-point' or spiritual core of the client.[70] Tolerance is shown in the response the group adopts towards new therapies, which tends to be open and experimental: members are seen as 'protean', constantly seeking new experiences. On the other hand, the central figure of Bert Potter, as guru and charismatic focus, has – at least for a long period of the group's development – given Centrepoint a more authoritarian basis: personal accounts by members constantly refer to his wise, but controlling, influence. Thus Centrepoint has to date been more of a *charismatic* than a *technical* movement,[71] though in the late 1980s the group was clearly in the process of change. In a 1987 announcement it was made clear that Bert's role was shifting as other members took over aspects of the group's publicly advertised workshops: 'The August/September 7-Day Intensive with Bert (listed in our previous calendar) will be his final workshop. Bert has devoted many years to the training and development of our team of leaders, who will now be responsible for the Centrepoint Workshop programme.'[72]

Symbolically, at this time Bert Potter's photograph ceased to feature as a central part of the group's presentation. One explanation of such changes is that the community had gathered a group of therapists of sufficient experience, and had acquired a sufficiently stable economic base, to have obviated the precariousness which leads to charisma-amplification. It appeared to be heading in a more technical direction; though the imprisonment of Bert Potter on drugs-related charges and legal actions against the community in 1991 on both drugs and sexual abuse charges may well result in more radical transformations in the community's life-style.

Syncretism is clearly evident in the range of sources from which Centrepoint's particular amalgam of beliefs and therapeutic techniques is drawn. A fruitful way of tracing these is provided by Wallis's 'map' of the Growth Movement[73] on which the following Centrepoint influences[74] can be located: psychodrama, group dynamics and sensitivity training, Schutz, encounter, Gestalt psychology, Rogers, Gestalt therapy, Jung, Reich (orgonomy), bioenergetics, primal therapy, psychoanalysis, Transactional Analysis and hypnotherapy. To this 'map' can be added the following: Dale Carnegie, Rajneesh (whence came Potter's initial inspiration for a community), Buddhism, Hinduism, Taoism, Perls and neuro-linguistic programming. On the one hand the range of inputs allows for a broad integration of the community around the theme of personal growth: on the other, it permits a degree of functional specialization through which different members can emphasize their particular therapeutic skills. In this respect, Centrepoint appears to be adapting in a similar way to other more traditional religious communities, in which a range of specialist activities and innovations can be accommodated, given a degree of consensus over expressive goals.[75]

The monistic theme is constantly reiterated in the literature of and about the community. One quotation, from a Centrepoint therapist, will serve as an illustration: 'At Centrepoint we see the whole of a person's life, and it's amazing how often a person's sickness is linked to his emotional state. The average GP doesn't get to see their patients as we do, but after a while it becomes obvious how much sickness, perhaps all of it, is basically a product of stress.'[76] And of course the purpose of this monistic approach to therapy is the 'moral re-making' or empowering of community members and clients. In the calendar (or brochure) mentioned, a 'write-yourself weekend' is described as 'An empowering workshop that puts you firmly in charge of your life' and quotes the adage, 'The acorn knows how to grow its Oak Tree'.[77]

At the time of writing, the future course of Centrepoint is uncertain. Bert Potter was charged in 1989 with possession for supply of illegal drugs and was subsequently imprisoned. Earlier this year the community was raided by a large number of police and charges are currently pending which involve not only drug offences but also sexual abuse. During previous vicissitudes – including a protracted period during which the community was forced to migrate to temporary premises because of local authority planning restrictions – the charismatic element in group maintenance seems to have been strong. Since there is evidence that, even before the most recent upheavals, the group was in a state of transition to a more rational and dispersed basis of authority, the future of the community cannot be predicted with any certainty.

Auckland is also the base for a range of New Age groups which are co-ordinated through a magazine called *Rainbow Network*. The Auckland location is entirely compatible with several key features of such groups. Its population includes a marked concentration of the wealthy, many of whom have sufficient leisure time to devote to the pursuit of spiritual and consciousness-raising goals. Furthermore, it is a pluralistic city with a polyglot population: while its Polynesian component is least involved in New Age groups – being more prominent in evangelical and Pentecostal churches – Auckland's international transport links attract European and North

American migrants to a greater extent than any other region of New Zealand. A further factor (one which has been little explored in relation to spiritual retreats and communitarian ventures) is climate: exposing one's spiritual core in the kind of natural settings favoured by a number of the centres, and by Centrepoint itself, is more congenial in Auckland's temperate environment than it might be, for example, in Wellington's notorious southerlies.

The Rainbow Network is very much in the genre of Oden's 'New Pietism', for his description of 'the socially mobile intelligentsia and cultural avant-garde who form the clientele of the encounter culture'[78] would be entirely appropriate to the clientele observed at public expositions of New Age culture, such as exhibitions and seminars, and the documented socio-economic backgrounds of Centrepoint members. The latter group contains a significant number of recruits from occupations characterized by 'emotional labour'[79] and can therefore be seen as offering reconstructed identities to those suffering from the commercialization of spontaneous feeling. Both the Network and Centrepoint eminently demonstrate the characteristics of Troeltsch's 'secret religion of the educated classes'.

Concluding Remarks

I have noted elsewhere[80] that one of the reasons for the vitality of minority religious groups in New Zealand has been the market opportunity presented by the relative weakness of mainline, institutional religion. The pluralistic religious environment of New Zealand society has fostered the emergence of new and experimental forms of belief in the absence of mainline religious monopoly. Nor is it surprising that minority religions in New Zealand are therapeutic and consumer-oriented. I find considerable plausibility in Keith Sinclair's assessment of New Zealanders as being a not very religious people and as practising a simple materialism in which the pursuit of health and possessions takes precedence over thoughts of salvation. He continues: 'The most respected personage in the community is the doctor, who is often regarded as both aristocrat and priest.'[81]

In the search for alternative meaning systems, New Zealanders have not rejected this basic cultural trait, but have merely sought health and well-being of a more esoteric and individualistically attuned kind. And the consumer ethic – which Campbell has identified as the modern counterpart of the Protestant ethic[82] – is strongly evident in the way that minority religions have created new needs and novel means of satisfying them. In line with the dominant culture of our society, these groups market *services* rather than products. (The contrast here is a fascinating one. The nineteenth-century new religious movements often marketed a product, so that Seventh-day Adventists perfected the cornflake, the Oneida community silverware, and the Shakers furniture. Today's new religions market specialist therapies, from TM's electroencephalograph to Scientology's E-meter, a form of skin galvanometer which is similar to the polygraph or lie-detector. (To the latter examples could be added a plethora of -punctures, -pressures and -bustions, together with a host of psychological and spiritual services.)

While consumer culture has usually been associated with the undermining of traditional Christianity, the relationship is a great deal more complex than would first appear; for even in the case of Christianity's more conservative and puritan forms, consumerist and market-oriented motifs have been strongly asserted. One of the first sociologists to detect the emergence of market-based motivation in the mainstream of Christianity was Peter Berger, who saw in the ecumenical movement a replication of strategies used by economic units in situations of oligopoly, when marginal differentiation of products was a more rational response than open competition.[83] He was later to extend the analogy by referring to the belief systems of modern societies as a spiritual supermarket.[84] Such a notion has appeared in a variety of sources, especially in accounts of religion in North America, of which the following is but one example:

> Religion in America was a vast multi-billion dollar industry, employing thousands of men and women and attracting people of talent and ambition. The earnings of men like Swaggart, Falwell, Robertson and Schuller ran into millions of dollars. They flew around the world in private jets, breakfasted with presidents, rubbed shoulders with prime ministers, and to outward appearances were indistinguishable from the tycoons and corporate chiefs who headed other, secular, multinational corporations. Competing as they did for audiences, funds and 'souls' in a market that was not expanding as fast as their ambitions, rivalries had sharpened between them, creating a context in which minor peccadilloes were blown up into major national scandals.[85]

While the above account refers specifically to televangelism, it can be set within the context of a broader observation about modern society, which sees it as being far from a symbolically impoverished material world in which goods and commodities are regarded as mere 'utilities': 'Consumer culture produces a vast shifting web of signs, images, and symbols and these symbols cannot be conceptualized as merely profane.'[86] In the case of 'self' religions and the cultic milieu of therapeutic and New Age products, one can trace a marked shift from the counter-cultural directions in the 1960s to the overtly capitalistic themes found in more recent movements – such as Exegesis, to give a striking example. The migration of TM and Rajneesh from India to the West was at least in part a response to the perceived potential of an untapped market.

Finally, there is value in Bibby's view of new religious movements as providing supplements for science. Since Spencer introduced the notion that religion's function was to plug the gaps left by science by postulating an 'unknowable' area which it was religion's job to service[87] attention has been paid to groups which operate on the boundaries of science. Bibby calls this the area of 'a-science' and suggests that 'a-science' explanations are drawn upon either because scientific explanations are unavailable or because the questions asked are not amenable to scientific answers: 'It is this potential for people to supplement science which creates a market for a-science.'[88] And, in line with the interpretation of such a-science products as an integral component of modern consumerism, he suggests that 'a-science advocates who can read and create consumer demand, as well as publicize and deliver their products stand to know market gains'.[89] For these reasons, the cult of humanity and the secret religion of the educated classes, while changing and adapting to the prevailing life-styles and preferences of its clientele, is likely to remain a resilient feature of modern societies. Far from being peripheral or a necessarily deviant growth, the cultic milieu – in New Zealand as in other western countries – is likely to provide a theology of individualism for those whose life and occupational experiences contain plausible resonances.

Chapter 14

Authority and Dependence in New Religious Movements

Eileen Barker

There are various ways in which authority may cease to be exerted over members of new religious movements (NRMs), and various ways in which a member may become dependent on the movement to which he or she belongs. My approach to these issues is sociological, focusing on social situations and processes. It may indeed be argued that it is necessary (but not sufficient) to examine the social aspects of such movements if one is to understand how authority 'works', and the extent and the degree to which individuals may find themselves dependent on the group of which they are, members.

Despite the fact that the movements are frequently characterized as having uniquely sinister methods of controlling those in their power, scholarly research into the movements has revealed nothing which cannot be observed in other parts of society. While it is true that the intensity and concentration of certain situations and processes may be different from those occurring in 'ordinary' situations, it is also true that one may find not altogether dissimilar manifestations of authority and dependence in the US Marines, in some monasteries, convents, prisons and other 'total institutions',[1] and within certain types of families throughout the world.

The potency that an authority figure may possess is a subject that has been of considerable concern in areas other than that of NRMs. One fact of recent history that has given rise to many still-unanswered questions is the co-operation that was given by men and women to the SS during the Second World War, even when their lives were not under threat. A related and just as important area of interest is the way in which people whose lives *were* under threat were brave and independent enough to refuse to obey instructions which they believed to be immoral. The extent to which an authority figure can convince people that they should do things which they would not dream of doing on their own account was strikingly demonstrated by Stanley Milgram's experiments, in which people were persuaded by an experimenter wearing a white coat in a 'scientific laboratory' to punish (allegedly as part of a teaching process) a planted participant in another room whenever he gave an incorrect answer – even to the point of apparently administering an electric shock that was clearly marked dangerous.[2] It is, however, important to note that others who were similarly tested refused to continue with the experiment once the planted participant expressed discomfort from the shock.

One of the most important points that needs to be made about groups that have been labelled 'cults' or NRMs, is that the only thing which they all have in common is that they have been so labelled. One cannot generalize about NRMs. There are vast differences in their beliefs, practices, organization and membership. By no means all of the situations or processes that are described in this paper are to be found in all NRMs; and even when they are present in several different movements, they are likely to take slightly different forms and be experienced with different degrees of forcefulness. It is also important to stress that the same process can affect different people in quite different ways. Furthermore, none of the processes or circumstances to be described results in complete control over everyone – or possibly even over anyone; individuals will be not absolutely, but only *more or less*, affected or unaffected by the situations in which they find themselves.

Related to this last point is the fact that the very terms 'social situation' and 'social process' assume, to some extent at least, an interactionist approach. It is true that people find themselves having to take account of a situation that exists independent of their own volition at that particular point in time; but if one thinks in terms only of 'something being done' to someone, there is a danger of ignoring the enormous range of potential responses to the situation. The social process is one in which the individual is a more or less active participant; the participation may take the form of a positive or negative reaction; it may involve conscious or subconscious deliberation or negotiation. But in any instance where authority (rather than naked power) is involved, there will be some degree of collaboration in the process of interaction between the authority figure and the person over whom he or she exerts authority. The relationship may well be lop-sided, but it will not be purely one-sided.

In other words, to understand the outcome of any particular situation, it is just as important to understand the role played by the led as it is to understand the role of the leader or of the movement as a social entity – even when the process which is being described is one that leads to a relationship of growing dependency. It is not irrelevant to this argument that far more people have left than have stayed in precisely those NRMs which are most frequently characterized by 'anti-cultists' and the more sensationalist media as engaged in brainwashing or as using mind-control techniques on their membership: people not only can, but do resist the influences and pressures that are discussed in this paper; people revolt against authority figures; and some people become more independent as a result of their membership of one or other of the NRMs.

That said, however, it may be noted that there are indubitably characteristics to be found in several of the movements which can contribute to the effectiveness with which authority may be wielded and dependency fostered. Such characteristics include a belief in a single, absolute truth held by the movement or its charismatic leader; and strong boundaries separating the evil and satanic 'them' from the good and godly 'us'. The fact that the movement is new and that most members have joined it, rather than having been born into it, means that the level of commitment, intensity and enthusiasm is liable to be greater than that found in sections of, say, the Church of England. There is frequently a tendency for the group to be seen as more important than the individual; the control of the group is likely to be particularly potent if there is social and/or geographical isolation from the rest of society, but it may be powerful even in segments of the Human Potential movement in which the goal is ostensibly one of freedom and individual self-development.

It is rare that these characteristics are carried to extremes, but in situations where they are, it is arguably the concentration on an exclusive, unquestionable Truth that is the most potentially dangerous in so far as it demands, at the expense of all else, total allegiance to that Truth. Edgar Mills, reflecting on the Jonestown suicides and murders, remarked upon the normative dissonance that was *not* present in the jungle community in Guyana: 'The ordinary morality of individuals is constrained by their contrasting loyalties to inconsistent standards, with the consequent necessity to keep correcting their behavior whenever allegiance to one norm threatens severe violation of another (thus we refer to "healthy skepticism").'[3]

Such healthy scepticism may, of course, be repressed in a number of different circumstances, but there is no doubt that such circumstances would include some fostered by a few NRMs: Jonestown and Rajneeshpuram providing obvious examples, with, perhaps, the erstwhile ISKCON[4] community at New Vrindaban, West Virginia, providing another. In such situations, where there is both geographical and social isolation from the rest of society, a single, unquestionable source of truth, an undermining of alternative views, tight control over the communication structure, and an undermining of relationships of trust, one may observe a process in which the generation of paranoia can lead to fear of both the enemy without and the enemy within – and a need for dependence upon a strong leadership. The leadership (which has itself created the need and dependency) can then demand increasingly unquestioning obedience, which may include the performance of illegal acts that are justified as a means of controlling the situation as it spirals towards the predicted disaster.

It is, of course, illegal in most western democracies to hold people against their will. In England both 'Kidnapping' and 'False Imprisonment' are criminal offences.[5] It has occasionally, very occasionally, been the case that people have been held against their will in an NRM. It is, for example, said that Synanon sometimes locked people up. For purely geographical reasons, it was not easy to leave the People's Temple (the Guyana jungle is not the most hospitable of environments); furthermore Jim Jones's followers had their passports locked away (a not insurmountable, but none the less considerable problem) and, even more persuasively, they risked getting shot in the back if they did attempt to escape. But such cases are very rare (in almost all respects, the People's Temple was significantly atypical of contemporary NRMs),[6] and the situation in which members of a new religious movement are most likely to find themselves restrained by physical coercion is when they are subjected to forcible deprogramming by people who want to remove them from their movement.

It has been frequently argued in the courts and elsewhere by Dr Margaret Singer and others that the process by which control has been exercised over people who have been held as prisoners-of-war is substantially similar to that used by the new religions. Most social scientists who have studied new religions have, however, disputed such claims. Not only do the NRMs not lock up their potential members, but the manner in which dependency and submission to the authority figures – the guards – was brought about in, for example, the situations that Bruno Bettelheim studied in Dachau and Buchenwald was radically different from the processes at work in new religions, where physical coercion is not a factor.[7] In the concentration camps, the prisoners started from an experience of shock and fear. Many of them suffered torture, and their initial reactions towards the guards were of hatred, anger and resentment. The changes that were brought about were responses to their finding themselves in this kind of a situation. Those who become members of a new religion do not have such experiences. The route to dependency and to accepting the Gestapo as father figures took a fundamentally different path from that followed by converts to NRMs with charismatic leaders, even if it may occasionally look as though there are some similarities in the final state.

The same point could be made about studies of prisoners-of-war in the hands of the North Koreans and the Chinese. The best-known of such studies, which are often cited by those who want to argue that the new religions use similar brainwashing techniques, are those carried out respectively by Edgar H. Schein[8] and Robert J. Lifton.[9] I do not wish to suggest that many of the characteristics which Lifton describes in the oft-quoted Chapter 22 of his *Thought Reform* can be found in several of the new religions; but I would want to insist that the process by which such characteristics come to be there is not the same when physical coercion is used as when it is not, and to confuse the two processes is to hinder rather than to help our understanding of authority and dependence in the new religions.

Before leaving the area of physical intervention, mention ought, perhaps, to be made of the possibility of interfering with the functioning of the brain in such a way that an individual is rendered dependent upon an authority figure or a movement. There are certain practices (to which I shall return) that can result in people becoming disoriented – at one extreme, such practices may result in 'altered states of consciousness' – but there is little or no evidence to suggest that NRMs employ techniques which have permanent effects on the brain; people subjected to practices that are meant to have such irresistible consequences have been able to resist the suggestion that they must submit to the wishes of, or become dependent upon, others. The processes that tend to be most influential, with the most long-lasting effects, are those which involve *understanding through the mind*, rather than mindless obedience that results from any significant malfunctioning of the brain.

Another theory that is sometimes used to explain authority and dependence in the new religions is that those who join the movements are, in some fundamental way, psychologically weaker or more suggestible than those who decide not to join the movements. There is no hard evidence that this is the case – indeed, psychological tests and sociological investigations have, on the whole, indicated that this is *not* the case.[10] In my own research into why people joined the Unification Church, I found that those who might be categorized as weak and/or pathetic were unlikely to be the ones who joined the movement, and, when they did join, they were likely to decide to leave within a few days or weeks at the most.[11]

While power is the general ability to get others to do what one wants, authority is power that is considered legitimate; those with authority are thought to have the right to expect others to do what they ask. Authority may be granted to individuals for a number of reasons and the scope and strength of the authority varies according to a number of different factors. The German sociologist Max Weber defined three 'ideal types' of authority: legal, traditional and charismatic.[12] Legal authority is the most limited in scope, it is the kind of authority that a bureaucrat might have by virtue of the office to which he has been appointed. Those who have such authority have it over only clearly defined areas of other people's lives: a policeman may have the authority to arrest someone, but not to tell that person whom he or she is to marry. Traditional authority stems from an assumption that things have always been done in a particular way, or because a person (such as a king or feudal lord) has inherited a status that commands respect and obedience according to the mores of the social system.

Charismatic authority is given to people because their followers believe that they have a special kind of 'grace' or personality, that they are in touch with the divine, or that they are themselves divine. Charismatic authority is constrained by neither rules nor tradition; the charismatic leader may be accorded the right to determine the minutest and most intimate details of his or her followers' lives. Charismatic leaders are not bound by even their own decisions – directives may be changed at any moment without either warning or reason being given. Perhaps one of the most important differences between most NRMs and most longer-established religions is that the charismatic leader of an NRM is rarely accountable to anyone or to any internal rules or traditions, while in the traditional religions, most leaders are subject to the constraints of a canon law or Shari'a: even the pronouncements of a Pope or an Ayatollah are considered infallible or irreversible within only a circumscribed sphere.

Clearly, in real life none of Weber's types is to be found in its pure form; authority may rest on a combination of the types and it may be more or less accepted by those over whom it is held. In some NRMs, charismatic leaders have a personality that by itself would appear to persuade people that they ought to be followed (Sai Baba and Bhagwan Shree Rajneesh are possible examples); but they will be recognized as having special powers only by certain kinds of people under certain kinds of conditions.[13] In fact, while carrying out research into the Unification Church, it became apparent that the members had not joined the movement because of any charismatic qualities which they had perceived in the person of the Reverend Sun Myung Moon: the vast majority of them had joined without ever having laid eyes on him, many had joined without even knowing that Moon was the leader of the movement. But once in the movement, they had *learned*, through finding themselves in a particular situation and taking part in a number of social processes, to see him as a charismatic leader who had the right to dictate where they should live, what kind of work they should do, whom they should marry, when they could sleep with their spouse – and numerous other details of their lives.

New converts to the Unification Church find themselves in a relatively authoritarian movement in that there is not only an expectation that members should comply with the dictates of the top leadership, but also with the orders of those above them in the hierarchical structure. The environment within which they find themselves is also relatively closed, in that there are few outside influences. They may be particularly vulnerable to suggestion in that they have acquired a new set of beliefs that have not been entirely internalized, and, in doing so, have been persuaded to reject the benchmarks with which they had previously evaluated new ideas.[14] The social attention of the members is focused inwards on the movement and its goals, and members are expected to affirm Unification beliefs and behave in a way that is deemed compatible with these. Moon is seen as the person who has revealed their new theology, the *Divine Principle*, and as they learn of the movement's internally circulated tenets, it is clear not only that Moon is accepted as the Messiah who can bring the Kingdom of Heaven on earth, but also that the whole of the world revolves around his actions. Moon is presented as the perfect example, who is prepared to sacrifice even his family for the purpose of establishing the Kingdom.

Personal stories and Unification myths telling of Moon's activities, achievements and insights are circulated, often defining him as one with super-human attributes; his photograph is to be found around the centres owned by the movement and in the members' pockets or handbags; members bow before his picture at the weekly 'pledge'; prayers are offered to God through Moon. Whatever happens in the movement – indeed in the world – Moon is automatically accorded the credit, with any blame for failures being levelled at second- or third-level leadership, the ignorance or intransigence of either members or non-members or both – or the power of Satan, who is said to be getting seriously troubled on account of Moon's incredible achievements. Individual members are unlikely to voice any misgivings about anything said or done by Moon – to do so would be disloyal to the movement, to Moon, to God. In other words, the whole ethos, practice and organization of the Unification Church is such that Moon is presented throughout each day as an omnipotent and omniscient presence, whose special attributes give him the right to expect those who wish to be part of the process of establishing God's Kingdom to do whatever he asks. And, of course, the commands of a person such as Moon, who is believed to have a direct line to God, will, for that reason if for no other, be accorded a very special legitimation.

The case should not be overstated. It is rare for even a charismatic leader to be able to persuade people to do absolutely anything just because he asks it of them. A step too far in the wrong direction, and the authenticity of his charisma may start to be questioned.[15] The process of 'charismatization' can be reversed – it is not unknown for a Unificationist to have a 'deconversion' experience, deciding, perhaps quite suddenly, that Moon's behaviour is not compatible with that of a Messiah.[16] Sometimes one can observe a more gradual disillusionment; some members never become convinced that Moon is a charismatic personality, but they are either sufficiently convinced of the truth of the teachings, or happy enough with life in the movement to be willing to 'flow with the tide' – at least for the time being.

Another point that should be stressed is that charisma can appear in a number of different guises.[17] Sometimes the leader denies that he is as divine as his followers wish to make him out to be: Krishnamurti is a well-known example; the leader of the Divine Light Mission (now known as Elan Vital) told his 'premies' not to regard him as a god. It should not, however, be thought that such a statement necessarily persuades devotees that their leader is not a charismatic person – it may even enhance his charisma in their eyes: 'neo-sannyasins' have frequently spoken of how Osho (Bhagwan Rajneesh) encouraged them to reject all dogmas and beliefs, including those that they had learned from him, yet this led many of them to believe more strongly than ever that his utterances were not only worth listening to, but should be faithfully complied with.

Once it is accepted that the exercise of authority involves a process of interaction, it is obvious that its character is likely to alter with the passage of time. Weber was particularly interested in the 'routinization' of charisma – a process whereby authority shifted to take on a more bureaucratic or legal–rational character. Although it is not common for those who take over from a leader to be imbued with a charismatic authority, this is by no means unknown – an example would be Elizabeth Clare Prophet who took over the leadership of the Summit Lighthouse (or Church Universal and Triumphant) on the death of her husband, Mark. On the other hand, it can happen that a successor appointed by a charismatic leader is later rejected by the membership – an example here would be Darwin Gross, who, having been pronounced by John Paul Twitchell to be the 972nd ECK master, was later ousted from the leadership of ECKANKAR.[18] There are, in fact, several different scenarios that can be realized with the death of a charismatic leader. Since the death of Bhagwan Rajneesh, his movement survives as a loose network of erstwhile sannyasins who continue to refer and defer to Osho's charismatic authority, which is now transmitted through videos, tape-recording, his books and those who can lay claim to having had personal contact with him during his lifetime. Alongside the charismatic authority of L. Ron Hubbard, the Church of Scientology had long had a bureaucratic quality; this became reinforced with Hubbard's death, with an interesting combination of the rational/legal authority being dependent upon the tradition of his charismatic leadership.

The ISKCON guru, His Divine Grace A. C. Bhaktivedanta Swami Prabhupada, who brought the Hare Krishna movement to the West, prepared for his death by devising a 'split level' authority structure: he appointed eleven gurus who were charged with the responsibility of spiritual leadership, and a 'Governing Body Commission' (GBC) which was to be responsible for more mundane organizational affairs. In fact, it was the non-charismatic GBC that was given authority to run the movement after it became apparent that nominating a devotee as a guru was not sufficient to guarantee that the aims and ideals of the movement would be ensured (indeed, half the gurus whom Prabhupada appointed have now left or been dismissed from the movement as a result of alleged offences such as gun-running, drug-trafficking, sexual peccadilloes and conspiracy to murder).[19]

However charismatic a leader may be, once a movement reaches a certain size, authority must, to some degree, be delegated. Lower-level leaders may be more or less authoritarian in character; they may be far less demanding than the leader, or they may be far more so. In the present wave of NRMs, there is a tendency for the lower-level leaders to be young and inexperienced. A hierarchical structure and/or the belief that there is an urgency to perform the tasks that God or some divine authority needs to be done can result in enthusiastically inept or power-hungry manipulators being in a position to wield an unpredictable or very heavy-handed authority over those placed under them. A reason that is sometimes given for following an authority figure, even when he or she is patently wrong, is that, if individuals were merely to follow their own conscience, the strength of the group would be lost; if, however, everyone does what the leader orders, the mistake will eventually be recognized (God will make it plain) and the group will retain its strength – an argument which, of course, gives the group (and its leadership) considerable control over its individual members. Several of the movements promote the belief that submitting to the discipline of a 'discipler', a 'shepherd' or (in Unification terminology) an 'Abel figure' is an essential path towards one's spiritual growth. Taken too far, however, this kind of authority can be counter-productive so far as increasing dependence on the movement is concerned: one former member of the London Church of Christ decided to leave the movement shortly after she had been told by her discipler that she was evil not to accept his interpretation of scripture.

There have been occasions when leaders have virtually handed over their authority to a second-in-command, who has then had the advantage of being the sole transmitter of the charismatic leader's message. Bhagwan Rajneesh's secretary in Oregon, Ma Anand Sheela, is a case in point. There, a situation developed in which Sheela and her most trusted associates initiated a process where all outsiders were, first, regarded with suspicion, and then defined as a dangerous threat to the Rajneesh community. Gradually, it became the insiders who were treated with suspicion, and eventually the ranch was fitted with electronic eavesdropping devices, and sannyasins developed sufficient paranoia to provide a rationale for a number of attempted and, perhaps, some actual murders.[20]

Although authority is most obvious when wielded by people in leadership positions, it should not be forgotten, however, that a peer group can exert considerable pressure on the individual to behave in a way that he or she might not otherwise have behaved. On a possibly somewhat trivial level, one can observe new members of a movement adopting styles of dress and hair, and speaking in new ways that are consistent with those of the other members. People joining the Unification Church do not need to be told by an authority figure that unkempt hair is 'out of place' in the movement – they themselves will feel out of place if they do not present a tidy appearance, if their clothes are 'unprincipled' or if they use 'bad language'. Their parents, having implored them for years to cut their hair and not to slouch about in scruffy jeans and a T-shirt, may become convinced that their sons have been brainwashed when they appear with short back and sides in grey flannels shortly after joining the movement. It is, however, unlikely that anyone has said anything to the convert – just as no one will have told new students to wear the scruffy jeans and T-shirt rather than the suit that their parents had given them when they left home to go to university.

More seriously, it is likely that the new convert may cease to mention doubts about the beliefs and practices of the movement, when he observes, not necessarily at a conscious level, that group mores do not encourage criticism of the movement – although they may approve criticism of the 'outside'. Such mores may convince a 'subversive' member that the fault lies in his or her perception. A series of now-classic experiments by Solomon Asch demonstrates the frequency with which people will agree to judgements about which there seems to be a group consensus, when they would have come to a quite different decision had they not been subjected to the group judgement.[21] For example, in one experiment, a college student was put in a room with a group of others who, without his knowing, had been primed to give the wrong answer in a 'test' to assess which of three unequal lines drawn on a blackboard was the same length as a fourth line. Thirty-two per cent of the students who were subjected to the experiment declared that they agreed with the verdict of the 'planted' members of the group despite the fact that the unanimous verdict patently went against the evidence of their own senses. Asch found, moreover, that if one of the 'plants' gave the correct answer, the 'naive' subjects' level of conformity to the majority dropped dramatically to 5.5 per cent. Other variations in the experiments indicated, perhaps not surprisingly, that the less obvious the differences, the more the conformity to the majority's judgement. In other words, Asch's work would support the propositions that (i) peer pressure can lead some people to suppress their independent evaluations and, in some cases, coming to doubt the evidence of their own eyes; (ii) individuals are more likely to doubt themselves if there seems to be *no one* who shares their perception of reality and (iii) if the differences in perception are not so easy to test; and (iv) this can happen in perfectly 'normal' situations.

Clearly in an NRM, where everyone is seemingly in agreement with a particular kind of perception of the world and the perception rests on claims that are not empirically testable, the new convert is more likely to go along with the majority (and thus reinforce the group influence on others) than he or she might do in an 'open' group where a variety of perspectives already exist. The fact that the presence of even one person who admits to seeing things in the same way as oneself can usually give people the confidence to express their doubts helps to explain why potential converts are sometimes kept apart from each other at introductory meetings or seminars, and why married couples or partners might come to leave a movement together as frequently as they do. At the same time, it should also be remembered that a sizeable proportion of individuals *do* defy the unanimously expressed majority view when it goes against their principles; and the majority of people who join the more well-known 'closed' movements, do in fact leave of their own accord in spite of the pressure to stay that is put upon them by both the leadership and their peers.[22]

Shifting away from the concept of authority towards the related but distinct subject of dependence, it can be argued that dependence, like authority, takes a variety of different forms, that it can be found in most non-NRM situations and that it is a 'more or less', rather than an absolute phenomenon. All of us are dependent on others more than we are likely to be aware of throughout most of our lives. The pertinent question here is whether there is anything peculiar to NRMs that leads to a special kind of dependence on the part of the individual on a movement and/or its leader(s). As with the wielding of authority, what knowledge we have of the NRMs does not suggest that there is; but some of the movements do exhibit characteristics that promote a tendency towards an increasing dependency among their membership.

It is, of course, important to note that the NRMs themselves tend to be dependent on the outside world for the provision of potential members, for economic exchange and material goods, and for services such as social security, medical care, legal protection and defence. This paper is, however, concerned primarily with processes, most of which are internal, but some of which are external, that lead to the individual members becoming increasingly dependent on the movement for decisions or resources such as personal identity, economic needs, friendship, direction in life, interpretations of particular experiences or a general world-view.

It is probably more often the case that a person becomes dependent on a movement to provide the key to the attainment of a goal that he or she had already valued, rather than to reveal the goal itself. There are, of course, numerous goals that individuals may be seeking, but which they find either impossible or extremely hard to achieve on their own. Often the goals are those that people who have no contact with an NRM would consider desirable: a closer relationship with God; a more spiritual life; better relationships with others; the development of one's 'true potential'; the establishment of a better (more godly, secure, peaceful or beautiful – or less materialistic, competitive, rational or unfair) society or world; and/or the attainment of salvation. Potential converts may have found themselves congratulated by members for being concerned about such goals and told that this in itself implies that they are truly kindred spirits of the movement in question. They are told that the movement not only desires the goal, but that it has the means of achieving it; the movement can provide the necessary techniques, the spiritual environment, the meaning, the direction, the reliable leadership, and the blueprint whereby the individual can develop (one way or the other), society can be transformed (one way or the other), a genuine relationship with God can be effected, and/or eternal salvation attained.[23]

Dependency on a movement to guide one towards a desired ideal or goal is dependency for day-to-day direction in life. This may be equally so when individuals depend on a movement to provide an ultimate meaning when, independently of the movement, they had already adopted certain values or a particular life-style. An example of this latter situation would be when an individual had decided to become a vegetarian and had then been told that this had really been a first step on the path towards Krishna Consciousness and a life of devotion – an ultimate goal, the understanding of which is dependent on obedience to the beliefs and practices of ISKCON.

In both these situations, that is, when individuals are dependent upon a movement to provide the means for a desired goal, and when they are dependent upon the movement to provide ultimate meaning for their everyday actions, there may come a time when faith in the connection between the means and the goal wavers.[24] It is possible that the member will then leave the movement; it is also possible that blatant discrepancies between means and end will result in a further dependency upon the movement to provide an even stronger statement of belief and commitment in order to justify or to make some kind of sense of an otherwise incongruous situation.

It has already been suggested that the more the members of a group are cut off from their family, their previous friends and acquaintances, the media and other alternative interpretations of what is going on, the more dependent on the group they are likely to become. One might expect the separation to be particularly acute if there is geographical or physical isolation, but social segregation may be almost as effective when members of a movement are meeting 'outsiders' during the course of their everyday lives but when discourse is restricted to exchanges about money or work, or, if deeper topics are touched upon, when members are concentrating on bearing witness to their own faith, rather than seeking or listening to alternative explanations about the meaning of life, the nature of reality, or the optimal methods of achieving salvation.

Isolation within and, thus, dependency upon a movement may also be fostered through a belief that for true spiritual development one has to relinquish all previous attachments, whether these involve ties to relatives, friends, interests, studies or whatever. Converts are expected to be not only born again in the Christian sense that they take Jesus into their hearts, but also in the sense that they become new people with no bond or loyalty (apart from that to the guru and/or the movement) distracting them from their path to self-realization. Again, it should be recognized that the desirability of detachment has been taught by most traditional religions and there, too, there have developed dependencies upon the immediate group and its interpretation of both ultimate and more mundane truths.

One of the most powerful resources that a movement may offer its members is friendship. The so-called 'love-bombing' that is showered upon potential converts in some movements is unlikely to last much beyond the stage at which a definite commitment to become, or not to become, a member has been made; but very genuine friendships do develop within NRMs – a fact that is hardly surprising considering that each of the movements tends to attract people who frequently have similar values and interests. It is true that the researcher may discover that members know surprisingly little about each other, but, especially in those movements that make a strong distinction between members and non-members, a shared identity and common experiences as members of the one group may bond at least some of them together with feelings of loyalty, trust and community that are often found lacking in the outside world. It is not uncommon for members to want to stay in a movement because they feel that they would be letting down their friends and that they would miss their companionship if they were to leave. Within a single movement, the degree to which the rift in friendship that leaving will impose may vary: leaving the Unification Church in the mid-1970s almost invariably resulted in there being a total break between the members and those who had departed; by the late 1980s, however, one of the numerous changes that had occurred in the movement was the sharpness with which membership was defined, and today it is not uncommon for ex-members to keep in touch not only with other ex-members, but also with some of the continuing membership.

The Unification Church in the 1970s, Ananda Marga, the Children of God, ISKCON, Sahaja Yoga and the Church of Scientology are among the NRMs that exhibit some of the characteristics which the anthropologist Mary Douglas has identified as typical of a strong 'group' control over the individual.[25] Where this kind of structuring of relationships occurs, people are defined primarily in terms of whether or not they are a member of a particular group: Ann, John, Mary and Timothy are seen by others and identify themselves first and foremost as a 'Moonie', a yogi, a Krishna devotee, a 'sannyasin', a 'premie' or a Scientologist. Within the clear boundary dividing 'them' and 'us', a parallel distinction is drawn between unambiguously opposed dichotomies such as godly and satanic, good and bad, righteous and evil. In such a situation, individuals depend upon the group for their very identity; it is of only secondary importance that the member is a musician, a mother, a kind person, or Mrs Smith's third child.

In such a group, it may be difficult to gain a sense of personal achievement; it is the group (or possibly the leader), not the individual, that is accorded praise or honour – although the individual may be apportioned blame for the group's or the leader's failures. With little apart from membership of the group to foster feelings of self-worth, fear of life 'outside' can be very threatening. To add to this, stories may be circulated about the terrible things that happen to apostates – one man told me how he had driven with extreme, almost dangerous, caution for several months after leaving a movement because, although he had publicly renounced his belief in his former guru, he still harboured the suspicion that she might get her revenge on him by causing a nasty accident. There are several cases of individuals who, having been forcibly removed by outsiders or told to leave by the movement itself, have experienced severe problems in coming to terms with themselves as individual persons. If one has come to accept oneself overwhelmingly in terms of the single characteristic of belonging to the group, then it is difficult to imagine *one's self* independent of the group identity.

Conversion, almost by definition, involves not only the adoption of a new set of beliefs, but also the *dropping*, or suspension of previously-held beliefs. Because most people are unlikely to be able immediately to grasp the whole of the new belief system, they will be dependent on others to fill in the details – and, perhaps, not only the details, but also the Gestalt, the full import and its implications. It may be that the movement not only determines what the correct answers to the converts' questions are, but also assumes the role of defining which questions can be asked – and which questions cannot be asked.

Although believers of any faith, particularly one of a more conservative or fundamentalist nature, can find themselves in a similar situation, individuals born into, or even converting into an older tradition in a relatively liberal or plural society are likely to enjoy more freedom in selecting and building up their own picture of reality and in exploring its implications, for there are likely to be a number of different perspectives that have been developed with the passage of time, accommodating to a number of different situations.[26]

Beliefs and practices leading to dependency are not confined to the more obviously authoritarian or closed groups; they may also be found in movements claiming to offer followers the opportunity of freeing themselves from constraints which are presumed to have arisen as a result of previous social conditioning. In such movements, the new truth, reality or approach is supposed to release one from previously obfuscating restrictions and thus enable the development of one's liberated, independent self. It is, indeed, possible to observe individuals who have joined such groups becoming more independent; but it is also possible to observe their becoming more dependent upon the guru or the group. Stripped of their erstwhile benchmarks, followers may find themselves as helpless as children who have not yet learned the ways of the world and are at the mercy of whatever situation they find themselves in. An assumption of many of the so-called 'self religions'[27] which celebrate the quest for 'the God within' is that, by removing layers of socialization from individuals, the true kernel of the individual will be revealed. This assumption needs to be carefully balanced against the alternative metaphor of an onion. Or, to make the point another way, individuals *without* social conditioning of one sort or another find it difficult, if not impossible, to function effectively as individuals.

A related way in which NRMs (and other traditions) may encourage dependency is by pouring scorn on rational thought. An emphasis is placed on the value of feeling, experience and 'allowing it to happen'; the 'reality' that one experiences with one's mind is defined as an unreal reality. It may be claimed that the proffered liberation is contingent upon surrendering to the guru, which, obviously enough, can lead to increased dependence. It may be claimed that 'real reality' is revealed in one's own dreams or during mystical experiences, in which case, it might be thought that individuals are enabled to grasp an understanding of their situation which, even if not that which others might agree upon, is dependent only upon their own subjective experiences rather than upon the whims or dictates of the group. This is, however, unlikely to be so. Anthropologists and historians have pointed out that most societies have had institutionalized explanations of otherwise inexplicable experiences, but, in modern western society, such explanations are not so readily available – one might, indeed, be tempted to say that in a predominantly secular society they are up for grabs.[28] A movement may be directly responsible for creating a situation in which individuals experience sensations, such as a cool breeze, or a deep calm, or an enhanced awareness of the senses so that colours seem more vivid, sounds more pure, and tastes more sweet, or they may fall into a trance or an 'altered state of consciousness'. But whether the experience is invoked by the movement, or appears to occur independently, as with a dream, the member may be dependent on the group, or at least some of the leaders in it, for an interpretation of the experience. It may not be very obvious that the interpretation is coming from the movement; it may, indeed, be presented as though the movement has nothing to do with it. Dubious converts might, for example, be told to ask God for a sign which will show them what they should believe. The next day they may be asked if they observed anything strange, or what they dreamed about during the night, only to be told with enthusiastic delight that what occurred is irrefutable confirmation that the movement is right. Alternatively, a movement may appear to be turning to an independent authority by providing the one and only true interpretation of Holy Scripture.

It was intimated earlier that dependency may be increased by certain techniques, beliefs or practices lowering an individual's resistance to suggestion. It has been claimed that within NRMs a lack of adequate sleep, a poor or unfamiliar diet, long hours of chanting, hyperventilation or (used in a very loose sense) hypnosis have left members incapable of being independent. It is true that in so far as people are kept very busy, without enough time to think about what they are doing, or in so far as they are physically run down or exhausted, they are less likely to make the effort to reach independent decisions; it is easier to drift with the tide. It is also true, however, that most of the members of most NRMs manage to keep as physically healthy and alert as others of their age, and as mentioned earlier, people can and do resist demands with which they do not wish to comply. Research has produced little evidence of long-term dependence on an NRM arising solely as the result of physical incapacity, although short-term suggestibility may sometimes be evoked by such methods.

Short-term compliance may also be invoked through a somewhat different process: that of deception. While 'heavenly deception', 'transcendental trickery' or any other form of 'economy with the truth' or outright lying is unlikely in itself to result directly in the deceived person becoming dependent on a movement, the deception can buy time for dependency to be fostered through other means. By the time that the deception has become apparent, it is possible that friendships and/or a sense of loyalty to the group has developed. It is also possible that some people, having acted as though something were true, will, for reasons of consistency, continue to act in that way in the face of evidence to the contrary.[29]

Occasionally a new religion may acquire a hold over its members by persuading them to confess to things that they have done in the past; the convert may be induced to do this as part of a cleansing, purifying or renewal process. Although assurances could have been given that the information is to be destroyed or kept utterly confidential, the fact that the secret has been revealed may be actually or potentially used to blackmail the confessor into a dependence on the group for silence. It may also be that a member will be persuaded to do something shameful or criminal while in the movement, and this, too, can result in a dependence upon those who know about the act to keep silent. The fear generated by guilt, shame and/or the threat of exposure may be generated even in instances where no one in the movement actually knows about the real or supposed sin, but it is believed that the leader has supernatural powers that allow him or her to 'see' the innermost secrets of others.

Both authority and dependency may be fostered through the employment of special concepts and language. Non-verbal language (such as the dress and self-presentation of Krishna devotees or the Brahma Kumaris) and special jargon (such as that used by Scientologists or Rastafarians) can reinforce the boundary between 'them' and 'us'. Jargon and catch-phrases can also reduce the complexities and complications of reality to simple ideas or distinctions of the either/or kind: people are either good or bad, godly or satanic; you are either with us or against us. Such sharp and, in most cases, misleading if not grossly inaccurate dichotomies can force people into taking positions that they might not really wish to embrace and, consequently, into complying with instructions or being dependent upon others to formulate actions they would not have considered necessary or appropriate had more than two options, each with its own pre-defined package of evaluation and implied action, been available. Members in an NRM have sometimes said that, although they were worried about some of the practices they observed in the movement, they still felt that there was something that they did not want to deny that was good, but, because of the black and white way in which the situation was defined, they would be forced to deny the good things and completely to sever relations with the friends that they had made in the movement – so they stayed in. If outsiders are defined as being in the power of Satan, a 'Potential Trouble Source', or 'giving out bad/dangerous vibrations', it is none too easy to have a relaxed or 'normal' relationship with them.

Such a situation can be reinforced by the propaganda of the anti-cultists who use similar either/or language – either one is totally against all cults, or one is on their side; ex-members who do not totally repudiate all their experiences in a movement are defined as having not 'really' left. Anti-cultists provide us with a further illustration of how language can be used to define a situation in a particular way through the frequent use they make of the passive tense to describe what 'happens to' members (victims) of the movements: how, for example, they *are* recruited, how they *are* forced to work for the organization, and, perhaps, how they had *to be* rescued – the implication being that the individual had no say in the matter, a device that can, in itself, lead to an increased dependency of the person who is defined as being so incapable of reaching independent decisions.

There are a number of other ways in which dependency on a movement can, paradoxically, be exacerbated by those outside the movement who want members to become less dependent and to leave. It is unhelpful for parents to persist in telling their children that they no longer have a mind of their own, or that they should stop being silly and return to their old selves when they may have joined the movement partly in an attempt to establish an identity independent of the one they feel their parents wish to impose upon them.[30] Members of NRMs have also felt inhibited from leaving when their parents have intimated that they want nothing more to do with their errant child – or when the members feel that there will be severe recrimination and/or 'I told you so's awaiting their return.

Members may be facing a very real difficulty in wondering what they could do, without becoming dependent on their parents, if they were to leave. A promising career or university place may have been abandoned; the local education authority may refuse to extend a grant for a second chance at getting a degree. Just as a hard-working wife might be dependent upon her husband for pocket money and permission to buy any personal items, so members who work long hours for a movement, or who are expected to hand over their earnings, may be dependent on the 'generosity' of the group if they want to purchase anything for themselves. Members in such a situation will not have accumulated a fat bank balance; they are unlikely to have made the down-payment for a mortgage; they will have little, if anything, in the way of furniture or other household goods – they may have donated any capital assets they had to the movement. Whatever skills they have developed while working for the movement are unlikely to be those that outside employers will readily recognize as relevant for any but the most menial of jobs; peers in the outside will have had more appropriate experience in the competition for jobs; the longer the time spent in an NRM, the more taxing the question of how to fill in one's *curriculum vitae* may become; health insurance and social security contributions may not have been paid since joining the movement. And friends and other previous contacts may have been dropped or drifted away.

Like the down-trodden wife who feels she cannot leave her husband because she has no other means of support for herself and, perhaps, her children, disillusioned members may come to feel that they cannot leave their movement because they are dependent upon it for their livelihood and shelter. They may, on the other hand, decide that the situation of dependence has become intolerable: one ex-member told me that he left his movement because he just could not bear the thought of continually having to ask for permission to buy a new tube of toothpaste or to beg for a pair of shoes when his old ones had been worn out by selling goods on the street all day.

In conclusion, there are many ways in which NRMs can exert authority and foster dependence, but all of these ways can be found in other situations. It is also the case that the outside world may be defined as threatening by some of the movements, but there are ways in which sections of the outside *do* threaten the member and may reinforce the belief that the movement is the only safe place in which to enjoy a real identity, friendship, work, economic support and so on. And, with the passage of time, the outside may come to appear less welcoming, and more strange – and some members may develop an increasing reluctance to risk losing the positive aspects of the movement in which they have invested so much of their time, energy and emotions. Under such circumstances, and after a period of not having to make major decisions about the direction of their life, the prospect of leading a potentially lonely life in the outside may appear increasingly daunting.

On the other hand, it is clear that the spirals of increasing authority and dependency can be, and frequently have been, reversed. Furthermore, several NRMs have given the individual time and the protective space in which to develop an independence from over-protective parents, to define themselves in their own terms, and to decide what they really want to do with their life, rather than drifting into the career planned by their parents or expected of them by the wider society.

Notes

Chapter 1   Religion, Modernity and Post-modernity

1 I am grateful to Dr Bryan Wilson for inviting me to try out some of the ideas in this chapter on the participants in his seminar at All Souls College, Oxford, in 1990. I benefited greatly from the participants' responses. I also appreciated the opportunity to learn from the responses made to an earlier version of this paper at a seminar given to the Department of Sociology, University of Edinburgh in the same year.

2 J. A. Beckford, 'The Insulation and Isolation of the Sociology of Religion', *Sociological Analysis*, 46, 4, 1985, pp. 347–54. See also K. Thompson, 'Transgressing the Boundary between the Sacred and the Secular/Profane: a Durkheimian Perspective on a Public Controversy', *Sociological Analysis*, 52, 3, 1991, pp. 277–91.

3 R. Wallis and S. Bruce, 'Religion: the British Contribution', *British Journal of Sociology*, 40, 3, 1989, pp. 493–520.

4 Ibid., p. 512.

5 See, for example, R. Robertson, 'The Globalization Paradigm: Thinking Globally', in D. Bromley, ed., *Religion and the Social Order. New Developments in Theory and Research*, Vol. 1, JAI Press, Greenwich, CT, 1991, pp. 207–24; G. Marshall, 'Which Way for the Sociology of Religion?', *Comparative Studies in Society and History*, 29, 1987, pp. 375–80; B. S. Turner, *Religion and Social Theory*, Heinemann, London, 1983; Thompson, op. cit.; and K. Thompson, 'Religion: the British Contribution', *British Journal of Sociology*, 41, 1990, pp. 531–5.

6 T. Parsons, *The Social System*, Free Press, New York, 1951; T. Parsons and E. Shils, eds, *Toward a General Theory of Action*, Harvard University Press, Cambridge, MA, 1951; T. Parsons, 'The Pattern of Religious Organization in the United States', *Daedalus*, Summer 1968, pp. 65–85; and 'Mental Illness and "Spiritual Malaise": the Roles of the Psychiatrist and of the Minister of Religion', in H. Hofmann ed., *The Ministry and Mental Health*, Association Press, New York, 1960.

7 'The supernatural order thus gives cognitive meaning to the moral–evaluative sentiments and norms of an action system . . . in the sense that they tend to be integrated with one another and that this integration is importantly related to the stabilization of the system' (Parsons, *The Social System*, op. cit., p. 369).

8 Economic productivity for the society may be translated into the valuation of achievement for the individual. There must be widespread motivation to active achievement in instrumental, 'worldly' activities,

essentially the type of pattern which Weber classically delineated for ascetic Protestantism, though it is now clear that Protestantism is not the only cultural base on which such a value-orientation can develop. (T. Parsons, 'Some Principal Characteristics of Industrial Societies', in his *Structure and Process in Modern Society*, Free Press, New York, 1960, p. 38)

9 R. N. Bellah, *Beyond Belief. Essays on Religion in a Post-Traditional World*, Harper & Row, New York, 1970, p. 39.

10 As Parsons put it:

In my opinion the Protestant ethic is far from dead. It continues to inform our orientations to a very important sector of life today as it did in the past. We do value systematic rational work in 'callings', and we do so out of what is at some level a religious background. In my opinion the instrumental apparatus of modern society could not function without a generous component of this kind of evaluation.
(T. Parsons, 'Religion in Postindustrial America: the Problem of Secularization', *Social Research*, 41, 2, 1974, p. 221)

11 R. N. Bellah, *Tokugawa Religion*, Free Press, New York, 1957, p. 121. Bellah has also argued that

Japanese religion never tires of stressing the importance of diligence and frugality and of attributing religious significance to them, both in terms of carrying out one's obligations to the sacred and in terms of purifying the self of evil impulses and desires. That such an ethic is profoundly favourable to economic rationalization was the major point of Weber's study of Protestantism and we must say that it seems similarly favourable in Japan . . . Such an ethic certainly seems favourable if not essential to industrialization, at least in its early stage.'
(Ibid., p. 196)

12 There are general statements of Berger's position in his *The Sacred Canopy: Elements of a Sociological Theory of Religion*, Doubleday, Garden City, NJ, 1967; *Pyramids of Sacrifice*, Penguin Books, Harmondsworth, 1974; and *Facing Up to Modernity*, Basic Books, New York, 1977.

13 This is one of the major themes of his *The Capitalist Revolution*, Basic Books, New York, 1986.

14 Bryan R. Wilson, *Religion in Sociological Perspective*, Oxford University Press, 1982, p. 155.

15 Ibid., pp. 159–61.

16 The best, but far from infallible, sources of evidence include P. Brierley, ed., *The UK Christian Handbook, 1990/91 Edition*, MARC Europe, London, 1990; A. D. Gilbert, *The Making of Post-Christian Britain*, Longman, London, 1980; and R. Gill, *Competing Convictions*, SCM Press, London, 1989.

17 See K. Knott, 'Other Major Religious Traditions', in T. Thomas, ed., *The British. Their Religious Beliefs and Practices 1800–1986*, Routledge, London, 1990, pp. 133–57; K. Knott, 'Hindu Communities in Britain', in P. Badham, ed., *Religion, State and Society in Modern Britain* (Texts and Studies in Religion, Vol. 43), Edwin Mellen Press, Lewiston, NY, 1989, pp. 243–57; J. Nielsen, 'Islamic Communities in Britain', in Badham, ed., op. cit., pp. 225–38; O. Cole, 'Sikhism', in Badham, ed., op. cit., pp. 259–76; R. Burghart, *Hinduism in Britain*, Routledge, London, 1989.

18 M. Abrams et al., eds, *Values and Social Change in Britain*, Macmillan, London, 1985.

19 R. W. Bibby and M. B. Brinkerhoff, 'The Circulation of the Saints: a Study of People who Join Conservative Churches', *Journal for the Scientific Study of Religion*, 12, 3, 1973, pp. 273–84.

20 A. M. Greeley, *Religious Change in America*, Harvard University Press, Cambridge, MA, 1989.

21 J. Seidler, 'Priest Resignations in a Lazy Monopoly', *American Sociological Review*, 44, 1979, pp. 763–83.

22 Gill, op. cit.

23 R. Towler, *The Need for Certainty. A Sociological Study of Conventional Religion*, Routledge & Kegan Paul, London, 1984.

24 J. A. Beckford, 'Religion and Politics in England and Wales', *Daedalus*, 120, 3, 1991, pp. 179–201.

25 J. A. Beckford, 'Great Britain: Voluntarism and Sectional Interests', in R. Wuthnow, ed., *Between States and Markets: The Voluntary Sector in Comparative Perspective*, Princeton University Press, 1991, pp. 30–63. For conservative protests against the growing affinity between religion and radical political causes, see E. Norman, *Christianity and the World Order*, Oxford University Press, 1979; and D. Anderson, ed., *The Kindness that Kills: the Churches' Simplistic Responses to Complex Social Issues*, SPCK, London, 1984.

26 See I. Hamnett, ed., *Religious Pluralism and Unbelief*, Routledge, London, 1990.

27 T. Luckmann, 'Shrinking Transcendence, Expanding Religion?', *Sociological Analysis*, 50, 2, 1990, pp. 127–38.

28 J. Gusfield, 'Social Movements and Social Change: Perspectives of Linearity and Fluidity', in L. Kriesberg, ed., *Research in Social Movements, Conflict and Change*, Vol. 4, JAI Press, Greenwich, CT, 1981, pp. 317–39.

29 A good example of this way of thinking is Ynestra King's description of what she calls 'ecofeminism':

> We come from the feminist movement, the anti-nuclear movement, the disarmament movement, the holistic health movement . . . Life on earth and the earth itself are in terrible danger . . . There are connections between all living things and indeed we women are the fact and flesh of connectedness . . . Feminism and ecology are where politics comes face to face with biology, and where the spiritual and the political come together . . . The crisis of this civilization which has led us to the brink of nuclear annihilation is spiritual as much as it is economic.
> (Y. King, 'Eco-feminism – Where the Spiritual and the Political Come Together', *Women for Life on Earth*, Winter 1984, pp. 4, 5)

30 Y. Lambert, *Dieu Change en Bretagne*, Cerf, Paris, 1985; and Y. Lambert, 'From Parish to Transcendent Humanism in France', in J. A. Beckford and T. Luckmann, eds, *The Changing Face of Religion*, Sage, London, 1989, pp. 49–63.

31 See, for example, accounts of the massive shifts of public opinion about such matters as ecology, peace, gender and health in R. Inglehart, *Culture Shift in Advanced Industrial Society*, Princeton University Press, 1990; see also the accounts of 'new' social movements on these themes in R. Dalton and M. Kuechler, eds, *Challenging the Political Order. New Social and Political Movements in Western Democracies*, Polity Press, Cambridge, 1990.

32 See Luckmann, *Invisible Religion*, op. cit.

33 See, for example, D. Harvey, *The Condition of Postmodernity*, Blackwell,

Oxford, 1989; and D. Kellner, 'Postmodernism as Social Theory: Some Challenges and Problems', *Theory, Culture and Society*, 5, 2–3, 1988, pp. 239–69.

34 See James S. Gordon, *The Golden Guru*, Stephen Greene Press, Lexington,
MA, 1987; J. Thompson and P. Heelas, *The Way of the Heart*, Aquarian Press,
Wellingborough, Northants, 1986.

35 R. N. Bellah, 'Christian Faithfulness in a Pluralist World', in F. B. Burnham,
ed., *Postmodern Theology*, Harper & Row, San Francisco, 1989, pp. 74–91.

36 R. Robertson and J. Chirico, 'Humanity, Globalization and Worldwide
Religious Resurgence: a Theoretical Exploration', *Sociological Analysis*, 46,
1985, pp. 219–42.

37   Modernity has given us a false pluralism because it has claimed to offer
      a new metalanguage which is really true, and to which all the particular
      languages of culture and religion must be reduced. The new metalangu-
      age is the language of facts, proven by scientific method to be truly,
      objectively there. [But] although science is alive and well, scientism,
      which is another way of designating the first language of modernity,
      is seriously undermined. The actual practice of science does not warrant
      the claim of scientism to be a universal language superior in its validity
      to all the beliefs and practices of mankind.
      (R. N. Bellah, 'Christian Faithfulness', op. cit., pp. 75, 78)

38 *Pace* Burnham (ed.), op. cit.
39 For example, the rapid proliferation of Protestant forms of religion in South
America has taken place largely outside the framework of traditional social
groupings. See D. A. Martin, *Tongues of Fire*, Blackwell, Oxford, 1990. Similarly in the UK, the 'house church' or restorationist movement has spread
through networks which cut across the traditional churches. See A. Walker,
Restoring the Kingdom. The Radical Christianity of the House Church Movement,
Hodder & Stoughton, London, 1985.

40 See J. A. Beckford, *Cult Controversies. The Societal Response to New Religious
Movements*, Tavistock, London, 1985, ch. 9.

Chapter 2   Religious Fundamentalism: Neo-traditionalism in Modern Societies

1 See, for example, Andrew Walker, 'Fundamentalism and Modernity: the
Restoration Movement in Britain', in Lionel Caplan, ed., *Studies in Religious
Fundamentalism*, State University of New York Press, Albany, 1987,
pp. 195–210.
2 Caplan (ed.), op. cit.
3 William Shepard, ' "Fundamentalism", Christian and Islamic', *Religion*, 17,
1987, pp. 355–78. Shepard was unable to provide a suitable alternative term
that would cover both Protestant fundamentalism and Islamic radicalism,
but he suggested that the term 'radical neo-traditionalism' might be used
when anti-modernist movements from what he calls non-scriptural religions
(that is, all religious traditions apart from Protestantism and Islam) are
brought into the comparison. 'Neo-traditionalism' in the sense of a fusion
of traditional and modernist forms has been used by Smart, by Friedman
with reference to the Jewish ultra-Orthodox, and, in a political context, by
Walder. Ninian Smart, 'Three Forms of Religious Convergence', in Richard
T. Antoun and Mary Elaine Hegland, eds, *Religious Resurgence: Contemporary
Cases in Islam, Christianity, and Judaism*, Syracuse University Press, Syracuse,

NY, 1987, pp. 223–32. Menachem Friedman, 'Jewish Zealots: Conservative versus Innovation', in Emmanuel Sivan and Menachem Friedman, eds, *Religious Radicalism and Politics in the Middle East*, State University of New York Press, Albany, 1990, pp. 127–41. Andrew G. Walder, *Communist Neo-Traditionalism: Work and Authority in Chinese Industry*, University of California Press, Berkeley, 1986.

4 Bruce B. Lawrence, *Defenders of God: the Fundamentalist Revolt Against the Modern Age*, I. B. Tauris & Co., London, 1990, pp. 90–5.

5 See, for example, Lionel Caplan, *Class and Culture in Urban India: Fundamentalism in a Christian Community*, Clarendon Press, Oxford, 1987, and Ian S. Lustick, *For the Land and the Lord: Jewish Fundamentalism in Israel*, Council on Foreign Relations, New York, 1988.

6 Nancy Tatom Ammerman, *Bible Believers: Fundamentalism in the Modern World*, Rutgers University Press, New Brunswick, NJ, 1987. This emphasis on a particular form of Christian millenarianism as a criterion of contemporary fundamentalism is in line with the argument that the roots of Christian fundamentalism are to be understood in relationship to the history of Christian millenarianism in the nineteenth and early twentieth centuries. See, Ernest R. Sandeen, *The Roots of Fundamentalism: British and American Millenarianism, 1800–1930*, University of Chicago Press, 1970. Lawrence criticizes Sandeen's representation of Protestant fundamentalism as a continuation of British and American millenarianism of the nineteenth century. Lawrence emphasizes that, by the late 1920s, the fundamentalist movement had undergone a transformation whereby its protest against modernism, and in particular its attack on evolutionism, had come to the fore in place of millenarianism (Lawrence, op. cit., pp. 167–70).

7 Grant Wacker, 'Uneasy in Zion: Evangelicals in Postmodern Society', in George Marsden, ed., *Evangelicalism and Modern America*, Erdmans, Grand Rapids, MI, 1984. Steve Bruce, *The Rise and Fall of the New Christian Right*, Clarendon Press, Oxford, 1988. John H. Simpson, 'Some Elementary Forms of Authority and Fundamentalist Politics', in Jeffrey K. Hadden and Anson Shupe, eds, *Prophetic Religions and Politics*, Paragon House, New York, 1986, pp. 391–409. Frank J. Lechner, 'Fundamentalism and Sociocultural Revitalization in America: a Sociological Interpretation', *Sociological Analysis*, 46, 1985, pp. 243–60.

8 Roland Robertson, 'Globalization, Politics, and Religion', in James A. Beckford and Thomas Luckmann, eds, *The Changing Face of Religion*, Sage, London, 1989, pp. 10–23. Roland Robertson and JoAnn Chirico, 'Humanity, Globalization, and Worldwide Religious Resurgence: a Theoretical Exploration', *Sociological Analysis*, 46, 1985, pp. 219–47.

9 Anson Shupe and Jeffrey K. Hadden, 'Is There Such a Thing as Global Fundamentalism', in Jeffrey K. Hadden and Anson Shupe, eds, *Secularization and Fundamentalism Reconsidered*, Paragon House, New York, 1989, pp. 109–22. Robertson and Shupe and Hadden contrast their attention to cultural features in the world setting with that of the world-system perspective associated with I. Wallenstein who has focused on economic and political relationships among nations within the world capitalist system. Wuthnow's attempt to categorize and account for the rise of different types of religious movements within the world-system perspective (Robert Wuthnow, 'World Order and Religious Movements', in Albert Bergesen, ed., *Studies of the Modern World-System*, Academic Press, New York, 1980, pp. 57–75) is also criticized by Robertson and Chirico (op. cit.) because

cultural factors come into Wuthnow's scheme only as intra-societal outcomes of inter-societal economic and political relationships. They, in contrast, want to emphasize the globalization of essentially cultural processes. As against the uncritical acceptance of secularization theory by the world-systems perspective, Shupe and Hadden claim that fundamentalism is an important form of the resacralization process that is triggered by the ceiling effect of secularization.

10 cf. Angela Dietrich, 'The Khalsa Resurrected: Sikh Fundamentalism in the Punjab', in Caplan (ed.), op. cit., pp. 122–37.

11 Hava Lazarus-Yafeh, 'Contemporary Fundamentalism – Judaism, Christianity, Islam', *Jerusalem Quarterly*, Summer 1988, pp. 27–39; Lawrence, op. cit.; Shepard, op. cit. Lawrence is the only book-length study of fundamentalism in the three monotheistic traditions, but it is less comparative in its framework than the other studies listed. Lawrence interprets all the fundamentalisms as radical opponents to ideological modernism, but each one is described and analysed in separate chapters and comparisons across the three religious traditions are few and tend to be incidental asides in the text. Shepard's comparison of Protestant fundamentalism and Islamic radicalism has been criticized by Lawrence who considers that what he calls Shepard's nominalist quest or search for definitional certitude avoids the real issue of fundamentalist movements which is their anti-modernist protest. Bruce B. Lawrence, 'Critique of William Shepard "Fundamentalism" Christian and Islamic', *Religion*, 19, 1989, pp. 275–80. This criticism is somewhat unfair because Shepard argues that it is the anti-modernist orientation that justifies a common term, but Shepard's defence of his efforts at semantic purification as necessary for understanding raises the question of the purpose of his comparative analysis beyond a classificatory scheme. William Shepard, 'Response to the Critiques of "Fundamentalism" Christian and Islamic by Bruce Lawrence and Azim Nanji', *Religion*, 19, 1989, pp. 285–92.

12 Lawrence, *Defenders of God*, op. cit., pp. 106–17.

13 Robin Gill, *Competing Convictions*, SCM Press, London, 1989, pp. 23, 32.

14 Lawrence, op. cit., pp. 5–6.

15 Shepard, op. cit.

16 Lawrence, op. cit., pp. 214–15, 222–4. Emmanuel Sivan, 'Islamic Radicalism: Sunni and Shiite', in Sivan and Friedman (eds), op. cit., pp. 39–75.

17 Malise Ruthven, *Islam in the World*, Oxford University Press, New York, 1984.

18 For general comparisons of Islam and Judaism see Daniel Pipes, *In the Path of God: Islam and Political Power*, Basic Books, New York, 1983, and Mervin F. Verbit, 'The Political Character of Judaism and Islam: Some Comparisons', in Michael Curtis, ed., *Religion and Politics in the Middle East*, Westview Press, Boulder, CO, 1981, pp. 69–76.

19 Lazarus-Yafeh, op. cit.

20 William Montgomery Watt, *Islamic Fundamentalism and Modernity*, Routledge, London, 1988.

21 Jonathan Webber, 'Rethinking Fundamentalism: the Readjustment of Jewish Society in the Modern World', in Caplan (ed.), op. cit., pp. 95–121.

22 Charles S. Liebman, *Deceptive Images: Toward a Redefinition of American Judaism*, Transaction Books, New Brunswick, 1988, p. 113.

23 In Islam there are, of course, the 'Five Pillars', the most important duties of all Muslims (profession of faith, daily prayer, almsgiving, fasting and

pilgrimage to Mecca), but because they are accepted, in theory at least, by almost all Muslims, they would not differentiate a fundamentalist stance.

24 Shepard, op. cit. See also Ammerman, op. cit., and James Davison Hunter, *American Evangelicalism: Conservative Religion and the Quandary of Modernity*, Rutgers University Press, New Brunswick, NJ, 1983, and *Evangelicalism: The Coming Generation*, University of Chicago Press, 1987.

25 R. Hrair Dekmejian, *Islam in Revolution: Fundamentalism in the Arab World*, Syracuse University Press, Syracuse, NY, 1985. Daniel Pipes, 'Fundamentalist Muslims in World Politics', in Hadden and Shupe (eds), op. cit., pp. 123–51. Gilles Kepel, *Muslim Extremism in Egypt: the Prophet and Pharaoh*, University of California Press, Berkeley, 1985. Fazlur Ruhman, 'Roots of Islamic Neo-Fundamentalism', in P. H. Stoddard, ed., *Change in the Muslim World*, Syracuse University Press, Syracuse, NY, 1981, pp. 23–35. Bruce B. Lawrence, 'Muslim Fundamentalist Movements: Reflections Toward a New Approach', in Barbara Freyer Stowasser, ed., *The Islamic Impulse*, Croom Helm, London, 1987, pp. 15–36. Said Amir Arjomand, 'The Emergence of Islamic Political Ideologies', in Beckford and Luckmann (eds), op. cit., pp. 109–23.

26 Janet Aviad, *Return to Judaism: Religious Renewal in Israel*, University of Chicago Press, 1983.

27 Menachem Friedman, 'Life Tradition and Book Tradition in the Development of Ultraorthodox Judaism', in Harvey E. Goldberg, ed., *Judaism Viewed from Within and from Without*, State University of New York Press, Albany, 1987, pp. 235–55.

28 Lazarus-Yafeh, op. cit.

29 Lawrence, *Defenders of God*, op. cit., pp. 100–1, 236.

30 Ibid., p. 6.

31 Lawrence, 'Muslim Fundamentalist', op. cit.

32 Razelle Frankl, *Televangelism: the Marketing of Popular Religion*, Southern Illinois University Press, Cardondale, 1987. Stewart M. Hoover, *Mass Media Religion: the Social Sources of the Electronic Church*, Sage, Newbury Park, 1989.

33 James Barr, *Fundamentalism*, Westminster Press, Philadelphia, 1977.

34 Gino Germani, *The Sociology of Modernization*, Transaction Books, New Brunswick, NJ, 1981.

35 Peter L. Berger et al., *The Homeless Mind*, Penguin Books, Harmondsworth, 1974.

36 Barr, op. cit.; Sandeen, op. cit.; Bruce, op. cit.; George Marsden, 'Preachers of Paradox: the Religious New Right in Historical Perspective', in Mary Douglas and Steven M. Tipton, eds, *Religion and America*, Beacon Press, Boston, 1983, pp. 150–68.

37 Hunter, *American Evangelicalism*, op. cit.; Hunter, *Evangelicalism*, op. cit.; Bruce, op. cit. Robert C. Liebman, 'The Making of the New Christian Right', in Robert C. Liebman and Robert Wuthnow, eds, *The New Christian Right*, Aldine Publishing, New York, 1983. Robert Wuthnow, *The Restructuring of American Religion: Society and Faith Since World War II*, Princeton University Press, 1988.

38 cf. Lynn Davidman, 'Accommodation and Resistance to Modernity; a Comparison of Two Contemporary Orthodox Jewish Groups', *Sociological Analysis*, 51, 1990, pp. 35–51.

39 Stephen Sharot, *Judaism: a Sociology*, Holmes and Meier, New York, 1976.

40 Robert Liberles, *Religious Conflict in Social Context; The Resurgence of Orthodox*

Judaism in Frankfurt Am Main, 1838–1877, Greenwood Press, Westport, CO, 1985.

41 Stephen Sharot, *Messianism, Mysticism, and Magic: A Sociological Analysis of Jewish Religious Movements*, University of North Carolina Press, Chapel Hill, 1982, pp. 206–24.

42 M. Ruthven, op. cit.; Bassam Tibi, 'Islam and Secularization: Religion and the Functional Differentiation of the Social System', *Archiv für Rechts-und Sozialphilosophie*, 66, 1980, pp. 207–27.

43 John O. Voll, 'Islamic Renewal and the "Failure of the West" ', in Antoun and Hegland (eds), op. cit., pp. 127–44. Emmanuel Sivan, *Radical Islam: Medieval Theology and Modern Politics*, Yale University Press, New Haven, 1985.

44 Lawrence, *Defenders of God*, op. cit., pp. 83–6.

45 Ibid., p. 222.

46 Amatzia Baram, 'The Radical Shiite Opposition Movements in Iraq', in Sivan and Friedman (eds), op. cit., pp. 95–125.

47 Lazarus-Yafeh, op. cit.; Lustick, op. cit.; Smart, op. cit.

48 The most extended comparison is Eric Davis, 'Religion Against the State; a Political Economy of Religious Radicalism in Egypt and Israel', in Antoun and Hegland (eds), op. cit., pp. 145–66.

49 Sharot, *Messianism*, op. cit., pp. 229–37. Tzvi Raanan, *Gush Emunim* (in Hebrew), Sifriat Po'alim, Tel Aviv, 1980. Janet Aviad, 'The Contemporary Israeli Pursuit of the Millennium', *Religion*, 14, 1984, pp. 199–222. David Newman, 'Gush Emunim Between Fundamentalism and Pragmatism', *Jerusalem Quarterly*, 39, 1986, pp. 33–43.

50 Emmanuel Sivan, 'Introduction', in Sivan and Friedman (eds), op. cit., pp. 1–9.

51 cf. Aviezer Ravitzky, 'Religious Radicalism and Political Messianism in Israel', in ibid., pp. 11–37. G. Aran, 'Redemption as a Catastrophe: the Gospel of Gush Emunim', in ibid., pp. 157–75. Menachem Friedman retains the label 'fundamentalist' for Gush Emunim by distinguishing between its 'innovative fundamentalism' and the 'conservative fundamentalism' of Neterei Karta. He defines fundamentalism as 'a religious outlook shared by a group of believers who base their belief on an ideal religious-political reality that has existed *or is expected to emerge in the future*' (my emphasis; 'Jewish Zealots', op. cit., pp. 127–41). This definition encompasses too wide a range of religious movements to be useful. I believe that it is more useful to distinguish between conservative and radical fundamentalist movements than between conservative and innovative. Friedman's own work ('Life Tradition', op. cit.) has shown that the ultra-Orthodox have been highly innovative in their conservatism.

52 Arjomand, op. cit.

53 Sivan, *Radical Islam*, op. cit., p. 86. Dekmejian, op. cit., p. 61.

54 Pipes, 'Fundamentalist Muslims', op. cit.

55 Charles S. Liebman and Eliezer Don-Yehiya, *Religion and Politics in Israel*, Indiana University Press, Bloomington, 1984.

56 Davidman, op. cit.; William Shaffir, *Life in a Religious Community: the Lubavitcher Chassidim in Montreal*, Holt, Reinhart, & Winston, Toronto, 1974.

57 Ammerman, op. cit.; Ted G. Jelen, 'The Effects of Religious Separatism on White Protestants in the 1984 Presidential Election', *Sociological Analysis*, 48, 1987, pp. 30–45.

58 Marsden, op. cit.; Wuthnow, *Reconstructuring*, op. cit.; Joel A. Carpenter,

'From Fundamentalism to the New Evangelical Coalition', in Marsden (ed.), op. cit., pp. 3–16. Wade Clark Roof, 'The New Fundamentalism: Rebirth of Political Religion in America', in Hadden and Shupe (eds), op. cit., pp. 18–34.
59 Shepard, op. cit.; Smart, op. cit.
60 Emmanuel Sivan, 'Islamic Radicalism', op. cit., pp. 39–75. Baram, op. cit.
61 David A. Snow and Susan E. Marshall, 'Cultural Imperialism, Social Movements, and the Islamic Revival', *Research in Social Movements, Conflict and Change*, 7, 1984, pp. 131–52.
62 R. C. Liebman, op. cit.; Roof, op. cit.; Bruce, op. cit. The analysis of Bryan Wilson of different types of sects and their chances of becoming denominations is of relevance here. The conversionist sects are among the most likely to become denominations and to accommodate to the wider society because their success in attracting members is likely to involve some relaxation and moderation of their rules and requirements. Bryan Wilson, *Religious Sects*, Weidenfeld & Nicolson, London, 1971.
63 Steve Bruce, 'Modernity and Fundamentalism: the New Christian Right in America', *British Journal of Sociology*, 41, 1990, pp. 477–96.
64 Michael M. J. Fischer, 'Islam and the Revolt of the Petit Bourgeoisie', *Daedalus*, 1982 (Winter), pp. 101–25.
65 Saad Eddin Ibrahim, 'Egypt's Islamic Militancy Revisited', in Hadden and Shupe (eds), op. cit., pp. 353–61. The student population of Egyptian universities increased rapidly in the 1970s and the radical Islamic associations also grew rapidly, pushing out the secular left associations, and by 1977 they had gained control of the student organizations. The Sadat regime at first encouraged them as a counterweight to the secular opposition groups, but in 1981, in response to their growing strength and challenge to the regime, the associations were dissolved and their leaders arrested. Kepel, op. cit.
66 Ibid.
67 The strata supporting Islamic rejectionist movements vary somewhat from country to country, but in the main the major support comes from urban strata who are no longer embedded in the traditional rural culture and have received little benefit from the partial forms of modernization that they have experienced. On Syria see Raymond A. Hinnebusch, 'Islamic Movement in Syria: Sectarian Conflict and Urban Rebellion in an Authoritarian-Populist Regime', in Ali E. Hillal Dessouki, ed., *Islamic Resurgence in the Arab World*, Praeger, New York, 1982, pp. 138–69. On Iran see Mary Elaine Hegland, 'Islamic Revival or Political and Cultural Revolution? An Iranian Case Study', in Antoun and Hegland (eds), op. cit., pp. 194–219. In contrast to Sunni countries where Islamic radicals tend to oppose the official *ulema* as servants of hated regimes, the rejectionist movement in Iran was spearheaded by the Shiite clergy who had been progressively excluded from the Shah's regime.
68 cf. Ammerman, op. cit.; Wuthnow, *Restructuring*, op. cit.
69 Sharot, *Messianism*, op. cit., pp. 189–205.
70 Wuthnow, op. cit.

Chapter 3   Religion, Identity and the Enforcement of Morality

1 Utilitarianism is often seen as a moral philosophy which has as its central goal the greatest good of the greatest number or the maximization of happiness. In today's moral debates, however, the negative short-term version of utilitarianism, which I have termed 'causalism', is more frequently

employed, i.e. it is argued that the aim of moral regulations is to minimize harm and suffering over-all, regardless of the moral desserts of the individuals involved. If the abolition of a moral regulation would produce, in the immediate future at least, a diminution of harm and suffering, then causalists will be in favour of abolition even if on balance the wicked benefit and the good lose out. For further discussion see Christie Davies, *Permissive Britain, Social Change in the Sixties and Seventies*, Pitman, London, 1975, ch. 1, 2; idem., 'How Our Rulers Argue about Censorship', in Rajeev Dhavan and Christie Davies, eds, *Censorship and Obscenity*, Martin Robertson, London, 1978, pp. 9–36; idem., 'Moralists, Causalists, Sex, Law and Morality', in W. H. G. Armytage, R. Chester and John Peel, eds, *Changing Patterns of Sexual Behaviour*, Academic Press, London, 1980, pp. 13–43.

2 David Martin, *A General Theory of Secularization*, Basil Blackwell, Oxford, 1978, pp. 100–67.

3 I have borrowed the phrase from Lord Devlin, *The Enforcement of Morals*, Oxford University Press, London, 1965.

4 Basil Mitchell, *Law, Religion and Morality in a Secular Society*, Oxford University Press, London, 1967.

5 Devlin, op. cit., and H. L. A. Hart, *Law, Liberty and Morality*, Oxford University Press, London, 1963.

6 Mitchell, op. cit., pp. 34–5.

7 See David Jenkins, *The British, Their Identity and Their Religion*, SCM Press, London, 1975, pp. 45–7; Martin, op. cit., p. 140; *Report of the Commission on the Church of England and Other Religious Bodies in Wales and Monmouthshire* (Cmnd. 5432), HMSO, London, 1910.

8 See Reginald Morrish, *To Whom Ye Yield*, Lord's Day Observance Society, London, 1959, pp. 135–7.

9 From a speech made when he was President of the Early Closing Association.

10 Terry Burke and J. R. Shackleton, *Sunday, Sunday, the Issues in Sunday Trading*, Adam Smith Institute, London, 1989, pp. 5–6.

11 Ibid.

12 Hansard Parliamentary Debates, House of Commons, Vol. 95, col. 639, 14 April 1986, Second Reading of Shops Bill (Lords).

13 Hansard, op. cit., col. 626.

14 Simon Jones, *Evidence on the European Sunday*, Jubilee Centre, Cambridge, 1988, p. 1; see also p. xi.

15 Ibid., p. xi.

16 Ibid., pp. 17, 21, 23, 28.

17 See Court of Justice of the European Communities, *Judgment of the Court in Case 145/88 Torfaen Borough Council v B and Q Plc*, Luxembourg Information Office, 23 November 1989.

18 Ben Roberts et al., *The Bruges Group Looks at the Charter of Fundamental Rights Issued by the Commission of the European Community on 2nd October 1989 (Preliminary Report)*, Bruges Group, London, 1989, p. 8. (italics added).

19 Ibid., pp. 9–10.

20 cf. Steve Bruce, *God Save Ulster, the Religion and Politics of Paisleyism*, Clarendon Press, Oxford, 1986, pp. 233–6 and Elim Papadakis, *The Green Movement in West Germany*, Croom Helm, London, 1984, pp. 31, 41–3, 213.

21 *Keep Sunday Special, Campaign Update*, 9, Spring 1991, p. 1.

22 Raymond P. Lang, *Scotland's Sunday Under Pressure, Survey of the Extent and*

Growth of Sunday Trading in Scotland 1977–1988, Jubilee Centre, Cambridge, 1989, p. 4.

23 Quoted by Rev. Keith M. Steven in foreword to Lang, op. cit., p. ii.

24 For a picture of a much earlier and fiercer Scottish Sabbatarianism that even drove out other virtues, see the Scottish anecdotes in John Kerr, *Memories Grave and Gay, Forty Years of School Inspection*, William Blackwood, Edinburgh, 1903, p. 283 and Dean Edward Bannerman Ramsay, *Reminiscences of Scottish Life and Character*, Gale and Inglis, Edinburgh, 1873 (27th edn,), pp. 21–2 and 35.

25 Lang, op. cit., p. 19.

26 Burke and Shackleton, op. cit., p. 8.

27 Ibid., pp. 22–4 and Lang, op. cit., pp. 21–6.

28 See Burke and Shackleton, op. cit., p. 24.

29 Jones, op. cit., p. 28.

30 Bruce, op. cit., p. 165.

31 See Bruce, op. cit., pp. 161–7 and 272–84.

32 Ibid., pp. 226–7.

33 Ibid., p. 148.

34 Ibid., p. 252.

35 Ibid., pp. 251–2, 252.

36 See Tom Inglis, *Moral Monopoly: the Catholic Church in Modern Irish Society*, Gill and Macmillan, Dublin, 1987, pp. 80–6.

37 See Institut National d'Etudes Demographiques (INED), *L'Interruption Voluntaire de Grosseuses dans l'Europe des Neuf* (Cahier No. 91), Presses Universitaires de la France, Paris, 1981, pp. 11, 25–6, 29–30, 47 and Inglis, op. cit., p. 81 concerning abortions carried out on Irish and Belgian women in British and Dutch clinics.

38 See Christie Davies, 'Religion, Politics and Permissive Legislation', in Paul Badham, ed., *Religion, State and Society in Modern Britain* (Texts and Studies in Religion, Vol. 43), Edwin Mellen Press, Lewiston, NY, 1989, pp. 319–40 and Peter G. Richards, *Parliament and Conscience*, Allen & Unwin, London, 1970.

39 See Giovanni Berlinguer, *La Legge Sull' Aborto*, Riunite, Rome, 1978, and INED, op. cit.

40 See Note 1, above.

41 See Martin, op. cit., pp. 120–6.

42 Ibid., pp. 42–3, 102, 126–7.

43 Christie Davies, 'Sexual Taboos and Social Boundaries', *American Journal of Sociology*, 87, 5, March 1982, pp. 1032–63; idem., 'Religious Boundaries and Sexual Morality', *Annual Review of the Social Sciences of Religion*, Vol. 6, Fall 1983, pp. 45–77.

44 See Leviticus 18: 22–4; 20: 13–27, and also Davies, 1982, op. cit.

45 See Note 43.

46 See Davies, 1975, op. cit.; and 1982, op. cit.

47 Hansard Parliamentary Debates, 5th Series, House of Lords, Vol. 266, col. 647, 24 May 1965.

48 See Davies, 1989, op. cit.

49 See European Court of Human Rights, Dudgeon Judgment, 24 February 1983 (Article 50), Series A, No. 59, Registry of the Court, Council of Europe, Strasbourg, Carl Heymans, Köln, 1983, paragraph 52.

50 Ibid., paragraph 60.

51 Bruce, op. cit., p. 150.

52 Ibid., pp. 150–1.
53 See Inglis, op. cit.
54 Bruce, op. cit., p. 152.
55 Martin, op. cit., p. 107.
56 See Bruce, op. cit., pp. 264–5.
57 Ibid., pp. 150–1.
58 See European Court of Human Rights, Norris Case, Decision of 30 November 1987 and Judgment of 26 October 1988, Series A, Vol. 142, Registry of the Court, Council of Europe, Strasbourg, Carl Heymans, Köln, 1989, Section IIA, paragraphs 12–13.
59 Ibid., Section III, paragraphs 21–4.
60 See European Court of Human Rights, Dudgeon Judgment, op. cit., and Norris Case, op. cit., Section III, paragraph 23.
61 European Court of Human Rights, Norris Case, op. cit., Section III, paragraph 24, consideration (i).
62 Ibid., paragraph 46.
63 Davies, 1975, op. cit.; 1978, op. cit.; and 1980, op. cit.
64 See Inglis, op. cit., pp. 80–9.
65 See the debates on the Prohibition of Racial, Religious and National Hatred Bill, *Dáil Eireann* Debates, 1988, Vol. 387, Part 9, cols 2175–238; Vol. 389, Part 2, cols 247–305 and 425–64; and *Seanad Eireann* Debates, 1988, Vol. 121, Part 8, cols 850–68.
66 See John Oliver Bartley, *Teague, Shenkin and Sawney*, Cork University Press, 1954, p. 208. Sir Boyle Roche was an Irish politician who sat in the Parliament in Dublin in the late eighteenth century. His speeches were famous for the self-contradictory phrases and arguments (known as Irish Bulls) that he employed. When it was argued that Parliament ought not to load posterity with a heavy debt, Sir Boyle replied: 'Why should we put ourselves out of our way to do anything for posterity: for what has posterity done for us?'
67 See Émile Durkheim, *The Division of Labor in Society*, Free Press, New York, 1964.
68 See ibid., pp. 70–110.
69 See ibid.
70 See ibid., pp. 115–22.
71 Burke and Shackleton, op. cit., p. 27.
72 Ibid., p. 28.
73 See Andrew M. Greeley, *The Denominational Society*, Scott Foresman, Glenview, 1972, pp. 86, 107, 181–2; Tom Luckmann, 'The Decline of Church Oriented Religion' in Roland Robertson, ed., *Sociology of Religion*, Penguin Books, Harmondsworth, pp. 141–62.
74 Burke and Shackleton, op. cit., p. 30.
75 See US Supreme Court Cases, Roe v Wade, 1973, especially section 8, and Doe v Bolton, 1973.
76 See Gillian Lindt, 'Religious Values and Social Conflict: the Abortion Controversy in the United States', in *Religion, Values and Daily Life, Acts 16, International Conference for the Sociology of Religion in Lausanne 1981*, CISR, Paris, 1981.
77 Martin, op. cit., pp. 66–9, 140–1.
78 Ibid., pp. 55, 105.

Chapter 4   Britain's Moral Majority

1 Representative critiques can be found in: D. Kavanagh, *Thatcherism and British Politics*, Clarendon Press, Oxford, 1987; R. Levitas, *The Ideology of the New Right*, Polity Press, Cambridge, 1986.

2 F. Mort, *Dangerous Sexualities*, Routledge & Kegan Paul, London, 1987. J. Weeks, *Sexuality and Its Discontents*, Routledge & Kegan Paul, London, 1985.

3 J. L. Himmelstein, 'The New Right', in R. C. Liebman and R. Wuthnow, eds, *The New Christian Right*, Aldine, New York, 1983.

4 Ibid. See also R. C. Liebman, 'Mobilising the Moral Majority', in Liebman and Wuthnow (eds), op. cit. For an insider's account, see W. Willoughby, *Does America Need a Moral Majority?*, Haven Books, Plainfield, 1981.

5 Himmelstein, op. cit.

6 Liebman, op. cit.

7 J. L. Guth, 'The New Christian Right', in Liebman and Wuthnow (eds), op. cit., For a detailed account see S. Bruce, *Pray TV: Televangelism in America*, Routledge, London, 1990.

8 A. Shupe and W. Stacey, 'The Moral Majority Constituency', in Liebman and Wuthnow (eds), op. cit.

9 S. Bruce, *The Rise and Fall of the New Christian Right*, Clarendon Press, Oxford, 1988.

10 S. M. Lipset, 'Religion and Politics in the American Past and Present', in R. Lee and M. Marty, *Religion and Social Conflict*, Oxford University Press, New York, 1964. For the purpose of this article only, I am using fundamentalist as a generic term to cover those of Pentecostalist, charismatic, evangelical and fundamentalist persuasion.

11 E. J. Bristow, *Vice and Vigilance*, Gill & MacMillan, Dublin, 1977.

12 L. Davidoff and C. Hall, *Family Fortunes*, Hutchinson, London, 1987.

13 Lipset, op. cit.

14 A precise summary of the history of the division that occurred can be found in S. Bruce, *God Save Ulster: the Religion and Politics of Paisleyism*, Clarendon Press, Oxford, 1986.

15 J. H. Simpson, 'Moral Issues and Status Politics', in Liebman and Wuthnow (eds), op. cit.

16 Liebman, op. cit., p. 1.

17 M. Wood and M. Hughes, 'The Moral Basis of Moral Reform', *American Sociological Review*, 49, 1984, pp. 86–99.

18 J. R. Gusfield, *Symbolic Crusades: Status Politics and the American Temperance Movement*, University of Illinois Press, Urbana, 1963.

19 M. Ammerman, *Bible Believers*, Rutgers University Press, London, 1987. R. Wuthnow, 'The Political Rebirth of American Evangelicals', in Liebman and Wuthnow (eds), op. cit.

20 J. L. Guth, 'The New Christian Right', in Liebman and Wuthnow (eds), op. cit.

21 Liebman, op. cit., p. 57.

22 C. Whittaker, *Great Revivals*, Marshall Pickering, Basingstoke, 1984.

23 E. England, *The Spirit of Renewal*, Kingsway, Eastbourne, 1982.

24 A. Walker, *Restoring the Kingdom*, Hodder & Stoughton, London, 1985.

25 Excellent insider accounts of the dynamics of growth can be found in both E. Gibbs, *Ten Growing Churches*, MARC Europe, London, 1984 and M. Griffiths, *Ten Sending Churches*, MARC Europe, Bromley, 1985.

26 *UK Christian Handbook*, 1989/90 edn, MARC Europe, Bromley, 1988.
27 Master Plan Publishing Ltd, *The 1988 Master List*, New Malden, 1988.
28 CARE Magazine, No. 1, Autumn 1990.
29 Walker, op. cit., *UK Christian Handbook*, op. cit.
30 Master Plan Publishing Ltd, op. cit.
31 M. Whitehouse, *Cleaning Up T.V.*, Blandford, London, 1967, p. 23.
32 M. Whitehouse, *Mightier than the Sword*, Kingsway, Eastbourne, 1985.
33 R. Wallis, 'Moral Indignation and the Media: an Analysis of the NVALA', *Sociology*, May 1976.
34 Cornwall CSA Membership Form, n.d.
35 Merseyside CSA Membership Leaflet, n.d.
36 Cornwall CSA No. 1, 1974. East Dorset CSA, Newsletters, 1984 and 1985. *Brief History of Enfield CSA*, n.d.
37 Merseyside CSA Newsletter, n.d.
38 Cornwall CSA No. 7, Winter 1978–9.
39 Taunton CSA Newsletter, September 1983.
40 W. Thompson, 'Porn-Wars: Moral Crusades, Pornography, and Social Policy,' unpublished PhD thesis. Essex University, 1987.
41 Cornwall CSA, No. 7, Winter 1978–9, and No. 10, Winter 1981–2.
42 Cornwall CSA, No. 7, Winter 1978–9.
43 Merseyside CSA, Annual Report, 1983.
44 Cornwall CSA, No. 8, Winter 1979–80.
45 Cornwall CSA, No. 7, Winter 1978–9 and No. 8, Winter 1979–80.
46 Cornwall CSA, No. 7, Winter 1978–9.
47 Cornwall CSA, No. 8, Winter 1979–80.
48 Ibid.
49 CARE News, No. 18, 1987; Nos 19 and 20, 1988.
50 Gusfield, op. cit.; S. Hall et al., *Policing the Crisis*, Macmillan, London, 1984; Kavanagh, op. cit.; A. Sked, *Britain's Decline*, Basil Blackwell, Oxford, 1987; L. A. Zurcher and R. G. Kirkpatrick, *Citizens for Decency: Anti Pornography Crusades as Status Defence*, Texas University Press, Austin, 1976.
51 M. Tracey and D. Morrison, *Whitehouse*, Papermac, London, 1979. Simpson, op. cit., p. 202.
52 R. Wallis, *Salvation and Protest*, Pinter, London, 1979.
53 Ibid.
54 Accounts of the modern fundamentalists' social status can be found in R. Wallis and R. Bland, 'Who Rallied to the Call?', *New Humanist*, Autumn 1978, and Liebman, op. cit.
55 H. Toch, *The Social Psychology of Social Movements*, Oxford University Press, London, 1965.
56 C. Davies, *Permissive Britain*, Pitman, London, 1978. D. J. Pivar, *Purity Crusade: Sexual Morality and Social Control. 1868–1900*, Greenwood Press, London, 1973. Bristow, op. cit. Wood and Hughes, op. cit.
57 Wood and Hughes, op. cit.
58 W. Thompson, 'Snuff, Sex and Satan: the Social Construction of Satanic Ritual Sex Abuse', unpublished paper presented at BSA conference, Manchester, 1991.
59 Toch, op. cit.
60 Davies, op. cit.
61 Whitehouse, *Mightier than the Sword*, op. cit., Introduction.
62 C. Hill, 'Address to the Order of Christian Unity', quoted in *New Humanism*, Autumn 1984.

63 H. E. Freeman, *Every Wind of Change*, Faith Ministries, Warsaw, IN, n.d.

64 D. S. Gardner, *The Trumpet Sounds for Britain*, Vol. 1, Christian Foundation Publications, Altringham, 1983, p. 99.

65 Gardner, op. cit., Vol. 2.

66 Gardner, op. cit., Vols 1 and 2.

67 1698 Royal Proclamation for Preventing and Punishing Immorality and Profaneness, quoted in Bristow, op. cit., p. 18.

68 Bristow, op. cit.

69 O. R. Johnston, *Who Needs the Family?*, Hodder & Stoughton, London, 1979.

70 Ibid., p. 134.

71 I have covered this aspect in W. Thompson, 'Moral Crusades and Media Censorship', *Franco-British Journal*, 9, Paris, 1990.

72 See, for example, M. Barker, *The Video Nasties*, Pluto, London, 1984.

73 Thompson, 'Moral Crusades', op. cit.

74 An account of the ambiguous nature of the reforms can be found in National Deviancy Conference, *Permissiveness and Control*, Macmillan, London, 1980.

75 M. Whitehouse, *Whatever Happened to Sex?*, Wayland, Hove, 1977.

76 Portsmouth City Council Archives File 1/27.

77 Home Office Circular, 88/71.

78 Home Office, *Report of the Committee on Obscenity and Film Censorship* (Cmnd. 7772), HMSO, London, 1979.

79 M. A. McCarthy and R. A. Moodie, 'Parliament and Pornography: the 1978 Child Protection Act', *Parliamentary Affairs*, Vol. XXXIV, 1, 1981.

80 Thompson, 'Porn-Wars', op. cit.

81 Ibid.

82 Whitehouse, *Mightier than the Sword*, op. cit.

83 C. Hill, *Towards the Dawn: What's Going to Happen to Britain?*, Fount, London, 1980. Barker, op. cit. G. Barlow and A. Hill, *Video Violence and Children*, Hodder & Stoughton, London, 1985.

84 Superintendent Michael Hames, head of the Obscene Publications Squad, was the major speaker at the NVALA's Campaign to Outlaw Pornography launch at the Conservative Party Conference, Bournemouth 1990. For details of CARE's link with the squad see CARE Magazine No. 4, 1991.

85 McCarthy and Moodie, op. cit.

86 See, for example, P. M. Marshall, *Thine is the Kingdom*, Marshall, Morgan and Scott, London, 1984.

87 Thompson, 'Porn-Wars', op. cit.

88 The most authoritative work in this area is J. Stott, *Issues Facing Christians Today*, Marshall, Morgan and Scott, London, 1984.

89 See CARE News No. 25, 1989–90 and CARE Magazine No. 4, 1991.

90 For an overview on the role of political disputes concerning norms and moral boundaries see N. Ben-Yehuda, *The Politics and Morality of Deviance*, NSUP, New York, 1990.

Chapter 5   The Distinctiveness and Effectiveness of Church Schools

1 M. Cruickshank, *Church and State in English Education*, Macmillan, London, 1963.

2 E. E. Rich, *The Education Act 1870*, Longmans, London, 1970.

3 G. F. Bartle, 'The Teaching Manuals and Lesson Books of the British and

Foreign School Society', *History of Education Society Bulletin*, 46, 1990, pp. 22–33.

4 H. J. Burgess, *Enterprise in Education*, National Society and SPCK, London, 1958.

5 J. Murphy, *Church, State and Schools in Britain 1800–1970*, Routledge & Kegan Paul, London, 1971.

6 D. R. Pugh, 'Wesleyan Methodism and the Education Crisis of 1902', *British Journal of Educational Studies*, 36, 1988, pp. 232–49.

7 H. J. Dent, *The Education Act 1944: Provisions, Possibilities and Some Problems*, University of London Press, 1947.

8 R. A. Butler, *The Art of the Possible*, Hamish Hamilton, London, 1971.

9 T. A. Fitzpatrick, *Catholic Secondary Education in South-West Scotland before 1972*, Aberdeen University Press, 1986.

10 Report of Diocesan Conference, 1947.

11 E. W. Kemp, *Kenneth Escot Kirk*, Hodder & Stoughton, London, 1959.

12 K. Brooksbank et al., *County and Voluntary Schools*, Longman, Harlow, 1982.

13 Ibid.

14 Murphy, op. cit.

15 Information provided by the Department of Education and Science and the Welsh Office.

16 See Note 15 above.

17 M. P. Hornsby-Smith, *Catholic Education: the Unobtrusive Partner*, Sheed & Ward, London, 1978.

18 W. H. Abbott, ed., *The Documents of Vatican II*, Chapman, London, 1966.

19 Sacred Congregation for Catholic Education, *The Catholic School*, Society of Saint Paul, Sydney, 1977.

20 *Signposts and Homecomings: the Educative Task of the Catholic Community*, St Paul Publications, Middlegreen, 1981.

21 *The Fourth R: the Report of the Commission on Religious Education in Schools* (Durham Report), National Society and SPCK, London, 1970.

22 *A Future in Partnership*, National Society, London, 1984.

23 G. Duncan, *The Church School*, National Society, London, 1990.

24 British Humanist Association, *Religion in Schools*, British Humanist Association, London, 1967.

25 Socialist Education Association, *The Dual System of Voluntary and County Schools*, Socialist Education Association, London, 1981.

26 P. H. Hirst, 'Education, Catechesis and the Church School', *British Journal of Religious Education*, 3, 1981, pp. 85–93.

27 P. H. Hirst, 'Christian Education: a Contradiction in Terms?', *Learning for Living*, 11, 4, 1972, pp. 6–11.

28 Swann Report, *Education for All*, HMSO, London, 1985.

29 Catholic Commission for Racial Justice, *Learning from Diversity*, Catholic Media Office, London, 1984.

30 General Synod of the Church of England Board of Education, *Schools and Multi-cultural Education*, Church House, London, 1984.

31 M. Flude and M. Hammar, eds, *The Education Reform Act 1988: Its Origins and Implications*, Falmer Press, London, 1990.

32 J. Astley, *How Faith Grows: Faith Development and Christian Education*, National Society and Church House Publishing, London, 1991.

33 G. Moyser, ed., *Church and Politics Today*, T & T Clark, Edinburgh, 1985.

34 L. J. Francis, 'School Influence and Pupil Attitude towards Religion', *British Journal of Educational Psychology*, 49, 1979, pp. 107–23.

35 K. E. Hyde, *Religion in Childhood and Adolescence*, Religious Education Press, Birmingham, AL, 1990.

36 R. Likert, 'A Technique for the Measurement of Attitudes', *Archives of Psychology*, 140, 1932, pp. 1–55.

37 L. J. Francis, 'Attitude and Longitude: a Study in Measurement', *Character Potential*, 8, 1978, pp. 119–30.

38 L. J. Francis, 'Monitoring Attitude towards Christianity During Childhood and Adolescence', in M. Pyysiainen, ed., *Kasvatus ja Uskonto: Professori Kalevi Tammisen Juhlakirja*, Werner Soderstrom Osakeghtio, Helsinki, 1988, pp. 230–47.

39 L. J. Francis, 'Measuring Attitude towards Christianity During Childhood and Adolescence', *Personality and Individual Differences*, 10, 1989, pp. 695–8.

40 C. H. Povall, 'Some Factors Affecting Pupils' Attitudes to Religious Education', unpublished MEd dissertation, University of Manchester, 1971.

41 K. E. Hyde, *Religious Learning in Adolescence*, Oliver & Boyd, London, 1965.

42 W. P. C. Johnson, 'The Religious Attitudes of Secondary Modern County School Pupils', unpublished MEd dissertation, University of Manchester, 1966.

43 J. E. Greer, 'Religious Belief and Church Attendance of Sixth Form Pupils and Their Parents', *Irish Journal of Education*, 5, 1971, pp. 98–106.

44 J. A. Jones, 'An Investigation into the Response of Boys and Girls to Scripture as a School Subject in Certain Co-educational Grammar Schools in Industrial South Wales', unpublished MA dissertation, University of Wales (Swansea), 1962.

45 Office of Population Censuses and Surveys, *Classification of Occupations 1980*, HMSO, London, 1980.

46 L. J. Francis, 'The Priest as Test Administrator in Attitude Research', *Journal for the Scientific Study of Religion*, 18, 1979, pp. 78–81.

47 J. P. Keeves, 'Path Analysis', in J. P. Keeves, ed., *Educational Research, Methodology, and Measurement: an International Handbook*, Pergamon Press, Oxford, 1988, pp. 723–31.

48 SPSS Inc., *SPSSX User's Guide*, McGraw-Hill, New York, 1988.

49 L. J. Francis et al., 'An Account of the Religious Attitude Research Project at the London Institute of Education', *Area*, 11, 1978, pp. 10–15.

50 L. J. Francis, 'Denominational Schools and Pupil Attitudes towards Christianity', *British Educational Research Journal*, 12, 1986, pp. 145–52.

51 Ibid.

52 L. J. Francis, *Religion in the Primary School*, Collins Liturgical Publications, London, 1987.

53 L. J. Francis, *Partnership in Rural Education*, Collins Liturgical Publications, London, 1986.

54 L. J. Francis, *Religion in the Primary School*, op. cit.

55 L. J. Francis, 'Anglican Voluntary Primary Schools and Child Church Attendance', *Research in Education*, 30, 1983, pp. 1–9.

56 L. J. Francis, *Rural Anglicanism*, Collins Liturgical Publications, London, 1985.

57 Board of Education, *Children in the Way: New Directions for the Church's Children*, National Society and Church House Publishing, London, 1988.

58 L. J. Francis and D. W. Lankshear, 'The Impact of Church Schools on Village Church Life', *Educational Studies*, 16, 1990, pp. 117–29.

59 L. J. Francis and D. W. Lankshear, 'The Impact of Church Schools on Urban Church Life', in press.

60 L. J. Francis and M. Carter, 'Church Aided Secondary Schools, Religious Education as an Examination Subject and Pupil Attitudes towards Religion', *British Journal of Educational Psychology*, 50, 1980, pp. 297–300.
61 L. J. Francis, 'Measuring Attitude towards Christianity During Childhood and Adolescence', op. cit.
62 L. J. Francis and L. B. Brown, 'The Influence of Home, Church and School on Prayer among Sixteen-year-old Adolescents in England', *Review of Religious Research*, in press.
63 L. J. Francis and L. B. Brown, 'The Predisposition to Pray: a Study of the Social Influence on the Predisposition to Pray among Eleven-year-old Children in England', *Journal of Empirical Theology*, 3, 2, 1990, pp. 23–34.
64 L. J. Francis and A. Jewell, 'Shaping Adolescent Attitude towards the Church: Comparison between Church of England and County Secondary Schools', in press.
65 L. J. Francis, 'Measuring Attitudes towards Christianity among 12- to 18-year-old Pupils in Catholic Schools', *Educational Research*, 29, 1987, pp. 230–3.
66 H. M. Gibson and L. J. Francis, 'Measuring Attitudes towards Christianity among 11- to 16-year-old pupils in Catholic Schools in Scotland', *Educational Research*, 31, 1989, pp. 65–9.
67 J. E. Greer and L. J. Francis, 'Measuring Attitudes towards Christianity among Pupils in Catholic Secondary Schools in Northern Ireland', *Educational Research*, 33, 1991, pp. 100–3.
68 L. J. Francis, 'Measuring Attitude towards Christianity During Childhood and Adolescence', op. cit.
69 H. M. Gibson, 'Measuring Attitude towards Christianity among 11–16-year-old Pupils in Non-denominational Schools in Scotland', *Educational Research*, 31, 1989, pp. 221–7.
70 L. J. Francis and J. E. Greer, 'Measuring Attitude towards Christianity among Pupils in Protestant Secondary Schools in Northern Ireland', *Personality and Individual Differences*, 11, 1990, pp. 853–6.
71 J. Rhymer, 'Religious Attitudes of Roman Catholic Secondary School Pupils in Strathclyde Region', unpublished PhD dissertation, University of Edinburgh, 1983.
72 J. Rhymer and L. J. Francis, 'Roman Catholic Secondary Schools in Scotland and Pupil Attitude towards religion', *Lumen Vitae*, 40, 1985, pp. 103–10.
73 W. A. L. Blyth and R. Perricott, *The Social Significance of Middle Schools*, Batsford, London, 1977.
74 J. J. Boyle, 'Catholic Children's Attitudes towards Christianity', unpublished MSc dissertation, University of Bradford, 1984.
75 J. J. Boyle and L. J. Francis, 'The Influence of Differing Church Aided School Systems on Pupil Attitude towards Religion', *Research in Education*, 35, 1986, pp. 7–12.
76 L. J. Francis, 'Roman Catholic Secondary Schools: Falling Rolls and Pupil Attitudes', *Educational Studies*, 12, 1986, pp. 119–27.
77 J. Egan, *Opting Out: Catholic Schools Today*, Fowler Wright, Leominster, 1988.
78 J. Egan and L. J. Francis, 'School Ethos in Wales: the Impact of Non-practising Catholic and non-Catholic Pupils on Catholic Secondary Schools', *Lumen Vitae*, 41, 1986, pp. 159–73.
79 L. J. Francis and J. Egan, 'Catholic Schools and the Communication of Faith', *Catholic School Studies*, 60, 2, 1987, pp. 27–34.
80 L. J. Francis and J. Egan, 'The Catholic School as "Faith Community": an Empirical Enquiry', *Religious Education*, 85, 1990, pp. 588–603.

81 Ibid.
82 L. J. Francis, 'Theology of Education', *British Journal of Educational Studies*, 38, 1990, pp. 349–64.

Chapter 6   Roman Catholicism: Function versus Performance, Universalism versus Particularism

1 I wish to thank my colleagues J. Billiet, R. Cipriani, T. M. Gannon, J. Swyngedouw, L. Voyé and B. Wilson for their critical remarks on an earlier version of this paper and their suggestions.
2 Thomas M. Gannon, ed., *World Catholicism in Transition*, Macmillan, New York, 1988.
3 Karel Dobbelaere and Liliane Voyé, 'From Pillar to Post-modernity: the Changing Situation in Belgium', *Sociological Analysis*, 51, 1990, S5–S6.
4 By 'performance', Luhmann understands the application of religion to solve problems generated in other sub-systems but not solved there. Niklas Luhmann, *Funktion der Religion*, Suhrkamp Verlag, Frankfurt am Main, 1977, pp. 54ff.
5 Karel Dobbelaere, 'Secularization, Pillarization, Religious Involvement, and Religious Change in the Low Countries', in Gannon (ed.), op. cit., pp. 82–90.
6 *De Standaard*, 23 May 1990.
7 Barbara Strassberg, 'Polish Catholicism in Transition', in Gannon (ed.), op. cit., p. 200.
8 Madeleine Adriance, 'Brazil and Chile: Seeds of Change in the Latin American Church', in Gannon (ed.), op. cit., p. 284.
9 Margaret E. Crahan, 'Cuba and Nicaragua: Religion and Revolution', in Gannon (ed.), op. cit., p. 268.
10 Adriance, op. cit., p. 293.
11 Karel Dobbelaere, *Het 'Volk-Gods' de mist in? Over de Kerk in België*, Acco, Leuven, 1988, pp. 81–140.
12 Meinrad P. Hebga, 'The Evolution of Catholicism in Western Africa: the Case of Cameroon', in Gannon (ed.), op. cit., p. 327.
13 Adrian Hastings, 'East, Central, and Southern Africa', in Gannon (ed.), op. cit., p. 310.
14 Ibid., p. 311.
15 Ibid., pp. 308–19; and Hebga, op. cit., pp. 320–32.
16 Hastings, op. cit., p. 312.
17 Hebga, op. cit., p. 325.
18 Ibid., p. 327.
19 Hastings, op. cit., pp. 316–17.
20 Ibid., p. 315.
21 Hebga, op. cit., p. 331.
22 Adriance, op. cit., p. 286.
23 Crahan, op. cit., pp. 265–82; and Adriance, op. cit., pp. 283–307.
24 Crahan, op. cit., p. 278.
25 Walter Fernandes, 'The Indian Catholic Community: a Minority in Search of Security', in Gannon (ed.), op. cit., pp. 370–6.
26 K. Dobbelaere, 'Secularization, Pillarization . . . ', op. cit., pp. 82–3; and Henri Madelin, 'The Paradoxical Evolution of the French Catholic Church', in Gannon (ed.), op. cit., p. 77.
27 Crahan, op. cit., p. 271.
28 Ibid., p. 271.

29 Hans Mol, 'Canada, Australia, and New Zealand', in Gannon (ed.), op. cit., p. 260.
30 Joseph Ratzinger, 'Moeilijkheden op het gebied van het geloof in het huidige Europa', *Kerkelijke Documentatie*, 18, 3, 1990, pp. 24–30.
31 Godfried Danneels with Leo Moulin, 'Het "geseculariseerde" Europa evangeliseren', *Collationes*, 15, 4, 1985, pp. 387–418.
32 Peter L. Berger, *The Heretical Perspective*, Doubleday, Garden City, 1979.
33 Leo Laeyendecker, 'Resistance to Change in a Religious Institution', *Netherlands' Journal of Social Sciences*, 25, 1, 1989, pp. 11–15.
34 The other topics are discussed in Dobbelaere and Voyé, op. cit. and Karel Dobbelaere and Liliane Voyé, 'Western European Catholicism Since Vatican II', in Helen R. Ebaugh, ed., *Vatican II and American Catholicism: Twenty-Five Years Later*, JAI Press, Greenwich, CT, 1991, pp. 215–24.
35 See also Chris Brekelmans et al., 'Probleemgebieden in de Kerk van Vandaag: Theologie en Kerk in nieuw perspectief', *Onze Alma Mater*, 89, 1989, pp. 311–59; and René Luneau, 'Introduction', in René Luneau with Paul Ladrière, eds, *Le rêve de Compostelle: Vers la restauration d'une Europe chrétienne?* Centurion, Paris, 1989, pp. 11–22.
36 Franz-Xaver Kaufmann, 'The Principle of Subsidiarity Viewed by the Sociology of Organizations', *The Jurist*, 48, 1, 1988, p. 290.
37 Dobbelaere and Voyé, 'Western European Catholicism . . . ', op. cit., P. 218; see also Hervé Legrand et al., eds, 'Acts of the Special Colloquium on the Nature and Future of Episcopal Conferences', *The Jurist*, 48, 1, 1988, pp. 1–412.
38 For a critical analysis, see Jean Séguy, 'Charisme de fonction et charisme personnel: Le cas de Jean-Paul II', in Jean Séguy et al., *Voyage de Jean-Paul II en France*, Cerf, Paris, 1988, pp. 11–34.
39 C. Castoriadis, *L'institution imaginaire de la société*, Editions du Seuil, Paris, 1975, pp. 161–77.
40 Liliane Voyé, 'Vision of the Church, Vision of the World: the Bishops' Conferences and the Principle of Subsidiarity', paper presented at the Annual Meeting of the Association for the Sociology of Religion, Atlanta, August 1988.
41 Laeyendecker, op. cit., p. 13.
42 See for example: Madelin, op. cit., pp. 72–4; Dobbelaere, 'Secularization, Pillarization . . . ', op. cit., pp. 102–4; and Aurelio Orensanz, 'Spanish Catholicism in Transition', in Gannon (ed.), op. cit., p. 139.
43 Hastings, op. cit., pp. 315–17.
44 Máire Nic Ghiolla Phádrarg, 'Ireland: the Exception that Proves Two Rules', in Gannon (ed.), op. cit., pp. 211–12.
45 Ratzinger, op. cit., pp. 25–6.
46 Bryan Wilson, *Religion in Sociological Perspective*, Oxford University Press, 1982, p. 80.
47 Ratzinger, op. cit., pp. 25 and 30.
48 Jef De Kesel, 'Kerk in de moderne samenleving. Een ecclesiologische bezinning', *Collationes*, 18, 3, 1988, pp. 335–61.
49 Karel Dobbelaere, 'De "overgangsrituelen", steunberen van een "Katholicisme buiten de muren"?', in Jef Bulckens and Paul Cooreman, eds, *Kerkelijk Leven in Vlaanderen anno 2000*, Acco, Leuven, 1989, pp. 35–8.
50 Gannon, op. cit.
51 Also in Africa, see Hastings, op. cit., pp. 313–14.

52 Karl Gabriel and Franz-Xaver Kaufmann, 'Catholicism in German-Speaking Central Europe', in Gannon, op. cit., p. 157.
53 Dobbelaere and Voyé, 'From Pillar to Post-modernity', op. cit.; and 'Western European Catholicism since Vatican II', op. cit.
54 Karel Dobbelaere, 'Church Involvement and Secularization: Making Sense of the European Case', in Eileen Barker et al., eds, *Secularization, Rationalization and Sectarianism*, Oxford University Press, 1992, forthcoming.
55 Paul F. Furlong, 'Authority, Change, and Conflict in Italian Catholicism', in Gannon, op. cit., pp. 125–6.
56 Orensanz, op. cit., p. 140.
57 Ibid., p. 141.
58 Martine Cohen, 'Les renouveaux catholique et juif en France', in Françoise Champion and Danièle Hervieu-Léger, eds, *De l'émotion en religion: Renouveaux et traditions*, Centurion, Paris, 1990, pp. 121–67.
59 Dobbelaere and Voyé, 'From Pillar to Post-modernity', op. cit., p. 511.
60 Jacques Zylberberg, 'Les transactions du sacré', in *Sociétés*, 1, 4, 1985, pp. 9–13.
61 Dobbelaere and Voyé, 'Western European Catholicism since Vatican II', op. cit.; see also Danièle Hervieu-Léger, 'Renouveaux émotionnels contemporains: Fin de la sécularisation ou fin de la religion?', in Champion and Hervieu-Léger (eds), op. cit., pp. 241–8; Jean-Louis Schlegel, 'L'Eglise catholique sur la mauvaise pente', *Esprit*, 148–9, 1989, pp. 70–81; Karel Dobbelaere, 'Secularization: a Multi-Dimensional Concept', in *Current Sociology*, 29, 2, 1981, pp. 1–213.
62 Jan Swyngedouw, 'The Awakening of a Local Church: Japanese Catholicism in Tension Between Particularistic and Universal Values', in Gannon, op. cit., pp. 384–5 and 387–90.
63 Kaufmann, op. cit., p. 289.
64 Louis de Vaucelles, 'Interrogations, déplacements et clivages provoqués ou sein du Catholicisme Français par les évolutions de la Laïcité', paper presented at the Colloque: Religion et Modernité Politique, CNRS, Paris, March 1990.
65 Dobbelaere and Voyé, 'Western European Catholicism since Vatican II', op. cit., pp. 220–23.
66 *De Standaard*, 27–8 October 1990.
67 *De Standaard*, 15 March 1990.

Chapter 7 Believing without Belonging? The Case of Roman Catholics in England

1 G. Davie, 'Believing without Belonging: Is This the Future of Religion in Britain?', *Social Compass*, 37, 4, 1990, pp. 455–69; idem., ' "An Ordinary God": the Paradox of Religion in Contemporary Britain', *British Journal of Sociology*, 41, 3, pp. 395–421.
2 Davie, 'Believing without Belonging', op. cit., pp. 457, 463.
3 Ibid., p. 458.
4 Ibid., p. 460.
5 Ibid.
6 M. P. Hornsby-Smith et al., 'A Typology of Progressive Catholics: a Study of the Delegates to the National Pastoral Congress', *Journal for the Scientific Study of Religion*, 26, 2, pp. 234–48.
7 Davie, 'Believing without Belonging', op. cit., p. 464.

8 Ibid., p. 466.

9 P. E. Hammond, 'Religion and the Persistence of Identity', *Journal for the Scientific Study of Religion*, 27, 1, pp. 1–11.

10 M. P. Hornsby-Smith, *The Changing Parish: a Study of Parishes, Priests and Parishioners After Vatican II*, Routledge, London, 1989, pp. 66–94.

11 R. Wuthnow, *The Restructuring of American Religion: Society and Faith Since World War II*, Princeton University Press, 1989.

12 Davie, 'Believing without Belonging', op. cit., p. 468, footnote 10.

13 M. P. Hornsby-Smith and R. M. Lee, *Roman Catholic Opinion: a Study of Roman Catholics in England and Wales in the 1970s*, University of Surrey, Guildford, 1979, pp. 14–19; M. P. Hornsby-Smith, *Roman Catholics in England: Studies in Social Structure Since the Second World War*, Cambridge University Press, 1987, pp. 26–31.

14 K. Thomas, *Religion and the Decline of Magic*, Penguin Books, Harmondsworth, 1973.

15 E. P. Thompson, *The Making of the English Working Class*, Pelican, Harmondsworth, 1968, p. 918.

16 H. McLeod, *Class and Religion in the Late Victorian City*, Croom Helm, London, 1974; idem., *Religion and the People of Western Europe, 1789–1970*, Oxford University Press, 1981.

17 R. Roberts, *The Classic Slum: Salford Life in the First Quarter of the Century*, Pelican, Harmondsworth, 1973.

18 G. Ahern and G. Davie, *Inner City God: The Nature of Belief in the Inner City*, Hodder & Stoughton, London, 1987.

19 Davie, 'Believing without Belonging', op. cit., p. 462.

20 Ibid., p. 464.

21 R. Wallis, 'Secularization: A Re-statement of the Orthodox Model', in S. Bruce, ed., *Secularization: Recent Trends in Theory and Data*, Oxford University Press, in press.

22 Davie, 'Believing without Belonging', op. cit., p. 465.

23 Ibid., p. 459.

24 P. Brierley, ed., *Prospects for the Eighties: from a Census of the Churches in 1979*, Bible Society, London, 1980, p. 23.

25 Hornsby-Smith and Lee, op. cit.

26 M. P. Hornsby-Smith, R. M. Lee and K. A. Turcan, 'A Typology of English Catholics', *Sociological Review*, 30, 3, pp. 433–59; Hornsby-Smith, *Roman Catholics in England*, op. cit., pp. 47–66.

27 Hornsby-Smith, *Roman Catholics in England*, op. cit.

28 M. Douglas, *Natural Symbols: Explorations in Cosmology*, Penguin Books, Harmondsworth, 1973, p. 67.

29 Hornsby-Smith, *Roman Catholics in England*, op. cit., p. 94.

30 D. Lodge, *How Far Can You Go?*, Secker & Warburg, London, 1980, pp. 113–27.

31 M. P. Hornsby-Smith, *Roman Catholic Beliefs in England: Customary Catholicism and Transformations of Religious Authority*, Cambridge University Press, 1991.

32 See, for example, E. Badone, ed., *Religious Orthodoxy and Popular Faith in European Society*, Princeton University Press, 1990.

33 A. Archer, *The Two Catholic Churches: a Study in Oppression*, SCM, London, 1986.

34 Hammond, op. cit.

35 Hornsby-Smith, *Roman Catholic Beliefs in England*, op. cit.

36 M. P. Hornsby-Smith, R. M. Lee and P. A. Reilly, 'Common Religion and

Customary Religion: a Critique and a Proposal', *Review of Religious Research*, 26, 3, 1985, pp. 244–52. The quotation is from p. 249. See also M. P. Hornsby-Smith, R. M. Lee and P. A. Reilly, 'Lapsation and Ideology', *The Month*, 10, 12, 1977, pp. 406–9.

37 R. Towler, *Homo Religiosus: Sociological Problems in the Study of Religion*, Constable, London, 1974, pp. 145–62; R. Towler and A. Chamberlain, 'Common Religion', in M. Hill, ed., *A Sociological Yearbook of Religion in Britain*, Vol. 6, SCM Press, London, 1973, pp. 1–28.

38 Hornsby-Smith, Lee and Reilly, 'Common Religion and Customary Religion', op. cit.

39 Hornsby-Smith, *Roman Catholic Beliefs in England*, op. cit., pp. 89–113.

40 M. P. Hornsby-Smith, 'Some Aspects of Popular Catholicism', in E. Bailey, ed., *A Workbook in Popular Religion*, Partners Publications, Dorchester, 1986, pp. 10–11.

41 As suggested by Grace Davie (private communication).

42 Wallis, op. cit.

43 Hammond, op. cit.

Chapter 8   The Demise of Liberal Christianity?

1 Donald E. Miller, *The Case for Liberal Christianity*, SCM Press, London, 1981, pp. 9–10.

2 Peter J. Gee, 'Responsibility without Power: the Dilemma Facing Christian Peace Groups', seminar paper presented to Bryan Wilson's Oxford Sociology of Religion Seminar, November 1989.

3 *Trust: a Newsletter of SCM Press Trust*, No. 1, October 1990.

4 Central Board of Finance of the Church of England, *Faith in the City: a Call for Action by Church and Nation*, Church House Publishing, London, 1985.

5 Many conservative Anglican clergy continued to complain of the domination of liberals, however, as the 1989 Crockford's Preface incident showed.

6 Dean M. Kelley, *Why Conservative Churches are Growing. A Study in the Sociology of Religion*, Harper & Row, New York, 1972.

7 Susan Budd, 'The Humanist Societies: the Consequences of a Diffuse Belief System', in Bryan R. Wilson, ed., *Patterns of Sectarianism*, Heinemann, London, 1967, pp. 403–40.

8 Bryan R. Wilson, *Religion in Secular Society*, Watts, London, 1966.

9 Variations in the pattern were explored by David Martin, *A General Theory of Secularization*, Basil Blackwell, Oxford, 1978. It is noteworthy that even in eastern Europe there are signs of decline, once the Church is no longer needed as a focus for opposition to communist regimes. In the former East Germany, churches were the centres for mass protest before the downfall of communism but attendances have now fallen.

10 I am grateful to James Beckford for stressing this point.

11 Peter L. Berger, *The Social Reality of Religion*, Penguin Books, Harmondsworth, 1973.

12 Peter L. Berger, 'A Sociological View of the Secularization of Theology', *Journal for the Scientific Study of Religion*, 6, 1, 1967, pp. 3–16.

13 See, for example, David Martin's defence of the Anglican Book of Common Prayer during the late 1970s. See David A. Martin, 'A Plea for our Common Prayer', in Brian Morris, ed., *Ritual Murder*, Carcanet Press, Manchester, 1980.

14 David A. Martin, 'Sociologist Fallen among Secular Theologians', in *The Religious and Secular*, Routledge & Kegan Paul, London, 1969.
15 The development of the role of the English clergy has of course been a much more complex phenomenon, associated with the development of the professions in the nineteenth and twentieth centuries. But much of this can be usefully seen as a response to marginalization. See Anthony Russell, *The Clerical Profession*, SPCK, London, 1980, and Robert Towler and A. P. M. Coxon, *The Fate of the Anglican Clergy*, Macmillan, London, 1979.
16 Gee, op. cit.
17 David A. Martin, *Tongues of Fire*, Basil Blackwell, Oxford, 1990, p. 295.
18 SCM Press Trust, op. cit.

Chapter 9   Does the Social Gospel Involve the Collapse of Christianity?

1 Charles Bremner, *The Times*, 17 April 1990.
2 Damian Thompson, 'Beating a Path to Sainthood', *Spectator*, 28 September 1991.
3 Edward Norman, *Christianity and the World Order*, Oxford University Press, 1979.
4 *Freedom Bulletin*, No. 13, May 1990.
5 Ibid.
6 Quoted in *Sunday Telegraph*, 19 November 1989.
7 Quoted by Graham Turner, 'Friars who Preach against Thatcher', *Sunday Telegraph*, 24 December 1989.
8 *The Times*, 29 January 1990.
9 *Sunday Telegraph*, 11 February 1990.
10 See Eric Voegelin, *The New Science of Politics*, University of Chicago Press, 1966.
11 In the 'Economic and Social Manuscripts', *Marx and Engels: Collected Works*, Vol. 3, London, 1976, p. 399.
12 Kenneth Leach, 'Caesar's Religion', *New Socialist*, April/May 1990, p. 10. Mr Leach is described as 'an Anglican priest for 25 years, mainly in the East End of London'.
13 John F. X. Harriott, 'Unwelcome Truths', *The Tablet*, 6 January 1990. It will be remembered that some social gospellers do not seem to welcome all truths about the conduct of liberation movements to which they commit themselves.
14 I have analysed one remarkable case of this kind of rhetoric in 'Societies Collapse, Faiths Linger On', in *Encounter*, March 1990, pp. 13–14.
15 Edmund Burke, *Reflections on the Revolution in France*, Penguin Books, Harmondsworth, 1969, p. 110.
16 Burke, op. cit., p. 157.
17 Referred to in my 'Societies Collapse . . . ', op. cit. See Note 14.

Chapter 10   Discourse on Women in the Clerical Profession: the Diaconate and Language-games in the Church of England

1 J. A. Beckford, 'The Restoration of "Power" to the Sociology of Religion', *Sociological Analysis*, 44, 1, 1983, pp. 11–32.
2 R. K. Fenn, *Liturgies and Trials*, Basil Blackwell, Oxford, 1981; B. R. Wilson, *The Social Dimensions of Sectarianism*, Oxford University Press, 1990.

3 A. E. Aldridge, 'Men, Women and Clergymen: Opinion and Authority in a Sacred Organization', *Sociological Review*, 37, 1, 1989, pp. 43–64.

4 M. Hill, *A Sociology of Religion*, Heinemann, London, 1973, p. 172.

5 W. S. F. Pickering, *Anglo-Catholicism*, Routledge & Kegan Paul, London, 1989; A. Wilkinson, 'Requiem for Anglican Catholicism?' *Theology*, 81, 679, 1978, pp. 40–5; F. Penhale, *Catholics in Crisis*, Mowbray, London, 1986.

6 E. R. Norman, *Anti-Catholicism in Victorian England*, Allen & Unwin, London, 1968.

7 D. A. Martin, *A Sociology of English Religion*, Heinemann, London, 1967, p. 71.

8 D. Newsome, *Godliness and Good Learning*, Murray, London, 1961, pp. 207–10; Norman, op. cit., pp. 108–10.

9 Pickering, op. cit., pp. 169–72.

10 T. W. Bamford, *The Rise of the Public Schools*, Nelson, London, 1967, pp. 45–6.

11 N. Perry and L. Echeverria, *Under the Heel of Mary*, Routledge & Kegan Paul, London, 1988.

12 Martin, op. cit., pp. 67–71.

13 E. Leach, 'Virgin Birth', in E. Leach, *Genesis as Myth and Other Essays*, Cape, London, 1969.

14 J. Barr, *Fundamentalism*, SCM Press, London, 1977, p. 176.

15 K. Barth, *Church Dogmatics*, Vol. 3, Pt 4, T. & T. Clark, Edinburgh, 1961, p. 161.

16 D. A. Martin, *A General Theory of Secularization*, Basil Blackwell, Oxford, 1978, p. 279.

17 R. R. Ruether, *Mary – the Feminine Face of the Church*, SCM Press, London, 1979, p. 62.

18 J. A. Beckford, *Religion and Advanced Industrial Society*, Unwin Hyman, London, 1989.

19 Ibid., pp. 170–2.

20 V. Turner, *The Ritual Process*, Routledge & Kegan Paul, London, 1969.

21 K. A. Thompson, *Bureaucracy and Church Reform*, Oxford University Press, 1970.

22 Brother Victor SSF, 'The Servant Leader: Impressions of Deacons in the USA', *ACCM Occasional Paper No. 27*, Advisory Council for the Church's Ministry, London, 1987, pp. 7–8.

23 Advisory Council for the Church's Ministry, *Deacons Now*, Advisory Council for the Church's Ministry, London, 1991.

24 In the summer of 1989 I sent a postal questionnaire to all the eighty-three women serving as deacons in four dioceses of the Church of England. The dioceses were selected to represent a diversity of socio-economic conditions and of diocesan policy and practice towards women in ordained ministry. The questionnaire, which did not seek to identify individuals, achieved a response rate of 85.5 per cent.

25 In the summer of 1985 I carried out a programme of semi-structured in-depth interviews with forty Anglican parish clergymen serving in one diocese. These interviewees were selected to represent a range of theological traditions, and were drawn from 178 respondents to a postal questionnaire sent to them in 1983. I also interviewed the two accredited women lay workers and sixteen of the eighteen deaconesses in the same diocese. These interviews were supported by a grant from Nottinghamshire County Council. For further details see A. E. Aldridge, 'In the Absence of the Minister:

Structures of Subordination in the Role of Deaconess in the Church of England', *Sociology*, 21, 3, 1987, pp. 377–92.

26 Aldridge, 'Men, Women and Clergymen', op. cit., pp. 60–1.
27 J. Robson, 'Ministry or Profession: Clergy Doubletalk', in M. Furlong, ed., *Mirror to the Church*, SPCK, London, 1988.
28 L. Wittgenstein, *Philosophical Investigations*, 2nd edn, trans. G. E. M. Anscombe, Basil Blackwell, Oxford, 1958.
29 D. Bloor, *Wittgenstein: a Social Theory of Knowledge*, Macmillan, London, 1983, pp. 137–59.
30 M. Douglas, *Natural Symbols*, Penguin Books, Harmondsworth, 1973.
31 Aldridge, 'Men, Women and Clergymen', op. cit., pp. 58–63.
32 Bloor, op. cit., p. 145.
33 Ibid., p. 144.
34 Ibid., p. 146.
35 House of Bishops of the General Synod of the Church of England, *Deacons in the Ministry of the Church* (The Portsmouth Report), Church House, London, 1988.
36 Advisory Council for the Church's Ministry, op. cit.

Chapter 11   Television, the 'Bartered Bride'; Broadcasting, Commerce and Religion: Transatlantic Perspectives

1 See Asa Briggs, *The Birth of Broadcasting*, Vol. I in *The History of Broadcasting in the UK*, Oxford University Press, 1961.
2 Quoted in the Pilkington Report, 1962, Ap. E.
3 Simon Jenkins, *Sunday Times*, 19 June 1988.
4 *Guardian*, 8 February 1986.
5 Peter G. Horsfield, *Religious Television: the American Experience*, Longman, London, 1984.
6 IBA Religious Consultation, *Proceedings Report*, 13 April 1983, p. 12.
7 R. Currie, A. Gilbert and L. Horsley, *Churches and Churchgoing*, Oxford University Press, 1977, p. 167.
8 *All Are Called*: Church Information Office: *Towards a Theology of Laity* London, 1985.
9 John Hull, *What Prevents Christians from Learning*, SCM Press, London, 1985, ch. 3.
10 Clifford Longley, *The Times*, 7 October 1985.
11 BCC/DES, 'The Training of Teachers of Religious Education', 1971.
12 David Martin, 'Why Spit on Our Luck?', *Poetry New Review*, 6, 5, 1977.
13 Timothy Hollings, *Beyond Broadcasting into the Cable Age*, London Broadcasting Research Unit, 1984, p. 327.
14 *The Times*, 27 December 1985.
15 Neil Postman, *Amusing Ourselves to Death*, Heinemann, London, 1986, ch. 8.
16 Pilkington Report, 1962, para. 402.
17 *The Army and Religion: An Inquiry and its Bearing on the Religious Life of the Nation*, Macmillan, London, 1919, pp. 425ff. See also Alan Wilkinson, *The Church of England and the First World War*, SPCK, London, 1980.
18 John Reith, *Broadcast over Britain*, Hodder, London, 1924, p. 220.
19 John Reith, *Into the Wind*, Hodder, London, 1949, p. 94.
20 *BBC Handbook*, 1929, p. 208; see also *Church Times*, 14 February 1986.

21 *The Future of Broadcasting* (Annan Report) (Cmnd. 6753), HMSO, London, 1977, p. 486.

22 R. E. Herzstein, *The War that Hitler Won – Nazi Propaganda*, Hamish Hamilton, London, 1979, pp. 30ff.

23 K. M. Wolfe, *The Churches and the BBC, 1922–56, the Politics of Broadcast Religion*, SCM Press, London, 1984, pp. 170ff.

24 William Temple, *Christianity and the Social Order*, Penguin Books, Harmondsworth, 1942.

25 William Haley, *Moral Values in Broadcasting*, BBC Publications, London, 1948.

26 *Goebbels' Diaries*, Doubleday, Garden City, NY, 1948, p. 56.

27 See review by Mark Lawson in *The Times*, 18 January 1986.

28 See Asa Briggs, *The First 50 Years*, Oxford University Press, 1985, pp. 279ff and Pt VI.

29 See Peter Brookes, *Communicating Conviction*, Epworth Press, London, 1983.

30 *The Agony of Deceit*, Moody Bible Institute, Chicago, 1990.

31 Steve Bruce, *Pray TV*, Routledge, London, 1990.

32 Peter Elvey, *Christian Broadcasting in Europe*, McCrimmon, Essex, 1990.

33 George Marsden, *Fundamentalism and American Culture*, Oxford University Press, New York, 1980, p. 177.

34 Gamaliel Bradford, *D. L. Moody: a Worker in Souls*, Doran, New York, 1927, pp. 227–63. See also Robert D. Cross, 'The Church and the City' in Kramer and Holborn, eds, *The City in American Life*, Capricorn Books, New York, 1971.

35 Charles Siepmann, *Radio, Television and Society*, Oxford University Press, 1950, ch. 1.

36 Briggs was co-editor of *The Hebrew Lexicon* (eds F. Brown, S. R. Driver and C. A. Briggs), Oxford, 1906.

37 George Schriver, ed., *American Religious Heretics*, Abingdon Press, Nashville, 1966, ch. 3; William J. Hynes, *Downside Review*, July 1987; and George Schriver, *Philip Schaff*, Mercer University Press, Macon, GA, 1987, pp. 88–93.

38 A. William Bluem, *Religious Television Programmes*, Hasting House, New York, 1969, pp. 203ff.

39 Horsfield, op. cit., p. 14.

40 Robert Bellah, *Habits of the Heart*, University of California Press, Berkeley, 1985, p. 220.

41 *Time* Magazine, 15 July 1988.

42 Bellah, op. cit., p. 238.

43 William Fore, *Television and Religion*, Augsburg, Minneapolis, 1987, p. 111.

44 See correspondence in the *Church Times* during October and November 1990.

45 See Horsfield, op. cit., p. 67., and Postman, op. cit.

46 *Religion and TV*, Report, Annenberg School, Philadelphia, 1984.

47 Frances Fitzgerald, *New Yorker*, 23 April 1990, p. 78.

48 Letter from CBN to R. L. Waugh, 27 December 1985. See also Bruce, op. cit., pp. 140ff.

49 Fore, op. cit., p. 125.

50 Robert Schuller, *The Be-Happy Attitudes*, World Books, Waco, Texas, 1985.

51 Horsfield, op. cit., p. 34.

52 See Paul Ferris, *Sir Huge: the Life of Sir Huw Wheldon*, Michael Joseph, London, 1990.

53 Bruce, op. cit., pp. 94ff.

54 *Time* Magazine, 17 February 1986, edition on the televangelists.

55 Bruce, op. cit., p. 66.

56 See Hull, op. cit., ch. 3.

57 See James Smart, *The Strange Silence of the Bible in the Church*, SCM Press, London, 1970, pp. 22ff.; and George C. Schriver, *American Religious Heretics*, Abingdon Press, New York, 1966.

58 Robert Runcie, 'Religious Broadcasting Today' in Dan Cohn-Sherbok, ed., *Essays on Religion and Society*, Canterbury Papers I, Bellew, London, 1990, p. 7.

59 Jeffrey K. Haddon and Charles Swann, *Prime-Time Preachers: the Rising Power of Television Evangelism*, Addison-Wesley, Reading, MA, 1981, pp. 101ff.

60 Fore, op. cit., pp. 87ff.

61 Colin Morris, 'God in a Box', documentary, BBC 2, 1984.

62 See Bibliography in Bruce, op. cit.

63 Bryan Wilson, *The Social Dimensions of Sectarianism*, Clarendon Press, Oxford, 1990, p. 147.

Chapter 12   Some Recent Developments in Seventh-day Adventism

1 Since this chapter makes frequent reference to the SdA organizational set-up, it is outlined here. At the top is the General Conference, which is the supreme governing body of the world Church. Locally, this functions through twelve divisions (e.g. the Trans-European Division, formerly the Northern Europe–West African Division, of which Britain is a part). Each division is divided into a number of Unions (e.g. the British Union, comprising the whole of the British Isles). The Unions, in turn, are divided into conferences and missions (e.g. in Britain, the South England Conference, the North British Conference, the Welsh and Irish Missions) which are made up of the local churches.

   At each level above that of the local church there is a comparable slate of officers – President, Secretary, Treasurer, and various departmental directors in charge of youth work, Sabbath Schools, etc.

   The General Conference meets in full session every five years, with many committees carrying out its work between sessions. The British Union also meets in session every five years, with its executive committee meeting frequently between sessions. The conference and mission sessions are held every three years, again with frequent meetings of their executive committees. The term 'conference' is somewhat misleading: it should be remembered that it designates a geographical area, and that its triennial meeting is referred to as a conference session.

2 See especially *Spectrum*, 2, 4, Autumn 1970, pp. 57–69; and 4, 2, Summer 1972, pp. 49–53.

3 *Ministry*, October 1990, pp. 4–7; and December 1990, pp. 11–15. *Ministry* is the journal of the SdA Ministerial Association.

4 Walter Rea, *The White Lie*, M & R Publications, Turlock, CA, 1982.

5 Geoffrey Paxton, *The Shaking of Adventism*, Baker Book House, Grand Rapids, MI, 1977.

6 On this, see particularly Robin H. Ward, 'Some Aspects of Religious Life in an Immigrant Area of Manchester', *A Sociological Yearbook of Religion in Britain*, 3, 1970, p. 18.

7 John Rex and Robert Moore, *Race, Community and Conflict: a Study of Sparkbrook*, Institute of Race Relations, London, 1967, p. 188.

8 Clifford Hill, *West Indian Migrants and the London Churches*, Institute of Race Relations, London, 1963, p. 27.
9 Roswith Gerloff, 'Black Christian Communities in Birmingham: the Problem of Basic Recognition', in Alan Bryman, ed., *Religion in the Birmingham Area: Essays in the Sociology of Religion*, n.d. (1975?) p. 70.
10 Malcolm Calley, *God's People*, Institute of Race Relations, London, 1964, p. 127.
11 Sheila Patterson, *Dark Strangers*, Tavistock, London, 1963, p. 261.
12 See the *Adventist Review*, 13 July 1989, pp. 13–15, esp. p. 14. This journal is the official church paper of the denomination world-wide.
13 Personal letter to the author.
14 Rex and Moore, loc cit.
15 Dilip Hiro, *Black British, White British*, 1973, p. 32.
16 Cynthia Handysides, 'West Indian Integration in the Seventh-day Adventist Church in Britain', unpublished BEd thesis, University of Reading, 1968.
17 Clifford Hill, 'Some Aspects of Race and Religion in Britain', *A Sociological Yearbook of Religion in Britain*, 3, 1970, pp. 35–6.
18 Gerloff, op. cit., p. 74.
19 In 1944, 'regional', or black, conferences had been established by the SdA Church in certain parts of the US. These covered the same, or similar, geographical areas to white conferences and were constituent parts of the same Unions, but were administered by blacks and their churches were pastored by blacks. There were no all-black Unions, but by the 1960s and '70s, demands for these began to be voiced.
20 Robin Theobald, 'The Politicization of a Religious Movement: British Adventism under the Impact of West Indian Immigration', *British Journal of Sociology*, 32, 2, June 1981, pp. 202–23.
21 In one church investigated by the present writer, the membership was 60 per cent black and 40 per cent white, but the tithe figures were 21 per cent and 79 per cent respectively. Even today, it has been estimated that in the South England Conference, the 26.3 per cent whites pay 35 per cent of the tithe.
22 As regards race relations, Mrs White, although an abolitionist in her younger days, had, in the era of Jim Crow legislation, come to advocate separation of the races.
23 Theobald, op. cit., p. 204.
24 See *Messenger*, 95, 21/2, 26 October 1990, for an account of this session. *Messenger* is the official church paper of the denomination in the British Isles.
25 See *Messenger*, 96, 15/6, 26 July 1991.

Chapter 13   New Zealand's Cultic Milieu: Individualism and the Logic of Consumerism

1 See B. S. Turner, *Religion and Social Theory*, Heinemann, London, 1983; K. A. Thompson, *Beliefs and Ideologies*, Tavistock, London, 1985; and J. A. Beckford, *Religion and Advanced Industrial Society*, Unwin Hyman, London, 1989.
2 See in particular, Talcott Parsons, *The Structure of Social Action*, Free Press, Glencoe, IL, 1949.
3 H. S. Hughes, *Consciousness and Society*, MacGibbon & Kee, London, 1959, ch. 2.

4 S. Lukes, *Emile Durkheim: His Life and Work*, Allen Lane, London, 1973, p. 460.

5 M. Weber, *The Sociology of Religion*, trans. E. Fischoff, Methuen, London, 1965.

6 H. R. Niebuhr, *The Social Sources of Denominationalism*, Henry Holt, New York, 1929.

7 J. Wach, *Sociology of Religion*, Chicago University Press, 1944.

8 C. Campbell, 'The Cult, the Cultic Milieu and Secularization', in Michael Hill, ed., *A Sociological Yearbook of Religion in Britain*, 5, SCM Press, London, 1972, pp. 119–36.

9 E. Durkheim, *The Elementary Forms of the Religious Life*, trans. J. W. Swain, Free Press, Glencoe, IL, 1954.

10 E. Durkheim, *The Division of Labor in Society*, trans. G. Simpson, Free Press, Glencoe, IL, 1960.

11 Lukes, op. cit., p. 139.

12 E. Durkheim, *Le Suicide – Etude de Sociologie*, Presses Universitaires de France (nouvelle édition), Paris, 1960, p. 382.

13 R. N. Bellah, ed., *Emile Durkheim on Morality and Society*, Chicago University Press, 1973, pp. 43–57; Lukes, op. cit.

14 Lukes, op. cit., p. 26.

15 Ibid., pp. 27–8.

16 Ibid., p. 18.

17 Ibid., p. 26.

18 F. Westley, *The Complex Forms of the Religious Life*, Scholars Press, Chico, CA, 1983, p. 9.

19 Durkheim, *Elementary Forms . . .* op. cit., pp. 427–8.

20 N. Abercrombie et al., *The Dominant Ideology Thesis*, Allen & Unwin, London, 1980, pp. 41–2.

21 G. Gehrig, *American Civil Religion: an Assessment*, SSSR, Norwich, CT, 1981.

22 M. Hill and W. Zwaga, 'Civil and Civic: Engineering a National Religious Consensus', *New Zealand Sociology*, 2, 1, 1987, pp. 25–357.

23 E. A. Tiryakian, 'A Problem for the Sociology of Knowledge: the Mutual Unawareness of Emile Durkheim and Max Weber', in E. A. Tiryakian, ed., *The Phenomenon of Sociology*, Appleton-Century-Crofts, New York, 1971, pp. 428–34.

24 E. Troeltsch, *The Social Teaching of the Christian Churches*, 2 vols, trans. O. Wyon, Allen & Unwin, London, 1931.

25 Ibid., p. 381.

26 Ibid.

27 C. Campbell, 'The Secret Religion of the Educated Classes', *Sociological Analysis*, 39, 2, 1978, p. 153.

28 Troeltsch, op. cit., p. 377.

29 F. W. Graf, 'Ernst Troeltsch', in M. Eliade, ed., *Encyclopaedia of Religion*, Vol. 15, Macmillan, New York.

30 Troeltsch, op. cit., p. 744.

31 Ibid., p. 794.

32 See especially, D. Cupitt, *Radicals and the Future of the Church*, SCM Press, London, 1989.

33 Idem., *The World to Come*, SCM Press, London, 1982, p. 121.

34 S. Cowdell, *Atheist Priest? Don Cupitt and Christianity*, SCM Press, London, 1988, pp. 72–3.

35 M. Hill, *A Sociology of Religion*, Heinemann, London, 1973, pp. 60–4.

36 H. Becker, *Systematic Sociology . . . of Leopold von Wiese*, John Wiley, New York, 1932, p. 628.

37 J. A. Beckford, *Cult Controversies*, Tavistock, London, 1985, pp. 75–6.

38 Campbell, 'The Cult . . . ', op. cit., and F. Westley, 'The Cult of Man . . . ', *Sociological Analysis*, 39, 2, pp. 135–45.

39 J. A. Beckford, 'The World Images of New Religious and Healing Movements', in R. Kenneth Jones, ed., *Sickness and Sectarianism*, Gower, Aldershot, 1985.

40 Hill, *A Sociology of Religion*, op. cit., p. 81; and idem., 'The Sectarian Contribution', in B. Colless and P. Donovan, eds, *Religion in New Zealand Society* (2nd edn), Dunmore Press, Palmerston North, 1985, pp. 122–4.

41 R. Wallis and S. Bruce, 'The Stark-Bainbridge Theory of Religion: a Critical Analysis and Counter Proposals', *Sociological Analysis*, 45, 1, 1984, pp. 11–28.

42 R. Wallis, *The Elementary Forms of the New Religious Life*, Routledge, London, 1984, pp. 86–118.

43 D. P. Johnson, 'Dilemmas of Charismatic Leadership: the Case of the People's Temple', *Sociological Analysis*, 40, 4, 1979, pp. 315–23.

44 R. Kohn, 'Radical Subjectivity in "Self Religions" and the Problem of Authority', in Alan W. Black, ed., *Religion in Australia*, Allen & Unwin, Sydney, 1991, p. 149.

45 Beckford, *Cult Controversies*, op. cit., ch. 2.

46 J. Liebrich et al., *In Search of Well-Being. Exploratory Research into Complementary Therapies*, Department of Health, Health Services Research and Development Unit, Wellington, 1987.

47 M. McGuire, 'Religion and Healing', in P. E. Hammond, ed., *The Sacred in a Secular Age*, University of California Press, Berkeley, 1985, p. 275.

48 Liebrich et al., op. cit.

49 Ibid., p. 13.

50 Ibid., pp. 96–7.

51 Ibid., pp. 42–4.

52 Ibid., pp. 93–5.

53 Ibid., p. 44.

54 Ibid., pp. 33–4.

55 Ibid., p. 99.

56 Ibid., pp. 29, 40.

57 Ibid., p. 39.

58 Ibid., p. 48.

59 Ibid., p. 84.

60 T. Posner, 'Transcendental Meditation, Perfect Health and the Millennium', in Jones (ed.), op. cit.

61 P. Hounam and A. Hogg, *Secret Cult*, Albatross, Tring, 1984.

62 Posner, op. cit.

63 D. W. Orme-Johnson et al., eds, *Introductions and Theoretical Papers Reprinted from Scientific Research on the Transcendental Meditation Program. Collected Papers*, Vol. 1, Maharishi European Research University Press, Seelisburg, Switzerland, 1977.

64 Wallis, op. cit., p. 3.

65 MERU, *Global Research Programme*, MERU Press, Seelisburg, Switzerland, 1978, pp. 10–11.

66 L. Oakes, *Inside Centrepoint. The Story of a New Zealand Community*, Benton Ross, Auckland, 1986, pp. 19–20.

67 Ibid., p. 20.

68 M. Hill, *A Sociology* . . . , op. cit., p. 61.

69 Oakes, op. cit., p. 91.

70 Ibid., p. 103.

71 Wallis, op. cit., p. 3.

72 Centrepoint, *Personal Development Calendar*, August 1987–January 1988.

73 R. Wallis, 'The Dynamics of Change in the Human Potential Movement', in Rodney Stark, ed., *Religious Movements: Genesis, Exodus and Numbers*, Paragon House, New York, 1985, pp. 129–56.

74 Cited in Oakes, op. cit.

75 S. Campbell-Jones, *In Habit. An Anthropological Study of Working Nuns*, Faber, London, 1979, esp. ch. 7.

76 Oakes, op. cit., p. 166.

77 Centrepoint, op. cit.

78 In E. Barker, ed., *New Religious Movements: a Perspective for Understanding Society*, Edwin Mellen, New York, 1982, p. 92.

79 A. R. Hochschild, *The Managed Heart. Commercialization of Human Feeling*, University of California Press, Berkeley, 1983.

80 M. Hill, 'The Cult of Humanity and the Secret Religion of the Educated Classes', *New Zealand Sociology*, 2, 2, 1987, pp. 112–27.

81 K. Sinclair, *A History of New Zealand*, Penguin Books, Harmondsworth, 1969, p. 288.

82 C. Campbell, 'Romanticism and the Consumer Ethic: Intimations of a Weber-style Thesis', *Sociological Analysis*, 44, 4, 1983, pp. 279–96.

83 P. L. Berger, 'A Market Model for the Analysis of Ecumenicity', *Social Research*, 30, 1, 1963, pp. 77–93.

84 P. L. Berger, *The Social Reality of Religion*, Faber, London, 1969.

85 M. Ruthven, *The Divine Supermarket: Travels in Search of the Soul of America*, Chatto & Windus, London, 1989, p. 2.

86 M. Featherstone, 'Consumer Culture, Postmodernism, and Global Disorder', in R. Robertson and W. R. Garrett, eds, *Religion and Global Disorder*, vol. 4, *Religion and the Public Order*, Paragon, New York, 1991, p. 146.

87 M. Hill, *A Sociology* . . . op. cit., pp. 29–30.

88 R. W. Bibby and H. R. Weaver, 'Cult Consumption in Canada: a Further Critique of Stark and Bainbridge', *Sociological Analysis*, 46, 4, 1985, p. 450.

89 Ibid., p. 451.

Chapter 14 Authority and Dependence in New Religious Movements

1 The concept of the 'total institution' is explored in Erving Goffman, *Asylums: Essays on the Social Situation of Mental Patients and Other Inmates*, Penguin Books, Harmondsworth, 1968.

2 Stanley Milgram, *Obedience to Authority*, Harper & Row, New York, 1974.

3 Edgar W. Mills, 'Cult Extremism: the Reduction of Normative Dissonance', in Ken Levi, ed., *Violence and Religious Commitment: Implications of Jim Jones's People's Temple Movement*, Pennsylvania State University, University Park and London, 1982.

4 ISKCON is the acronym used for the International Society for Krishna Consciousness.

5 Archibold, *Criminal Pleading, Evidence and Practice*, 43rd edn, Vol. 2, p. 2038ff.

6 See James T. Richardson, 'People's Temple and Jonestown: a Corrective

Comparison and Critique', *Journal for the Scientific Study of Religion*, 19, 3, 1980, pp. 239–55.

7 Bruno Bettelheim, 'Individual and Mass Behavior in Extreme Situations', *Journal of Abnormal and Social Psychology*, XXXVIII, 1983, pp. 417–52.

8 Edgar H. Schein, 'The Chinese Indoctrination Program for Prisoners of War: a Study of Attempted Brainwashing', in Eleanor E. Maccoby et al., eds, *Readings in Social Psychology*, Methuen, London, 3rd edn, 1959, pp. 311–34.

9 Robert J. Lifton, *Thought Reform: a Psychiatric Study of 'Brainwashing' in China*, Gollancz, London, 1961.

10 See, for example, R. Marc Galanter et al., 'The "Moonies": a Psychological Study of Conversion and Membership in a Contemporary Religious Sect', *American Journal of Psychiatry*, 136, 2, February 1979; Marc Galanter, *Cults: Faith, Healing and Coercion*, Oxford University Press, 1989; Wolfgang Kuner, 'New Religious Movements and Mental Health', in E. Barker, ed., *Of Gods and Men: New Religious Movements in the West*, Mercer University Press, Macon, GA, 1983; Tom Robbins and Dick Anthony, 'New Religious Movements and the Social System: Integration, Disintegration and Transformation', *Annual Review of the Social Sciences of Religion*, 21, 1978, pp. 1–27; Michael W. Ross, 'Mental Health in Hare Krishna Devotees: a Longitudinal Study', *American Journal of Social Psychiatry*, 5, 4, Fall 1985, pp. 65–7. See also Eileen Barker, *New Religious Movements: a Practical Introduction*, HMSO, London, 1989, ch. 6.

11 Eileen Barker, *The Making of a Moonie: Brainwashing or Choice?*, Basil Blackwell, Oxford, 1984, ch. 8.

12 Max Weber, *The Theory of Social and Economic Organization*, Free Press, New York, 1964 edn, pp. 324–92.

13 See Weber, op. cit.; and, for example, Bryan Wilson, *The Noble Savage: the Primitive Origins of Charisma and its Contemporary Survival*, University of California Press, Berkeley, 1975. See also Roy Wallis, 'The Social Construction of Charisma', *Social Compass*, 29, 1982, pp. 25–39, for an analysis of the conditions under which David 'Moses' Berg came to be accorded charismatic authority by his followers in the Children of God/Family of Love.

14 It should be noted that new converts are also most likely to reject the whole new set of beliefs and to leave the movement at this stage.

15 For some examples, see Roy Wallis, ed., *Millennialism and Charisma*, The Queen's University, Belfast, 1982.

16 See, for example, Norman Skonovd, 'Leaving the "Cultic" Milieu', in David G. Bromley and James T. Richardson, eds, *The Brainwashing/Deprogramming Controversy: Sociological, Psychological, Legal and Historical Perspectives*, Edwin Mellen, New York and Toronto, 1983, pp. 95–8.

17 Ibid.

18 David Christopher Lane, ed., *Understanding Cults and Spiritual Movements*, 2, 1, 1987, pp. 1–6; 2, 2/3, 1987, pp. 1–13.

19 See Burke E. Rochford, *Hare Krishna in America*, Rutgers University Press, New Brunswick, NJ, 1985.

20 See Hugh Milne, *Bhagwan: the God that Failed*, Caliban, London, 1986; and Frances Fitzgerald, *Cities on a Hill*, Simon & Schuster, New York and London, 1986, pp. 247–414 for descriptions of the process by which Sheela built up and lost an empire at Rajneeshpuram.

21 See, for example, S. E. Asch, 'Effects of Group Pressure upon the Modification and Distortion of Judgements', in Eleanor E. Maccoby et al. (eds), op. cit., pp. 174–83.

22 See Barker, *New Religious Movements*, op. cit., pp. 145–55.
23 See Eileen Barker, 'Kingdoms of Heaven on Earth: New Religious Movements and Political Orders', in Dan Cohn-Sherbok ed., *The Canterbury Papers 1: Essays on Religion and Society*, Bellew, London, 1990, pp. 190–209, for a discussion concerning the variety of goals that are to be found in NRMs, and some of the methods advocated by the movements for achieving these.
24 Ibid.
25 Mary Douglas, *Natural Symbols: Explorations in Cosmology*, Barrie & Rockliff, London, 1970.
26 See Robert Towler, *The Need for Certainty: a Sociological Study of Conventional Religion*, Routledge & Kegan Paul, London, 1984, for an account of the beliefs that were considered appropriate for the Church of England by people responding to John Robinson's *Honest to God*.
27 See Paul Heelas, 'Western Europe: Self-Religions', in Stewart Sutherland and Peter Clarke, eds, *The Study of Religion, Traditional and New Religion*, Routledge, London, 1991, pp. 167–73.
28 See Erika Bourguignon, 'Cross-Cultural Perspectives on the Religious Uses of Altered States of Consciousness', in Irving I. Zaretsky and Mark P. Leone, eds, *Religious Movements in Contemporary America*, Princeton University Press, 1974, pp. 230–1.
29 Leon Festinger et al., *When Prophecy Fails*, Harper & Row, New York, 1956, produced the study that formed a basis for explanations in terms of the 'principle of consistency', explored further in, for example, Festinger's *A Theory of Cognitive Dissonance*, Row, Peterson, New York, 1957. There have, however, been several criticisms of Festinger's work; see, for example, Jane Allyn Hardyck and Marcia Braden, 'Prophecy Fails Again: a Report of a Failure to Replicate', *Journal of Abnormal and Social Psychology*, 65, 1962, pp. 136–41; and J. Gordon Melton, 'Spiritualization and Reaffirmation: What Really Happens when Prophecy Fails', Institute for the Study of American Religion, Santa Barbara, CA, 1989.
30 See Saul Levine, *Radical Departures: Desperate Detours to Growing Up*, Harcourt Brace Jovanovich, San Diego, CA, 1984, for analysis of this process.

Contributors

Alan Aldridge is a lecturer in the School of Social Studies, University of Nottingham. His recent research has been concerned with social change in the clerical profession. He acted as consultant to a Church of England working party on women's career development which produced the report *Deacons Now* (Advisory Council for the Church's Ministry, London, 1991).

Eileen Barker is Reader in Sociology at the London School of Economics. She is the Founder and Honorary Director of INFORM, a charity supported by the Home Office and mainstream churches, which provides information about new religions. She is currently President of the Society for the Scientific Study of Religion. Her publications include *New Religious Movements: A Practical Introduction* (HMSO, London, 1989).

James A. Beckford is Professor of Sociology at the University of Warwick. His books include *Religion and Advanced Industrial Society* (Unwin Hyman, London, 1989). His current research is on self-help groups and the spiritual aspects of social movements.

Christie Davies is Professor of Sociology at the University of Reading. He is the author of *Wrongful Imprisonment* (with R. Brandon), 1973; *Permissive Britain*, 1974; *Censorship and Obscenity* (with R. Dhavan), 1978; *Ethnic Humor around the World: a Comparative Analysis*, 1990; and many articles about the sociology of morality, and religious and ethnic identity in edited volumes and learned journals.

Karel Dobbelaere is Professor of Sociology and Sociology of Religion at the Catholic University of Leuven, and Professor of Sociological Research at the University of Antwerp (UFSIA). He has published extensively on secularization, pillarization and church involvement.

Leslie J. Francis is Mansel Jones Fellow at Trinity College, Carmarthen, in Wales. His most recent books are *The Country Parson* (1989); *Christian Perspectives for Education* (1990); and *Churches in Fellowship* (1991). His current research projects include the relationship between personality, religion and values among thirteen- to fifteen-year-olds, and a survey of the rural church.

P. J. Gee is Publications and Information Technology Officer at the Overseas Development Institute, London. He recently edited (with John Fulton) *Religion and Power, Decline and Growth: Sociological Analyses of Religion in Britain,*

Poland, and the Americas, BSA Sociology of Religion Study Group, London, 1991.

Michael Hill is Professor of Sociology at the Victoria University of Wellington, New Zealand, and the author of *A Sociology of Religion*, and *The Religious Order*. He co-edited *Shades of Deviance*, and has contributed to Frank Whaling's *Contemporary Approaches to the Study of Religion*, and to Mircea Eliade (ed.), *Encyclopaedia of Religion*.

Michael Hornsby-Smith is Senior Lecturer in Sociology at the University of Surrey, and the author of *Catholic Education* (Sheed and Ward, 1978); *Roman Catholics in England* (Cambridge University Press, 1987); *The Changing Parish* (Routledge, 1989); and *Roman Catholic Beliefs in England* (Cambridge University Press, 1991).

Kenneth Minogue is Professor of Political Science at the London School of Economics. He is author of *The Liberal Mind*; *Nationalism*; *The Concept of a University*; and *Alien Powers: the Pure Theory of Ideology*. He has written widely both for academic journals and for wider publication in *Encounter*; *The Times Literary Supplement*; *The National Interest*; and *The National Review*. His 'Societies Collapse: Faith Lingers On' in *Encounter*, March 1990, deals also with religion and politics.

D. S. Porter was formerly Senior Assistant Librarian in the Department of Western Manuscripts, Bodleian Library, Oxford. Since taking early retirement in 1988, he has worked on manuscripts at Manchester, Oriel and St Hilda's Colleges, Oxford, and has continued to edit the *Bodleian Library Record*. He has published *A Century of Adventism in the British Isles* (1974).

Stephen Sharot is Professor of Sociology in the Department of Behavioural Sciences, Ben Gurion University of the Negev, Beer-Sheva, Israel. His most recent publications include *Ethnicity, Religion, and Class in Israeli Society* (co-authored with Eliezer Ben-Rafael), (Cambridge University Press, 1991); and 'Judaism and the Secularization Debate', *Sociological Analysis*, 52, 3, 1991.

Dr William Thompson is a lecturer in Sociology at the University of Reading. Articles related to the one published in this volume include 'Moral Crusades and Media Censorship', *Franco-British Studies*, 9, Spring 1990. He is currently engaged in research on the rise of satanic abuse allegations in Britain, and is editing a collection of essays on moral panics.

Dr Kenneth Wolfe is Director of the Centre for the Study of Religion and Society at the University of Kent, and is joint editor of the *Canterbury Papers* series. He is preparing a second volume in the history of broadcast religion in the UK: the first was published by SCM Press in 1984, *The Churches and the BBC: The Politics of Broadcast Religion*.

Index

church, *see* Church schools
Education Act 1944, provisions
   of 94–5
religious life and
   curriculum 103–4
school ethos in Gloucestershire,
   study of 103–5
Seventh-day Adventist 207
Science and technology
   human control, religious attempt
   to bring under 21
Scotland
   Catholic secondary schools
      in 107
   Sunday trading in 51–2
Secularization 3, 11, 12, 36, 46, 56,
   82, 111, 112, 113, 138, 139
   trend in 11
Seventh-day Adventism
   administration of 199
   Britain, in
      black ministers 206, 213
      British Union session 1991,
      213, 214
      evangelistic centre 206–7
      London Laymen's
      Forum 208–10
      New Gallery 206–7
      North British conference
      session, 1990 213–14
      Pierson Package 211–13
      politicization of 208–15
      racial discrimination in 207
      regional conferences 209–10
      West Indian
      membership 200–6
      white membership, level
      of 203–4, 215
      withholding of tithe
      from 210–11
   character of 193–4
   church workers 196
   correct beliefs, importance
      of 201
   Dingo Baby case, effect of 192,
   195
   doctrinal deviance 199
   emergence of 192

health reform, emphasis on 194
independent ministries 199
Investigative Judgement,
   doctrine of 192–3, 197–8
Mrs White, accusations
   against 195–7
nineteenth century, history
   in 194–5
non-Americans in 199–200
non-Christian cult, considered
   as 193
perfectionism, drift to 198
plagiarism, accusations of 195–6
recommendations
   committee 214
representative government 213
schools 207
Spirit of Prophecy 192–3
Ten Point Critique 198
Third World dominance 215
tithe 209
uniformity 201
Sheppard, Dick 173
Short, Clare 90
Simmel, Georg 22
Simmonds, Richard 90
Smith, Uriah 195
Societalization
   process of 14
Society
   modern, influence of religion
      in 4
   secularization, question of 3
Sociology of religion
   Church, role in society 5
   development, stimuli 2
   minority religious
      organizations 8
   other parts of sociology, effect of
      developments in 11
   power, analysis of 155–6
Soper, Lord 174
Specialist therapies
   marketing 235
Spiritual absolutism
   fundamentalism as 30
   meaning 27